ALSO EDITED BY GEREMIE BARMÉ

Seeds of Fire: Chinese Voices of Conscience
(with John Minford)

NEW GHOSTS, OLD DREAMS

NEW
O   l   d
GHOSTS
D   r   e   a   m   s

CHINESE REBEL VOICES

Edited by Geremie Barmé
and Linda Jaivin

TIMES BOOKS

RANDOM HOUSE

Library of Congress Cataloging-in-Publication Data
New ghosts, old dreams: Chinese rebel voices/edited by Geremie
Barmé and Linda Jaivin.
    p.   cm.
Includes bibliographical references.
ISBN 0-8129-1927-0   ISBN 0-8129-1909-2 (paper)
1. China—History—Tiananmen Square Incident, 1989.
I. Barmé, Geremie. II. Jaivin, Linda.
DS779.32.N48   1992
951.05—dc20   90-71447

Manufactured in the United States of America

9 8 7 6 5 4 3 2

First Edition

Book design by Susan Hood

Foreword

New Ghosts, Old Dreams by Geremie Barmé and Linda Jaivin is an extraordinary work. It outdoes even Barmé and John Minford's earlier edited book, *Seeds of Fire* (which I reviewed for the *New York Times Book Review*), as a vibrant, probing guided tour of the Chinese mind today.

Barmé and Jaivin know contemporary China as no one else does—from the heights of philosophical speculation to the lows of popular superstition; from the literary tradition to literary gossip; from political theories to power games. They recognize the historical references and appreciate the historical resonances which lend Chinese intellectual life a dimension that is often hidden from Western readers. They appreciate the subtleties of the Chinese language, and they know how the personal loves and hates of the Chinese elite affect even their apparently most abstract discourse.

They see the picture whole and they see each of its parts in accurate detail. Their affection for China is the honest kind that embraces the absurdities as well as the greatness of this all-too-human civilization.

By dint of extraordinarily skillful editing, they guide the reader through a quick course in today's Chinese literature, philosophy, and politics. Artfully arranged excerpts and incisive commentaries weave a text that is integrated without oversimplification, readable without vulgarization, consistently entertaining yet deeply serious.

—ANDREW J. NATHAN
Professor of Political Science,
Columbia University
Author of *Chinese Democracy* and
China's Crisis: Dilemmas of Reform and Prospects for Democracy

Acknowledgments

This book was conceived as a sequel to *Seeds of Fire,* and John Minford, the co-editor on that book, was involved in the early stages of the planning of the work. Although illness prevented him from editing the book with us, his contribution was considerable.

It would not have been possible in terms of either time or technology to complete this work without the generous support of the Tiananmen Documentation Project of the Australian National University and the Division of Pacific and Asian History and the Contemporary China Center of the Research School of Pacific Studies at the Australian National University.

Our special thanks go to W. J. F. Jenner, who was painstaking and thorough in reading drafts of many of the translations and finally the whole manuscript, making numerous valuable suggestions. Mary Farquhar also offered creative comments on the organization of some of the earlier sections, for which we are very grateful.

Shelley Kay read a number of the translations as a writer without any China background, and her observations were always stimulating and useful. Jonathan (B. J.) and Melissa Jaivin suggested a range of contemporary slang for use in the story "Rocking Tiananmen."

Jonathan Hutt, an energetic, creative translator and our man in Auckland, played a crucial role in coordinating work done there for the book. Nicholas Jose, the tireless Australian cultural counselor in Peking, helped us find Chinese materials difficult to obtain after June 1989 as well as some of the more unusual examples of official propaganda. In Canberra, X. D. Fan devotedly searched through university and national library holdings for relevant materials, and also in Australia, Da Jun kept a sharp eye out for new and obscure works that might be used in the book.

We would like to thank Pang Bingjun for his suggestion concerning the title and Duncan Campbell, Brigette Holland, and Don J. Cohn in

Acknowledgments

New Zealand for their help and encouragement. We are also indebted to many other friends: Bo Yang and Chang Hsiang-hua, Cao Changqing of the *Press Freedom Herald* (now *Press Freedom Guardian*), Johnson Chang of Hanart 2 Gallery in Hong Kong, Chen Ruoxi, Chin Heng-wei of Taiwan's *Contemporary Monthly,* Geoff Crothall of the *South China Morning Post,* Emily Lau and Margaret Scott of *The Far Eastern Economic Review,* Mark Elvin, John Fincher, Fong Su and Lee Yee of *The Nineties Monthly,* Romain Franklin of *Libération,* Victoria Godfrey, Richard Gordon and Carma Hinton of the Long Bow Group, David Hawkes, Hou Dejian, Jin Zhong of *Emancipation Monthly* (now known as *Open Magazine*), Daniel Kane, Nigel Kat, David Kelly, Kuang Hsiang-hsia of China Television in Taipei, Gabriel Lafitte, Jane Macartney, Mi Qiu, Andrew Nathan, Richard Rigby, Pierre Ryckmans, Orville Schell and Liu Baifang, Shu Kei, Diane Stacey, Lung-kee Sun, Jonathan Unger, Wang Keping, Wang Yanni and Yu Junwu, Marion Weeks, Kristian Whittaker, Wu Shaoxiang, Danny Yung of Zuni Icosohedron, Zhang Hongtu, and Zhang Langlang. We'd also like to thank Amnesty International's New South Wales branch.

We are particularly grateful to Steve Wasserman, who commissioned the book for Hill and Wang before leaving to become editorial director of Times Books and welcomed it onto his publication list there. We owe a special debt of gratitude to Ken Gellman and the other editors at Times Books who helped shepherd the book through to completion. We wish to thank Susan Hood for creating a design that has so elegantly accommodated our unwieldy manuscript.

Huang Miaozi wrote the calligraphy for the title page, for which we are most grateful.

This book owes much to many other friends in China and Hong Kong who for reasons of their own safety must remain unnamed.

Contents

Contents

Introduction

I can but stand by, looking on as friends become new ghosts,
I seek an angry poem from among the swords.

—*Lu Xun, 1931*

In early 1931, Lu Xun, one of China's foremost literary figures, composed these lines upon hearing of the execution of five young writers. He
mourned the murdered young as "new ghosts."

In early June 1989, at least a thousand (and possibly many more)
"new ghosts" were created when the Chinese government brutally
crushed the peaceful student-led Protest Movement of that spring and
began a political purge on a scale not seen in China since the Cultural
Revolution (1966–1976).*

New Ghosts, Old Dreams: Chinese Rebel Voices is an anthology of
Chinese writings. Although we were inspired to compile this book by the
events of 1989, we have not limited its contents to writings concerning
them. Instead, through a selection of fiction, poetry, songs, essays,
speeches, plays, petitions, reportage, documents, satire, newspaper articles, and even excerpts from the script of a television miniseries, we
explore the social and cultural roots of the 1989 Protest Movement and
provide a basis for understanding what has occurred in China since then.

Underlying many of the writings is a profound awareness of crisis—
social, economic, political, cultural, and environmental—and an agonized concern for the dilemmas faced by China as it approaches the
twenty-first century. The feeling that the Chinese government would not
honestly confront the nation's problems, many of them caused by its
own mistaken or inept policies, was one factor that drove so many
ordinary citizens in Peking, Shanghai, Chengdu, and other cities into the

---

* According to carefully documented reports produced by Amnesty International and
the International League for Human Rights together with the Ad Hoc Study Group
on Human Rights in China, the number of people killed in Peking alone on June 3–4
was at least one thousand, with thousands more wounded. There were reportedly
many deaths in other cities, and a spate of executions took place around the country
in the general clampdown on dissent that followed.

streets in the first half of 1989 to support what were initially student demonstrations.

The second part of the book's title, "old dreams," refers to the dreams of freedom and self-expression that Chinese individuals have pursued for millennia; the dreams of a modern, democratic, and equitable polity cherished by reformist intellectuals for nearly a century; and the dreams of being on an equal footing with the rest of humanity, true members of the international community.

While this book focuses on the sounds of discontent, protest, and despair that formed the chorus of Chinese urban life in the late 1980s, they also contain clear echoes of both the recent and distant past. There are resonances from the Tiananmen Incident of 1976, in which the popular mourning for Premier Zhou Enlai turned into a massive expression of protest against the Cultural Revolution, Jiang Qing, and indeed Mao Zedong himself. There are also reverberations from the Democracy Wall Movement of 1979, when thousands of young people in cities all over China demanded the redressing of past wrongs and called for increased democracy and human rights so that a disaster like the Cultural Revolution could never occur again. Indeed, the tenth anniversary of the imprisonment of Wei Jingsheng, a Democracy Wall activist and China's most famous political prisoner, was one of the causes of the protests in 1989.

But 1989 was also the seventieth anniversary of the May Fourth Movement, which involved the first serious reevaluation of China's traditional culture. In 1919 students demonstrated en masse for the first time against their new government, agitating for reform under the banner of "democracy and science." Seventy years later, many Chinese felt that the issues of the May Fourth Movement were as relevant as they had ever been. Both the slogans of the original May Fourth Movement and references to it were prominent in the 1989 Protest Movement. Two members of the original May Fourth Movement generation, the Shanghai-based writer Ba Jin and the novelist and poet Bing Xin, even played a small but significant supporting role in the 1989 movement.

As the authors of the controversial television miniseries *River Elegy* put it, "It is as though so many things in China must start all over again from the May Fourth Movement."

This "recycling" of history is one of the main themes of the book. While Part IV ("Wheels") is devoted to illustrating the cycles of recent Chinese history, other examples are inserted throughout the text. That is why, for example, in "The Cry," we use an essay about the dispersing of a student demonstration in 1919 just before touching on the subject of the massacre of 1989.

We have chosen to call the events of the first half of 1989 the Protest Movement. Other writers, in Chinese and English, have variously called it the Student Movement, the Democracy Movement, or the Peking Spring. Although the street demonstrations of April and May 1989 were led to a great extent by students from Peking's major educational institutions, they had already been developing from events earlier in the year (and even in 1988) and from late April grew to become a widely based movement involving leading intellectuals and writers of several generations, journalists, central government cadres, factory workers, private entrepreneurs, members of nearly every profession from medical doctors to hotel chefs, and to some extent even peasants (who helped stop army trucks from getting into Peking from the surrounding countryside).

While the movement claimed democracy to be one of its major goals, it came to encompass grievances and demands as varied as its participants. Journalists demanded greater independence for the press, students lobbied for better conditions in the universities, intellectuals petitioned for a greater role in the polity, and nearly everyone wanted an end to official nepotism and corruption. For many, the protests were actually aimed against the inequalities and unsettling social changes resulting from the party's 1980s' reform policies themselves. The aims of the movement were vaguely described as freedom and democracy, but as some of the selections in "The Cry" illustrate, democracy was not one of the movement's strongest points. Rather, its overriding theme was that of protest—against dictatorial one-party rule, a lack of both individual and group autonomy, economic and political mismanagement, and government unresponsiveness to its people's concerns.

New Ghosts, Old Dreams is a sequel to an earlier anthology, *Seeds of Fire: Chinese Voices of Conscience.** Like *Seeds of Fire*, it contains selections or excerpts from a wide range of translated materials, put together in such a way as to illustrate common concerns or points of conflict and

---

* John Minford, the other editor of *Seeds of Fire*, although unable to edit the present volume with us, was closely involved in the early stages of planning this book. It is thus very much a continuation, conceptually and otherwise, of that earlier work.

controversy. The style of juxtaposition is what Mao Zedong would have called "reactionary editing" *(fandong bianpai)*.

In many cases, particularly where the original work was a novel, television script, or longer essay, our selection consists of excerpts or quotations. To publish the works in full would mean producing a book of many volumes.

Most of the material in this anthology has never been published in English before, and some of it hasn't even been published in Chinese—a poem smuggled out after the massacre, for example, and a letter (quoted with permission) from a government academic.

In *New Ghosts, Old Dreams*, we hear again from many of the people featured in *Seeds of Fire*. There are members of the rusticated Red Guard, or "Urbling" generation, as we have called them previously, Bei Dao and Yang Lian for example, though their preoccupations have shifted somewhat in recent times. There are also older figures like Liu Xinwu, Chen Ruoxi, and Wang Meng, as well as the irrepressible dissident astrophysicist Fang Lizhi and the senior writers Ba Jin, Wu Zuguang, and Yang Jiang. The Taiwan essayist Bo Yang, author of "The Ugly Chinaman," appears here as well, though this time after making his first visit to Mainland China in forty years, in 1988, and the American-based academic Lung-kee Sun also reappears. Liu Xiaobo, the iconoclastic literary critic, is back as well. He was also an activist in the Protest Movement, and his observations on democracy, intellectual life, and other topics form something of a running commentary throughout the book.

We also introduce many new voices. Liu Xiaobo is joined by the Shanghai literary and film critic Zhu Dake, who like Liu holds an irreverent attitude toward state-approved culture and the writings of the aging ex–Red Guard generation. And the Taiwanese writer Li Ao, one of the most striking essayists in the Chinese language today and certainly one of the wittiest, also appears several times, as does Hong Kong's Ni Kuang.

On the mainland, the Red Guard generation is still producing extraordinary personalities, and we introduce several who were not featured in *Seeds of Fire*. These include Dai Qing, a "historical investigative journalist" whose efforts to undo the party's control over modern Chinese history represent one of the most intriguing intellectual projects undertaken by anyone in China in the late 1980s. They also include Su Xiaokang, like Dai Qing a journalist, but whose own quest led to a radical questioning of tradition and dedication to the goal of national salvation; Su was one of the main authors of *River Elegy*, a television miniseries featured in Part II ("Bindings"). The conservative scholar He Xin is another member of the generation that grew to maturity during the Cultural Revolution. He became after the 1989 massacre an adviser to the government and a fierce critic of Liu Xiaobo and Su Xiaokang, as well as of what he decries as the "hippie spirit" throughout Chinese history, a spirit he saw as being particularly manifest from the mid-1980s on.

We also introduce the brasher, more confident voices of a younger generation. The members of this generation were too young to participate directly in the Cultural Revolution, but the complex influences on them are reflected in their outlook on life and their work. Their writings, songs, and paintings express the ambience of anarchy, desire for personal freedom, and general irreverence that characterized so much of Chinese urban society in the late eighties (and continues to do so in the early nineties), particularly the youth subcultures. In their work, they tend to write the way people speak—slang, vulgarities, and all—and to treat sex and anomie in a natural, nondidactic manner. As a result, their work, if not necessarily great literature, is readable, unpretentious, and often true to life.

We start off the book with an excerpt from just such a story, Liu Yiran's "Rock 'n' Roll Youth," which we have called "Rocking Tiananmen." Other examples include "Hot and Cold, Measure for Measure" by Wang Shuo, the "entrepreneur-writer" who became one of the most popular Peking writers in the late 1980s, and Xu Xing's "Variations Without a Theme."

The voices in this book are not always pleasant or nice. Some of them, like Liu Xiaobo, have managed to antagonize both China's conservative rulers and its liberal intellectuals. Their rebelliousness, irreverence, and cynicism are in a sense products of both the Cultural Revolution and the free-for-all age of reform, and that is perhaps why they rankle the party so much—they are, in fact, its own creations.

Many of these people were active to one extent or another in the Protest Movement and have paid a heavy price for both their involvement and their previous impertinence toward authority. Following the June massacre, Liu Xiaobo, Dai Qing, Wang Peigong, Wang Ruowang, and other people represented in these pages were detained or interrogated by the police. Others, like Zhu Dake, were put under intense investigation for supposedly "counterrevolutionary" activities, and their future went under a cloud. Fang Lizhi took refuge in the American embassy and the singer Hou Dejian hid in the Australian embassy, leaving seventy days later only after receiving assurances from the government that he would not be arrested. In mid-1990, both Fang and Hou were forced overseas. Still others, like Su Xiaokang, fled into exile.

Not all the voices are Chinese. Simon Leys (Pierre Ryckmans), Timothy Richard, John Minford, Nicholas Jose, and Michael Dutton also have their place in our "Tiananmen Square." We believe their observations on Chinese history and society add much of interest to the anthology. In the case of Nicholas Jose's "And the Beat Goes On," about the mood of Peking after the massacre, he speaks in part for those who were silenced.

This book is divided into five interconnected sections. In the first of these, "The Cry," we concentrate on the events of 1989, in particular the Protest Movement. Behind the protests was a complex skein of dissatisfaction, an accumulation of social, cultural, political, and economic problems. The materials in the following three sections, "Bindings," "Red Noise," and "Wheels," highlight the nature of those problems. The final major section, "Floating," covers the topics of Hong Kong, survival, and exile. On the whole the material is organized by theme, rather than chronologically.

"The Cry" begins with the disquiet of "Rocking Tiananmen" and moves on to the protests of 1989. The approach to the protests and petitions is generally more documentary than journalistic, though the section includes one piece of journalism, Hong Kong writer Jimmy Ngai's "Tiananmen Days." The massacre itself and its aftermath are described in poems and essays.

In Part II, "Bindings," we look at the types of restraints imposed on the Chinese by history, culture, society, and the Communist system. This section takes as a central symbol the bound foot, representative of the feudal past, the oppressive nature of a massive, agricultural society, and subjugation to patriarchal authority. We set the mood with a description of the binding of a girl's feet from Feng Jicai's story "Three-Inch Golden Lotuses." But restrictions are not limited to the feet. In the past, the individual was bound by the demands of Confucian propriety and the extended family; under socialism, people are tied to their work units. The miniseries *River Elegy* presents a China weighed down by a five-thousand-year history and bound in crisis by stagnation and a land-locked economy, as well as oppressed by national icons such as the Yellow River, the Great Wall, and the dragon. We see the reformist intellectuals, many of whom were active in the 1989 Protest Movement, as people who have tried to loosen the bindings. There are also the "natural feet," the true individualists, from republican and even imperial times as well as the 1980s, who have tried—often with fatal consequences—to live an unfettered existence.

Part III, "Red Noise," uses long excerpts from contemporary Chinese fiction, criticism, and reportage to reflect the "ambience of anarchy" of urban China in the late 1980s. The Communist Party's reforms created relative prosperity, but they also unleashed new, unruly, and chaotic elements in the society. "Red Noise" is, in one sense, the sound of the snapping of the ties of social and political convention. The hedonistic, rebellious atmosphere deeply unsettled both conservative thinkers like He Xin and the Communist leadership, who, even before the Protest Movement erupted in 1989, sought to reign in what from their standpoint had become a feral society.

Part IV, "Wheels," deals with the cycles of binding and unbinding experienced by the Chinese throughout the last century, cycles many believe they will never escape. Indeed, the fatalistic belief in the cyclical nature of Chinese history itself may condemn so many to repeat the tragedies of the past. There are the cycles of political movements, of the May Fourth Movement, of superstition and debates about China's "national characteristics." In some cases, the selections directly address the question of cycles—Xu Jilin's essay "The Vicious Cycle of the May Fourth Movement" and Fang Lizhi's ironic "Chinese Democracy: The View from the Peking Observatory." In others, the theme is brought out by the juxtaposition of texts, like the pairing of Chen Ruoxi's story "The Old Man," about someone caught up in the Tiananmen Incident of 1976, with an article from the *Peking Daily* in August 1989.

The final section, "Floating," takes survival as its theme, whether it is in Hong Kong, inside China, or in exile. It looks first at the dilemma of Hong Kong, which will be reunited with the mainland in 1997. The section starts off with Xi Xi's "The Floating City," a lyrical allegory about the territory. The other selections here tend heavily to satire. The Hong Kong Chinese have been allowed little say about and no control over their future, which has been decided by the mandarins in Whitehall and Zhongnanhai (China's Kremlin), so perhaps humor is the last weapon they have against total control by the northern Communists. Li Ao also makes a few suggestions about how to cope with repression in general in "The Art of Survival." Yang Jiang believes the best defense is a "cloak of invisibility." Among the diverse voices from exile are those of the Dalai Lama and the exiled poets Bei Ling and Duo Duo.

In the Epilogue, we give the last word to Dai Qing and the rock singer Xie Chengqiang.

Like *Seeds of Fire, New Ghosts, Old Dreams* is in essence an "anti-reader" on China but not an "anti-China" reader.

It attempts to expose Western readers to the Chinese world's range of debate on her problems. In these pages there is much humor and some hope, but little optimism and few solutions. By the late 1980s, China was facing a series of unprecedented crises in almost every sphere and optimism was restricted to propaganda and official speeches.

The Protest Movement, with its moving scenes of street marches and young and forceful leaders and the horrible massacre that followed, have lent the first half of 1989 a rather holy aura. It is easy, even tempting, to gloss over the more complicated reality—the motivating energy and humor and the social and cultural complexities of the period.

New Ghosts, Old Dreams attempts to demonstrate that the elements of conflict present in 1989 predated the Protest Movement itself by many years, and that certain of these existed before Communist rule—some Chinese writers even feel they are indigenous to Chinese culture itself. We have tried to offer Western readers a path through the labyrinthine intricacies of the Chinese cultural and political dilemma, presenting as their guides some of that nation's most extraordinary contemporary writers.

We have made no attempt to be "representative." The selections do not, by and large, address the situation in the Chinese countryside, for example, though the issues of unchecked population growth and impending environmental catastrophe raised by urban intellectuals are directly relevant to the future of all Chinese citizens—and indeed to the rest of the world. Nor have we dwelt on the political infighting that has been part and parcel of every upheaval in Mainland Chinese history.

In general, we chose the materials translated here with an eye to content and style, and in both we have preferred the spicy over the bland, even if the bland is more typical of contemporary Chinese writing. It is a book intended, after all, to be provocative. We hope that allowing these Chinese men and women of conscience (and some of their detractors) to speak directly to Western readers will challenge accepted Western views on China, stimulate discussion, and create a greater awareness of China's difficult situation.

There are no simple answers to the range of questions facing China in the 1990s that are posed in this anthology. But we do suggest that if one knows where China has been, it is a little easier to imagine where it is headed, or at least to understand where it is today.

—*Canberra, Australia*

A Note on Section Titles: The title page of each section features a one-character Chinese equivalent of the section title, reproduced here in the calligraphy of Wang Xizhi (fourth century), with the exception of Part II, "Bindings," the calligraphy for which was done by Dong Qichang (sixteenth century).

"The Cry" is represented by *ku,* which encompasses both the meaning of "shedding tears" and "crying out." "Bindings" is *chan,* or "entanglement." *Hun* is used for "Red Noise"; it means muddy, turbid, unsophisticated, whole. "Wheels" is *hui,* which means return, transmigration, the Buddhist wheel of life. "Floating" is *fu,* which implies instability and impermanence. The "Epilogue" uses *e,* which means outspokenness and truthfulness.

HUABIAO, *TIANANMEN, AND MAO ZEDONG*

Just outside Tiananmen Gate stand two *huabiao,* sculpted marble pillars with small decorative wings. The wings are said to represent the Board of Criticism and Protests, or the "wood of direct speech" *(feibang zhi mu),* placed outside the imperial court for common people to write their complaints on. Even though the *huabiao* are ornamental rather than

Huabiao

functional, they symbolize the right to speak up against official injustice and the need for conscientious government.

> Walking past Tiananmen Gate as a child, I would look up at the *huabiao,* which reached up into the clouds. At the time, I only thought how beautiful they were. I had no idea what they stood for. Now, after much reading and reflection, I understand: The *huabiao* are a debased symbol, tools of expression that have lost their function. They are the tears of China; the *huabiao* is China's cross.
>
> —*Li Ao, 1980*

Stretching out from the gate where the *huabiao* stand is Tiananmen Square, the scene of successive demonstrations, protests, celebrations, and political incidents for over seventy years.*

The square itself was created after the Qing dynasty was overthrown in 1911 as a parade ground for the military displays of the new Republic of China. Originally, there had simply been an open area in front of the Tiananmen Gate of the Imperial Palace where ministers and subjects would gather to hear the proclamation of imperial edicts. Mao Zedong chose this same site to announce the founding of the People's Republic on October 1, 1949, and during the 1950s it was expanded into a T shape including the eastern and western approaches of the Avenue of Eternal Peace.†

For forty years, Tiananmen Square was used for orchestrated displays of popular will. But during early April 1976, and again in 1986 and 1989, the square was also the scene of popular protest against the government. While the *huabiao* may long ago have lost any real meaning, the image of Mao Zedong has, even long after his death, continued to dominate the political life of Peking. During the 1989 protests, the image and the specter of Mao Zedong loomed over the square. His huge portrait stared out from Tiananmen Gate, while his mummified body lay in state in the Chairman Mao Memorial Hall directly south of the Monument to the People's Heroes.

On the afternoon of May 23, 1989, the third day of martial law in

---

* For more on Tiananmen Square as the historical stage of the 1989 Protest Movement, see the introduction to the 1989 edition of *Seeds of Fire,* pp. xxxiii–iv.
† Until the Peking Massacre, when it became expedient for the government to declare that the approaches, where much of the slaughter took place, were not part of the square, Tiananmen Square was officially considered to stretch from Xidan in the west to Dongdan in the east and Qianmen in the south.

"Women!" Zhang Hongtu, Chairmen Mao Series

Peking, the portrait of Mao Zedong on Tiananmen Gate was splattered with colored paint (see the cover of this book) by three men from Hunan, Mao's home province. Even the student demonstrators were shocked by this unprecedented and irreverent gesture, and student marshals immediately apprehended the culprits and turned them over to the police. Some were delighted by this sign of rebellion, while others were outraged, for they cherished Mao as a symbol of probity and leadership; for all his radical excesses, they considered him superior to the likes of Deng Xiaoping and Li Peng. A few cynics speculated that the paint throwers were government *agents provocateur*. Shortly after the incident, a violent storm struck Peking. The skies turned an ominous yellow and angry winds and pelting rain lashed the demonstrators, felling a tree by the moat in the Imperial Palace. Many took the storm to be a portent of approaching doom.

The portrait, first covered over, was replaced that evening.

Perhaps it was in unconscious response to the iconic nature of Mao's portrait that when the students raised their own version of the Statue of Liberty across from it, they felt compelled to call it the Goddess of Democracy, rather than a Statue of Democracy.

> Seen solely within the context of Chinese history, Mao Zedong was undoubtedly the most successful individual of all. Nobody understood the Chinese better; no one was more skillful at factional politics within the autocratic structure; no one was more cruel and merciless; none more chameleonlike. Certainly no one else would have portrayed himself as a brilliant and effulgent sun.
> —*Liu Xiaobo, November 1988*

Although there are few direct references to Mao in these pages and only two direct quotations from him, his spirit permeates this volume. For many Chinese writers and thinkers, coming to terms with such concepts as democracy and personal freedom (whether expressed through fiction, poetry, or essays) is tantamount to a struggle to be released from Mao's hold over them. This effort is made explicit in the work of the Chinese artist Zhang Hongtu, formerly of the Central Art Academy in Peking and now resident in New York, whose reconstructed portraits of Mao provide a visual theme throughout this book. In December 1989, Zhang explained why he had embarked on this series of paintings:

> The audience response to my Mao series is not informed solely by artistic considerations; the Mao image has a charisma of its own. It's still so powerful that the first time I cut up an official portrait of Mao for a collage I felt a pang of guilt, something gnawing away inside me. Other people, in particular other Chinese, may well feel the same. As long as this "power to intimidate" exists, I will continue to do Mao.

PART I

The Cry

We should not be alarmed when we hear moaning, sighing, crying, or pleading. It's only when we are confronted by stark silence that we should beware. When we see a venomous serpent weaving its way through a forest of corpses, and malevolent ghosts stealing through the dark, we should take care, for these announce the approach of true wrath.

LU XUN, MAY 5, 1925

I could see it coming. I warned them, but I failed. No one would listen to me.

DAI QING, JUNE 10, 1989

This section is about the Protest Movement of 1989 and takes the "cry" as its theme. The cry is made up of many voices, some strident, others plaintive; voices calling for personal and political freedom, democracy, and human rights.

We begin with a short story that has no direct connection with the Protest Movement. As is so often the case, it is a work of literature that best encapsulates the mood of the times, in this instance the unfocused and inarticulate restlessness of China's urban youth in the late 1980s. "Rocking Tiananmen," an excerpt from a story written by a Peking-based army writer in 1988, gives expression to the almost palpable ambience of discontent that helped fuel mass support for the student-led protests of 1989. "Rocking Tiananmen" is a young man's cry for attention and freedom. The Protest Movement too was a cry for attention—as witnessed by the students' demand for recognition by and dialogue with party leaders—and greater freedom for society as well as the individual.

In many ways, the concerns of the 1989 Protest Movement echoed those of the Democracy Wall Movement ten years earlier. The cries of that movement had been silenced when the party clamped down on dissent and jailed leading activists, including Wei Jingsheng.

The cry found its voice again in the petitions and letters of protest written or signed by Chinese men and women of conscience in the first six months of 1989. They asked the government for the release of political prisoners, including Wei, for a free press, and for more democracy. But these measured and rational cries were ignored or condemned by the government, and the chorus of protest swelled and grew more vociferous. The cries of protest gave way to screams of anguish, outrage, and pain when the government decided to use military force to crush the peaceful rebellion.

This is not meant to be a comprehensive history of the 1989 Protest Movement. A number of excellent accounts of the events have already appeared. Instead, it is a selection of cries: cries appealing for reason and justice; cries of frustration, passion, and fury; cries of despair.

Rocking Tiananmen

LIU YIRAN

Now, *this* is what I call turmoil.

Can anyone really describe just how fuckin' good this feels? This is, like, the longest kiss I've ever had in my whole life. It's even longer than the Avenue of Eternal Peace. It knocks my soul right out of my ears and sends it flying into the ozone. I relax and feel something totally wild sprouting in every cell of my body. Hot desire leaves my more rational impulses groping on the floor for their teeth. In the dim light, I get a second wind and pull her closer to me.

She has this incredible smell, it drives me wild, it psychs me up, it's a scent with her signature on it. My lips are locked to her warm fragrant mouth by an electric current; sparks are going to start flying any second now. Trembling has become an indescribable pleasure; nothing else exists. I don't know where this amazing high comes from. The skin on my face is about to blister under her hot breath. It's like I'm dead or dreaming. The face of the goddamn moon is green, and the sun is coarse, no way you'd catch me kissing them. Nothing exists outside this kiss. I silently savor every lingering detail. I feel like her soul is mingling with mine, pulsing through me to the tips of my fingers and toes, riding on the blood that is racing through my veins faster than a spaceship through the galaxy. I feel it: uproar, rebellion in my most private parts. Vaguely, distinctly, I can smell it now too, that elusive smell of life itself, unbearable and real comfortable—you figure it out. There's a milky-white fog floating before my eyes, and I ride a roaring surf out to the realm of pure nothingness. I swear my heart's stopped.

Now that we've inhaled the life out of each other, we start using the tips of our tongues to explore, create whole new feelings, communicate messages of love that might shock people of more refined tastes. She's getting into it even more than me, she's got those gorgeous eyes so tightly shut that nothing can get in the way of these tender emotions. I wonder

(Wide World Photos)

if all women do that? She's softly writhing against my chest; I suddenly think of glutinous rice fermenting in a cauldron. Of waves stroked by gusty winds. Of white snails. She puts a hand on my neck. What a turn-on. It's just occurred to me that this is why God made men taller than women. Thank you, God.

A water truck drives by slowly, spraying the street, its headlights lingering on our bodies for what seems like an eternity. It's awful, like being stripped naked in broad daylight. What an asshole, bet the driver got a good eyeful out of that one. Oh! she exclaims in this happy voice, and there's nothing in the world that sounds so good.

Ding! The elevator doors close with a thud.

How the hell we came to be here is anyone's guess. We don't have supernatural powers. But just a moment ago we were in our dark little corner under the trees. Anyway, we're still "inhaling life." If only the elevator light were red. Red lights drive me wild.

Our passions soar with the elevator as we peak with it on the sixteenth floor. The doors slide open softly. No way I'm getting out. If we go to her place there'll be no more tonsil hockey for us tonight. Her father, the old stiff, is just itching to connect his Parisian-clad feet with my behind. She clings to me more tightly and the doors thud closed once more. We go down and so does our sexual freedom.

Last time I came to see Yuanyuan the elevator broke down between the eighth and ninth floors. Hey, I even wrote my last will and testament. If only the elevator would break down now, however, we would be real happy.

Apparently Americans suck face in elevators all the time. It's so fuckin' cut off from the rest of the world that your desires get seriously out of control.

Ding! The elevator doors open softly. An old woman is standing outside; her gaze is so cold you could skate on it. We pay no attention, we don't even see her—we're wrapped up in our work.

Your polite little cough isn't going to force us apart, old lady. You underestimate the adhesive power of young passion! If you can't take the heat, stay out of the elevator. Once more the doors thud together. The elevator goes up again; our passion rises with it, then falls away. When the doors open this time, it's a real bummer. The old girl is surrounded by a crowd of people looking like some plenary session, all of them as serious as death. Party's over. All I can do is sigh with frustration and gaze tenderly at my love object. A truly moving sight. I pick up my black sweatshirt that's fallen on the floor and grin at Yuanyuan. She grins back. Very politely, I turn sideways to let in the wrinklies and try to stop myself from laughing. Yuanyuan is in control. God, she's cool—smoothing her hair like nothing's happened. But her face is flushed. Just then her almost uncontrollable lust had nearly landed us in a real mess, for she was guiding my hand to that firm, luscious breast of hers when the doors opened. Fortunately, I was quick enough to block the view. I'm not going to let strangers gawk at us in midgrope. They don't deserve the pleasure.

I tell her I'm going. I mean it this time.

She laughs, a laugh tinged with charming melancholy.

The old bag pretends she doesn't see a thing. She's definitely a relic from the Qing dynasty, a practitioner of longevity kung fu. She wouldn't know what the hell a kiss is!

Ding! The elevator doors slam violently behind me. I'm gone. Not one for wasting time. I stand outside the apartment building and look up toward the top floor. I can't see a thing. But I've got this feeling that she's gonna stick her head out and wave and all of a sudden there she is waving, then she disappears. If only I were Superman. If only your father and those French shoes weren't home. If only . . .

I'm now wandering along the street sharing my feelings with the evening breeze, letting its warm fingers run over my body. I stroll along in its warm embrace, savoring the flavor of Yuanyuan's kisses. Tomato? Coffee? Sugar? The flavor, mysterious and indistinct, lingers in my consciousness. I'm on fire. My legs are all energy. I find myself doing a moonwalk, my whole body floating like some god up in the clouds.

Recently I've really gotten into break dancing and rock 'n' roll. I've heard that millions of break dancers think that tall, ugly black guy in the American film *Breakin'* is a superstud. They just about go down on their knees in front of the screen. But what's he got that I don't? I'm one funky kinda dude, and one day I'll be in some movie or I'll do a benefit gig in Tiananmen Square for African famine victims. Then you'll know who's king!

But it really pisses me off how the heads of my dance troupe refuse to let me break dance. They're so fake it makes me puke. What's wrong with break dancing? What's wrong with rock music? All around the world kids are dancing and singing. Don't tell me they're all a pack of hooligans. The fuckers can barely afford to pay us our salaries. Not long ago a friend of mine in a rock band was banned from performing—no excuse given—and this routine I did for TV combining disco and break dancing wasn't allowed to be screened: too "suggestive," they said. What

Hey, you: Don't go treating this crock of shit as if it were literature or anything. You'll regret it if you do. Fiction's the kinda stuff "artists" scribble on God's toilet paper. This is just a rave between friends. It'll be over in the time it takes to do a crap. Hang loose.
—Liu Yiran

Liu Yiran was a thirty-three-year-old writer in the People's Liberation Army (PLA) in 1988 when this story was published.

a joke! If a foreign rock star visited Peking, these same bosses would be all smiles, lining up to kiss his ass. But Chinese people aren't allowed to dance. Our lives are so lousy to begin with, and now these guys won't let us do anything. Shit!

I quicken my pace. The last bus has gone by now. A few guys with shoulder-length hair and stubbly beards are hanging around the bus stop. They've got electric and bass guitars and they're howling away, trying to sound like John Lennon. There's also some chick singing, her hair and clothes a total mess, looks like a real slut. Their eyes look like they're full of tears; I'm touched. If only they could use our auditorium for a few jam sessions, a few concerts—then fuck me if you didn't see people really rockin' for reform!

I run from them like a madman. If I listen I'll start to cry. Makes me think of my baby, always telling me to get serious and dance according to the rules. Tells me not to hang around with "The Demolition Crew" or the "QUAKE-ers." But hey, *bo*-ring, like, that's not where I'm at. If a dog wants to eat shit, can you stop it? I'd rather face a butcher's knife than spend a lifetime dancing that traditional crap. People should have more fun. Just thinking that tomorrow I'll probably be selected to take part in the Arts Festival gives me the shits—doing the "seagull," which "expresses" the fuckin' "spirit" of the ethnic minorities. Every step is fixed by the choreographer; if she tells you to stick your ass in the air, you don't give anything else a wiggle. Forget emotion, forget letting go, you're an unthinking lump of flesh. If only I could break dance instead; it'd freak them out and put Yuanyuan on the warpath. It'd be like I pissed on the Bible or something. My knees turn to jelly when she gets mad. Damn!

Life sucks.

. . . I smell the difference in the air the second I enter the auditorium the next morning. All my darling competitors have become beauty queens, their faces glazed an absurd, saintly greasepaint white. What the hell for? It's just a contest to see who'll get into the Arts Festival. So you might score an award, big deal. Or get to wiggle your ass on some New York stage. So what? No reason to sink this low—the guys with their hair permed so they look like fluffy Pekinese, the girls with so much eyeliner on they look like those cretinous pandas. Talk about over the top. Even the girls who are usually real cool are talking like bimbos. A feeling of steely dejection comes over me, it's soon replaced by smoldering anger, and now I'm in the throes of a wild, rebellious mood. I look over at them, shower them with contempt. Fuckin' geeks.

I calm down as soon as I spot Yuanyuan. My field of vision is filled with a mass of raised red arms, round and voluptuous, moving like a film on fast forward, a surging red wave. A red sea, real groovy. Anyone who prefers their seas blue would have to be missing a few marbles. Just look at Yuanyuan, leading a pack of men and women in the red ribbon dance. They're so into it. The music is soothing. She's beautiful. I can't take my eyes off her; she's mine.

At this moment a warm stream of yellow light comes flooding through the window. The dust in the air is lit like a blue curtain. The ribbon dance goes on and on. Our grandparents danced this stuff, but they can't hack it anymore, so now it's our turn. If we gave it up people'd think we weren't Chinese anymore.

I strip off my jacket without taking my hungry eyes off Yuanyuan. I'm, like, cool but real edgy, too. I think of wild horses galloping across the grasslands. Now that's dancing.

Our choreographer is standing in front of the practice mirror, smiling. She used to be the lead dancer. Yuanyuan probably reminds her of what she was like in her prime. She's a good old stick. Sometimes I feel like finding her some of that ginseng from the Changbai Mountains that's supposed to make you young again. Maybe then she could take over from Yuanyuan. The action climaxes as I'm daydreaming. Yuanyuan strikes the final pose—classic, I mean seriously beautiful. It's over at last. Thank God.

Yuanyuan rushes over to me, her face glistening, smelling of perspiration. Looks up at me, fishing for compliments. No way, babe. I'm gonna make 'em squirm a little. What do they think they're doing, wasting their youth doing that fossil dance? It's criminal. I do a takeoff on them, wriggling my bum real offensively. Yuanyuan looks super-uncomfortable but only gives me a playful smack. Whip me instead, baby, that'd turn me on.

Suddenly, over all the noise, I hear the choreographer calling my name. I swing my head around in this really suave way. Man, such a good look.

Knock 'em dead, goes Yuanyuan, blowing a kiss.

Right on, my lady. Today I will. No way you guys are getting off that easy.

A Phantom 2000 flies overhead. I streak past the mirror to the tape

> *Liu's story is written entirely in the patois of Peking youth. The use of slang and sometimes offensive language was perhaps as liberating for the writer as break dancing is for his hero. There was a time, not so long ago, when poker-faced citizens of Mao's China would tell foreigners that there were no swear words in Chinese. Even in the early 1980s, when vulgar language began to find its way into literature, X's were substituted for the cruder terms. It was only in the late 1980s that the real language of the "masses," both urban and rural, belatedly found a place in literature.*
>
> *Some readers may find the "Americanisms" of the translation and the profusion of Western imagery slightly jarring. In fact, certain unlikely expressions, such as "pissing on the Bible," and references to God, are actually direct translations from the Chinese; terms like "geeks" and "dudes" have been chosen to convey the feeling of the Peking slang in the original and the tone of the story. The hero fervently desires to identify with international, specifically American, youth culture, to free himself from the bonds of tradition and convention. He may be a case study in urban cultural confusion, but while he may be somewhat extreme in his rebellion, he's not all that atypical.*

recorder and slip in my tape at supersonic speed. I'm so fast I surprise myself. Being slow gets you nowhere. Slow means the seagull, and if they put that music on, the show's over.

How ya doin', Michael Jackson? Blood brother across the seas, you really turn us on. The second I flick on the tape, the music, that totally universal music, comes just rock-'n'-rollin' out over the room. The choreographer and party bosses don't even have time to take a breath. Sorry, folks, today I'm gonna party. Outrageous? Yeah, it's a fuckin' rebellion all right. But it's a hell of a lot more fun than that boring old ribbon dance.

I collect myself, take up a position in the middle of the hall. The funky beat fills every inch of the place; we're in the mood for turmoil. I tie a black band around my head: outrageous. Black break dance gear, black fingerless gloves on hands crossed over my chest. I send out my message, the only message: black temptation.

I'm superconfident. A new historical age has crept up on the sly. Bend, shake those arms, arch the head and neck till they form an "A." A little top footwork. A front glide combined with a body wave. Hit the dirt, elbows and shoulders into a backspin and spin like a twister. Scrambled features. Electric shock. A phantom. Music rules, carries me into a state of non-ego. Nothing can hold me back, not even gravity. Every bone sends off sparks of feeling, every muscle is in ecstasy. My eyes shine with the electricity of freedom. My arms and legs move, change, do things I never knew they could. This isn't just goddamn dancing, it's pure release. I howl joyfully with a wild primitive cry like a Steppenwolf. Oh yeah! Now this is what life's all about. Just as I'm tripping out in that state of enlightenment they talk about in Chinese esthetics, the music stops dead. I crumple back to earth. What a fuckin' bummer. I see the shaking hand of the Youth League boss pull away from the tape recorder. Like a foul, sallow hand that's just been feeling up a beautiful white breast. The worst associations. Everyone's standing there dumbstruck. A pack of penguins, beaks agape, eyes staring. The sight tickles me.

The choreographer's face is bright red. Can't tell if she's excited or pissed off. It's a face that spells Big Trouble.

"And what was that all about?"

"Just what it looked like."

"All I saw was madness. Perverted madness."

"You ain't wrong there. Why make life more of a bore than it has to be? I dance as the mood takes me. If I feel crazy, I dance crazy. It's, like, breakin' out."

"Such dancing is totally unsuitable for the Arts Festival."

"Yeah, sure. But what's wrong with trying something different? People can't eat cabbage every day of their lives."

"Come on, it's getting late. Get ready to do the seagull."

"Thanks a lot." I've wasted enough time.

I go over to the exercise bar and grab my clothes. All of a sudden, I'm real uncomfortable. Yuanyuan is shooting me this seriously pained and angry glare and it gets me right in the heart.

Damn. Forgot to nod at my girl. I gaze upon the face I love more than anything else in the universe.

What's up, Yuanyuan? Don't look so sour, I can't handle it.

She's biting her lip. I know the second she stops, tears will come pouring out of her eyes.

"Don't get like that," I say huskily.

She turns on her heel and runs off just as the music for the seagull starts up. Go for it, geeks. I'm outa here. I put on my clothes, toss them this supercool look, and split; I'm one impressive dude.

Lousy seagull, fuck you!

"I swear to God I didn't mean to hurt you."

I'm standing in front of her like I'm taking an oath. Yuanyuan's thin shoulders are heaving with every sob. Never thought my baby would take it so badly. I draw her to me, hold her to my chest like a wounded deer. She pushes me away, gently but with determination. Her shoulders are still shaking. I feel like a turd. I can't think of any way to lighten things up. I never thought she'd freak out like this. I know she wants me to make a name for myself, take on the world, but that dinosaur dance bores me shitless. It cramps my style; might as well put me in a strait-jacket. Maybe that's how the Chinese have always squandered their creativity; otherwise we'd surely have worn out that little bit of civilization our ancestors left us by now.

Yuanyuan's still sitting there being real heavy. Well, fuck me if I know how love and freedom came to be enemies. I bend down and kiss her tenderly on her white neck, just under her earring. No reaction. A big zero. Usually it makes her smile, then she grabs me and we're into lip-lock mode in no time. It's not working today.

"Don't you like it when I kiss you there?" I take her face in my hands. Shit, she's still crying.

"Get serious," she goes, real serious herself. "Will you just listen to me for a second? Can you stop fooling around for just one moment? Stop jerking off, just for once, okay?"

"All right, all right, all right already." I'm in repeat-action mode. It must be a real thrill to fire a machine gun.

"Stop treating your future like some sort of joke."

"Who's joking?" I go. "Our teachers have been doing the red ribbon dance all their lives. What have they got to show for it? I'm not saying it's no good, but we're living off the past. We can't keep doing the same steps our grandparents did, can we? They spent their whole lives on their knees. Do we have to do that, too? Come on! I just wanna try something new, live a bit more freely. When you've got nothing to live for, life sucks. Why not try—"

"Try, try, try! What else do you want to try? How about trying to become premier of China then? At least I'll have a good time, too."

"Give me a break. They wouldn't even let me be head of a street committee."

"Let me ask you something: How long do you think a dancer's career lasts? Why waste your time on that rubbish? So you think you're the only one with any talent and the other ten hundred million of us are just time servers, is that it?"

"But why not dance something you like? Why not live life the way you want to?" I throw in all the theory I've learned at break dance classes these past few days.

"I like the moon. Can you pluck it from the sky for me? Anyway, do you really think those dances you like are really for us Chinese?"

"They're international. If you're looking for a pedigree, I guess they come from black Africa . . . don't forget, our ancestors were all monkeys once." *

"You're really far gone." Yuanyuan smiled.

Timing. Everything's a matter of timing, and I'm not one to let an opportunity slip. I put a hand on Yuanyuan's waist, right on the place an expert in these matters says is one of a woman's most vulnerable spots.

"Come on, let's go have some fun." My voice catches in my throat and makes a pitiful sound I hardly recognize as my own.

. . . The people in charge of the Youth League want to see me at nine tomorrow morning. I know for sure: I'm dead meat. At best I'll get a stay of execution. Anyway, I'm definitely in deep shit. Those fuckers never did like me.

So I head for the Noon Gate [in the Forbidden City right behind Tiananmen] to spend the evening. A good night there is just incredible, all of China's break dance elite in one place. They're all "problem youths" infected with "initial stage syndrome." † Can't hack their parents, can't deal with the traditional love scenario, hate their bosses. They

---

* Racist attitudes against blacks are far from uncommon in China and can be found in writings as far back as the Tang dynasty. The protagonist doesn't seem to be aware of the contradiction between his racism and his adoration of Michael Jackson and the break-dance culture. He later also makes a disparaging comment about homosexuality that reflects another typical prejudice. Even many university students thoughtlessly share these general views, and in 1988–1989 there were scattered demonstrations against black African students dating Chinese women.

† A reference to the theory of the "initial stage of socialism" propounded by the party in 1987. This is supposedly the stage of social development in which capitalist and socialist reality intermingle.

The Cry

In the past ten years China has achieved satisfactory progress. Our biggest mistake is in the field of education; ideological and political work has weakened and education has not been developed enough.

—Deng Xiaoping to Ugandan President Yoweri Kaguta Museveni, March 23, 1989

all go there to cut loose. What could be better: dancing to rock music where the old Qing emperors slept. It's a real turn-on.

As I reach the Bridge of the Golden Waters all I can hear is the thunderous wave of rock music pouring out of the five massive doors in the palace gate. These dudes are dead set on rockin' the place until those red walls and green tiles come a-tumblin' down. . . .

When I reach the Noon Gate the place is exploding with break dancing. Rock music hits me on all sides: ghetto blasters of every shape and size on the ground, stuck on the backs of bikes, hung in the trees. Sorry, Your Imperial Highness, we couldn't be bothered to prostrate ourselves on the ground, kowtow, and cry out "Ten Thousand Years" tonight. Instead, our thunder is shaking you from your dreams.

I squeeze my way in and spot a crowd of happenin' dudes. They're doing finger curls, the whip, glides, and shoulder pops. They are fuckin' ace. There's this old fella there mumbling away, abusing our ancestors —perfectly quiet spot like this destroyed by a gang of punks, yakety yakety yak. He's still carping on when this guy bops over and says, What's eating you, granddad? The emperor left this for all of us. I don't start bitching when Your Reverence practices tai chi here, so why does our break dancing bother you? Take a good look. Can you do this? He suddenly drops to the ground backwards and, balancing on his shoulders, does this really radical backspin. Then he jumps up, snatching up the worn old carpet he'd been dancing on, and, with a weird chuckle, walks off. The old boy, pissed, splits too.

Meanwhile, the boys and girls are getting hot. A lot of their moves are off the wall, some of it's dork city. But everyone is having a good time, hanging loose. Their hot, sweaty faces raise the temperature, you can feel the satisfaction in the air. This is it, the smell of life itself. The only thing the wankers in our dance troupe smell of is bullshit. Mineral water and insecticide.

Don't know whose idea it is to turn off all the blasters. Someone climbs up a tree and beams a light down, a spotlight like they use on-

The Noon Gate

stage. He must have nicked it. A band appears in the lit circle. They're skinheads in blue Chinese jackets and cloth-soled shoes. Fuckin' amazing. Western rock in Chinese rig. Breakin' out is international. They're living free. But, wow, are they lousy musicians. Barf-city rock. Everyone screams and mobs into the square to dance anyway. There are people with brooms and umbrellas,* all the fuckers are my age. It's like they're showing off their youth and having a pavement-pounding competition at the same time.

Right then I think: Over in the land of the Mississippi, Tyson and Spinks are fighting for the title. The boys and girls in the Paris Métro are smoking dope.

A few girls who've put on the Hong Kong look are dancing disco. One

---

* Presumably inspired by the dance Tony a.k.a. "Turbo" (played by Shrimp) does in the 1984 American film *Breakin'* when he's supposed to be sweeping outside a shop. The "tall, ugly black guy" the protagonist referred to earlier is Tony's partner Otis, a.k.a. "Ozone" (played by Shabba-Doo). *Breakin'* played in theaters throughout China in 1988 and was enormously popular.

Still from the film *Rock 'n' Roll Youth*

with shoulder-length hair looks like Yuanyuan. She turns me on. If only it were Yuanyuan. Damn it, why won't she ever come out and have some fun?

Then these ugly dudes get up and start dancing real wild, like they don't know what to do with all their energy. It's like every muscle and bone just gets in their way, they're thrashing and bouncing around and suddenly one of them dives for the ground and does a really awesome headspin. People cry out; I'm seriously impressed. Then a young guy with a punk haircut does a big glide, like he's skimming on water. Then a moonwalk. Unbelievable.

This squid standing next to me suddenly screams and grabs my arm. She's shaking with excitement. I give her a real warm smile and she releases me with a dumb, slack-jaw laugh. I turn to look at these kids who are really letting go now, generating waves of excitement. It's like being in a wild, totally free world. I feel like I'm on fire. Then I see some seriously amazing kung fu.

Some high school kids are doing somersaults, handstands, and splits, just like acrobats in the Peking opera. One of them does a Thomas flair and the whole of the Noon Gate begins to spin.

I can't resist this black temptation another second. I tear off my jacket. Believe me, no normal person could have kept back. Unless, of course, you're a fuckin' nutcase or some mummy out of the Mawangdui Tomb.

A BREAK DANCER'S CONFESSION

When I'm break dancing I feel passionate and uninhibited. That's why people assume I'm a wild, crazy kind of girl. In fact, I'm normally very quiet and soft-spoken, introverted even, and quite straight. When we have visitors, it's all I can do to stammer out a few polite words, and even then I turn bright red. Often I turn around and go a bit out of my way rather than have to stop and say hello to people I know on the street. But when I hear that entrancing music my feet start tapping and I feel like waving my arms. The last drop of adolescent shyness evaporates as hot blood surges through my veins. After all, I'm a child of the eighties!

—Jin Hua, a nineteen-year-old salesgirl in
an electrical appliance shop in Tianjin

I throw down my jacket, tighten my belt, and dive into the break dance whirlpool.

How's Tyson doing? Will he be world champ? If I could make a bet, I'd put my money on him for sure. 'Cause he's young.

—Hey, dude, playing our game now? What happened to the red ribbon dance? Isn't this stuff beneath you?

—You trying to embarrass me or what?

—You're a real talent; you could be king of the square in three days if you wanted. Of course, you're still a bit rough around the edges.

The more I dance, the crazier I get, every cell in my body is rockin' 'n' rollin'. Fuckin' ecstasy! Not some robotic performance, but total liberty. My life starts now. Clenching my fists, I raise them high in the air, waving my arms. I enter a realm of pure freedom. I want to give Gullit a call. This cool, long-haired soccer star has just scored in Naples, pushing even Maradona out of the limelight. A new "King of Soccer" is born. Why can't there be a new "King of Dance"? The world will know of my triumph, my freedom. Suddenly I see four suns in the sky, I can't tell north from south, east from west. Who said the earth is the center of the universe? How come we should be the center of everything? Why say the sun rises in the east? Does the universe have an east or west? They say Nixon made a real fool of himself with the astronauts who landed on the moon. Like a dope he asked them, What's it like up there? I mean, like, where's "up there"?

Forget it, just dance. To hell with the future.

I'm dancing with two real artistic units, guys with long hair and beards. These days that's really hip. If you're not a skinhead, you've got to have long hair.

We're always having to repress our feelings. So the second you get the chance to let it all out on the dance floor, you're on fire. People have been singing Shaanxi folk tunes for thousands of years, but add a little rock music and everyone goes crazy. It's the Northwest Wind.* But that's not really enough, you've still got to let off steam.

Gradually I feel like my movements are a flood of pure excitement, my muscular body is shimmering like the summer sun. Youthful strength surges through my veins like I'm twenty again, forever in the black groove of break dance, forever in the groove of rock 'n' roll. Blood-red life! The freedom of night! I feel like I'm drunk, crazed, totally spaced out. Hey, all you "freaks" on the Berlin U-bahn! Brothers, sisters—we're all sexy, we're all funky. What's so great about smack, man? Forget shooting up; those needle-pocked arms ought to be dancing. Come down to the Noon Gate and break dance. We'll give you the ultimate high. You'll forget all that heavy shit the world throws at you. Forget drugs, forget being gay, don't get into all that prostitution shit.

It's getting real late. Suddenly, this guy with long, messy hair and a guitar on his back leaps onto one of the stone lions and starts singing with a throaty voice and everyone sings along as the band thumps out the beat. I'm going clear out of my head:

Dancing our favorite dance
*   so ecstatic*
singing our favorite song
*   so laid-back*
the ground is breaking up under our feet
we're the funkiest people you'll ever meet
singing and dancing, happy and free
your happiness has sure won over me
and I win your love with my energy
forget your worries, go to town
cut the chains that hold you down.
Be happy, yeah, be free!

* In 1988, rock and disco versions of folk tunes from Shaanxi Province in Northwest China became the rage. The fad was called the Northwest Wind. The popular soundtrack album of *Red Sorghum*, the directorial debut of Zhang Yimou (see *Seeds of Fire*, pp. 252, 259), featured songs belonging to this genre.

Everyone cheers. No one gives a damn if old granny Cixi * can't sleep. Time passes too quickly; I still haven't had enough. It's like how unsatisfied Uncle Sam and the blond chicks in the audience must've felt when Tyson knocked out Leon Spinks after ninety-seven seconds. I suddenly remember that I've got an appointment with Yuanyuan in our elevator, so I slip on my jacket real slick and push my way through the crowd. . . .

Buttoning my jacket, I raise my head only to see this incredibly sad sight. Sitting in a wheelchair is a beautiful young student. Her bright, beautiful eyes are fixed on me. I'm taken aback. She's so beautiful it hurts. Life's so unfair. Who says she has to be crippled while all those dog-faced girls get off being healthy? I walk over. I want to comfort her, to stroke her face. No, people will say I'm a hooligan. So all I can do is smile at her. That makes things worse. She smiles back, somewhat strangely, and those sparkling eyes cloud over and fill with tears, tears like I've never seen before, sticky, translucent drops of crystal. Those eyes are full of tenderness. I can't take it, I think I'm going to cry. A gust of cold wind chills me to the core and a shiver runs down my spine, as if the sweat has frozen on my body. How can I help you? If you need a healthy pair of legs, I'd give you mine, truly, I wouldn't mind. Only don't look so sad, so pitiful.

There'll be no sweets for me tonight. The elevator has been off for ages. It probably didn't know we had a date. I hate that old bag who locked it on me. Why not leave it on for us? We wouldn't wreck it. We're real civilized.

Yuanyuan throws me a fierce glare. She's so pretty when she's angry! I want to make her laugh, but it's not working. It looks like humor won't go very far tonight. Maybe I should fart—sometimes when I'm training I fart, and that always makes her laugh. Says I'm destroying the ambience. But where are my farts tonight? Lost in the "elixir field" below my navel, I guess. Bad luck.

"Well, have a good dance? Getting yourself mixed up with the types that go to a place like that! Have you found someone prettier than me there?"

* The Qing dowager empress (1835–1908).

"No way!"

"Humph! Why'd you waste your time going to the dance academy? What's next? Break dancing in Zhongnanhai?" *

The hero quits the dance troupe, breaks up with Yuanyuan, and gets a job working for a fashion designer. He directs a hit fashion show, has a short-lived affair with the designer, and finally leaves the company. He ends up living with a woman sign painter and artist whose name he doesn't even know.

The story ends with him lying in bed after their first night together. She's made him breakfast and left him her keys before going out.

I take a long, satisfying stretch. My calves feel a little soft. Time to get out of bed. In a while Tian Zhuangzhuang's coming over to see me. He's the Fifth Generation director who made *On the Hunting Ground* and *Horse Thief*. He's a guy who doesn't quite play the game. Reckons he wants to make a film of my story, likes it 'cause it's not over the top, nor is it about heroes. We're real thick, he talks my language. Neither of us likes to make life a hassle, we're also into dumping on the usual worldly crap.

I don't care if no one understands me. But I'm worried about Zhuangzhuang. Will he be able to express the anxiety, loss, anger, frustrations, and rebelliousness of my generation? Will the censors pass it? All I can say is: Good luck, Zhuangzhuang.

Tian Zhuangzhuang went on to make the film Rock 'n' Roll Youth, *which screened in Peking in early 1989 and again in the months after the massacre. Although recognizing the significance of Liu Yiran's story, Tian completely failed to capture the spirit of the original.*

Tian was the only member of China's film community to sign the Petition of 33 in February 1989, which called for the party to release

---

* Zhongnanhai is the headquarters of the Communist Party and formerly part of the imperial palace. During the 1989 Protest Movement, the entrance to Zhongnanhai was besieged a number of times by students and other petitioners, some of whom staged a hunger strike there. While there was no break dancing in Zhongnanhai, the student protesters camped out on the square nearby sometimes amused themselves at night by break dancing there.

Wei Jingsheng and other political prisoners. In mid-1990, Tian Zhuang-zhuang completed a film about Li Lianying, the eunuch favorite of the Dowager Empress Cixi. The final scene shows the aged empress dying while being carried by the eunuch. He collapses under her weight. This is seen by many as a political allegory with contemporary significance.

Petitions and Protest

What is now most required of Chinese intellectuals, in particular enlightened intellectuals, is neither to mourn Hu Yaobang nor to eulogize him, but rather to confront the figures of the imprisoned Wei Jingsheng and Xu Wenli and to engage in a collective act of repentance. The petition movement, rather than being seen as a heroic undertaking, would best be understood as the first step toward such repentance.

—Liu Xiaobo, April 1989

There is a venerable tradition in China of petitioning rulers, and an equally ancient tradition of rulers punishing those who dare petition them. Bi Gan, an argumentative minister of the Shang dynasty (twelfth century B.C.), so infuriated the tyrant Zhou that Zhou, saying, "They tell me sages have seven holes in their hearts," ordered the minister's chest cut open so he could see for himself.

But appeals to the throne were not always so hazardous. Outside the court, from early days, a drum was placed that could be beaten by petitioners who wanted the court's attention. The marble huabiao pillars on either side of Tiananmen Gate were also a reminder to emperors to accept petitions with equanimity.

Petitioning was a major element of the 1989 Protest Movement. While the Student Movement, or Democracy Movement as it is often called by the Chinese, is generally considered to have begun with the overt student agitation that followed the death of Hu Yaobang in April, we see the 1989 Protest Movement as beginning in early January at the initiation of Fang Lizhi, the astrophysicist who was purged from the party for his outspokenness in 1987 and was the first prominent Chinese intellectual to publicly declare himself to be carrying on from where Wei Jingsheng left off in 1979.* Official Chinese denunciations of the movement also identify Fang's letter as its starting point.

---

* For more on Fang Lizhi and Wei Jingsheng, see *Seeds of Fire*, pp. xxxi–xxxiii, 277–89, 328–40.

On January 6, 1989, Fang Lizhi wrote the following open letter to Deng Xiaoping:

Chairman Deng Xiaoping
Central Military Commission
Communist Party of China

This year marks the fortieth anniversary of the founding of the People's Republic of China. It is also the seventieth anniversary of the May Fourth Movement. There are sure to be many commemorative activities surrounding these two events. However, people may well be less interested in reflecting on the past than on the present and the future. They hope that these two anniversaries will give them cause for optimism.

In view of this, I would most sincerely suggest that as these anniversaries approach, a nationwide amnesty be declared for all political prisoners, and particularly Wei Jingsheng.

I believe that no matter what opinion one has of Wei Jingsheng, to release him now after he has served some ten years of imprisonment would be a humanitarian gesture that would contribute to a healthy social atmosphere.

This year also happens to be the bicentenary of the French Revolution, and however one views it, the slogans of liberty, equality, fraternity, and human rights have gained universal respect. For these reasons, it is my sincere hope that you will consider my suggestion, thereby earning even greater respect in the future.

    Felicitations,
    Fang Lizhi

Over the next two months Fang's petition inspired a series of similar appeals to the government from writers, scholars, and scientists, emboldened by the government's failure to retaliate against Fang. Later petitioners generally sought safety in numbers. Their appeals were aimed as much at other ordinary Chinese as at the government, for they called for the awakening of conscience, for fairness and justice. They were also cries of desperation, urging people to act before the economic, political, and cultural crises facing China in the late 1980s (see pp. 213–320) drove the country to catastrophe.

Fang Lizhi (Mi Qiu)

Some of the petitions originated in Chinese communities in Europe and the United States. In Hong Kong the response was particularly strong: A petition organized in February calling for the release of China's political prisoners was signed by more than 12,700 people.

The Protest Movement often took on the appearance of a rebellion of the young against the old. The picture the Western media presented was largely one of a movement led by students in their early twenties. Indeed, many of the slogans that appeared during the massive street marches attacked China's leaders as being too old to govern. Despite the youthful image of the movement, however, the young did not enjoy a monopoly on rebellion.

A number of the masterminds of the movement's ever-changing strategies were intellectuals in their thirties and forties who generally stayed behind the scenes. And as we read these petitions we also hear the voices of much older people. These include Bing Xin and Ba Jin, writers in their eighties and members of the original May Fourth generation who had called for democracy and freedom in the late 1910s and '20s, and others like Wang Ruowang, a Shanghai writer in his seventies. Fang Lizhi himself was in his fifties. In fact, Deng and the other party leaders felt most threatened by the protests of the older generations.

On January 28, Fang, Wang Ruoshui, and Su Shaozhi (see below) were among those present at a salon organized by the independent intellectual journal New Enlightenment, *whose title had been inspired by the May Fourth Movement—also called the "Enlightenment Movement."*

The gathering was held at the Dule Bookstore in southwest Peking. A number of the guests made statements to the effect that China was facing a crisis of which a central feature was the reappearance of "feudalism in the guise of Marxism-Leninism."

On February 13, a petition in support of Fang Lizhi's letter was organized by the poet Bei Dao* along with Chen Jun, an entrepreneur cum political activist. Bei Dao and Chen Jun collected thirty-three signatures for their petition. A number of the signatories were controversial figures in their own right; others, like Bing Xin (born 1900), were important members of the cultural establishment. The letter was distributed publicly along with Fang's January petition at a press conference held at Chen Jun's JJ Café in Peking on February 16. The JJ Café was used as a venue for the gathering of more signatures for the letter.

On February 22, a spokesperson for the party judiciary made an official response to the petition:

This letter calling for the release of Wei Jingsheng is aimed at influencing public opinion, bringing pressure to bear on the government, and interfering with the judicial decisions of the State . . . this contravenes the principles of legality in China and as such is erroneous.

Even after this letter was attacked by the authorities in the Chinese media, Bing Xin defended her action by saying that Wei Jingsheng may have been guilty of treason as accused, but it was normal to announce an amnesty on an occasion such as the fortieth anniversary of the state. After all, she commented to a reporter from an official newspaper, Pu Yi, the last emperor of the Qing dynasty and the puppet ruler of the Japanese state of Manchukuo, was released in the 1950s under just such an amnesty. She hinted that if a traitor like Pu Yi could be the object of such official magnanimity, so could Wei Jingsheng.

On February 26, another petition signed by forty-two intellectuals, mostly scientists, was sent to party and state leaders.

Also on February 26, Fang Lizhi and his wife, Li Shuxian, were prevented by Chinese security personnel from attending a Texas-style barbeque hosted by U.S. President Bush at Peking's Great Wall Sheraton, to which they had been invited by the president. The Chinese authorities, who had vetted the guest list, had not indicated beforehand to either

---

* For more on Bei Dao, see *Seeds of Fire*, pp. 2–17, 236–37, 388–93.

Bing Xin (Deng Wei, Joint Publishing Company)

Fang and his wife or the Americans that they would object to Fang's presence at the banquet. On February 27, Bei Dao wrote an outraged letter to the government in which he captured a sentiment shared by many people in the Chinese capital at the time.

Our Rulers Must Get Used to Hearing Different Voices

Last night (February 26) the police physically prevented Professor Fang Lizhi and his wife, Li Shuxian, from attending U.S. President Bush's farewell banquet at the Great Wall Sheraton Hotel. The actions of the police constitute a gross violation of the human rights of Fang and Li. This incident has deeply shocked me; it is without question a great blot on China's human rights record.

Professor Fang represents the cream of Chinese intellectuals. The crude infringement of his rights is an insult to every self-respecting Chinese intellectual. If this incident is to be construed as the government's response to Professor Fang's open letter of January 6 and the Petition of 33, which I initiated on February 13, then I feel nothing but profound sorrow.

When I initiated that petition I trusted the government would react in a rational and enlightened way. I thought the government would at least listen in a spirit of forbearance to a suggestion made by writers and scholars, especially as our voice was so mild. But if even this cannot be tolerated it shows how fragile democracy and legality are in China. Capitalism has no monopoly on the protection of human rights and freedom of speech; they are the standard of any modern, civilized society.

I believe every Chinese intellectual realizes how extremely tortuous China's path to Reform is. However, during this process, the rulers must become accustomed to hearing different, even discordant, voices. It is beneficial to develop such a habit; it will mark the beginning of China's progress toward becoming a modern and civilized society.

I am a poet with no interest in politics. Nor do I wish to become an object of media attention. Originally I hoped to withdraw after the publication of our petition, to return once more to my desk, to return to the world of my imagination. Yet if in a country the size of China there is no room for a writer's desk, I feel I can remain silent no longer.

Bei Dao
Peking

Shock at Fang's treatment and growing concern over political and legal rights in China led to an overwhelming response among Hong Kong Chinese, overseas Chinese intellectuals, and China scholars and writers.

Meanwhile, from early March onward, posters attacking the government and supporting Fang Lizhi and calling for demonstrations in support of "freedom" and "democracy" began appearing at Peking University. Since May 4, 1988, concerned intellectuals had met at Peking University in unofficial gatherings called Democracy Salons. On March 9, such a salon was organized by Wang Dan, a history student who later became one of the movement's leaders. The speakers called for action. They included the former Democracy Wall activist Ren Wanding, a dissident and founder of the Chinese Human Rights League who had only recently been released from jail.

In April the government attempted to close down the salon at Peking University.

On March 17, forty-three important cultural figures in Peking wrote to the Chinese congress in support of the call for an amnesty for political

"There is no longer enough room for a quiet writing desk in the whole of North China." This statement was originally part of the student manifesto of the December 9 Movement [which called for national unity in the face of the invading Japanese] of 1935. For Bei Dao to paraphrase this declaration shows the level of anger and shock among young people at the repressive attitude of the Communist Party of China regarding the question of human rights.
—Lee Yee, *editor of* The Nineties Monthly*

* For more on Lee Yee, see *Seeds of Fire*, pp. 274–76, 373–77.

prisoners. *They stressed their belief that such an action would accord with the constitution as well as reflect the popular will.*

This letter was initiated by a scholar in the Chinese Academy of Social Sciences. First on the list of signatories, however, was Dai Qing, a prominent journalist, party member, and member of the privileged circle of elite party families. When Dai Qing was later accused of "instigating rebellion" against the party, her involvement with this letter was construed as one of her criminal acts. At the time she defended her action in a telephone interview with the sometime correspondent for The Nineties Monthly *in Hong Kong, Zhang Langlang (who also writes under just the name Langlang):*

LANGLANG: Does the appearance of your petition have anything to do with the upcoming sessions of the National People's Congress and the Political Consultative Congress?

DAI: Of course; we're aiming the petition at these meetings.

LANGLANG: So you are hoping for some concrete results?

DAI: I hold out no such hope. But I think we have to speak up. Now I feel at least I can look myself in the face. What type of person would I be if I didn't even dare make this type of statement?

On March 28, seven members of the Hong Kong "Delegation Calling for the Release of Wei Jingsheng" flew to Peking via Tianjin to deliver a petition signed by more than three thousand people from some thirty countries to the National People's Congress. One of the delegates, a former prisoner on the mainland, was forced to return to Hong Kong, and the petition and other materials were confiscated by border officials. This led to widespread outrage in Hong Kong, where confidence in the territory's future took yet another plunge. After all, critics pointed out, the delegation was only trying to deliver a petition to the congress; this did not bode well for the ability of Hong Kong citizens to make legitimate representations to the body that would be governing them after 1997. But Ni Kuang, one of Hong Kong's most popular and prolific writers and formerly a soldier on the mainland, took issue with the whole idea of petitions.

What Political Prisoners?

NI KUANG

I think the people behind the petitions are making a big mistake by asking the Chinese Communist authorities to release political prisoners: They don't have any political prisoners on the mainland, only counterrevolutionaries. Wei Jingsheng went to prison on charges of counterrevolution; in the eyes of the Chinese Communist Party there's no such thing as a political prisoner, so who have they got to release? The petitioners ought to be calling for the release of all counterrevolutionaries.*

Of course, to be even more accurate, no one should be using the term "counterrevolutionary" either. What is a "counterrevolutionary"? It's someone who opposes the Communist Party—but does the party really represent revolution? Mainland intellectuals always approach problems in the most simplistic manner; it's useless. You can achieve democracy, human rights, and freedom only through fundamental opposition to the Communist Party; to bargain with the Communist Party for democracy and freedom is like trying to talk a tiger into giving up its skin—forget it! Chinese intellectuals keep making the same mistakes; they inevitably yield before the mighty. They beg for a little largess from the powers-that-be; they dare not rebel. What good is it going to do even if tens of thousands of intellectuals put their names to the petitions? The only way to fight for democracy is to rebel against the Communists.

---

* At least two prominent academics declined to sign Bei Dao's letter because they felt the call for the release of political prisoners could be seen as including clemency for Jiang Qing and other detained members of the hated "Gang of Four."

(Morgan Chua)

On April 5, the thirteenth anniversary of the 1976 Tiananmen Incident, an issue of The New May Fourth, *a journal put out by the Institute for Research into Problems of Contemporary Society under the Philology Society (Xuehaishe) of Peking University, published an article by Wang Dan. The following are excerpts from that article, one of the few theoretical works written by any student leader of the 1989 Protest Movement. Wang was arrested after the massacre and sentenced in early 1991 to four years' imprisonment for his role in the protests.*

In Wang Dan's stolid prose (marked in the Chinese original by the use of Maoist terminology and abstract, "scientific" prose), we see none of the style or flair of Fang Lizhi, Wei Jingsheng, or Liu Xiaobo. Note too that in the penultimate paragraph Wang stops short of endorsing absolute freedom of speech.

On Freedom of Speech

WANG DAN

Although freedom of speech is an important principle enshrined in the Constitution, it has long been savagely and tyrannically trampled underfoot. This is strikingly demonstrated by the way the authorities violently and illegally ban the expression of opposing views in political life. These bans amount to the open imposition of the formula: Truth = The Proletarian World View = Marxism = The Party's World View = Declarations by the Party's Leading Organs = The Highest Leaders

Themselves. This reasoning is so clearly absurd that there is no need to refute it. . . .

I must make perfectly clear that we do not advocate absolute freedom of speech. Any development has its internally dictated limitations, making absolute freedom impossible. But we oppose any restrictions that are imposed from the outside, particularly by violent means.

In the current movement for a New Enlightenment in China, the intellectual elite must place first priority on freedom of speech and have the courage to criticize injustice, including unjust decision making and actions by the party and the government. For the only social role intellectuals have is to speak out, and if we lose our freedom of speech and are unable to aid the progress of China's democratization or take an independent critical stance, we will continue to be expendable dependents on the party and the government, and our fate will be no better than it has been for the last forty years.

The death on April 15 of Hu Yaobang, the former party general secretary forced to resign in early 1987, marked the beginning of a new level and style of protest. The "cry" now included tearful eulogies for the dead party leader by China's most influential and reformist intellectuals. These were accompanied by calls to the party and state to reassess Hu's career favorably and exonerate him from charges of "bourgeois liberalization," or Bourgelib. Student protests and agitation among intellectuals became increasingly public; those who, like Hu, had been accused of Bourgelib in 1987 now demanded that the leadership reverse the "verdict" against them as well. *

A common sentiment was summed up in the slogan:

The man who ought not to have died is dead, those who ought to be dead are still alive.

For most activists, the aim of the protests was to achieve official recognition of a spectrum of problems: the unfairness of the official verdict on Hu Yaobang, the need to carry out political reform, the elimination of corruption and nepotism within the party and its business sector, an improvement of the poor living and studying conditions in the universi-

* See *Seeds of Fire*, pp. 341–84, especially page 350, for an elucidation of Bourgelib.

ties, and a positive response to students' concern about their job assignments. These and other more concrete demands were often subsumed under vague slogans of democracy and freedom.

The Tragedy of a "Tragic Hero": A Critique of the Hu Yaobang Phenomenon

LIU XIAOBO

In August 1988, Liu Xiaobo, a literary critic in his early thirties,* traveled to Norway to lecture, after which he spent some months in the United States. During his sojourn abroad he wrote a series of devastating critiques of the mainland government and a book-length study of contemporary Chinese intellectuals. Like those of Wei Jingsheng and Fang Lizhi, Liu Xiaobo's political writings (most of which were composed overseas) did much to reveal the limitations and hypocrisy of his contemporaries. One of the truly independent voices of China and an admirer of Nietzsche, Liu decided to return to Peking in late April at the height of the student demonstrations, claiming it was necessary to participate in the protest rather than discuss it at a safe distance. Indeed, he returned only days after the following analysis of Chinese intellectuals' response to Hu Yaobang's death was published. His example proved embarrassing to many other intellectual dissidents overseas.

This article was first published in Chinese in New York and was reprinted in full in the appendix of an officially sponsored volume of denunciations of Liu produced on the mainland after June. The clarity of thought and good sense expressed in this essay stand in strong contrast to the sentimental and bombastic pronouncements of many other Chinese intellectuals who were overseas at the time of Hu's demise. It also helps explain why Liu is so unpopular both with reformist intellectuals and with more conservative elements.

Liu's point about Hu Yaobang having been a member of a privileged elite is an important one. The issue of privilege and nepotism in the party was one of the most emotive issues of the 1989 Protest Movement, and one that mobilized the people of Peking and the nation.

---

* See *Seeds of Fire*, pp. 395–97.

> I would believe in a revolution, any revolution, and in a party, any party, that would replace the present government by Face, Fate, and Favor by a government by law. These three have made the rule of Justice and the weeding out of official corruption impossible. The only reason why official corruption remains is that we have never shot the officials, not one of them. We couldn't so long as these three goddesses still remain. The only way to deal with corruption in the officials is just to shoot them. The matter is really as simple as that. And democracy is an easy thing when we can impeach an official for breaking the law with a chance of winning the case. The people do not have to be trained for democracy, they will fall into it. When the officials are democratic enough to appear before a law court and answer an impeachment, the people can be made democratic enough overnight to impeach them. Take off from the people the incubus of official privilege and corruption and the people of China will take care of themselves. For greater than all the other virtues is the virtue of Justice, and that is what China wants. This is my faith and this is my conviction, won from long and weary thoughts.
>
> —*Lin Yutang, 1936*

All I felt when I heard about Hu Yaobang's death was indifference. People die when they get old. What did shock me was the emotional response to his death of intellectuals both in China and overseas, in particular among proponents of democratization. It made me suspicious of my own indifference; it unsettled me. Was I being too callous, unfeeling—amoral, even? These doubts led me earnestly, you could even say solemnly, to set about reading the various news items, commentaries, and memorials concerning Hu. My surprise, doubt, and unease turned to despair, a cool despair. This was not on account of Hu Yaobang's death, nor was I becoming infected by the national mood of mourning; I despaired because of the excessive response of the Chinese to his death.

A TRAGEDY OF THE SYSTEM, NOT THE INDIVIDUAL

When Hu Yaobang was forced to resign from his position as party general secretary in early 1987 during the Anti-Bourgelib Campaign, someone dubbed him a "tragic hero." But popular sympathy gradually faded, and when he failed to do anything to defend himself after his fall it turned to apathy. Things changed dramatically between February and April of this year. Leading to these changes were the series of failures surrounding the Reforms in 1988 and 1989, the weakening of party and state power, and the growing sense of despondency and discontent among the populace. Fang Lizhi's appeal to the government for the release of political prisoners led to a host of joint letters and petitions, and the sudden demise of Hu Yaobang finally ignited a broad-based Protest Movement. It was as if everyone had been transported back to the time of mourning for Zhou Enlai and the Tiananmen Incident of April 5, 1976. Hu Yaobang's spirit, like that of Zhou Enlai, had gained a heroic stature as a result of popular sorrow and protest.

But I am tempted to ask: Why do the Chinese always go in for this particular brand of tragedy—starting with Qu Yuan, who drowned himself in the Miluo River? Why is it the Chinese feel so much more deeply for tragic heroes like Zhou Enlai, Peng Dehuai, and Hu Yaobang than for ones like Wei Jingsheng?* Is the last really worth so much less than the others as a person and a political victim? The answer to my first question should be obvious to everyone: Authoritarianism brooks no opponents, not even well-intentioned, helpful ones. For this reason the tragedies of Hu Yaobang and the rest of them are not personal tragedies but tragedies of the system itself; they are bound to be repeated as long as our authoritarian system remains. All of these tragic heroes have one thing in common: They were loyal but not trusted, they told the truth and were condemned for it.

HU YAOBANG AND WEI JINGSHENG

The second question calls for a somewhat deeper analysis. To be quite fair, Wei Jingsheng, Xu Wenli, and other tragic figures of the Democracy Wall period were far more progressive in both word and deed than Hu Yaobang and other members of the party's enlightened faction. I think there is a basic difference between the two.

Hu Yaobang attempted reform within the parameters of an authoritarian system. The fact that he was able to perform countless good deeds

---

* Qu Yuan (ca. 340–278 B.C.), supposed author of the *Chuci* poems, was banished by his king for offering unwanted advice and is said to have drowned himself in the Miluo River. He is a traditional icon of tragic loyalty. Peng Dehuai (1898–1974) was a famous Red Army general and China's minister of defense until 1959, when he was purged for criticizing Mao Zedong's ruinous Great Leap Forward.

Liu Xiaobo *(Emancipation Monthly)*

was not a mark of the system's superiority, but rather the result of the huge amount of personal privilege he enjoyed as party general secretary. To use privilege to protect people fighting for democracy is an antinomy and self-parody, for the protector as well as the protected.

The Democracy Wall activists, on the other hand, were calling for the abolition of the authoritarian system itself. They devoted themselves to the struggle for individual rights and independence, and the authoritarian system could not tolerate this. The publication of fiercely critical articles in official journals does not amount to freedom of speech; the ability to print the most politically conservative articles in an independent journal run by ordinary people, on the other hand, does. For example, in 1979 the party could tolerate writers like Liu Binyan publishing highly critical works (such as "The She-wolf," * in which there is the line "The Communists keep everything under control, everything, that is, except for themselves"), yet it could not countenance a samizdat publication like the literary journal *Today*. Many of the articles published in the samizdat journals of the Democracy Wall period were no less in favor of Deng Xiaoping's Reform than those in official publications were; yet the former were banned, while the latter were encouraged.

Furthermore, Hu Yaobang had to suffer nothing more than being forced to resign his post; Wei Jingsheng and his fellows, on the other hand, were clapped in irons and thrown into prison. The inhuman pun-

---

* *"Renyao zhi jian"* in Chinese. The title of what is perhaps Liu's most famous work of reportage is also translated as "Between Man and Demon."

ishments they have suffered are far, far worse than anything ever meted out to Hu. Whereas Hu, as a member of the privileged elite, was humiliated by being stripped of his power, prison is the fate of commoners like Wei Jingsheng. I believe that in a Western democracy, anyone who, for example, commits murder would be treated equally before the law, whether they be Ronald Reagan or an office clerk. But in China the system of privilege determines not only what you can enjoy, but how severely you may be punished.

No matter what criticisms he made of the party, Hu Yaobang was always seen as wanting to protect its authoritarian rule. Thus his treatment was different in its nature from that of people like Wei Jingsheng. Hu was the victim of an internal party conflict; Wei Jingsheng and his fellows were destroyed because they opposed the dictatorship itself.

INTELLECTUALS AS COURTIERS

I believe, therefore, that courageous pro-democracy intellectuals must be more enthusiastic and active in their support and concern for the pioneers of the democracy movement; they should at least speak up as loudly for Wei Jingsheng as they do for Hu Yaobang. Recent events, however, have shown quite the opposite tendency.

Ten years ago there was a tragic, even chilling, silence when Wei was jailed. Even now appeals for the release of political prisoners are still cast in the mildest of terms. This is in stark contrast to the powerful groundswell of mourning for Hu Yaobang. Even intellectuals regarded by the government as dissidents have not only eulogized Hu to the skies, but also made a big show of phoning or visiting his family to pay their respects. Here, in far-off America, Li Chunguang phoned Hu Deping, Hu Yaobang's son, on behalf of Liu Binyan, Wang Ruoshui, and [the political commentator] Ruan Ming, to express their grief.* The depth and sincerity of emotion are redolent with an air of servitude normally seen only in the relationship between loyal mandarins and their emperor. Not even in his wildest dreams could Wei Jingsheng or his fellows ever hope for such treatment. If Fang Lizhi hadn't come forward and made an appeal on Wei's behalf in January, there might never have been a petition movement at all. The agonies Wei Jingsheng, Xu Wenli, and others have suffered in prison have been far greater than anything Hu

---

* For Liu Binyan and Wang Ruoshui, see *Seeds of Fire*, pp. 354–60 and 150–51, respectively.

Yaobang experienced following his fall from power, but have any Chinese intellectuals ever attempted to contact their families and express their concern?

There are complex reasons for all of this: strategic considerations, the concern for personal safety, and, even more important, that typically Chinese phenomenon of power worship. If it's true that the student demonstrations are motivated by more than just a desire to mourn Hu Yaobang, intellectuals should give the students public support instead of belittling them. The least one can ask is that they show some understanding.

We have to be critical about the attitude of some of our most famous intellectuals. They have always been extremely grateful to Hu for the way, directly or indirectly, he used his position and power to protect them or allow them greater freedom of speech. What developed was the ideal relationship between an enlightened ruler and his enlightened thinkers. To put it more bluntly, over the years they developed a mutually beneficial relationship. Basking in the shade of Hu Yaobang's patronage, these people enjoyed both personal safety and official support. They knew full well how dangerous it would be for them to get too close to the Democracy Wall activists. After all, what could Wei Jingsheng or the others do to protect them? They couldn't even protect themselves.

A DOUBLE STANDARD

It's disturbing how in recent years China's pro-democracy intellectuals have done their best to get in good with the enlightened faction in the party. In their desperate quest to become court advisers they pride themselves on the "capital" accrued by cultivating intimate relationships with senior bureaucrats. They speak in mysterious, conspiratorial whispers of their contacts with important figures. But they assiduously avoid the question of the Democracy Wall activists and China Spring,* the pro-democracy organization of Chinese students overseas. (Even though there is much about this group that is disappointing, even unacceptable, it is nonetheless an association that was formed spontaneously as an

---

* China Spring, or the Chinese Alliance for Democracy, has its headquarters in New York and was at the time headed by Hu Ping, a democratic activist persecuted in China since the early 1980s. Liu Xiaobo was later accused by the Chinese media of being an operative for this organization sent back to China to foment student and civilian unrest.

On April 19, the leading reformist publications World Economic
Herald, *based in Shanghai, and Peking's* New Observer *jointly
sponsored a memorial meeting in Peking entitled "Comrade Yaobang Lives On in Our Hearts" at which friends of the dead party
leader and prominent intellectuals and writers reflected on the significance of Hu's passing. The participants called on the government to "rehabilitate" Hu and negate the 1987 purge of Bourgelib;
a transcript of the meeting was then published in a special issue of
the* World Economic Herald *on April 24. That issue was banned by
Jiang Zemin, then party secretary of Shanghai, and its editor, Qin
Benli,* was suspended from his post. This led to mass protests by
the rank-and-file journalists of Shanghai and Peking and, after the
Protest Movement as a whole was crushed in June, was a factor in
the party's decision to promote Jiang to the job of party general
secretary. Following are excerpts from the banned transcript.*

YU HAOCHENG (*legal expert*): I feel the passing of the Great Marxist, our beloved leader, Comrade Hu Yaobang, as a devastating
loss! . . . Yaobang was our dear teacher; in particular, he was the
wise mentor and good friend of the intellectuals.

QIN CHUAN (*former head of* People's Daily): Comrade Yaobang's
sudden death has left us all deeply shaken and sorrowful. . . . For
he was not only a Great Marxist, he was also a friend who knew
and understood us. . . . After having to resign he said on a number
of occasions that under no circumstances should the party mistreat
intellectuals or young people. We must not punish the students.

SU SHAOZHI (*Marxist theoretician*): Comrade Hu Yaobang was a
Great Marxist. He was open-minded, and he respected knowledge and theoretical work. He was a leader who was of one mind
with intellectuals.

SUN CHANGJIANG (*theorist, assistant chief editor* of Science Daily):
Why is the whole society mourning Yaobang? Because Yaobang
was a real person, honest and down to earth, not one of those
duplicitous schemers.

YU GUANGYUAN (*scientist and member of the Central Advisory
Commission of old party leaders*): It's not enough to be mournful.
We must think a little further, work on, and do what must be done;
in particular we must continue to develop Marxism. . . . I'd like to
know who counts as a Great Marxist. Comrade Yaobang didn't

* Qin Benli, along with many of the other people who attended this meeting, appears in the "Gallery of Reformers" on p. 171.

(l. to r.) Yan Jiaqi, Yu Haocheng, Dai Qing, and Chen Ziming at the memorial meeting on April 19, 1989 (Jane Macartney)

even rate that [description in his official obituary]; they say he didn't make the grade.

HU JIWEI (*former* People's Daily *editor and a leading lawmaker*): Comrade Yaobang made a special contribution to reasserting the Marxist ideological line of our party [after the Cultural Revolution]. The correct ideological line is the very soul of the party's correct political and organizational line.

YAN JIAQI (*political scientist*): Yaobang's death has left me very heavy-hearted. This is because he left us while still under a cloud, having been treated unfairly. The people will certainly make their dissatisfaction with this known.

ZHANG LANGLANG (*writer and artist*): Certainly he lives on in our hearts, but do we have the courage of our convictions or are we just a group of intellectuals indulging in empty talk? How come we're all so courageous now that he's gone? What did we ever do or say on his behalf when he was alive?

DAI QING (*journalist and writer*): Yaobang was not forced to resign during a period of emergency. It was entirely in contravention of correct party procedure. Furthermore, he was forced to make a self-criticism against his will. I think that self-crit was probably the most painful thing he had to do in his whole life. The party was established seventy years ago. Why is there this shadow? The general secretary of the party represents all party members (he's elected by them) to run the day-to-day affairs of the party. But all of them [the five general secretaries up to and including Hu Yaobang] were removed in the most questionable circumstances. Isn't there a serious lack of democracy in this party of the proletariat?

"Soul of China" banner on Tiananmen Square *(Liu Dong, Science Daily)*

> **LIU ZHANQIU** *(poet, editor of the official monthly* Poetry*)*: I cried when I saw the words "Soul of China" on Tiananmen Square. If we lose this opportunity and let the people's passion fade away into despondency once more, we'll be making a very grave mistake.

experiment in democratic organization and process among young Chinese intellectuals. At its worst it still has to be better than the present ruling party.) Intellectuals in China, however, tacitly acknowledge the party's dictatorial definition of China Spring as a reactionary group. The mere mention of its name makes people blanch with fear. In the final analysis, these intellectuals are not only interested in their personal safety: They want power, too. I believe, however, that if they could openly support Wei Jingsheng, the other jailed activists, and China Spring at the same time as offering their support for the enlightened faction within the party, they would speed up the process of democratization within China.

The different responses among intellectuals to the cases of Hu Yaobang and Wei Jingsheng, both reformers, are evidence of a double standard. While they boldly demand fair treatment for Hu Yaobang, they draw the line at calling for justice for the student movement and the Democracy Wall Movement. This double standard reveals the true difference between Hu and Wei: The former was an enlightened autocrat, the latter a fighter for democracy.

In essence, although Hu Yaobang is viewed as a tragic hero, he did not sacrifice himself for the cause of democracy. Wei Jingsheng and his fellows did, but for the most part they have been forgotten. This is China's real tragedy.

> Yaobang made mistakes. Now that he's dead, however, we should not speak ill of him. He did many good things, too, like supporting Reform and the Open Door Policy. But confronted by the tide of Bourgelib, he was weak and submissive. . . . We gave him an appropriate memorial service, but there are those who want him named a Great Marxist. He didn't make the grade. None of us makes the grade, not even me. Don't call me that when I'm dead.
>
> —Deng Xiaoping, April 25, 1989

PERFECTING THE SYSTEM OR CREATING THE PERFECT LEADER

There is something oddly melodramatic about the way Chinese intellectuals have reacted to Hu's passing, giving vent to their feelings by recounting personal anecdotes and commenting on his political achievements and personality. Both in the students' slogans and in commemorative articles by intellectuals, Hu has been transformed from a victim of an internal party power struggle into an outstanding politician and moral superman. "Long live Yaobang!" is a slogan that has appeared in the ranks of the marching students, and banners praising Hu vie for room at the foot of the Monument to the People's Heroes. Chinese students and scholars overseas have also been taking part in various mourning activities. Even Fang Lizhi has called Hu Yaobang a respected politician and says that under his tutelage "Chinese intellectuals enjoyed halcyon days."

I'm quite prepared to admit that the student demonstrations sparked off by Hu's death can play a positive role in China's democratization. I agree that Hu was treated unjustly and, in comparison with other top party leaders, was enlightened and did much that met with popular approval. And I was always particularly impressed by his strong individuality, quite unlike the wooden and bureaucratic personae cultivated by other party leaders. However, objectively speaking, Hu Yaobang was not an outstanding politician. It is simply that within a mediocre party apparatus he appeared as a relatively fair-minded, tolerant, and uncorrupt man who was willing to learn. At most you could say he was an upright official.

Hu's performance after his ouster, however, was extremely disappointing. His public appearances and attendance at Politburo meetings were nothing more than political window dressing. That he could toler-ate the humiliation must have been the result of decades of party train-ing. No matter how disgruntled he must have been with his treatment, he never said a word about it in public; his silence amounted to acqui-escence. Boris Yeltsin, the former Moscow party secretary and a radical reformer, offers a striking contrast. He, too, was forced out of his job, but although he had been much less powerful than Hu, he nonetheless has taken every opportunity to express his opinions. What he is saying now is far more extreme than what he said when he was in power. His faith in the justice of his cause, his courage, and his unrelentingly critical attitude enabled him to score an overwhelming victory over a party candidate in the recent elections. The two men are separated by a chasm of difference. Hu Yaobang lacked the necessary acumen and tactical know-how to survive as a politician. And as an individual he lacked the courage of his convictions. Take, for example, the long article he pub-lished in *People's Daily* in 1985 in which he reiterated the policy that the media must be the "tool" of totalitarian thought control. Just on the basis of the passivity he displayed after his ouster, I don't think he deserves such high marks.

One can look at it from another angle: Let's suppose that all the high-flown praise is objective and fair and that Hu was an extraordinary individual both politically and morally. Then why was it possible for him to have been dumped with so little effort? As the mourners create an image of the ideal leader, they seem to be overlooking the dangers inherent in such idealization. Chinese intellectuals find it difficult to get away from their traditional quest for a savior, an individual ruler in whom they can place their trust [rather than rule by law]. Even now, deep down, these people are pinning their hopes for China's democrati-zation on the appearance of an enlightened monarch.

Every age has thrown up its Hu Yaobangs, but none of them has ever been able to save China. Why don't we abandon the search for an enlightened ruler as a means of reform and experiment instead with changing the system itself? I simply do not believe that even if they had all the power in the world people like Hu Yaobang could lead China successfully in the direction of reform. To say that under Hu Yaobang "Chinese intellectuals enjoyed halcyon days" is nothing less than a slave's expression of gratitude to an indulgent lord. Isn't this the greatest insult to democracy? What a supreme irony that such a statement should come from the mouth of Fang Lizhi, the democratic fighter. Fang's con-tribution to the democratization of China is plain for all to see, and the movement still needs people like Fang. However, I fear that by mourning

Hu Yaobang in this fashion he has regressed. I hope this is just a temporary aberration.

Chinese intellectuals must achieve independence through their own efforts; they must create their own halcyon days. What binds us to the authorities should be not the presence of fine and upright individuals among the leaders but rather a fine political system and legal structure. The relationship between rulers and ruled should not be that of superiors bestowing munificence on their inferiors in return for their loyalty, like that of an emperor and his subjects; it should be a relationship based on equality and mutually advantageous cooperation. As long as they long for a savior, be it Hu Yaobang or Zhou Enlai, Chinese intellectuals will never really be free. Of course, people will argue that you must take Chinese realities into account. Certainly, strategy and tactics are important in the struggle for democracy, but the struggle itself must be founded on the principles of democracy rather than the rules of totalitarianism. Rationality and order, calmness and moderation must be the rules of our struggle; hatred must be avoided at all costs. Popular resentment toward authoritarianism in China can never lead us to wisdom, only to an identical form of blind ignorance, for hatred corrupts wisdom. If our strategy in the struggle for democracy is to act like slaves rebelling against their master, assuming for ourselves a position of inequality, then we might as well give up right here and now. Yet that's what the majority of enlightened Chinese intellectuals are doing at this very moment.

Basically, for the realization of democracy in China we need a system perfected by concrete and practical processes, not one dictated by a perfect and enlightened ruler.

THE AIMS AND PROCESS OF CHINA'S DEMOCRATIZATION

Their response to Hu Yaobang's death has revealed the superficiality of the Chinese intelligentsia's understanding of the aims and process of democratization. Democracy has been a goal for at least seventy years, ever since its banner was first raised in the May Fourth Movement. But most participants in the movement for democracy over the years have had only the most cursory understanding of its aims. This can be seen from the fact that many of them enthusiastically joined or allied themselves with either the Nationalist or the Communist Party in the name of freedom and democracy, even though both parties early on turned into machines for the practice of totalitarian politics—particularly the Communist Party, which began a reign of violence the day it achieved power. For more than thirty years the majority of progressive intellectuals have identified themselves with the Communist Party, faithfully accepting Mao Zedong's analysis of the relationship between dictatorship and democracy: that dictatorship should replace democracy. Only after countless disasters have they begun to wake up to the anti-democratic nature of Communist power.

More important, although Chinese intellectuals can grasp the theory of democracy, when it comes to its practical application they are at a complete loss. . . . In China, the democracy movement is strong on sloganizing but weak on practical implementation. Chinese intellectuals are full of sound and fury but lack the patience required for detailed and concrete work. There is something very old hat about the present large-scale student movement. Chinese university students have been using the same methods to agitate for democracy since 1919: mass demonstrations. They're spontaneous and very exciting for a while, but they invariably peter out. The students lack creativity. In China, people have been shouting slogans about democracy for nearly a century, but no actual progress has been made toward the realization of it for the last seventy years. Surely this is food for thought.

It's not that I oppose the radical actions of the students; I support them wholeheartedly. But the students should be more patient and rational. In their efforts to find practical ways of implementing democratic methods and processes they should use concrete and pluralistic methods that actually get results.

At the same time as staging mass political demonstrations within the wider political sphere, people have to engage in detailed, down-to-earth, constructive actions for democratization in their immediate environment. For example, democratization can start within a student group, an independent student organization, a nonofficial publication, or even the family. We can also carry out studies of the nondemocratic way we live in China and consciously attempt to put democratic ideals into practice in our own personal relationships (between teachers and students, fathers and sons, husbands and wives, and friends). The enormous price paid in the struggle for democracy in the thirteen years since 1976 might have at least won us a popularly run democratic organization or an independent journal with the right of free speech.

Of course, we know full well that people feel safer participating in mass demonstrations; small-scale practical undertakings are far more dangerous. But there's no way around it. If, following the suppression of Democracy Wall, other people had continued its work, we would have

DEMOCRACY IS A WAY OF LIFE
Bo Yang *

Bo Yang, a controversial Taiwan-based writer, made the following remarks to an audience at Peking University when he visited the mainland in 1988.

Ever since the Western term "democracy" was translated as *minzhu* and introduced to China, democracy has been the most sonorous of political catchphrases. Any Joe Blow who gets into politics claims to be a great defender of democracy, even to the extent where he sees himself as democracy incarnate. Before long, however, he invariably reveals his true nature, and all those who have fought for democracy, including those who are sitting in prison, are said not to have understood the real meaning of the word. Things have been like this for many years, and it's thus that everyone pays allegiance to and struggles for something they have never experienced.

Something most astonishing and quite unforgettable once happened in Taipei. A friend of mine had been locked up for five years for having criticized the Nationalists as undemocratic. After getting out of prison he became chief editor of a magazine. One day he got into an argument with one of the publishers over the cover design for a series of books. He was confident that most of the other board members would agree with him and insisted on a vote. But the result was that, with the exception of his wife—who abstained—everyone voted against him. My friend sat there for a little while, his face drained of color, then suddenly stood up and, pointing at all those present, shouted, "You people disgust me! I despise you all!" after which he strode out of the room. Everyone, including his wife, watched him leave in stunned silence. After some time, the board member whose disagreement with him had brought on the crisis muttered: "But he demanded a vote!"

I can assert categorically that if this friend of mine ever got into power there'd be helmets on the streets. . . .

With each new dynasty and each new reign throughout Chinese history, the throne has never changed, only the ass that is on it. We've always believed, as though it's an iron law, that so long as the tyrant whom we see before us is overthrown and a new rear end with its democratic slogans can sit down in his place, everything will take a turn for the better and the country will be at

* See *Seeds of Fire*, pp. 168–78, 373–77.

> peace. But in the end we discover that this new ass, despite all the carrying on about democracy, is even worse than the old one. . . .
>
> Democracy is a way of life—family life, school life, and community life. Once you have a democratic way of life—and only then —will you be able to have democratic politics. To try to pass over this stage, in which you make your life democratic, is like a primary school student skipping high school and university to take up postgraduate studies. To put it simply, democracy matures in the process of daily life.
>
> My suggestion is that we leave the task of trying to replace asses on the throne to our elected representatives (whether they be members of the Legislative Yuan or People's Congress) and concentrate our efforts on self-improvement. This is different from saying we should each simply cultivate our own garden, for we need to unambiguously and openly embrace an idea that does not come naturally to us: that of equality among people. Equality is the most beautiful thing of all and the basis for social ethics. Everyone must comprehend that others are people just like themselves, with a similar need for respect and dignity. Then and only then will it be possible to communicate and join hands with others, to work together and be flexible, to exercise self-restraint. Communication, unity, cooperation, a spirit of give and take, and self-restraint are the constituents of a democratic life-style.

seen some real achievements over the past decade. In China, a truly independent publication or a self-regulating body would be far more significant in terms of democratization than any reform policies by the government. In Taiwan it took more than thirty years for people to achieve freedom of speech and the right to establish an opposition party. This work started back in the 1950s with the journal *Independent China* and continued with *Democracy Review, University,* and other such magazines. Is it really impossible to do the same on the mainland?

Chinese intellectuals have hoped for too much from the government during the past dozen or so years of Reform. They have too readily ignored the push for democracy among the people. The cool indifference of everyone in China to Wei Jingsheng's sentencing in 1979 is proof of that attitude. (Here I include myself, for at the time I was just one of the ignorant mob.) The various student movements that came after Wei Jingsheng soon fell apart because they lacked both a tight-knit organization and [democratic] procedures. As I have said before, I see the shadow of China's numerous peasant rebellions in the hotheaded enthu-

> Either you take part in the student movement or shut up about it.
> —Liu Xiaobo, April 1989
>
> By deciding to go back, [Liu Xiaobo] was little better than a moth being drawn to a flame.
> —Liu Binyan, June 1989

siasm of these movements. If they could only both organize themselves and establish processes to maintain public enthusiasm for democracy and democratic action, I believe there would be a healthy future for democratization in China.

But the present movement for democracy in China is abnormal. It places its hopes on the enlightened faction of the party, while popular democratic forces are assigned a supporting role at best and more often pushed aside. It should be quite the opposite, with autonomous popular democratic forces at the core and enlightened bureaucrats playing only supporting roles. The strengthened popular activism that would emerge could result in a pressure group that could force the authorities to make concessions and undertake fundamental reforms in the direction of democratization. Democratization is a process as well as a goal, and it is in the realization of that process that the real significance of democracy lies. In other words, the democratization and formalization of the process itself is the way to realize the goals of democracy. Yet in China, although the aims are invariably democratic, the means are not. Chinese-style mass democracy can easily degenerate into mob rule. . . .

What is now most required of Chinese intellectuals, in particular enlightened intellectuals, is neither to mourn Hu Yaobang nor to eulogize him, but rather to face up to the figures of the imprisoned Wei Jingsheng and Xu Wenli and to engage in a collective act of repentance. The petition movement, rather than being seen as a heroic undertaking, would best be understood as the first step toward such repentance.

Arriving back in Peking in late April, Liu joined the students and spent most of May on Tiananmen Square. Many knew Liu from his lectures or as a teacher at the Peking Normal University. He helped organize logistical support for the student hunger strikers—which included, he said, supplying the students with condoms as well as blankets and medicines—and he, along with the singer Hou Dejian, later became an ad-

> Among primitive tribes, idiots and madmen are the objects of particular respect and enjoy certain privileges; since their condition frees them from the normal constraints of prudence and wisdom, they alone can be forgiven for speaking the truth—an activity that would naturally not be tolerated from any sane person. For Truth, by its very nature, is ugly, savage, and cruel; it disturbs, it frightens, it hurts, and it kills. If, in some extreme situations, it is to be used at all, it must be taken only in small doses, in strict isolation, and with the most rigorous prophylactic precautions. Whoever would be willing to spread it wildly, or to unload it in large quantities, just as it comes, is a dangerous and irresponsible person who should be restrained in the interest of his own safety, as well as for the protection of social harmony.
>
> Ancient Chinese wisdom already expounded this notion; there is in the book of Liezi (third century B.C.) a parable about a man whose particular talent enabled him to identify thieves at first sight: he only needed to look at a certain spot between the eye and the brow, and he could recognize instantly whether a person was a thief. The king naturally decided to give him a position in the Ministry of Justice, but before the man could take up his appointment, the thieves of the kingdom banded together and had him assassinated. For this reason, clearsighted people were generally considered cripples, bound to come to a bad end; this was also known proverbially in Chinese as "the curse of the man who can see the little fish at the bottom of the ocean."
>
> —Simon Leys

viser to the student leader Wuer Kaixi (also known as Uerkesh Daolet in his native language of Uighur).

Following the death of Hu Yaobang, petitions for the release of political prisoners gave way in April and May to signed appeals in support of the student demonstrators. New and varied petitions were produced virtually every day. During the funeral for Hu on April 22, a group of students actually emulated feudal practice by kneeling outside the Great Hall of the People, holding high a petition for Premier Li Peng.

The plight of Wei Jingsheng and China's other political prisoners was forgotten by the majority as the student demonstrations gained momentum and political factions, both within the Communist Party and on its fringes, plotted to manipulate the outpouring of popular sentiment in their own favor.

Still Out of Control

Wang Ruowang, a writer who had been expelled from the party in 1987 after Deng Xiaoping declared he was "absolutely out of control there in Shanghai," * *wrote an open letter to Deng shortly after the state funeral for Hu Yaobang, excerpts from which are produced below. It was finished on the evening of April 25, the same day Deng first ordered the crushing of the students and after a* People's Daily *editorial was broadcast nationwide (before being published on April 26) declaring that the student disturbances were being manipulated by a small group plotting to overthrow the party.*

The letter is written like a memorial to the throne, and Wang even avails himself of the traditional language of the outspoken loyal minister. As he was unable to publish anything in Mainland China, Wang was forced to have the letter issued in Hong Kong and Taiwan. He knew that both this act as well as the contents of the letter could lead to his arrest.

Like Liu Xiaobo, Wang was detained after the massacre and vilified in the national press. He was finally released from custody in late 1990. It was not his first stint in jail: He'd been a political prisoner at various times under both the Nationalists and the Communists, and had once said he preferred the jails of the former.

Comrade Xiaoping:

. . . It seems inappropriate for a true Marxist to view a mass movement of students demonstrating for democracy and freedom as "floodwaters and wild beasts." Rather, it should be seen as a force that can help further the progress of history. Mao Zedong warned us all that "anyone who crushes a popular movement will come to no good end." But your comments on and policies toward the 1986 Student Movement contravened this principle. In early 1987, you launched a nationwide Anti-Bourgelib Movement and were unconcerned about forcing General Secretary Hu Yaobang, a man devoted to Reform, from office. You did not hesitate to punish severely the most forward-thinking intellectuals in the party, availing yourself instead of experts in political purges and extreme "leftist" plotters. All of this is proof that the direction you chose was incorrect, and

* See *Seeds of Fire*, pp. 361–67.

as a result every concrete policy decision was wrong and perverse. The year 1987 was a historical turning point. Once more the heinous methods of the Maoist era and the sense of personal insecurity of the past reappeared. The prestige of the party suffered a disastrous decline among the people.

You have been the object of great veneration and respect both at home and abroad. Internationally, you were even dubbed Man of the Year. During the National Day parade [of 1984, when Deng turned eighty], university students held up a placard that read "How are you, Xiaoping!" and so on. But from 1987 your reputation has suffered badly. Sycophantic advisers have used Maoist methods and fed you daily reports of good news. Allowing yourself to be surrounded by distortions and baseless optimism, you have failed to distinguish between loyal and scheming officials, or even between good and evil. In addition, due to your physical and mental frailty, you have been unable to travel to the isolated and impoverished parts of the country as Comrade Yaobang had done. You have become divorced from reality and divorced from the masses. You have issued incorrect directives that have had the most serious and disastrous consequences. . . . In the early 1980s, you returned from your visit to the United States deeply impressed by our industrial backwardness and were willing to admit that there were problems with our party's leadership. You proposed emphasizing knowledge and respect for talented people. But how is it that within a few years of taking the throne Mao had occupied for so many years you became so totally unrecognizable?

I have reflected on this long and hard, and the conclusion I have reached is virtually the same as your own: Our political system is a hotbed of bureaucratism. But I'll add something: If the political system and the party in power are not reformed, it doesn't matter how many good people there are, the moment any of them get into power, they will become autocratic, arrogant, and corrupt. And the monopoly control of the print media only encourages the protection of evil people, nefarious activities, and the abuse of power. For this reason I say that not only has this anti-democratic dictatorship failed to mobilize the creativity of the people, it also makes difficult the continuation of economic Reform itself. It harms not only the party, but also our most dearly beloved Comrade Xiaoping.

The student movement calling for democracy and freedom inspired by the unfortunate passing of Comrade Yaobang this April is

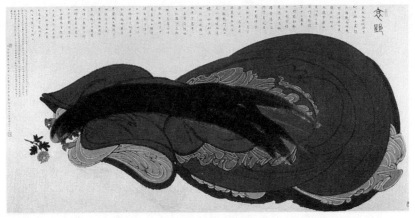

Qu Yuan, by Huang Yongyu. The inscribed poem is "In Lament for Ying" by Qu Yuan:

High Heaven is not constant in its dispensations:
See how the country is moved to unrest and error!
The people are scattered and men cut off from their fellows
In the middle of spring the move to the east began . . .
                    (Kusada Yuen, *The Nineties Monthly*)

the sequela of the inappropriate fashion in which the students were dealt with two years ago. Forgive my boldness, but it is punishment for your own policy errors. . . .

I wish to give you a few words of sincere advice:

When Chun Doo-hwan in South Korea did repentance in front of the Buddha for using the army during his rule to mercilessly crush the mass protests at Kwangju and Wonsan, he shed tears of sorrow, deeply regretful of his actions. When you meet Gorbachev [in mid-May] you can learn from his experience in dealing with the demonstrations in the minority republics of the Soviet Union that are demanding autonomy . . . that these are incidents which have occurred in neighboring parts of Asia in the past year. I advise our policy makers, who have already revealed their bloodlust, to learn from them and, above all, not to act impetuously.

If you feel that the experience of the Soviet Union and South Korea do not conform to our national characteristics, then perhaps you could learn something from President Chiang Ching-kuo in Taiwan.* In the last year of his life he made a series of farsighted political decisions that are widely admired. The Taiwanese are of

* For more on the notion of China's "national characteristics," see the section on *guoqing* on pp. 366–69.

the same race and language as we are; and like us they have a one-party dictatorship.

You are in a unique position, and I hope you will use your unparalleled prestige to do some real good for the Chinese nation while you still have the time. Do something for which you will be remembered by history and future generations. You are at the crossroads of history; will you be remembered as a good official or as a tyrant? I pray you will consider this very, very carefully. Whatever you do, don't compound your past mistakes!

As I write this I am overcome by emotion and my tears prevent me from continuing.

> Wang Ruowang,
> a writer and citizen of Shanghai

An Analysis of the Current Student Protests and Forecasts Concerning the Situation

H E   X I N

Deng Xiaoping denounced the student movement as being manipulated by plotters who planned to overthrow the Communist Party itself. The People's Daily *editorial of April 26 dubbed the student agitation that threatened the state and Reform "turmoil." Troops and police were stationed around the city to prevent further demonstrations; party cadres and members were cautioned not to support the students. The reaction to the April 26 editorial and its implicit threat of violence was one of public defiance and civil disobedience. On April 27, students staged the largest popular demonstration ever seen in Peking.*

He Xin, a forty-year-old scholar in the Chinese Academy of Social Sciences and cultural conservative who was eager to advise the Politburo, wrote a letter to the leadership offering his own analysis of the mounting crisis and urging caution. The letter was sent as a confidential petition to the Politburo immediately after the April 27 demonstration. Coincidentally or not, his charges of foreign involvement in the popular agitation and his naming of the River Elegy *school, Fang Lizhi, and Liu*

Xiaobo as key troublemakers were later echoed in official speeches and reports. Despite the well-balanced advice of this document, after the massacre He Xin surprised many by joining in the denunciation campaigns. It is significant, however, that he was generally only repeating the attacks he had made on reformist intellectuals before June.

CAUSES OF THE STUDENT PROTESTS

1. The current student protests are, in fact, the outcome of a variety of both internal and external factors that have reinforced and prompted one another's development in recent years. If the immediate cause of the protests is arbitrarily and simplistically defined as the product of a fortuitous development (Comrade Hu Yaobang's death), and from this an attempt is made to blame the situation on "a minority of bad elements" (plotters or enemy spies), then the actual background to the unrest will not be subjected to exacting and careful analysis. Such one-sidedness will be dangerous. An erroneous political analysis of the situation will lead to an inability to comprehend the crises that are inherent in the nationwide situation; this in turn will lead to a series of miscalculations and policy errors. In the forty years since the founding of the People's Republic, the party has been taught many lessons by its economic and political miscalculations. In view of the extreme seriousness of the present situation facing China both internally and internationally, we can say that if [the party] makes further major policy errors, it is quite possible that it will lose forever the support of the people. This is a question of the utmost gravity. The Chinese nation cannot endure yet another major policy miscalculation.

2. If I may be permitted to be truthful, then I request that leaders in the center note the following: After the *People's Daily* editorial of April 26 was published and the speeches of the relevant leading comrades were transmitted to the lower echelons, the response was one of panic and resistance, especially within cultural and intellectual circles. People felt that the center was preparing to launch another [political] movement. Sympathy with the students is general among the citizens and various social strata of the capital. During the demonstration [of April 27] countless citizens gathered along the route [of the marchers] to cheer the students on and to lend their support (although central organs and enterprises had carried out ideological work and forbidden this). They gave

the students money, bread, and drinks. Even the citizens who generally show no interest in politics felt that the government's way of dealing with the situation was inappropriate; they felt the government was being excessively heavy-handed in employing such a tough line. This is now causing new political disappointment and dissatisfaction. (The speeches printed in the press supporting the April 26 editorial are no different from the endless articles that appeared after the Tiananmen Incident in 1976, insincere products of political inducement. The political consequences of such speeches may be delusory for policymakers, who will in fact be greeted by the public with indifference and ridicule. The end result is the exact opposite of the desired effect.)

3. There are complex political and economic factors behind the present student unrest. The following is a tentative analysis:

a. There is widespread dissatisfaction among students and spontaneous demands for speeding up political reform;

b. Under the influence of three main currents of thought—ideas favoring extremist reform, Western thought, and cultural nihilism (represented by the *River Elegy* school, Fang Lizhi, and Liu Xiaobo)—university students in recent years have become an extremist lobby;

c. Behind-the-scenes encouragement has been offered by some extremist political factions within China;

d. There has been secret support from overseas enemy powers.

The complex and extremely serious social background of the student unrest may be outlined as follows:

a. Inequality in incomes over recent years has resulted in polarization with a small number of officials and new bourgeois elements developing direct conflicts of interest with the majority of middle- and lower-strata workers. This has resulted in widespread discontent. These economic realities have caused the people to doubt the socialist nature of the system itself;

b. Due to the repeated errors [of recent years], people's confidence in [the party's] general and specific policies has declined;

c. Rising inflation has made inroads on the standard of living of middle- and low-income earners, leading to widespread dissatisfaction.

Apart from the above, there are three other latent but dangerous factors within the social environment:

a. The concealed labor/capital contradictions between workers and management in certain enterprises may well result in widespread industrial unrest;

b. The emergence of a rootless, mobile part of the rural population has created a huge unorganized force. (It is already a hotbed of crime.) Once they form organizations with an educated leadership and a political program, the floating peasant population could be molded into a political force, a mobile, armed, and formidable antisocial coalition;

c. Separatist social forces exist in national minority regions.

Thus, people from various strata throughout the country are following the student protests with keen interest. If the center is incapable of smoothly and effectively resolving these contradictions and of finding rational solutions, then [I predict]:

a. A deterioration of the situation will spark new and unpredictable incidents in other cities and regions; and

b. Movements in other regions will emulate the "Peking model."

TWO POSSIBLE SCENARIOS

I am of the opinion that there are two possible scenarios of how the present student protests may be resolved. One is positive, the other negative. If through well-chosen measures the government is able to turn the situation in its favor, then the general demands made by the protesters, such as calls for Reform, support for the party (even though this is superficial), and patriotism can be harnessed for speeding up political reform, building a more democratic system, cleaning up government, and doing away with corruption. By so doing, the patriotic and progressive tendency of the students will be inspired, and this will lead to a new consensus within the Chinese nation, as well as unity and cooperation among different social strata. In this way we will be able to weather the present serious problems and usher in a new period of political democratization and economic development.

If, on the other hand, inappropriate measures are taken to resolve the crisis—measures that lead to a deepening of conflicts, further dissatisfaction throughout society, and an increased sense of hopelessness—political reform and democratization will be delayed yet again. It is even possible that the achievements of the Reform program of the past decade will be forfeited. China will enter a period of political turmoil with constant outbreaks of unrest on varying scales. Political unrest and a loss of popular support will invariably result in a failure to achieve economic goals. The inevitable worsening of the economy along with the exacerbation of class contradictions will, in the long run, lead to further small-scale disturbances that will spark mass turmoil. Civil war, military coups, and popular uprisings in China for decades to come are now far from unthinkable.

For these reasons I am of the opinion that the leading comrades at Party Central must not underestimate the contradictions and dangers within society at the moment; it is also crucial that [leading comrades] not underestimate the pervasive sense of public disappointment and discontent. The student unrest can trigger other protests. If the problems [raised by this unrest] are not resolved and diffused in an appropriate and suitable manner, continuing and indeed ceaseless disturbances will take place throughout the country, a situation that, in the long run, will quite possibly result in the collapse of the present [political and social] structure in its entirety. This is the very danger of "destruction of the party and the state" Mao Zedong often warned against.

Some comrades will no doubt find the above analysis excessively gloomy. However, as a social scientist it is my duty to make a cool and realistic appraisal of problems. Although the Communist Party of China has many faults and has made various errors, I am of the belief that in view of the size of China and its massive population, and given the complex problems it is facing at the moment, China's sole hope lies in reliance on the Communist Party and on the force of political leadership to unite our nation's best and brightest and to revitalize the Chinese nation. . . .

China's traditional art of politics sets great store by "ruling with virtue, maintaining prestige through laws" and warns that "those who depend on moral power will prosper, while those who rely on force will perish." It should be remembered that in the first years of the People's Republic the authority and leadership of the Communist Party was built on the basis of a shiningly uncorrupt morality that made it extremely popular. Over the past twenty years, this moral image has been increasingly tarnished by corrupt officials. This is extremely painful. In my opinion this must be the starting point for restoring the party's image, for only by so doing can the causes of political turmoil be fundamentally eliminated, the dissatisfaction of the people abated, and the permanent security of the state ensured.

—*Peking, April 28, 1989*

Even the calculated and balanced advice of He Xin was ignored, and in early May, as the Protest Movement continued to gain momentum, factions within the Communist Party drew their own battle lines and played out a deadly game of power politics, using the students and citizens of Peking and more than a dozen other Chinese cities as their pawns.

After Hu Yaobang's ouster in 1987, he had been replaced by Zhao Ziyang, the former premier. Zhao reportedly had helped push Hu from power. As the Protest Movement grew, Zhao's close association with Reform had not prevented him from becoming a major target of student dissatisfaction along with Deng Xiaoping and his own successor in the premier's job, the highly unpopular Li Peng.

But then, on the seventieth anniversary of the May Fourth Movement, at a meeting with representatives of the Asian Development Bank, Zhao expressed his opposition to the party line by calling the students "patriotic." Along with a temporary lifting of restrictions on reporting in the official media, this encouraged an escalation of the protests.

An unofficial newspaper, the News Herald, *was founded after the successful April 27 demonstration, and on May 12 it published details of a proposal signed by thirty-eight of the capital's leading intellectuals, including Li Honglin, Yu Haocheng, Yan Jiaqi, Dai Qing,* Fan Yong (the former editor-in-chief of Joint Publishing and the controversial intellectual monthly* Reading), *the translator Yang Xianyi, the cartoonist Ding Cong, and Dong Leshan, the translator of George Orwell's* 1984:

. . . The proposal opposes the view that democracy is "turmoil"; it insists that democracy is compatible with unity and stability. It objects to using the excuse that China's situation is unique and therefore that democracy, freedom, human rights, and rule by law are irrelevant. The signatories call on the government to persist with Reform, to establish the authority of democracy and legality, to use the spirit of legality to advance the

* See pp. 173–74, 176, 181–82, for more on Dai Qing, Li Honglin, Yan Jiaqi, and Yu Haocheng.

cause of Reform, and to protect the citizens' rights of freedom of speech and so on that are guaranteed in the Constitution. They also call for the principle of separation of party and state in order that truly democratic elections can be held and the independence of the judiciary assured. Finally, the proposal calls for progress along the path forged by the Communist Party so that the enterprise of Reform may advance in the radiant spirit of the May Fourth Movement.

On May 13, the eve of Mikhail Gorbachev's official visit to China, when officials still hadn't satisfied student demands for dialogue, student leaders began a hunger strike in which they were joined by thousands of supporters in Peking and elsewhere. A few days later, a dozen students refused water as well as food. The danger that students might actually die in their quest for dialogue galvanized the capital and led its citizens into an unprecedented state of peaceful rebellion against both the Peking Municipal Government and their overlords, the rulers in Zhongnanhai.

(China Daily)

Human Rights for Chinese Writers

Meanwhile, also on May 13, in Shanghai, a group of young writers issued a strongly worded appeal for human rights.

Drafted by the poet Song Lin, who was subsequently detained by the police, one of the first signatories was Song's friend Zhu Dake, a controversial film and literary critic, who was later put under intense investigation. Song was finally released in May 1990, and Zhu was to have a collection of his cultural critiques published later in 1991.

We have been forced to speak up by the fact that for many years the basic human rights of Chinese writers and citizens have not been guaranteed.

In the past, writers have been threatened, subjected to surveillance, investigation, exile, and imprisonment, and even executed. What's more, there is absolutely no guarantee against such things happening in the future. Not only do such acts violate the basic principle of universal respect for human rights, they now also constitute a major obstacle to the progress of Chinese civilization and the process of democratization.

In response to this, we make the following appeal and statement:

1. We express our outrage and wish to register the strongest protest against the various forms of persecution suffered by Chinese writers over the past forty years, in particular during political campaigns. We have the inalienable right to expose these.
2. We demand an immediate end to the illegal interference with the creation or publication of artistic works by any political force. All obstructions must be removed immediately, including an end to all actions that constitute an invasion of the human rights of Chinese writers (such as tailing, bugging, the reading of mail, etc.).
3. Writers must have the freedom to analyze, explain, and publish their views on all aspects of Chinese reality both historical and present, in particular political incidents. For a party official to use his position or administrative powers to restrict or interfere with writers or deprive them of their freedom of expression or publication is not only an abuse of power but illegal.
4. The rights of writers to form associations, hold meetings, and publish their own newspapers and journals must be protected. Any interference by the government must be regarded as illegal.

5. In light of the fact that the international situation is moving toward conciliation, dialogue is replacing confrontation, and there is a consensus on the need for democratization, Chinese writers claim the right to publish their works in the country or territory of their own choice.
6. The writer's conscience and sense of responsibility oblige him or her to uncover lies and speak the truth. Any limitation on or deprivation of this right constitutes an attack on creative freedom and an interference in human rights.

We have the deepest respect for all the writers, intellectuals, and students who have made sacrifices for democracy and human rights since the May Fourth Movement.

We give our unconditional support to the students who are continuing this struggle today.

We appeal to all Chinese writers and citizens of good conscience to arise and protect their dignity and inalienable rights!

We appeal to all those who are concerned with the fate of humanity and all writers to stand with us now!

In Peking, on May 16, Zhu Xuefan, the chairman of the Revolutionary Kuomintang, a democratic party of communist fellow travelers, sent an urgent appeal to Party Central to meet with the leaders of the eight democratic parties to discuss a solution to the dilemma resulting from the student hunger strike. These parties had been allowed to survive after 1949 but were gradually stripped of any real power. This appeal and the subsequent letters and activities of other members of these usually tame organizations must have struck Deng Xiaoping and his coevals as particularly ominous. In 1957 Deng had led the administrative purge of "rightists," and many of the leading critics of the Communist Party's dictatorship at that time were members of the democratic parties. For the heads of these parties to join the Protest Movement now must have appeared to be a continuation of the struggles of the 1950s.

In his meeting with Gorbachev on May 16, General Secretary Zhao Ziyang had stated that despite his semiretirement in 1987,* Deng Xiaoping was the de facto ruler of China and by implication ultimately responsible for the unrest in the capital. Zhao's conflict with Deng was

---

* See *Seeds of Fire*, p. 352.

now out in the open, and opposition forces quickly rallied around the previously unpopular general secretary. On May 17, Yan Jiaqi, a former Zhao adviser, together with the academic Bao Zunxin and others, drafted the "May 17 Proclamation," the most strident public attack on Deng Xiaoping since Wei Jingsheng's arrest:

Now the crucial problem of our nation has been exposed to both ourselves and the whole world. The problem is that we are ruled by a dictator with unlimited power. The government has lost its sense of responsibility and humanity. This irresponsible, inhumane government cannot be accepted as the government of the republic; it is nothing more than a government under the control of a dictator.

The Qing dynasty has been dead for seventy-six years, but China still has an uncrowned emperor, an aged and muddleheaded autocrat.

MIDDLEMEN
Lung-kee Sun

Although the following passage was inspired by the wave of political activism that swept Hong Kong and Taiwan in the 1970s, it is equally relevant to the 1989 Protest Movement on the mainland. The special role played by Liu Xiaobo, Wang Peigong, and others in their thirties and forties is but the latest example of the role "intermediary generations" have played in China's "youth rebellions" since the May Fourth Movement.

The Chinese try to maintain harmonious relations between generations, something usually achieved by the young surrendering to the old. The propensity of the young to yield to their elders has made Chinese culture the world's most successful conservative ideology, one that has resisted change for thousands of years. Entry into the modern world and all its unpredictability, however, has led to an assault on the traditional hierarchy of intergenerational relations. . . .

Because the authority of the older generation in China is so obdurately rooted and the youth so thoroughly repressed, however, it is not easy for young people to gain the self-confidence necessary to challenge their elders. That is, unless there is an intermediary generation—relatively young teachers and so on—to lend a helping hand. The intermediary generation's rebellion is a postponed one, carried out after they have attained a place in society.

During the May Fourth period, a clear cultural conflict between traditional culture and Western intellectual trends informed the generation gap. In the course of this "cultural revolution," members of the intermediary generation felt they could play only a transitional role, for while they were advocates of the new culture, they also felt themselves to be mired in tradition. For example, Li Dazhao, himself nearly at middle age, wrote essays extolling "today" and "youth" and placed all his hope in the next generation.* Lu Xun, too, felt that at most his generation would be able only to open the "gate of darkness" to let the next generation pass through.† The younger May Fourth generation eventually took the road to revolution; among them were some of the founders of the Chinese Communist Party.

Only a complete split between the generations can bring an end to the perennial gloom of Chinese history. But the "gate of darkness" has yet to let a single generation of Chinese pass through.

* Li Dazhao (1889–1927), officially considered China's "first Marxist," was a founding member of the Chinese Communist Party and a lecturer in economics at Peking University.
† In his essay "The Obligations of Today's Fathers" (1919), Lu Xun argued that the traditional view that children should serve and obey their parents should be abandoned; the liberation of the young required parents to hold open the gate of darkness through which their children could pass into a brighter future.

One of the most impressive petitions to the government was organized by Wang Peigong, the former PLA playwright; this was also published as an urgent appeal on the evening of May 17. Among its signatories were the elderly writer Xia Yan, Bing Xin, the scholar Qian Zhongshu and his wife, the writer Yang Jiang.* Apart from calling for immediate action to bring an end to the hunger strike and begin a direct dialogue with the students, this appeal contained a passage central to the demands of all of the protests:

The party and the government should make an earnest and realistic attempt to learn a lesson from this Student Movement. They should stand together with the broad majority of the people, speed up the process of political reform, rid the party of corruption, and push on with

* For Xia Yan, see *Seeds of Fire*, p. 260; for Wang Peigong's play *W.M.*, see pp. 105–17; an excerpt from Yang Jiang's Cultural Revolution memoir is to be found on pp. 80–87. Wang Peigong was detained shortly after the massacre. His play, *W.M.*, was denounced again in October 1990. He was released without charge, only in early 1991.

democratization and the establishment of a legal system, thereby creating a situation where there is a political atmosphere of real stability and unity and ensuring the smooth advancement of Reform and the Open Door Policy.

On May 18, after nearly a week of hunger strikes and massive demonstrations in Peking, Shanghai, and other cities, and the day before Li Peng and Yang Shangkun publicly ordered units of the People's Liberation Army to enter Peking "to restore order," Ba Jin,* one of China's most highly regarded writers and a member of the May Fourth generation, wrote a letter to the demonstrating students.

Seventy years ago, during the May Fourth Movement, a group of patriotic students [demonstrated] for the cause of science and democracy in our motherland. Seventy years have passed, and we are still a backward country. I believe that the students' demands are completely reasonable. What they are doing today is completing the task we were unable to finish. They are the hope of China.

I am a sickly and decrepit old man, but I feel deeply encouraged by the example of these young people. I trust that all Chinese who are patriotic, upright, and of good conscience will nurture and protect them.

Ba Jin,
from my sickbed

On the morning of May 19, Zhao Ziyang suddenly appeared on the square to address the students. He apologized for "coming too late." Bidding them a lachrymose farewell, he signed a few T-shirts for the students and left with Premier Li Peng, who had followed him there, in hot pursuit. Zhao's televised message, coupled with the events of the following weeks, helped to transmogrify him into a tragic and sympathetic figure, as had happened with Hu Yaobang after his fall.

That evening, at a meeting of leading party, state, and army cadres on the outskirts of Peking, Li Peng and Yang Shangkun announced the

---

* See *Seeds of Fire*, pp. 381–84.

Ba Jin (Deng Wei, Joint Publishing Company)

decision to crush the Protest Movement by force. As the troops massed to invade the city, Li Ximing, the Peking party secretary, made a secret speech outlining the history of the Protest Movement and explicating the dangers it posed to party rule. Li claimed that the municipal government had done its utmost to bring a conclusion to the protests, while failing to mention that throughout the week of the hunger strike it had in fact tried in numerous ways to incite the participants in the peaceful protests to rebellion and violence. In his lengthy speech, Li Ximing gave a hair-raising description of the demonstrations.

All of our efforts to defuse the student agitation have been unsuccessful. On the contrary, due to the erroneous lead and encouragement of the media and the continued instigations of an extremely small handful of people, as well as to the extreme emotionalism of some students and the fact that the broad masses are ignorant of the true situation, the student disturbances have escalated rapidly. Suddenly, it is thought "unpatriotic" not to take part in the demonstrations. The number of people in the streets has increased dramatically since May 15, from tens to hundreds of thousands and finally nearly one million people. The demonstrators have not all been students; they include workers, peasants, government cadres, and members of the democratic parties, as well as middle and primary school students and small children. Even some cadres and operatives in the organs of Proledic * and some lecturers and students at military academies have been participating. More than twenty thousand students from outside Peking have flooded into the capital by train to show their support. In fact, this is forcing the hunger strikers into a corner. Part of the media has not only failed to take an appropriate stance, but has churned out harmful propaganda, fanning the flames of protest. What's worse is that in the midst of the massive and continuous demonstrations, a small group of people have taken heart and raised slogans not heard for some time, attacking and vilifying the Communist Party and socialism. They have concentrated their attacks on Comrade Deng Xiaoping. Some have gone so far as to say: "Get out of office, Deng Xiaoping," "We demand Xiaoping resign from the party," "We don't want a bogus government with Chinese characteristics," "Oppose rule by a single man, bring an end to the gerontocracy." Other banners have read: "Deng Xiaoping is cruel, Zhao Ziyang's a slime," "Li Peng must resign to appease the country and the people." One banner has openly called out: "China's Walesa, where are you?"

All of this proves beyond a doubt that this is not a simple student disturbance. It has spread to the whole society. The student movement has been instigated by a small group and turned into turmoil. This is a most serious political struggle. . . .

Xinhuamen [the entrance to Zhongnanhai] has been stormed four times, and Tiananmen Square has been occupied on numerous occasions. This never occurred even during the Ten Years of Chaos [of the Cultural Revolution]. This is also the first time in the history of the People's Republic of China that thousands of students have been on a week-long hunger strike in Tiananmen Square. The strike was timed to coincide with the visit of Gorbachev, and this has seriously disrupted a major foreign affairs activity and damaged our international image. The mass demonstrations of tens of thousands to more than one million people incited by the hunger strikers have exceeded even the "revolutionary linkups" of the Red Guards during the Cultural Revolution, resulting in the reappearance of anarchy. State laws and regulations have been flouted, resulting in extreme social disruption. Particularly insidious and evil have been the rumor-mongering, the vicious libel, the personal attacks, and the anti-democratic, illegal incidents that have occurred. They have reached an unprecedented level.

—*Li Ximing*

* Proledic, or the "dictatorship of the proletariat." The organs of Proledic referred to here include the police and the judiciary. For more on Proledic, see *Seeds of Fire*, p. 65.

*That evening, while the cadres were meeting in the suburbs, a group of
organizations linked to Zhao Ziyang had a prepared announcement repeatedly read out to the crowds in the square. The "Six-Point Declaration Concerning the Situation" claimed to give details of the inner
workings of the Politburo and Zhao Ziyang's attempts to overcome the
crisis. Although it seems to give a somewhat fanciful version of events,
the announcement did help mobilize the people of the city to prevent the
entry of the army.*

. . . On May 16, at a meeting of the Standing Committee of the Politburo attended by Deng Xiaoping, Zhao made a number of suggestions:

1. That Deng Xiaoping's *People's Daily* editorial of April 26 be
   negated;
2. That Zhao take responsibility for the publication of the editorial;
3. That the National People's Congress set up a special commission
   to investigate the corrupt practices of high-level cadres' children
   (including Zhao's own two sons);
4. That the personal background of all cadres of vice-ministerial
   level and above be made public; and
5. That the income and fringe benefits of all high-level cadres be
   made public and that privileges for these cadres be eliminated.

The other four members of the Standing Committee rejected Zhao's
proposal.

At a meeting of the Politburo on May 17, Zhao was voted out of
power by a slight majority and Li Peng was appointed acting general
secretary.

Martial law is about to be announced. The crushing of the Tiananmen
Incident of April 5, 1976, is about to be reenacted. . . .

*After the declaration of martial law in Peking and the encirclement of
the city by the army on May 20, numerous new petitions to the government were issued that called for the sacking of Premier Li Peng and the
lifting of martial law. Liu Xiaobo, however, now urged the citizens and
students of Peking to organize their own democratically elected autonomous groups. He and his fellow activists wanted to turn the movement
away from one of demonstrations and calls for change in the party
leadership toward a civil movement similar, as it turned out, to those*

that occurred in Eastern Europe later in the year. One of the most impressive statements for this cause was "Our Suggestions," issued on May 23 in the name of the Autonomous Student Union of Peking Normal University but written by Liu Xiaobo.

Whereas many writers had discussed the matter of civil consciousness in the pages of newspapers like the World Economic Herald, *Liu made a concerted effort to actually put the theories into practice. He encouraged the student leaders to organize citywide democratic student elections for their organizations. They considered his suggestion, but then certain student leaders, including Wuer Kaixi, objected, Liu said privately, on the grounds that they might not be elected. Nevertheless, "Our Suggestions" introduced a new element into the political debate on the square, for it was not the petition of a subject to his ruler, nor was it the condescending appeal of an intellectual trying to rally support among the masses; rather, it was the statement of a citizen to his equals, appealing to their common sense and judgment:*

Each stage in the expansion and escalation of this student movement and its development into a civil movement has been prompted by the government's political folly. The slogans and demands of the movement have primarily been aimed at the erroneous policies of the government, and the movement has followed a path dictated by the government's mistakes and popular discontent. The mutual passivity that has resulted can in no way help us to move beyond the stage of ideological sloganizing and enter a phase of democratic construction that emphasizes regularity, means, and process. Thus it is necessary for all strata of the society to reach actively beyond short-term slogans and aims. We must attempt to change the government's long-standing inability to listen to the voice of the people and its ideology of privilege that denies the people the rights to demonstrate, strike, and establish popular organizations. We must teach the government to accept the people's desire to use the powers accorded to them in the Constitution to supervise the government and express their demands. We must teach the government how to rule the country democratically. . . .

The highly charged emotionalism of the movement is proof that the deep-seated motivation behind it is the traditional peasant mentality of narrow hatred and revenge. It has the flavor of a revolution staged by those who have "suffered greatly and hate deeply." Even more striking has been the antagonism and hatred evinced by members of the government. But democracy has nothing to do with the psychology of hatred. Hatred can only lead to violence and dictatorship. Thus in spreading a democratic mentality throughout the nation the crucial thing is to eliminate the long-standing hatred and animosity that result from the peasant revolution and class struggle. No matter how serious Li Peng's errors, even though he must fall from power, he is not an enemy. He is a Chinese citizen like everyone else. It is this type of hatred, particularly the hatred the government has for the students and the people of the nation, that has resulted in the intensification of this movement, martial law, and some violent incidents. Democratization in China cannot be achieved on the basis of popular dissatisfaction, hatred, or the overthrowing of an unpopular leader, but only through a rational and peaceful process.

Our slogan should now be: Don't let hatred poison our wisdom and the cause of democratization in China.

—*Liu Xiaobo*

Although the students called off their hunger strike just before martial law was declared, the war of petitions and appeals continued in the two weeks that followed. Students, intellectuals, and others called on the government to abandon the enforcement of martial law on Peking, especially as the city remained well ordered and peaceful. They also demanded the sacking of Li Peng and the establishment of an emergency interim government.

In the last days of May and early June, government propaganda against the protesters intensified as the media once again fell under strict party control. On May 27, a joint session of all the autonomous organizations involved in the protests agreed unanimously to declare the movement a victory and quit the square before the government had a

"The students love the nation; I love the students," calligraphy by Bing Xin, June 1, 1989 *(Ming Pao Daily)*

chance to take violent action. However, a small group of student dema-
gogues decided on their own to go against the decision and declared that
the square would not be abandoned.

To revive the flagging morale of the movement, art students erected
their Styrofoam Goddess of Democracy and a group of four lone pro-
testers declared they were going on a hunger strike. It was June 2, and
the hunger strikers, Liu Xiaobo, Hou Dejian (a singer-songwriter from
Taiwan), and two friends, Zhou Duo and Gao Xin, published their
hunger-strike proclamation:

We are on a hunger strike! We protest! We appeal! We repent!

We search not for death, but for true life.

Under the violent military pressure of the irrational Li Peng government, Chinese intellectuals must bring an end to their millennia-old and
weak-kneed tradition of only talking and never acting. We must engage
in direct action to oppose martial law; through our actions we appeal
for the birth of a new political culture; through our actions we repent
the mistakes resulting from our long years of decrepitude. Every Chinese
must share in the responsibility for the backwardness of the Chinese
nation. . . .

The quartet was not only critical of the machinations of the government
before and during martial law, they also called on the student leaders, a
chaotic and willful group that at times acted as though inspired by
William Golding's Lord of the Flies, *to clean their own house:*

The errors of the students, meanwhile, are evident in the internal chaos
of their organization, their general lack of efficiency and democratic
process. For example, although their aims are democratic and they es-
pouse the theory of democracy, in dealing with concrete problems they
have acted undemocratically. They lack a spirit of cooperation, and their
power groups are mutually destructive. This has resulted in the complete
collapse of the decision-making process; there is an excess of attention
to privilege and a serious lack of equality, etc. Over the last one hundred
years few of the struggles for democracy in China have ever gone beyond
ideology and sloganizing. There's always been a lot of talk about intellectual awakening but no discussion of practical application, a great deal
of talk about ends but a neglect of means and processes. We believe that
the true realization of political democracy requires the democratization

The events in Eastern Europe and the Soviet Union in late 1989 and 1990 excited the exiled Chinese activists and gave them encouragement for the future. Some were openly jealous of the Europeans, who, they felt, had benefited from China's tragedy. One intellectual, however, was driven to reflect critically on the role he and his fellows had played in the 1989 Protest Movement. Yuan Zhiming is a philosopher in his thirties and one of the authors of the television series River Elegy *(see "Bindings"). He escaped into exile with Su Xiaokang after the massacre.*

I've been speculating as to how things would have turned out if, during the initial stages of the Democracy Movement or at the height of the movement, Fang Lizhi, Liu Binyan, Yan Jiaqi, Chen Yizi, Wan Runnan, and Su Xiaokang, as well as the rest of us, the large group people refer to as the "elite," had courageously stood forward and led the movement. If we had formulated some mature, rational, and feasible plan of action and organized a democratic front incorporating the students and civilians. If we had worked together harmoniously to struggle for dialogue with the authorities. How would it have turned out? Of course, we might still have been defeated, but we would have done everything in our power to prevent defeat.

. . . but all we intellectual leaders did was to voice our support and protest . . .

Of course, we had done much more: We'd taught the young students the need to fight for democracy. We'd inspired them, and it was our thinking and patriotism that in the last analysis affected them and incited them to action. We'd caused them to throw themselves into the struggle for democracy heedless of the dangers, to the point that they were crushed by the tanks. But what about us?

Shortly after June 4, the Communist press published a major denunciation entitled "Grabbing Liu Xiaobo's Black Hand." In fact, Liu Xiaobo's hand was the cleanest of all. He stood forward without fear, and at the most critical moment he started a hunger strike in Tiananmen Square. He always made his appeals directly and without artifice. He didn't play those games where you attack people and then run away when there's a danger of being caught. As for the rest of the intellectual world, if we did get involved, you could say our hands really were black. . . .

A few days ago, in a telephone conversation, I told Yan Jiaqi what I've been thinking. "Next time things will be different," Mr. Yan replied. But I'm more interested in why things turned out the way they did this time. If we don't get this straight and arrive at a

consensus, a recurrence of events will be unavoidable. That's because a strong, nationwide opposition group can only evolve if
there are many courageous people willing to sacrifice themselves
and to unite in struggle. . . .

In recent years, there has been a rebirth of humanism on the
mainland. Many intellectuals have courageously and in all good
conscience used their writings and speeches to do many remarkable things. Yet when the time came for real action they were
struck impotent. Suddenly there was no sign of all that heroism.
Keeping ourselves clean, evading responsibility, knowing when to
stop, being wise, playing safe—that's what we're good at. We
never wanted to be standard-bearers; we did our level best to
keep out of it. But now? Why, we're all heroes! Forgive my caustic
tone, but none of us, neither you nor I, and none of the intellectuals
on the mainland, can avoid the shameful truth.

I sincerely hope that when a new democratic tide sweeps China,
the heroic students and civilians and the new oppositionists who
appear will simply ignore us all.

—Yuan Zhiming, January 1990

of the process, means, and structure [of politics]. For this reason we
appeal to the Chinese to abandon their vacuous, traditional, simplistic,
ideological, sloganizing, and end-oriented approach to democracy and
engage in the democratization of the political process itself, starting with
small, practical matters. We appeal to the students to examine their own
actions and make their priority the democratic reorganization of the
student body on Tiananmen Square itself.

*On the evening of June 3, the People's Liberation Army forced its way
into Peking, beginning the Peking Massacre. In the early hours of
June 4, as the PLA surrounded Tiananmen Square and Hou Dejian
negotiated with the troops to give the protesters time to withdraw, Liu
Xiaobo prevented students and workers from using captured weapons
against the army and successfully organized a voice vote among the
students in which they agreed to evacuate. After escaping the massacre
with Hou Dejian, Liu was detained by plainclothesmen on June 6 and
subsequently vilified in the Chinese press. As part of the campaign
against him, many of Liu's articles were printed in book form and widely
distributed for criticism. It is reported that as a result, many people who*

had previously considered him just an iconoclastic literary critic—if they knew of him at all—soon came to regard him as something of a hero. He was convicted of "counterrevolutionary agitation" in late January 1991 but exempted from punishment and released from prison as a result of his "meritorious service" in preventing the use of weapons by protesters and helping organize the evacuation from the square.

Petitioning is common enough in every country. It doesn't necessarily end in death—except, of course, in China.

—*Lu Xun, April 10, 1926*

The following is a partial list of people who signed petitions or appeals and whose names or works appear in this book. Some of these people signed a number of petitions.

January 6: Fang Lizhi
February 13: Bao Zunxin, Bei Dao, Bing Xin, Jin Guantao, Li Zehou, Liu Qingfeng, Mang Ke, Tian Zhuangzhuang, Su Shaozhi, Su Xiaokang, Wang Ruoshui, Wu Zuguang
February 20: Chen Ruoxi
February 26: Yu Haocheng, Li Honglin, Ge Yang
March 1: Simon Leys, Yang Lian, John Minford
March 14: Dai Qing, Yan Jiaqi, Yuan Zhiming
March 17: Chen Ying-chen, Liu Binyan, Zhang Langlang
March (Cheng Ming *petition started by Wang Keping and others on January 1*): Bo Yang, Lee Yee, Liu Xiaobo, Wang Keping
April 25: Wang Ruowang
May 12: Ding Cong
May 16: Gao Gao, Ke Yunlu, Liu Zaifu, Xie Xuanjun, Xu Xing
May 17: Huang Miaozi, Qian Zhongshu, Wang Peigong, Yang Jiang, Yang Xianyi
May 18: Feng Jicai, Liu Xinwu
May 24: Wang Juntao, Wang Luxiang
June 2: Hou Dejian

Tiananmen Days

JIMMY NGAI SIU-YAN

The Protest Movement spread to other cities throughout China, but nowhere outside the mainland did it have such an impact as in Hong Kong. A wave of national pride and activism dispelled the image of the Hong Kong citizen as the quintessential materialistic and apathetic colonial. With just eight years before Great Britain was to return sovereignty over the territory to China, the people of Hong Kong opened up their hearts, purses, and telecommunications lines to Peking: They marched in the hundreds of thousands through the streets of Hong Kong in support, donated generous amounts of money and supplies, and flooded mainland fax machines with news, information, and encouragement when the Peking authorities imposed a news blockade after the declaration of martial law. (The Hong Kong dispatches were immediately photocopied by sympathizers in Peking offices that had fax machines and posted on the streets.) Everyone, it seemed, was involved: Taxis and buses in the territory were plastered with pro-democracy slogans, Hong Kong's top pop singers held a benefit concert for the movement, and Protest Movement T-shirts were quickly produced for sale at boutiques and streets stalls alike.

In the past Peking Chinese had generally despised Hong Kong people. They ridiculed their heavily accented Mandarin and felt both resentful toward and superior to Hong Kong Chinese, whom they considered "tainted" by the West and somehow not really Chinese. They were also deeply jealous of their relative wealth and the special status that allowed them entry to mainland hotels and stores barred to ordinary mainlanders. Hong Kong's massive show of solidarity with the students and people of Peking from mid-May suddenly changed all this. Finally, for the movement's supporters, the Hong Kong people were true compatriots.

Some Hong Kong Chinese, moved by the images of the protests that filled their television screens nightly, actually made the pilgrimage to

Peking. They approached Tiananmen with awe, slowly making their way to the epicenter of popular rebellion, the "sacrosanct" Monument to the People's Heroes, a veritable altar on which they laid their offerings of Hong Kong dollars, pup tents, communications equipment, and so on. Coordinating the effort were the Hong Kong Federation of Students and the newly formed Hong Kong Alliance in Support of Democratic Movements in China.

Among those who went to Peking was a thirty-four-year-old writer named Jimmy Ngai Siu-yan, who flew there at the end of May. He wrote up his experiences for the Hong Kong edition of Esquire.

The first thing that caught my eye was Chairman Mao's portrait on Tiananmen. Turning, I saw the Monument to the People's Heroes some way back. There were people everywhere around the square. . . .

I moved toward the southern part of the square, past the tents that had been weatherbeaten by the sun and rain, past students whose exhaustion was written all over their faces, past all those people who believed that their collective will was like a wall of iron. This is it, I thought, this is really it.

From the students' loudspeakers came the strains of the "Internationale."

I approached the steps of the monument, showed my press pass, and was allowed up the steps by the student pickets. On the third level, there were some beat-up tents in the corners that served as the students' general headquarters and financial department.

Students moved about busily in little groups. Reporters hung around, cigarettes dangling out the sides of their mouths, ready to cover whatever happened next.

From the steps you could see the back of the Goddess of Democracy, who stood in the center of the vast square, holding her torch in a face-off with Chairman Mao. . . .

Leaving the square, [the Hong Kong writer Fung Wai Choi] and I walked east on the Avenue of Eternal Peace toward the Peking Hotel. It was a walk of about ten minutes. In the next few days I was to travel this route countless times. . . .

There weren't many people in the hotel. Walking in from the western door, you passed through a dark corridor to get to the Chinese restaurant. Inside there were only five or six tables of diners, about half of them foreign reporters.

As we ordered, the waitress asked if we'd come from Tiananmen.

"Uh-huh."

"What's happening there?"

"Nothing. It's real quiet."

She fell into silence. We asked her, "Have you been there to have a look yourself?"

"I can't, I've got to work."

"What do you think of it all?"

She paused a moment and answered that the students were good.

After dinner we got as far as the door of the East Wing when we discovered it had begun to rain.

We repaired to the hotel bar. Reporters from Hong Kong bustled in and out. The hotel's location had made it something of a press center.

After the rain stopped we took a stroll down Wangfujing, the street running alongside the hotel, and then returned to Tiananmen Square.

Although it had been raining and it was already eight o'clock at night, the Peking twilight stretched out for a long time; at the edges of Tiananmen people were dimly visible walking their bikes, here to support the students, check out the scene, or listen to the broadcasts.

"Serve the People," Zhang Hongtu, Chairmen Mao Series

Some people felt the Student Movement had gone on long enough and that the enthusiasm of Peking citizens was cooling off. I found the sight of these anxious and concerned faces clustered under the streetlights gratifying.

If the movement couldn't depend on the support of the masses, what could it depend on? Under the three-tiered lights, the clamorous masses on the cold and rainy square formed a shield in my imagination, a shield constructed of flesh and blood. . . .

In the morning I went to the Air China office in the hotel to arrange for my return flight on June 5. They told me that passengers had to go in person to Air China's head office in town to reconfirm their seats. I asked if it was possible to get it all done in the branch office. Of course—for an extra fee of five yuan in Foreign Exchange Certificates (FEC). I laughed. Such a bizarre system.

We had lunch at the restaurant "Window on the World," on the top floor of the CITIC (China International Trade and Investment Corporation) building in Jianguomenwai. . . .

On the south side of the square close to the Chairman Mao Memorial Hall there was an orderly encampment of dozens of red and blue tents resembling Mongolian yurts. These tents lent an unintentionally discordant holiday atmosphere to the whole setup.

John Shum* was standing near the broadcasting station at the foot of the steps to the monument, directing things. He smiled as I approached and reached out to shake my hand. As far as I can recall, this was the first time I had ever shaken hands with Shum; we hadn't even shaken hands when he'd returned to Hong Kong all those years ago. The entire delegation from the Hong Kong Alliance in Support of Democratic Movements in China had arrived just three days earlier. Shum seemed to be enjoying himself immensely. He introduced me to the delegate from the Hong Kong Federation of Students, Lam Yiu Keung.

I asked Shum what he made of all this; he smiled but didn't say anything.

Only when I reached the top level of the steps, where there was a view over the whole square, did I realize there was a major cleanup operation underway. Much of the rubbish had been swept into heaps, and some of

---

* John Shum (Cen Jianxun) was a Trotskyist and political activist in Hong Kong in the late 1960s and '70s who went on to edit the trendy *City Magazine* and in the '80s became a popular film producer, actor, and scriptwriter.

the most dilapidated tents had been taken down. Over by the Great Hall of the People, newly erected bamboo structures covered with thick green sailcloth formed a dazzlingly fresh encampment.

I thought that if the students were planning to hold on until at least June 20 [when the National People's Congress was scheduled to meet] it wasn't a bad idea to clean the place up a bit.

The students and reporters on the steps of the monument were laughing and smiling, perhaps influenced by the newly salubrious atmosphere of the square itself—or was this just my imagination? But I must say that of the days I spent on Tiananmen Square, the only time I felt truly lighthearted and relaxed was close to sunset on June 1.

Regretfully, like all twilights, this one was not to last.

A young fellow rushed over to me. I recognized him as the reporter for *Youth News* I'd met on the steps of the monument the day before.

We strolled toward the Goddess of Democracy. This was my first opportunity to have a good look at her close up. I stood at her feet and, craning my neck, gave her the once-over.

If I could turn back the clock, I'd go back to her and weep. I'd tell her about her fate, about the fate assigned to her by Deng Xiaoping and his cronies, but comfort her too with the thought that for every one who fell there, thousands upon thousands will stand up in the future. . . .

At the Palace Hotel we found Shum just about to order some food from room service. "Hey, you guys, I don't know when I'll have another chance to eat."

I smiled and listened respectfully as he told me his views on [the student leader] Chai Ling. He had had a long talk with her just two days before.

"She's incredible. When the army was about to enter the city, this tiny little girl rushed over to a car by the square, locked the door, and poured kerosene all over her body, saying that if the troops entered the city she'd set herself on fire." He took a drag on a cigarette. "You wouldn't believe it just from looking at her."

"She may be commander in chief of the Defend Tiananmen Headquarters, but it seems that Hong Kong reporters aren't all that wild about her." This was my big discovery of the last two days.

"She's tired, exhausted, naturally sometimes she finds it hard to keep up appearances. Anyway, she's a tough cookie."

The food arrived, and Shum attacked it with gusto. When my reporter friend went to the bathroom, Shum asked me if I'd checked his identity card or press pass.

From the time I'd appeared, Shum had been trying to contact [the Taiwan singer] Hou Dejian by phone. When someone at his home said he'd gone to the Palace Hotel for dinner, Shum hastened downstairs to find him. No luck.

About nine o'clock Shum called for room service to take away the tray. He spoke to them in English. After hanging up, he said, "Don't take it the wrong way. Speaking all this Mandarin ties my tongue up in knots."

I told him I knew the feeling.

After half an hour we went to the Yuexiu Garden restaurant downstairs for dinner.

Lam Yiu Keung arrived with another representative of the Hong Kong Federation of Students, Chan Chong Yee. He had just arrived that day,

OFF THE BLOODY STAGE! (a song)
Hou Dejian

Off the bloody stage! * I'm getting old and a little senile too.
Get off the bloody stage! This stage seems to belong not to me
   but you.
Off the bloody stage! You were applauding me only yesterday.
Get off the bloody stage! What's turned you against me today?

Off the bloody stage! I'm not sure what I still can do.
Get off the bloody stage! I'm not sure what I still can say.
Off the bloody stage! I sing and play for all of you.
Get off the bloody stage! But what you want I've not a clue.

No one's said what's on their mind for years.
But there's a fire in their guts that sears.
You hate him, and he hates you and me.
But we haven't done anything wrong, really.

It's just that we're not doing as well as we'd hoped,
Still, that's not your fault, or his, and don't blame me.
I still want to sing for a few more years,
Why is the applause no longer resounding in my ears?

* Audience shouts out the lines in italics.

toting a fax machine. Shortly afterwards, Lee Wai Kit, Lee Chuk Yan, and Tam Yee Wah of the Hong Kong Alliance also turned up.

Shum naturally took on himself the responsibility of choosing what we would all eat.

Conversation Topic One: Should Shum and Lee Wai Kit follow their original schedule and return to Hong Kong on the following day? Or should they wait until they'd seen the completion of the drive to clean up the square?

Topic Two: When the Hong Kong customs people discovered that Chan Chong Yee was a student on his way to Peking, why did they insist on double-checking his fax machine before allowing him on his way?

Resolution of Topic One: The original schedule was to be maintained. The reasons were as follows: Shum was scared to death of flying Air

THE HONG KONG ROLE

Even though areas of the Peking municipality had been placed under martial law, Hong Kong people like Lee Chuk Yan entered China—indeed, came right into Tiananmen Square itself to provide money, provisions, and even communications equipment in order to encourage, support, and finance illegal activities in contravention of martial law. Their actions violated Chinese law and order. According to the principle of "one country, two systems," China will allow Hong Kong to maintain a capitalist system for fifty years after 1997. Hong Kong people can express any opinion they like in Hong Kong; that's their business. But when they are in China, they must respect the law of the land. The recent illegal activities of certain Hong Kong people in China who encouraged, supported, and participated in an attempt to overthrow the People's Republic of China and the socialist system cannot be tolerated by Chinese law.

Lee Chuk Yan and his ilk came to Peking expressly to participate in the turmoil. People of conscience cannot help but ponder the role that their support for the instigators of turmoil played. They raised their so-called morale and encouraged them in their long-term illegal occupation of Tiananmen Square, which led in the end to a counterrevolutionary rebellion.

—*Eight Members of the Staff of the Standing Committee of the National People's Congress, writing in the* People's Daily, *June 15, 1989*

China and the next Cathay Pacific flight was four days away, on Tuesday. Neither Shum nor Li was willing to stay that long.

Resolution of Topic Two: No one could figure it out. Maybe it was like the old saying: The palace eunuch is always more uptight than the emperor.

Just as we were finishing dinner, Chan Ching Wah and Lee Lan Kuk of the Hong Kong Federation of Students rushed in.

The team returned to the square in small groups.

We arrived there about eleven o'clock to find a dense crowd of pedestrians and bicyclists surging about in the darkness. Because the taxi driver had been arguing with us about Mao's portrait and the Mao Memorial Hall, he had taken a long way around. We ended up on a part of the road that had been closed off, so we got out of the cab and walked over to the supply station.

Some members of the federation were doing a bit of stocktaking. I watched from the sidelines. Stocktaking requires a lot of patience—I had to respect the students for that.

About midnight we heard that another row had broken out between the autonomous student union of Peking and that of the provinces; several groups from the Hong Kong Federation of Students and the Hong Kong Alliance hurried over to see if they could help negotiate a truce.

By midnight, most of the bicyclists had gone home. I sauntered over to the monument and mounted the steps. The Peking nights were a bit chilly, and many of the student pickets were wearing windbreakers. A handful of foreign reporters, their cameras strapped around their necks, were enjoying a leisurely smoke. Some students were already fast asleep in their tents. The soft, throaty strains of the "Internationale" came floating by from somewhere in the darkness. The sole illumination was that of the streetlights. . . .

While having breakfast in the hotel coffee shop, I kept trying to reach Shum by phone to find out the latest news.

By eleven I still hadn't found him. Fung Wai Choi and I left the hotel for the square.

It was a sunny day. The taxi dropped us off on the side of the square by the Great Hall of the People. It was clear that there were more people here today than in the previous two days. Spectators in sunglasses were wandering around everywhere. Students holding soft drinks or sucking on ice bars were strolling around with blank expressions on their faces. There were a lot of new tents.

At the top level of the monument, the general headquarters and financial department had also had a facelift. Bamboo poles had been set up on the front side of the monument. Someone told me that they were tents for the four people who were beginning a hunger strike at four o'clock in the afternoon and the medical team that was to attend them.*

Time was running out, though no one could have known this.

Going into the Peking Hotel, I bumped into Lee Lan Kuk. She asked if I knew where Shum was, and I said no. She told me that the Hong Kong Federation of Students was going to hold a small press conference that afternoon at the hotel.

While I was having a lunch of soup noodles, Shum returned to his hotel room with Chai Ling. I raced over to join them.

Shum answered the door. He was wearing a "Concert for a Democratic China" † T-shirt.

Inside, two people sat having lunch, their backs to the window. The girl lifted her head, slightly suspicious. Shum introduced us. Relieved, she smiled faintly and stopped eating.

The fellow by her side stood up to shake my hand: "How do you do —I'm Ma Ben." ‡ Ma Ben was Chai Ling's assistant.

Even though I'd read so many interviews with Chai Ling and seen so many photographs of her, I was surprised by this first encounter. Here was the commander in chief of the students' Defend Tiananmen Headquarters, a leader of the patriotic Student Movement for democracy, and yet to look at her she seemed so delicate, so vulnerable!

It's hard to express my amazement. She looked perfectly ordinary, the kind of person you'd pass on the street without a second look. But she did have a special quality about her, one that could make you feel protective and affectionate toward her before she'd even said a single word. She looked terribly tired and yet determined, unwilling to let other people see how exhausted she was. There was something special, too, in that steely gaze of hers, a sense of strength she projected quite unconsciously. She had lost her voice, and I had to strain to hear what she said.

"Have some more to eat," Shum urged her.

Smiling faintly, she sat in the armchair by the window.

Ma Ben pushed the room service cart into a corner of the room.

* Hou Dejian, Liu Xiaobo, Gao Xin, and Zhou Duo.
† The name of the benefit concert for the Protest Movement in Hong Kong on May 27 that John Shum helped organize.
‡ Not his real name.

"Art Appreciation": The picture is of a stool, or *deng* in Chinese, turned over, meaning "overthrow Deng" (Kristian Whittaker, *Direct Action*)

"So you're with some journal in Hong Kong, are you?" Chai Ling asked, running her hand through her hair.

"Well, not exactly, I've just come to get the feel of things and write a piece for this magazine." I pulled a copy of *Esquire* out of my knapsack and handed it to her.

As she was skimming through it, Shum said, "It's a very *middle-class* magazine." He said the words "middle-class" in English.

She raised her head. "Are you just letting me have a look, or are you giving this to me?"

"It's a gift."

She smiled. Actually, she smiled quite a lot. In the two days that I knew her I often saw her smiling—sometimes she grinned with real happiness, other times she had a strained, encouraging smile on her face —and her smile was enough to melt anybody's heart.

Lee Wai Kit and the other students from the federation arrived next, and they discussed the afternoon's arrangements with Chai Ling. Ma Ben took the copy of *Esquire,* sat down beside me, and struck up a conversation.

"You must all be very tired," I blurted out.

He smiled softly. Despite their exhaustion and the heavy load on their shoulders, they always seemed to be able to smile. They were ready to take whatever risks they had to. "Last night there was a bit of trouble with the school reps from outside Peking. I didn't get back to the tent until five A.M. and got up again two hours later." He flipped the magazine open to an advertisement and stared at it in a daze for a while.

Looking back, I now realize I ought to have known it would have been impossible to fully comprehend what they were going through—no matter how hard I tried.

"So if you don't run the magazine, what is it exactly that you do?" he asked.

And so it was that on a hot and sunny day I sat inside a room at the Palace Hotel exchanging life histories with this student who'd come from the provinces to join the student movement in Peking.

At three o'clock Shum, Chai Ling, Ma Ben, and I shifted to another room in the Palace where the BBC was to videotape an interview with Chai Ling.

One side of the room had been made into a makeshift studio. Originally they had planned to attach a small mike to Chai Ling's collar, but as her voice had gone this wouldn't work, so the sound recordist had to use an extremely sensitive handheld microphone instead.

In a soft, hoarse voice, Chai Ling began to tell the story of the movement from its beginnings.

In front of the lens, Chai's fighting spirit returned. She gesticulated boldly as she spoke, trying to communicate to the rest of the world, and put into some kind of order, the story of these young people's struggle. Their peaceful struggle. Sometimes she seemed to lose the thread, but she plunged on regardless. She wasn't the sort to stop and go back.

Forty minutes later, Ma Ben and I took advantage of a break in the filming to step out into the corridor for a cigarette. Not long afterward Shum joined us, and we each took a photo with Ma Ben as a memento.

Shum and Lee Wai Kit had to pack and hurry off to catch their five-thirty flight. The students from the federation returned to their hotel room to repair their fax, and I remained at the Palace to wait for the end of the interview so I could accompany Chai Ling and Ma Ben back to Tiananmen Square.

Inside the taxi, the driver asked uncertainly, "Are you students?"

"Sure thing," answered Ma Ben, who was sitting next to the driver. "Are you for the Student Movement?"

"Of course."

"Do you know who the leaders are?" Ma Ben asked, giggling.

The driver thought for a moment: "I've heard of Wuer Kaixi."

"How about the one called Chai Ling. Have you heard of her?" Ma Ben turned around to smile at us.

Chai Ling put her head down on the back of the driver's seat.

After a while, the driver said, "You know, this movement shouldn't go on for much longer."

Very slowly, very softly, she answered, "I know." She knew this all

OLD CHINA HANDS

The news that [Zhao Ziyang] wants to resign has been leaked, and now everyone outside is talking about it. They're asking how a bunch of seventy- and eighty-year-olds can cope with the nation's problems! In my opinion the answer is obvious. . . . Our older comrades have the greatest prestige and the longest involvement with the party; they have made important contributions to the party and the nation. It goes without saying that this is true of Comrade [Deng] Xiaoping. [Li] Xiannian, Chen Yun, Marshal Xu [Xiang-qian], Marshal Nie [Rongzhen], Elder Sister Deng [Yingchao, Madame Zhou Enlai], Peng Zhen, and of course our revered Comrade Wang [Zhen] have also all made great contributions. How could they remain silent at such a critical juncture! They certainly are not going to stand idly by as the country teeters on the brink of disaster. It is the rightful responsibility of a member of the Communist Party to speak up. There are people who are spreading rumors that there's no party to speak of, that all decisions are made by one person. This is quite wrong. A correct decision on this issue has been made by the majority of members of the Politburo and the Standing Committee. It has the wholehearted support of Chen Yun, Xiannian, Comrade Xiaoping, and the other older revolutionaries.

*—President Yang Shangkun, eighty-two
years old, May 24, 1989*

FROM WALL POSTERS AND POPULAR RHYMES

Xiaoping, Xiaoping, a venerable eighty-five,
He may still be walking but his brain's half alive.

Who says I'm old? I'm just a tad over eighty!

Black cats, white cats—they're all old cats!

too well, and yet there was nothing she could do about it.

"Are you very busy tonight?" I asked as we approached the square. Ma Ben nodded.

"How about tomorrow? Would you have time tomorrow? If you could make some time, I'd like to sit down with you and talk properly."

"Tomorrow . . ." Ma Ben frowned, running over the following day's schedule in his mind.

"See what you can do," Chai Ling said to him.

"All right, then, I'll give you a call at your hotel before nine o'clock tomorrow morning," Ma Ben said. "Be careful, the square is crawling with undercover policemen."

Standing in the sunshine, I watched them disappear into the crowd.

The hunger-strike activities had already begun, and there was a solid mass of people crowded around the side of the monument facing the Goddess of Democracy. The reporters pushed their way through. The four hunger strikers had greatly revived the movement's flagging morale. More people were flooding in all the time.

The spaces between the new, neatly arranged tents were packed with people. People were continually pushing up the steps from the foot of the monument.

Hou Dejian, one of the four hunger strikers, addressed the crowd. He was wearing a "Concert for a Democratic China" T-shirt covered with the signatures of all the other artists who'd been in the concert. He told the crowd that although the other singers, including Teresa Teng,* couldn't be there that day, they were with all their mainland compatriots in spirit. Afterwards, he led the crowd in singing "Heirs of the Dragon." †

I'd sung "Heirs of the Dragon" countless times—in Chater Garden, in Victoria Park, on King's Road, at the racecourse, outside the gates of the Xinhua News Agency—but I still wasn't prepared for how deeply moved I would be hearing this song sung here in the capital of the "land of the dragon," in the "far off East" itself.

The last pieces of the puzzle were falling into place; the whole picture was at last appearing before our eyes. . . .

On the steps of the monument, I ran into the young reporter. As we were exchanging greetings, he suddenly pointed at someone, exclaiming, "Wuer Kaixi!"

I had underestimated this star of the student leaders. Although sturdily built, he was neither tall nor particularly handsome. But there was something very striking in the way he moved; he stood out from the crowd. He was quite full of himself, and he deliberately used his arrogance to give himself the air of a star.

Surrounded by about ten reporters and students, he looked a bit im-

---

* A famous Taiwan songstress.
† For the words to this song, Hou's most famous work, see pp. 153–4.

patient but said little. He bent his head slightly to listen to the reporters' questions. Every so often he would answer with a sentence or two.

About five minutes later he discreetly nodded at the bodyguards by his side, and the four of them immediately clustered around and helped him down the steps. Two tireless women reporters followed him off into the distance.

There had been a steady stream of rumors showing Wuer Kaixi in a bad light. I could understand this: It was the way he was. You either loved him or hated him, there was no middle way. Personally, I found it hard to believe reports of his illegal appropriation of funds. Surely he wouldn't have stooped to that.

I tried one of the iced soft drinks they were selling on the square. It wasn't bad. The almost pathological fear of dirt I'd had in Hong Kong had almost completely melted away in these few days—the smell of filth and sweat had become part of the air itself. When students spat close to me, I simply stepped aside. When the fate of the nation was at stake, such trifling concerns seemed irrelevant.

You've got to be able to live before you can talk about the art of living.

By the time I got to Room 8016 in the Peking Hotel, it was close to six o'clock. Only about ten reporters were present. Lam Yiu Keung, Chan Chong Yee, Chan Ching Wah, and Lee Lan Kuk of the Hong Kong Student Federation were perched on the edge of the bed or sitting on the floor. They were casually discussing the power struggle between the autonomous student associations of Peking and the provinces; whether the two factions within the Hong Kong Student Federation were really at each other's throats; whether the enormous sum of money brought to Peking by the Hong Kong Alliance would put indirect pressure on the Peking students to prolong the movement; methods for distributing the money; how the federation, as a behind-the-scenes supporter, could assist the Peking students; and so on.

More gossipy topics included whether Chai Ling and Feng Congde had been kidnapped by Wang Li as everyone said they had; * whether Wuer Kaixi had really taken seven suites and rooms in the Great Wall Hotel; and so on.

The unofficial press conference came to an end forty-five minutes later. I went down to the lobby coffee shop to space out for a while.

---

* They had been and reportedly were questioned extensively over the alleged misuse of funds. Later, so as not to damage the image of the movement, the results of the questioning were kept secret.

I decided to relax a bit. I suggested to Fung Wai Choi that we have dinner at the teahouse on West Qianmen Avenue. . . .

The Peking twilight lasts for such a long time. After dinner we strolled back to the square, dragging elongated shadows behind us.

As we approached the side of the monument and began climbing up the steps, student marshals hurried up to us. "Reporters? Quick, there's a press conference over by the Goddess of Democracy."

Only about a dozen foreign reporters attended the press conference, which had been called by the students of the eight Peking universities. All around the platform at the goddess's feet were posted copies of the manifesto issued when the statue was raised. A pack of photographers was taking pictures of the spokesmen.

We walked along the side of the square nearest to Tiananmen Gate. It was Friday night, and there were countless people on bicycles. The government's official loudspeakers were trying to broadcast the martial law order and the speeches of Li Peng and the others. The people were all facing the monument to try to hear the much weaker broadcast of the students, cupping their ears with their hands. I discovered that this actually worked.

It was announced that the three workers who'd been arrested by the Public Security Bureau several days earlier had been released. There was thunderous applause.

Once more we made our way to the Hong Kong supply station. There were boxes upon boxes arranged neatly within the tent. Student representatives were lining up to exchange tickets for goods.

Things were moving along preordained paths. The first steps had been taken to reorganize Tiananmen Square according to plans drawn up by the polytechnic students. The plan included a library and rest areas on either side of the square. There was also hope that a water truck could be used to set up a bathhouse. It seemed as though the students would soon make living here a bit more comfortable.

As it turned out, the new encampment was theirs for only one day, one last glorious, sunny day. The plans for Tiananmen Square turned out to be nothing more than a pipe dream. . . .

I woke up to a broadcast by the American Cable News Network describing how young, unarmed soldiers had entered the city in the wee hours only to be stopped by the masses. The soldiers, dressed in white shirts and khaki trousers, had been sent on an exercise. Unaware of what was going on, they had jogged all the way from the airport to the Avenue of Eternal Peace.

I figured Chai Ling and Ma Ben wouldn't be phoning.

Fung Wai Choi had arranged to meet Wang Dan at ten o'clock, so we rushed over to Peking University. After losing our way several times, we finally reached Building 32, where Wang Dan lived. His roommate said that when they'd received the news of an emergency in town, Wang Dan had left and hadn't returned.

The rectangular room was probably about a hundred square feet. It looked a mess. On either side stood double-tiered iron beds; four people slept here. Their books were piled up alongside the wall on their beds, along with bedding, pillows, and clothes. All three of Wang Dan's roommates were in. For some reason the whole scene gave me an anxiety attack.

From Building 32 we went to Building 29, where the Peking University Autonomous Students' Union had its headquarters. The loudspeaker in the courtyard was urgently calling on volunteers to gather at eleven-thirty to join a funeral procession* scheduled to leave Fuxingmen for Tiananmen Square at one o'clock.

Fistfuls of flyers in their hands, students rode off in all directions.

We went to the small campus shop, where I bought a T-shirt and tank top on which was printed "Peking University."

Along the side of the road were notice boards covered with handwritten posters. Teachers and students stopped to read them as they walked by. Others had come by bike and some read as they ate from lunchboxes.

They all wore grave expressions. . . .

By three-thirty in the afternoon, the Xidan area was already in a state of chaos. A foreign reporter ran stumbling into the Jianguo Hotel [where we were having coffee] and said that the troops were using tear gas on the people. His camera had been knocked to the ground; he'd come back for another lens.

It's so strange to reflect back on that moment: There was a life-and-death struggle unfolding around me, and I really hadn't the foggiest notion of it.

At four o'clock, Fung Wai Choi and I returned to the Peking Hotel to hang out for a while before returning to the square.

---

* To mourn the three people killed the night before by an army jeep on loan to Central Television that had been driven recklessly down the Avenue of Eternal Peace.

There were lots of people in the coffee shop—it was wickedly hot outside. A young guy with long hair sat down at our table.

He was wearing a tattered old T-shirt on which was stamped "Tiananmen Square Democracy University." I couldn't control my curiosity. "What's that?" I asked.

He answered proudly, "A university that's yet to be founded."

"Pardon? I don't get it."

"You're from Hong Kong, aren't you? Some people from your Chinese University have gotten together with the autonomous student associations of Peking and the provinces to set up a university. The opening ceremony is tonight." He showed us the heavy thing he was holding in his hand: "This is the seal."

I laughed. "I want to use it too."

"Feel free." He put the seal on the table. It was about four inches tall and two inches square. "What do you want to stamp with it?"

"Ah!" I pulled the two Peking University souvenirs out of my backpack. "Not bad, eh?"

He smiled faintly.

Fung Wai Choi, infinite in his resources, went to borrow an inkpad from the hotel post office. Chuckling with amusement, we stamped our T-shirts in the middle of the coffee shop.

"Why do you have this seal?" I asked as I stamped.

"I carved it," he answered languorously.

"Really?"

"No shit. I'm a sculptor—and a painter too."

"Are you a member of the Stars?"

"The Stars have broken up. But yeah, I used to be."

At this point Fung Wai Choi decided to leave us and go back to the Lido for a rest. Lao Men and I ordered another drink.

"I've just come back from the square. I was hanging out in the tent where Hou Dejian and the others are fasting. The atmosphere there's a real downer."

He showed me his trousers, which were covered with signatures. "Hou Dejian just gave me his autograph."

"Will he be able to make it through the fast?"

"No problem. It's only for forty-eight hours."

"Wasn't it supposed to be three days?"

"That's for Liu Xiaobo, Zhou Duo, and Gao Xin. Hou has to get to Hong Kong to cut a record, so he's only fasting for two days."

"Well, two days isn't easy."

"He'll survive," he said.

Lao Men was living in Shanghai. He'd come to Peking for the Student Movement and had spent all his money. He'd been living in the tents on the square, but it was so hot in the afternoon that he'd come to the Peking Hotel to pass the time. He was great pals with the waiters in the coffee shop. "These waiters are pretty cool. They see a lot of foreigners, so they're pretty world-wise."

We drank beer.

"Democracy is the only hope for China," he declared, taking up his beer. "A friend of mine has been to Hong Kong. He drove on those fabulous highways. When he came back he said to me, you know, in a way I'm now rather grateful for the Opium Wars."

There was nothing I could say.

Could I even pretend to understand them?

We had dinner at the Donglaishun Restaurant on Wangfujing. As we crossed the road Lao Men put his arm through mine as if it were the most natural thing in the world, as if by so doing he could protect me from the traffic. Why? Was it because I was from Hong Kong? Or because of what I could do for them? Perhaps they didn't expect anything from me at all. Maybe they were just grateful I was there. I don't know.

"You'll be at the opening of the Democracy University tonight?" he asked again as we left the restaurant. Stuffing the seal into my backpack, he said, "In that case, watch this for me, will you?"

It was seven-thirty when we passed through the Peking Hotel. At the shop I bought the day's *South China Morning Post*. The front page had pictures of troops entering the city.

"The troops are coming in again," I said.

"That's right. They've already moved into Dongdan."

When we entered the square, Lao Men said to me, "I'll meet you at Hou's tent in a while. Have a look around and then meet me there."

As I reached the stairs of the monument, I noticed Chai Ling discussing something with several students, a serious expression on her face. She saw me and cracked a smile. I stood not far away, smoking a cigarette and watching the tide of people wash over the square.

Shortly afterwards she came over. "I'm so sorry about this morning . . ."

"I understand. You had to deal with the troops."

She raised her head. "It's a real crisis."

A student patrol approached and asked her to attend to some business on the other side of the monument.

Ma Ben wandered up.

I smiled at him and said, "Good to see you—I'm out of cigarettes." We sat down by the side, and he pulled a pack of Chinese Dachongjiu cigarettes out of his bag and handed it to me. "Yesterday my father came to see me and gave me these. They're not bad. Try them."

"He's gone?"

"Yes, he left this morning."

We sat wrapped in our thoughts for a while.

Eventually Ma said, "There was really nothing we could do about this morning. Sorry to keep you hanging around like that."

"Don't worry about it. There's always tomorrow, isn't there?"

He smiled softly.

I said, "So you didn't get much sleep last night?"

"It wasn't that bad. I managed to sneak in four hours."

Chai Ling came running over, spoke briefly to Ma, and then ran off again. Ma called out to her, "Is it all right to give him an interview tomorrow?"

She stopped. "Who?"

"Him!" Ma pointed at me.

She laughed. "Sure. Make the appointment, will you?"

"Done."

We lit up again. I'd become a heavy smoker in Peking.

"Let's set up a time and place to meet tomorrow morning. I promise we'll keep our word this time." He pulled on my sleeve. "But I think you should leave now."

"I can't," I protested. "I want to see the opening ceremony of the Democracy University."

He pondered this. "Well, don't stay too long. Go home at the end of the ceremony, all right?"

As he ran off, he said, "Be careful."

How I regret not saying the same to him!

Sitting under the monument, I watched as people came and went from the fasting tent nearby. Two young doctors wearing the uniforms of the Capital Hospital and holding their dinners were trying to find a place to sit down and eat. I moved over. "Sit here."

They sat down and began to eat. Neither of them had shaved in days; their chins were covered with stubble. They looked exhausted but calm as they shoveled in the food.

I wonder if those young doctors are still alive.

"How's it going?" Lao Men had reappeared.

We strolled to the side of the monument, where Wuer Kaixi was speaking, surrounded by a crowd of reporters and other people.

"You've met him, haven't you?" asked Lao Men.

I shook my head. "Haven't had the chance."

"That's quite an achievement."

We walked down the steps. Lao Men shouted out, "Kaixi!" Without a word, Wuer Kaixi extricated himself from the crowd and came over.

He first smiled politely at me and then asked, "What's up?"

"My friend." Lao Men had his usual cheeky grin on his face. "From Hong Kong."

Wuer Kaixi nodded in my direction and spoke to Lao Men. "Why haven't I seen you around these last few days?"

"I've been lying low." Lao Men turned to me. "Lend me your pen a second." He took the pen and handed it to Wuer Kaixi. "Sign this for me, will you?"

"Untitled," Zhang Hongtu, Chairmen Mao Series

Wuer Kaixi, shaking his head, knelt down to write his autograph on Lao Men's thigh.

"Hey, give this guy an interview. He's with a magazine," Lao Men said as he inspected his souvenir.

"I'm afraid it's not on tonight. Things are a bit tense." He gazed at the people standing to one side.

"Tomorrow would be okay." I looked at him.

"I don't think there'd be any problem with tomorrow." He paused. "Come to my tent."

"What time?" I persisted.

"In the afternoon . . . say around two or three o'clock."

Lao Men pulled Wuer Kaixi over to the side and had a few words with him in private. I walked in the direction of the Goddess of Democracy. The location of the Democracy University was close to the base of the goddess.

I sat down for a minute, quietly watching the excited, happy people who were slowly gathering round. Ma Ben appeared at my side and whispered, "If you sit so far away you won't see anything." I followed him up to a place in the front of the platform, right in the middle. I took out the packet of Dachongjiu cigarettes and offered him one.

"If you ever come back to China, write to me first. The place I come from is really nice."

"So I understand."

"Have you heard? The army's coming in to crush us tonight."

I was dumbfounded. "No, it couldn't be true, could it?"

"Listen, I think you'd better leave now."

I looked around. There were students and other people as far as the eye could see. I couldn't even begin to estimate the size of the crowd. It was just people, people, everywhere.

"If they're not afraid, why should I be?" I replied.

"You don't understand." After a while he said, "They're coming in soon."

We lit up again. The army was coming in, and there I was, sitting in the middle of Tiananmen Square smoking a cigarette.

After a long while, Ma looked at his watch, said, "I'm going to get Chai Ling," and left.

Lao Men appeared with his wife, Yang Yi, in tow. He was extremely anxious as he spoke to her. "You can sit here awhile, but then you must go home. Do you understand?" Yang Yi explained, "We've come to an agreement so that our child won't become an orphan. He does what has to be done here and I take care of the child. Our kid's only three years old."

Yang Yi was also a painter. She was twenty-three, a spirited, pretty northern girl with clear features. I took out the notebook in which I'd stamped the seal of the Democracy University and asked the two of them to sign their names. Lao Men took the seal up to the headquarters. "When can the students get their T-shirts stamped with the seal?" I asked innocently.

"Hell," said Lao Men. "That's a university seal. It's not for stamping T-shirts."

I burst out laughing. It was the last time for many days that I was to feel so happy.

"It's nine-thirty. You'd better be off," Lao Men ordered his wife.

"I'll just stick around a while longer."

"If you leave now, it'll be easier to get back home."

"You know, I think you ought to prepare some Molotov cocktails for the troops."

"But," I interrupted, "that's too violent!"

At nine-thirty, Yang Yi left the square.

At nine forty-five, the loudspeaker at the Democracy University command platform asked Wuer Kaixi, Chai Ling, Feng Congde, and Wang Dan to come to the platform; the opening ceremony was about to begin.

At ten to ten, Chai Ling arrived, surrounded by people. It had been two days, and she was still wearing the shirt with wide white and green stripes. Ma Ben had just returned and sat down next to me.

"Don't you need to look after Chai Ling?"

"We've organized a bodyguard of thirty people to look after her to-night."

I ran over to take a photo of Chai Ling, who waved a greeting.

At exactly ten o'clock, the ceremony began. Zhang Deli, the vice commander of the Defend Tiananmen Headquarters and president of the Democracy University, stood up to speak. "We have reliable news that the troops will begin their attack at one in the morning. We will conduct this ceremony as quickly as possible in order to ensure everyone's safety."

After the ceremonial cutting of the ribbon, the guests of honor took the stage one after another to speak. Wuer Kaixi, Feng Congde, and Wang Dan still hadn't appeared.

When it was Chai Ling's turn to speak, she stressed that the establishment of the Democracy University was a symbol of the fight for democracy on the square; anyone who shared their ideals counted as a student of the university. Finally she apologized: "I have to return to the command post. Tonight the situation is extremely critical, and as the commander in chief, I must work out tactics with the other students."

She tried to raise that worn-out voice of hers so the excited crowd could hear every word. She held up both hands in the sign of victory and grinned widely.

Ma Ben pulled on my sleeve. "We must go." He started to run off. I called out, "Don't forget about tomorrow." He turned his head and yelled, "Remember, as soon as the ceremony is over, go back to your hotel." He caught up with Chai Ling, and the two of them waved good-bye to me in the distance.

That was the last time I saw them.

At eleven-thirty I left the square with Lao Men to drink a toast to the establishment of the Democracy University.

Just as blackness was about to descend on the land, Lao Men and I sat at the Peking Hotel throwing back vodka in a toast to the new university.

Lao Men suggested that I get a taste of life on the square—he could arrange for me to move into one of the tents.

Maybe tomorrow night? I asked.

At the hotel, Lao Men planned the following day's itinerary for me:

BLOOD OATHS

I swear that I will devote my young life to protect Tiananmen and the republic. I may be beheaded, my blood may flow, but the people's square will not be lost. We are willing to use our young lives to fight to the very last person.

> —From an oath sworn by the students on
> Tiananmen Square, led by Chai Ling, 9 P.M.,
> June 3, 1989

If I can wake up the people with my blood, then I am willing to let my blood run dry;
If by giving my life the people will awake, then happily do I go to my death.

> —Oath sworn by Martial Law Enforcement
> Troops before entering Peking

We'd first have lunch together and then go spend the afternoon with Wuer Kaixi.

At this juncture between life and death, I was sitting inside the hotel cracking jokes and enjoying myself.

As we left the hotel a tank with the number 003 painted on it raced past on the Avenue of Eternal Peace away from Tiananmen. There was a crowd of people on bikes chasing the tank.

"Things are bad. I'd better get back to the square," Lao Men said. He looked at me. "Get back to your hotel."

"But the square—"

"Just return to your hotel," he interrupted. "See you tomorrow."

That was the last time I saw the Avenue of Eternal Peace.

One Night in Peking

An editorial in today's *Liberation Army Daily* says: "A most serious counterrevolutionary riot occurred in the capital in the early hours of June 3."

At approximately 2200 hours on June 3 the sound of firing was heard in the vicinity of the Military Museum. Martial Law Enforcement Troops were entering the city.

From midnight until early morning we received continual phone calls from the Friendship Hospital, Fuwai Hospital, Municipal First Aid Clinic, Railroad Hospital, Fuxing Hospital, Capital Hospital, and Guang'anmen Hospital reporting on the admission of dead and wounded.

At the time the paper went to press, Martial Law Enforcement Troops had already forced their way onto Tiananmen Square.

—Front-page news item, People's Daily,
June 4, 1989

An Encounter with Mounted Troops at Qianmen

ZHOU ZUOREN

Zhou Zuoren was the brother of Lu Xun and a well-known writer in his own right.

It was after three o'clock on the afternoon of June 5, 1919. I was walking from Beichizi next to the Forbidden City to Qianmen to do some shopping when to my surprise I saw many pedestrians along the long lane flanking the former Imperial Clan Court. The sidewalks on both sides of the street near the Police Department were packed. Many troops and policemen were standing guard in the middle of the road. Further down the street I saw groups of young students in long gowns. Each group was holding a Chinese flag, and they were surrounded by police and troops.

Soldiers blocked my way. Usually, the very thought of soldiers is terrifying, but I felt sure that as they were ordinary Chinese just like myself there was nothing to be scared of. Sure enough, they asked me amiably enough not to go any further. "But they're just ordinary, unarmed civilians. What possible danger could there be?" I asked. "Search me," one soldier replied. "We're just obeying orders. You'll be able to get through in a minute." With this reassurance, I stood there and waited.

Suddenly the air was rent by yells of "Move back!" followed by the clatter of horses' hooves. My right shoulder seemed to collide with the head of a chestnut horse. The crowd panicked, and we all ran north. Behind us we could hear shouting and more clatter of hooves.

By the time I felt the danger was over and I'd stopped, I found myself under a memorial arch with the word *lüzhong* [Walking the Middle Path] written on it. I collected my thoughts and tried to plot my way south out of Qianmen, the front gate of the inner city, so as to avoid another confrontation with the cavalry. I approached a policeman who kindly advised me that the safest route would be to head south from Tiananmen, passing through the wall at the Zhonghua Gate. I thanked him and followed his advice, thereby avoiding any more danger.

As I walked I kept going over the events of the afternoon in my head. The soldiers and policemen had been perfectly civil; it was those mounted troops who had caused such terror. Their horses were stupid beasts who knew nothing about the republic or laws but simply charged about wildly. But shouldn't the troops or policemen on the horses have had minds of their own? What could possibly have made them want to trample over their own people?

Instead of panicking and fleeing, I told myself, I should have tried to talk to the "humans" on horseback. I was sure they would have been quite friendly and reasonable, perfectly capable of protecting us. I hated myself for panicking and running away, dropping all my money into the bargain.

Lost in this meditation, I found myself before tent number 39 outside Tiananmen. It was now too late to turn back and talk to the troops. When I recalled the incident at home that night, I was both pleased and angry with myself: pleased that I'd been lucky enough to escape the horses' hooves, angry for not having spoken to the troops. I picked up my brush and wrote this essay as a memoir.

In the old days, when educated Chinese gentlemen had some dangerous encounter, they were wont to write "Anguished Reminiscences" or "Tales of a Survivor." My experience was hardly so dramatic. But it was my first such encounter.

When living overseas, I was never shouted at or hunted down by troops or police. I never had to flee for my life. But today, in the capital of my own country, I have had such an unexpected experience, one that was quite beyond my imagination. No wonder I'm making so much of it, writing about it at such length.

I don't regret my walk this afternoon. It has taught me a lesson that is far more significant than the humiliation it inflicted on me.

The Howl

ANONYMOUS

*F*ollowing *are the last two sections of a lengthy prose poem by a young poet from the provinces, completed just after the June massacre and smuggled out of China. In the poet's own recording of it, smuggled out with the words, he at times screams, weeps, and repeats phrases again and again, conveying a mood of hysteria. Writers connected with this poem and its distribution in a number of provincial cities were reportedly arrested in May and June of 1990.*

But another sort of slaughter takes place at Utopia's core

The prime minister catches cold, the people cough, martial law is declared again and again

The toothless old machinery of the state rolls on toward those with the courage to resist the sickness

Unarmed hooligans fall by the thousands, ironclad professional killers swim in a sea of blood, set fires beneath tightly closed windows, wipe their army regulation boots on the skirts of dead maidens. They're incapable of trembling

These heartless robots are incapable of trembling!

Their electronic brains possess only one program, an official document full of holes

In the name of the motherland slaughter the Constitution! Replace the Constitution and slaughter righteousness! In the name of mothers throttle children! In the name of children sodomize fathers! In the name of wives murder husbands! In the name of the citizens blow up cities! OPEN FIRE! FIRE!FIRE!FIRE! Upon the

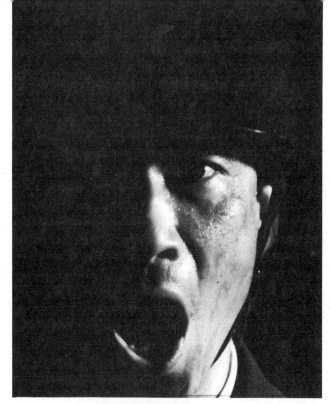

Still from the *The Big Parade*, a film by Chen Kaige, 1985

elderly! Upon the children! OPEN FIRE on women! On students!
Workers! Teachers! OPEN FIRE on peddlers! OPEN FIRE!
BLAST AWAY! Take aim at those angry faces. Horrified faces.
Convulsing faces. Empty all barrels at despairing and peaceful
faces! FIRE AWAY to your heart's content! These faces that come
on like a tide and in the next moment are dead are so beautiful!
These faces that will be going up to heaven and down to hell are so
beautiful! Beautiful. A beauty that turns men into beasts! A beauty
that lures men on to ravage, vilify, possess, despoil! Do away with
all beauty! Do away with flowers! Forests. Campuses. Love.
Guitars and pure clean air! Do away with flights of folly! OPEN
FIRE! BLAST AWAY! IT FEELS SO GOOD! SOOOO GOOD!
Just like smoking dope. Taking a crap. Back on base giving the old
lady a good fuck! OPEN FIRE! ALL BARRELS! BLAST AWAY!
FEELS GOOD! SOOO GOOD! Smash open a skull! Fry his
scalp! Spill the brains out. Spill the soul out. Splatter on the
overpass. Gatehouse. Railings. Splatter on the road! Splatter
toward the sky where the drops of blood become stars! Stars on the
run! Stars with legs! Sky and earth have changed places. Mankind

*wears bright shining hats. Bright shining metal helmets. A troop of
soldiers comes charging out of the moon. OPEN FIRE! ALL
BARRELS! BLAST AWAY! SUCH A HIGH! Mankind and the
stars fall together. Flee together. Can't make out one from the
other. Chase them up to the clouds! Chase them into the cracks of
the earth and into their flesh and WASTE THEM! Blow another
hole in the soul! Blow another hole in the stars! Souls in red skirts!
Souls with white belts! Souls in running shoes doing exercises to the
radio! Where can you run? We will dig you out of the mud. Tear
you out of the flesh. Scoop you out of the air and water. OPEN
FIRE! BLAST AWAY! IT FEELS GOOD! SOOO GOOD! The
slaughter takes place in three worlds. On the wings of birds. In the
stomachs of fish. In the fine dust. In countless species of living
things. LEAP! HOWL! FLY! RUN! You can't pass over wall after
wall of fire. Can't swim across pool after pool of blood. IT FEELS
SO GOOD! Freedom feels SO GOOD! Snuffing out freedom feels
SO GOOD! Power will always triumph. Will be passed down
forever from generation to generation. Freedom will also be
resurrected. Generation after generation. Like that dim light just
before the dawn. No. There's no light. At Utopia's core there can
never be light. Our hearts are pitch black. Black. Scalding. Like a
crematorium. Phantoms of the burnt dead. We will survive. The
government that dominates us will survive. Daylight comes
quickly. IT FEELS SO GOOD! SOOOO GOOD! The butchers
are still howling! Children. Children with cold bodies. Children
whose hands grasp stones. Let's go home. Girls, your lips drawn
and pale. Let's go home. Brothers and sisters, your shattered bodies
littering the earth. Let's go home. We walk noiselessly. Walk three
feet above the ground. Forward, on and on, there must be a place
to rest. There must be a place where sounds of gunfire and
explosions can't be heard. We yearn to hide within a stalk of grass.
A leaf. Uncle. Auntie. Grandpa. Granny. Daddy. Mommy. How
much farther till we're home? We have no home. Everyone knows.
The Chinese have no home. Home is a gentle desire. Let us die in
this desire! OPEN FIRE! BLAST AWAY! FIRE! Let us die in
freedom. Righteousness. Equality. Universal love. Peace. In these
vague desires. Let us become these desires. Stand on the horizon.
Attract more of the living to death! It rains. Don't know which is
falling, raindrops or transparent ashes. Run quickly, mommy! Run
quickly, son! Run quickly, elder brother! Run quickly, little*

brother! The butchers will not let up. An even more terrifying day approaches.

OPEN FIRE! BLAST AWAY! FIRE! IT FEELS GOOD! FEELS SOOO GOOD!

Cry Cry Cry Cry Crycrycrycrycrycrycrycry

Before you've been surrounded and annihilated, while you still have the strength left to suckle, crycrycry

Let your sobs cast you off, fuse into radio, television, radar, testify to the slaughter again and again

Let your sobs cast you off, fuse into plant life, semivegetable life and microorganisms, blossom into flower after flower, year after year mourning the dead, mourning yourself

Let your sobs be distorted, twisted, annihilated by the tumult of the sacred battle

The butchers come from the east of the city, from the west, from the south, from the north

Metal helmets glint in the light. They're singing—

The sun rises in the east, the sun rises in the west, the sun rises in the south and north

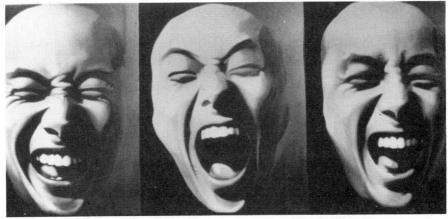

"A Second State," by Geng Jianyi (Modern Chinese Art Exhibition, February 1989)

Putrid, sweltering summer, people and ghosts sing—

Don't go to the east, don't go to the west, don't go to the south and north

In the midst of brilliance we stand blind
On a great road but we cannot walk
In the midst of a cacophony all are mute
In the midst of heat and thirst all refuse to drink

People who misunderstand the times, people who think they're surrounded, people who plot to shoot down the sun

You can only cry, you're still crying, crycrycrycrycrycrycry! CRY! CRY! CRY!

You've been smothered to death, baked to death, your whole body is on fire! And yet you're crying

You get up on the stage and act out a farce, you're paraded before the crowds in the streets, and yet you're crying

We forget all too quickly. The Cultural Revolution, Wei Jingsheng, "eliminating Spiritual Pollution," the "Four Basic Principles"—the crystal-clear executioner's manifesto of Deng Xiaoping. Has the slaughter ever stopped? What difference does it make if the blood is shed on Tiananmen Square or in the labor camps of Qinghai? If the shock of the Peking Massacre comes as something totally new and disturbing, it is proof that people forget their past all too easily.

How can I trust the repeated cries of the mourners? In the cycles of farce there are always those who shed tears in silence. The dead cannot weep; nor can those who remember the past. That young lives were lost is tragic, for they believed that their sacrifice was a novel thing. But no, everyone has gone through the motions of dying many times before. They are worn out, like the cries themselves.

Cry we must, but let us hope that memory is not washed away in the flood of tears.

—Yang Lian*

* Yang Lian, a poet from Peking who was in New Zealand at the time of the massacre and is now living in exile, wrote this comment on "The Howl" in October 1989 in Auckland. For samples of Yang Lian's poetry, see *Seeds of Fire*, pp. 36, 135, 246–49, 398–99, 434–37.

The Cry

Your eyeballs explode, scald the surrounding crowd, and yet you're crying

You offer a bounty on yourself, track yourself down, frame yourself, you say you were mistaken, this accursed epoch is all wrong! And yet you're crying

You are trampled, you cry

You are pulverized, you cry

A dog licks up the paste, inside a dog's belly you cry! CRYCRYCRY!

In this historically unprecedented slaughter only the sons of bitches can survive.

(Alain Keler/ODYSSEY)

In the First Light of Dawn

XI XI

In the first gray light of dawn,
We curl into the air,
Trailing from the ground
Up into the open sky above the square.
Limp, leaden, dumdum-pocked
The corpses lie
Mashed into the concrete.
Suddenly weightless
We drift
Like balloons.

We hear the sound
Of your weeping.

Mother, I beg you
Not to look for us again in the square,
The wasteland, where
Crushed tents, banners, command posts,
Public address stations
Strew the ground.
Teachers, students, friends
Are all gone.
The acrid smoke of gunfire
Fades as
Thousands of lives
Turn to ash.

Tomorrow will be Environment Day—
A Sanitation Show is planned,
The square will be scrubbed

The Cry

Nice and clean,
As if nothing ever happened.

We hear the sound
Of your weeping.

We fell together,
Together we rise,
Joining once more our parted hands,
Holding our torches ever higher.
A wound gapes
On one man's chest;
A tank tread
Furrows one man's brow.
But these wounds lie
On the body's husk;
We are beautiful beyond compare.
Nothing can hurt us now.
We will share
The city's splendor
With the stone beasts—
They, on their carved columns,
We, on the People's Monument—
Calling
Across the square.

A Tiny Handful . . .

During late spring and early summer, from mid-April to
early June of 1989, a tiny handful of people exploited
student unrest to unleash planned, organized, and
premeditated political turmoil, which later developed into
a counterrevolutionary rebellion in the capital, Peking. . . .
—*Chen Xitong, Mayor of Peking,*
June 30, 1989

Some indication of the amount of damage done by this "tiny handful"
of people is given in the following excerpt from a front-page report in
the Peking Evening News of August 3, 1989.

. . . After June 4, under the guidance of the district and municipal governments, neighborhood committees organized 649 work teams with
156,000 members to participate in the task of restoring order to traffic
and society. Neighborhood committee cadres and activists joined forces
with Martial Law Enforcement Troops and the People's Police to clear
away roadblocks, remove posters and slogans, and clean up the city.
Altogether they cleared away roadblocks in more than 570 places,
washed away or painted over more than 30,000 slogans, and picked up
more than 80 tons of bricks and stones, making a great contribution
toward the early restoration of normal traffic and a stable situation in
the capital.

"The Iron Cross of June 4," sculpture by
Wang Keping (Taiwan Art Gallery).

An Unfortunate Incident

CHEN YING-CHEN

While most Chinese throughout the world were appalled by the massacre, not everyone saw the events of 1989 in the same light. Here, Chen Ying-chen, a middle-aged Taiwan writer who spent years in a Taiwanese prison for his pro-Communist stance, gives his perspective on what he calls the "unfortunate Tiananmen Incident." Chen's views on the massacre and his decision to lead an unofficial delegation to Peking in February 1990 to meet with top Communist officials, including Party General Secretary Jiang Zemin, reportedly upset a number of his friends and colleagues.

The reformist line of Deng Xiaoping, Hu Yaobang, and Zhao Ziyang, although undoubtedly based on the "best of intentions," has undeniably developed into a revisionist, semicapitalist line. It has created intensely sharp contradictions in the areas of life-style and ideology. In May 1989, these contradictions finally led to an explosion among the students, the most sensitive group in the society.

The contradictions arising from the revisionist and semicapitalist Deng-Hu-Zhao line helped foster the Peking Student Movement. In ideological terms the movement not only failed to criticize revisionism and semicapitalism, it actually demanded further moves in that direction! The students opposed corruption and bureaucratism and demanded a greater role for the masses in production, distribution, and political life ("Long Live Democracy!" "Long Live Freedom!"). But they didn't criticize the roots of corruption and the bureaucratic system—the social contradictions caused by the decentralization of power, the Open Door Policy, and Reform—they actually called for these to be further enhanced! The Peking students and liberal intellectuals were endorsing the very source of the official racketeering and bureaucratism they found so intolerable! This is in fact the greatest internal contradiction and tragedy of this unfortunate Tiananmen Incident.

These contradictions and sorrows have propagated even more contradictions and sorrows:

In one night, the astoundingly harmonious relationship between the People's Liberation Army and the masses as well as the tolerance and administrative "support" shown by the Chinese Communist authorities toward demonstrations involving millions of people were completely obliterated. . . .

Taiwan aside, the Tiananmen Incident has resulted in the most extensive chorus of anti-Communist and anti-Chinese sentiments the world has seen since 1950. Anti-Communist fascist elements have become the guardian angels of democracy and freedom; international anti-Communist espionage organizations and human rights warriors and the language of the Cold War, not heard for such a long time, are suddenly everywhere you look. Clearheaded people can only stand by helplessly as the truth is willfully distorted, liars take the stage, and the unscrupulous appear as veritable Bodhisattvas, while the soldiers and people who have fallen on Tiananmen must remain silent.

Furthermore, as long as the true meaning of the unfortunate Tiananmen Incident is not brought to light and crystallized, those who fervently desire upright government, democracy, and freedom for China in a pure and honest way will continue in the dark night of nihilism, cynicism, and even total hopelessness. Official speculators will become more rapacious than ever, and just as in the Cultural Revolution, bureaucratism, far from having been conquered, will go from strength to strength!

What could be more perverse? What contradictions are more topsy-turvy than these? What misery could be more profound than this?

This is the main reason why I so bitterly condemn those who opened fire in front of Tiananmen.

—July 1989

My Home Is Next to Tiananmen Square

ZHANG LANGLANG

The old men of the party who sent in the troops to slaughter the students and citizens who had been protesting in Peking were all provincials, people from outside the capital. For the better part of forty years, they have occupied the ancient imperial city, living in its secluded princely mansions and palaces. They never walk in the streets with their own citizens; the lost pleasures described in this essay are entirely foreign to them. These cadres, the old men and their toadies, come mostly from the rural south or the west; they are peasants who hate the self-sufficient, proud culture of the old imperial city and have connived to destroy it since 1949. (Mao once reportedly even contemplated tearing down the Imperial Palace.) They never felt at home in Peking, and when the city rebelled in May, albeit peacefully, they had their revenge, using as tools provincial soldiers who, like themselves, deeply distrusted and resented the city.

Our small courtyard house is just off Nanchizi Road, right next to Tiananmen. Everyone agrees it's a very special place.

It's the tiniest courtyard imaginable, but somehow there's room enough in it for a big tree of heaven, with a trunk as thick as a washbasin. Our friends envy us; the whole courtyard is shaded by the leafy parasol of the tree. And it gives us fruit every year. . . .

Friends and relatives who came visiting could find us just by following the scent of the tree. They came in groups—well, packs really—armed with their baskets and bags. They walked straight in and went clambering up the tree without a by-your-leave. There were always people around at that time of year, up in the tree or gathered beneath, talking or playing, joking and laughing. The fruit rained down on the courtyard. Nobody ever went away empty-handed, dissatisfied. But they always left a dish of the best fruit, saving us the trouble of picking it ourselves. A grand tree, that. This was in early spring, when the weather can turn hot and cold without warning.

When the real spring came, our lilac tree stole the limelight. A few white flowers would permeate the whole alley with their fragrance, so sweet it would follow you down the street, filling your lungs. You could never get too much of it. I suppose that's why they put it into medicine. The fragrance itself is like a tonic.

In the early morning we'd go out to do our exercises. The old people and kids living along the alley would all be up and about as well, calling out a greeting and smiling as you walked past. In Peking they say neighbors are closer than relatives.

Every day, regardless of the weather, there'd be groups of young and old men by the red walls of the old palace, brandishing their spears and cudgels, practicing with as much conviction as if they were really fighting. Even the old man in the white jacket, who used to stay behind closed doors for the rest of the day, would be out there doing his tai chi, convinced he was every bit as good as Grand Master Zhang Sanfeng. You couldn't help admiring him for his total dedication. He didn't think much of us joggers—too newfangled and Western for him. But to give him his due, he'd always give us the thumbs-up anyway, just to encourage us. We'd smile back, and that'd make him happy. To him we'd always be kids.

The Cultural Palace is just a short run from our place. We call it "our backyard"; it really is the cheapest imperial garden in the world: three cents a head to get in. I won't bore you by listing all the types of trees and plants in the park; there must be a few hundred of those massive pines, the ones that take several people with outstretched arms to reach around. There's no other place that can compare with it. It's very special; worth every cent.

In the morning haze, gaggles of old men and women gather to practice the mysteries of *qigong*. They belong to every school and sect, and they each think they're the best. Just eavesdrop on any one of the groups talking among themselves for a few minutes, and I guarantee you'll go away in hysterics.

By the imperial canal just outside the palace, you'll find people doing voice training; nowadays fewer of them practice Peking opera, they all do bel canto. Fattening their tongues to sing foreign songs, warbling away like nobody's business. By the time the sound reaches the imperial yellow tiles on the turrets or the emerald leaves of the willows by the red palace walls, you can be sure it will have warbled itself out of key. This must rate as one of the new "sights" of Peking.

In the evening we'd go out for a stroll with my younger brother's family—they've just had a baby girl, so they push her along on a bike. The pack of us would go clomping down the street in our thongs and have a "spin" around the square. The silken evening breeze seemed to summon everybody out of doors: the old and the young, many of them charging around flying kites: "paired swallows," "black woks," "split pants." Some people are only happy flying massive things: great big "centipedes," huge "flying hexagrams," or "double dragons." A bobbing flotilla filled the sky. The high flyers stood there looking very proud of themselves, while the spectators added their tuppence, commenting on each of them. If by accident a couple of kite strings got twisted, there'd always be people ready to help get them untangled; there'd be people waiting to start a fight; and there'd be others to smooth things over. . . . The whole business is all very good for you, really: gets rid of bile, keeps the juices running, quenches your thirst. . . . An evening stroll on the square was an essential part of our daily life.

One turn around the square with us, and friends from Hong Kong and Taiwan were converted. They praised it to the skies, each in their own unbearably out-of-key attempt at a Peking accent. They weren't joking, either: Who else has a massive courtyard like Tiananmen Square right at their front doorstep? That's the way we are: Peking people are used to space, and lots of it. Our hearts are bigger than most, can never get used to the small-minded.

Our lives have been linked with those streets, that huge garden, the square; they are all part of us.

Then the students came. When we heard them sing their songs, our hearts beat faster. Tears filled our eyes when we heard them speak to the crowds, their voices growing hoarse. We felt sick at heart when we heard they were going on a hunger strike.

What did they want? It was something for us; they wanted something more for all of us. Each of us could judge in his own heart; no one could deny the justness of their cause. They'll win for sure, we thought. Our fathers and grandfathers had always been so submissive, they'd never had the courage of the students. Even though they'd wanted the same things.

People said they were all from outside Peking, but we treated them like they were our own children. They were polite, a little shy, just kids.

(Mi Qiu)

We'd drag them into our courtyard and give them a drink. They'd always say: a glass of cold water would be fine. But we'd always prepare some jasmine tea; too hot for them, they'd say, then we'd add some cold boiled water to the cup. Sometimes they wouldn't even wait for it to cool off.

When the people from our alley, men and women, old and young, went out to keep the army from getting to the square, none of them were scared in the least. They didn't give a thought to the danger. All we knew was: "We are Peking people, we can't let the army beat up the students on our own doorstep, can we?"

Later . . . but I can't go on. What use is what I have to say? They didn't just beat up the students, they killed them. They murdered our neighbors too. Remember that old man who did tai chi every morning? The old boy never bothered anyone in his whole life, all he ever wanted to do was practice his shadowboxing in peace. Well, he's gone. Just like that.

And what about those kids who came up our alley for a drink of water? Which of them survived? No one knows. And the road outside our alley. All torn up by the tanks. And the square . . . Words aren't enough. But we're not sad, not now. Now we understand. It's too late for talk.

One day the road will be repaired, the square resurfaced, hosed down, cleaned up. But how can we go out for our morning exercise as though nothing had ever happened? How can we take a stroll around the corner to the square or go flying kites? . . . How can we ever be happy here again?

I'd never seen such a thing before, never even thought it possible. No one in that city could ever have imagined it.

We shouldn't have had to witness so much. But one day, one day . . .

Zhang Langlang was born in 1943 and raised in Peking, the son of Zhang Ding, a famous painter and a veteran Yan'an cadre. After graduating from the Central Art Academy in 1968, he was imprisoned for most of the Cultural Revolution and at one time even sentenced to death. An artist and writer, he also worked for foreign businesses in Peking for some years. During April–May 1989, his brother's courtyard house was a key liaison point for protesting students, intellectuals, their Hong Kong supporters, select government negotiators, reporters, and interested observers. Langlang fled Peking just prior to the massacre and sought refuge in the United States. In 1990 part of his brother's courtyard house was still under police seal.

PART II

Bindings

A calamitous destiny is now unfolding in China. It has been brought about by the evils committed by generations of tyrannical rulers, and also by the karmic deeds of the people during incalculable cycles of transmigration. When I look at China, I know that a great disaster is at hand.

TAN SITONG, 1897

All of China's tragedies are authored, directed, performed, and appreciated by the Chinese themselves. There's no need to blame anyone else.

LIU XIAOBO, NOVEMBER 1988

This section takes as its central theme the concept of binding—foot binding, mind binding, and being bound to the collective. The bound foot, or the "three-inch golden lotus" (as the tiniest possible and therefore most ideal bound foot is poetically called in Chinese) is used by the Tianjin writer Feng Jicai as the ultimate symbol of subservience in traditional culture.

We also use the bound foot as a symbol of the bound self, the bones of individuality broken by intellectual convention, social conformism, ideological dogma, and patriarchal power. It is these bindings that dissidents attempted to cast aside in the 1978–79 Democracy Wall Movement and from which demonstrators in 1986 and 1989 struggled to free themselves. Although the bindings on the individual and society in Mainland China had been loosened by Reform and the freeing up of intellectual debate during the 1980s, they were still perceived as constricting, even unbearable—as illustrated in the cries of 1989.

Young girls may no longer have their toes crushed to form "three-inch golden lotuses," but people of all ages and both sexes can be made to "wear small shoes." You can cause people pain for daring to defy social convention, cripple them by denouncing them for some political misdemeanor, tie them up in political study sessions and rounds of confession writing. Just as in the past the family and the bureaucracy were used to restrict the movements of their members, in the post-1949 era neighborhood committees and work units have controlled theirs.

Now, as in the past, there are those who delight in the special perfume of broken and mummified flesh. Just as men once titillated themselves by fondling bound feet and drinking wine from cups placed in their amorosas' tiny shoes, today there are those who take extreme delight in participating in political movements or the persecution of nonconformists.

"Yellow Cloth, People, Environment: I," performance art by Zhang Guoliang, Ding Yi, and Qin Yifeng *(Fine Arts in China)*

We think of true individuals as people who have never allowed their feet to be bound, who have natural, unbound feet—*tianzu* in Chinese; people who are generally deemed by the rest of society to have grown "too big for their boots." The reformers, who would loosen the bindings not only for themselves but also for their fellows, are more like women whose bindings have been taken off after some years of binding. While the crushed bones and toes of their "liberated feet" (*fangzu* or *jie-fangjiao*) gradually may assume a more natural appearance, they are forever condemned to hobble. Both groups have been made to suffer for their freedom of movement, just as the students and workers in the Protest Movement suffered for daring to establish autonomous organizations.

Of the pre-1989 discussions of China's intellectual, economic, political, and cultural dilemma, none was more popular or controversial than the 1988 television miniseries *River Elegy*. The authors of *River Elegy* see the Chinese as still being bound to the land and tied to their rulers in semifeudal bondage. In this section we include excerpts from that series and reactions, both positive and negative, to it. The series and many of the books that were published in 1988–89 helped create a "crisis consciousness" that both fed into the Protest Movement and highlighted the urgency of the issues raised during it.

Fragrant Lotus

FENG JICAI

Fragrant Lotus found the way Granny was bustling about a little frightening. The old woman first took a big piece of blue cloth and cut it into strips. Starching the strips in a basin, she beat them with a wooden hammer until they became smooth and glossy. She then hung them in rows on the clothesline in the back courtyard. They twisted and flapped in the gentle breeze, making a faint slapping sound when they struck one another. Occasionally they became entangled like cinnamon twists, and then, when they could turn no more, they unwound in the opposite direction. Often the strips on one side of the yard were unwinding while those on the other side were just twisting up.

Later, Granny went to the market and returned with two bags, one big, one small. Putting the big one aside, she opened the other and laid out many good things to eat on the *kang**: dried apple slices, sour pear cakes, malt sugar, crispy broad beans, and cotton candy—Fragrant Lotus's favorite—as soft and white as the fresh cotton Granny placed in the lining of padded winter coats. It quickly melted away in the mouth, leaving only an aftertaste of sweetness. Even during the New Year's holidays, Fragrant Lotus never received such an array of sweets and goodies.

"Why are you being so nice to me, Granny?"

Granny smiled.

Fragrant Lotus always felt safe in Granny's presence. When Granny was there, she feared nothing, because Granny knew everything. The neighbors all called Granny "The Genius." Last winter, it had been time for Fragrant Lotus to have her ears pierced. She was terrified, because all the girls who'd had it done said it was torture when they punched a

---

* A raised brick platform found in northern Chinese peasant homes that is hollow and can be heated. The *kang* is used as both a bed and a sitting area.

hole big enough to see through in your nice, healthy ear. How could it not hurt? But Granny insisted it wouldn't. Weeks earlier, she had threaded a length of silk floss through a needle and placed it to soak in a bowl of sesame oil. She waited for a day when it snowed and then rubbed Fragrant Lotus's ears with handfuls of snow until they became red and numb. When Granny jabbed the needle through the lobe, Fragrant Lotus felt no pain at all. After passing the needle through, Granny tied together the two ends of the silk thread. Each day she pulled the thread back and forth a few times. Since it had been soaked in sesame oil, the blood didn't adhere to it, and as it slid through the lobe, it didn't hurt, it only tickled a little. After two weeks, Granny gave her a pair of earrings, metal rings from which dangled tiny blue glass balls. When Fragrant Lotus shook her head, she could feel the earrings sliding coolly on her neck. So she asked Granny if binding her feet would be as pleasant as piercing her ears. Granny, momentarily stunned by the question, could only say, "I have a way." And so she believed Granny would somehow get her through this new difficulty as well.

The day before it happened, while playing in the courtyard, Fragrant Lotus noticed some strange little objects—red, blue, and black—on the windowsill. They were pairs of small shoes. She had never seen such tiny shoes, as narrow as melon strips and as pointed as the pyramid-shaped *zongzi* people ate during the Dragon Boat Festival in spring. Even Granny's shoes were bigger than these. Picking up one of the shoes, Fragrant Lotus placed it against her own foot. A cold bolt of fear brought her suddenly upright, and she imagined the tendons in her feet cramping,

(Shouhuo)

twisting, tying into knots. Clutching the shoe in her hand, she rushed into the house.

"Granny, whose is this?"

Granny smiled. "It's yours, dear. Isn't it pretty?"

Fragrant Lotus hurled the tiny slipper across the room and ran into Granny's arms.

"I won't bind my feet, I won't, I won't!"

The muscles supporting Granny's strained smile sagged; the corners of her mouth and eyes drooped and pearl-sized tears began to cascade down her cheeks. She was speechless.

Fragrant Lotus spent the night whimpering, passing in and out of the mist of sleep. She thought she saw Granny sitting beside her throughout the night. She felt Granny massaging her feet with those old, callused hands. And once in a while she felt Granny raise her feet to those wizened old lips and kiss them gently.

Dawn marked the day of Fragrant Lotus's foot binding.

That morning, Granny's normally lively face was set hard. The skin was stretched taut and the muscles twitched from time to time. She did not even glance at Fragrant Lotus. And Fragrant Lotus dared not speak. When she peered into the courtyard through the crack of the door, she shivered at the gruesome scene: The gate was shut tight and secured with a huge bar. The big black dog was tied to a post. A pair of red-crested, white-feathered roosters had appeared as if from nowhere and lay flopping helplessly on the ground. Their rough, finger-thin legs were tied with twine. What did roosters have to do with foot binding? A small table, some stools, a cleaver, a pair of scissors, a jar of alum, a jar of sugar, a kettle, some cotton, and some rags were laid out in the middle of the courtyard. The starched bandages lay coiled in neat rolls on the table. Several huge needles normally used for sewing quilts were pinned to the front of Granny's tunic; from the eyes of the needles trailed lengths of white cotton thread. Despite her tender years, Fragrant Lotus understood the scene before her and the agony it portended.

Granny sat her down on the stool and took off Fragrant Lotus's shoes and socks. Fragrant Lotus's eyes were red and swollen.

"Granny, just one more day. Tomorrow—let's wait till tomorrow," she begged.

Granny pretended not to hear a word. Sitting opposite Fragrant Lotus, she pulled the two roosters over to the spot between her and her grand-daughter. She held the necks of the roosters together and stepped on them with one foot. With the other foot she stepped on the roosters' feet. Her hands quickly plucked several clumps of feathers from the roosters' breasts, and with the cleaver she sliced the breasts open. Before the blood could begin to flow, Granny grabbed Fragrant Lotus's feet and forced them, first one, then the other, into the roosters' stomachs. The hot, burning, sticky sensation and the convulsions of the dying roosters so shocked Fragrant Lotus that she tried to pull her feet back. But Granny screamed frantically:

"Don't move!"

Fragrant Lotus had never heard Granny use such a tone, and she froze. She just watched as Granny pressed her feet into the roosters. Granny's own feet stood hard on the two roosters to hold them down. Fragrant Lotus trembled, the roosters heaved, Granny's arms and legs shook from exhaustion, and they all shivered as one. To press even harder, Granny lifted her hips off the stool. Fragrant Lotus feared Granny could not maintain her balance and might fall forward onto her.

After a short while, Granny relaxed her grip and pulled Fragrant Lotus's feet out. The blood flowed freely and her feet were covered with it, scarlet and sticky. Granny flung the two roosters aside, one stiffened and already dead, the other near death but still flapping weakly. She pulled over a wooden basin, washed and dried her granddaughter's feet, and held them in her lap. The binding was to begin. Fragrant Lotus was so confused she wondered if she should cry, or beg, or throw a fit, but all she did was watch as Granny grabbed her feet, first the right, then the left. She left the big toe alone, but she pressed the other four toes downward and back at a slight angle, toward the arch. With a muted crack, the bones in the toes broke and gave way. Fragrant Lotus cried out, mostly in surprise. Granny had already shaken loose a roll of bandage and tied the four toes securely down. Fragrant Lotus saw the new shape of her feet, and even before she felt the pain, she began to cry.

Granny's hands worked fast. Fearing that Fragrant Lotus would start to kick and scream, she completed the binding quickly. She wrapped the bandage around the four toes, down to the arch, up over the instep,

> The beauty of Chinese women is entirely the result of foot binding. After the feet are bound the blood of the foot and leg is forced to concentrate upwards, and the thighs and buttocks become more voluptuous. This is why our women appear so dainty and wistful.
> —Gu Hongming, 1925

behind the heel, and then quickly forward, over the four toes once again. On the next round, when the bandage came over the toes and back toward the instep, she gave it a sharp tug toward the heel so the four toes bent even more downward toward the sole. Fragrant Lotus's head was filled with waves of pain and pinching, folding and breaking. But before she was overcome by these feelings, Granny rapidly completed two more rounds. She pulled the bandage forward and wrapped it tightly around the big toe, which was still free. She wrapped from front to back, layer upon layer, until the four toes, now next to the arch, were locked firmly in place, as if by metal bands. They were totally unable to move, even a minute fraction of an inch.

In her pain and fright Fragrant Lotus shrieked like a pig being butchered. A band of neighborhood boys stood outside shouting, "She's having her feet bound, she's having her feet bound!" They pounded on the gate and threw clods of earth into the courtyard. The black dog jumped up and down, barking furiously at the gate and at Granny. It tugged so forcefully that the pole to which it was tied began to tilt. In the breeze, the roosters' feathers swirled with the dust on the ground. Fragrant Lotus clutched at Granny so hard her fingernails drew blood from Granny's arms. But even if heaven had fallen now, Granny would have ignored it. Her hands kept moving around and around, and with each wrap the bandage became shorter and shorter, until it eventually came to an end. Then she plucked the needle and thread from the front of her tunic and sewed the bandage up tightly with one hundred or so close stitches. She

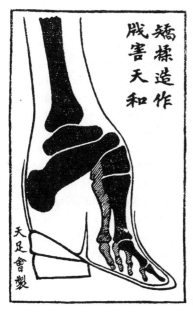

(*Shouhuo*)

then picked up a pair of small red shoes and placed them on Fragrant Lotus's newly bound feet. She brushed back the crescent locks of hair stuck to her sweaty forehead. The muscles of her face relaxed, and she asked,

"Well, it's over. Aren't they nice?"

—From *Three-Inch Golden Lotuses*

Feng Jicai on Bound Feet

Feng Jicai, a Tianjin novelist in his forties, wrote Three-Inch Golden Lotuses *as part of a trilogy,* Curious Tales of a Strange World, *the other two novels being* The Magical Queue *and* Yin-yang Eight Hexagrams. *Apart from using cultural symbols to create entertaining tales, Feng also employs them in a literary investigation of the mysteries of the Chinese national character.*

I'm not really writing about feet at all. I'm using them as a symbol for our cultural psychology. And it would be a misinterpretation to say I approve of foot binding, for I've written of the agony and grotesqueness of small feet, not their beauty. Despite the horror and hideousness of it, Chinese women bound their feet for a thousand years. Why? It's not as though they were forced into it, for women did it to themselves and even deemed it attractive. That's what I'm writing about. . . .

There's something very potent about Chinese culture; it turns restrictions and taboos into immutable and acceptable rules. If they were just taboos, the Chinese could easily be rid of them. Even today the greatest obstacle to Reform is that the old ways have been turned into sacred Truth, and this clouds people's judgment, they assume it is right and proper. The moment you liberate them they feel uneasy and oppose their freedom. When feet are unbound people fight against it heart and soul; they can't walk with unbound feet anymore. It's not just that the feet have been bound too long; they become their own raison d'être, a self-regulation that has also become an esthetic in its own right, a value system. Once this has happened, you can't do anything to get rid of it. . . . The reason Reform is making such slow headway is that people don't dare let go of all those things they once found attractive. Release their feet today, and tomorrow they will bind them up again. Release is capitalism, liberalization. I've observed the overall problems of the society, so I'm not writing about one factory manager who wants Reform and another who opposes it. In my opinion it's a question of the culture as a whole. I've found a symbol through which I can analyze the culture. That symbol is the bound foot; it reveals the characteristics of the culture.

Superior Customs

HU SHI

Feng Jicai's story Three-Inch Golden Lotuses *is by no means the first fictional description of foot binding in Chinese literature. Hu Shi, a leading May Fourth period intellectual and an outspoken critic of the traditional treatment of women, declared the early nineteenth-century novel* Jinghuayuan *by Li Ruzhen to be an "immortal work of women's rights literature."* Jinghuayuan *is something of a Chinese* Gulliver's Travels; *one episode depicts the matriarchal "country of women" where men are subjected to the humiliations common to women in Chinese society. Li describes the torment of men having their feet bound in exquisite detail. In his last public lecture Hu Shi scornfully reviewed Chinese civilization, pointing out the significance of foot binding.*

We have to rid ourselves of a prejudice that although the West is superior in terms of its material civilization, we in the East can remain proud of our superior spiritual civilization. . . .

I am of the opinion that there is nothing particularly spiritual about our ancient civilization at all. What type of spiritual civilization could tolerate for over one millennium the cruel and inhuman practice of foot binding without even one peep of opposition?

—*Hu Shi, November 1961*

On Big Feet

LIN YUTANG

Democracy isn't doing very well. The Chinese mind has been tied up like a bound foot for two thousand years. With the advent of Western thought, it's as though these bound feet finally have the chance to be set free; it's time to regain the intellectual independence of the pre-Qin period [before the second century B.C.]. But two thousand years is a long time, and people are used to their bound feet. The invisible power of tradition remains implacable, you just can't budge it; you can't cut yourself loose. So although the imperial house has fallen, tradition still holds sway, and the thinking condoned by tradition is still playing havoc with us. You overthrow the old only to have a new tradition set up in its place. Today both the leftists and the rightists think, *l'état, c'est moi*, and are determined to get everyone's feet back into those bindings. All the talk about ideological unity means everyone has to have the same bound, smelly feet. Unless they stink you're branded a traitor or a rebel. . . .

Everyone has the spark of individuality; ideological unity is not so easily achieved. Unity means the individual has to be manacled, has to conform to the pattern. This leads people to despise any spark of individuality and individualism. It's like saying: Get those feet back into bindings, otherwise the nation will collapse. Alas, who would ever think that humanity could come to this? Who would think that people hate natural feet so much?

1934

Intellectuals in a Bind

LI AO

Li Ao (born 1935), one of the prize students of Hu Shi, is one of Taiwan's most talented writers. A Monologue on Tradition, a collection of essays on history and the Chinese national character from which the following quotation was taken, was finally published in a mainland edition by the People's Literature Publishing House in August 1989.

THE EMASCULATED EGO

A person with a weak and fragile sense of self will feel very self-conscious in public situations, as though under the constant scrutiny of all around him, and as a result he will appear awkward and unnatural. If he must pass in front of a crowd, he will stagger; at a lecture or in a classroom he may have questions to ask of the speaker but chances are he won't ask them, at least not until someone else has raised a hand first. But even then, in his nervousness the blood will rush to his head, causing him to blush and stammer, with the result that his question, when he finally spits it out, is inarticulate and confused.

When such a person is confronted with a stronger individual, he invariably feels as though he has fallen under the sway of some powerful force. Despite himself he will bow, smile on cue, and even try to adapt himself to the other's thinking. Many Chinese simply cave in when faced with someone who expresses an opinion antithetic to their own, hastily abandoning their own position even if they know it to be superior. Unable to establish themselves as individuals, they find it difficult to stand up for their own ideas.

Even in matters of great importance, a person with a weakened sense of self feels himself bound hand and foot, helplessly yielding to the manipulations of fate. He doesn't resist even if he ends up being destroyed. Lu Xun's Ah Q [and numerous other characters in Chinese fiction] are perfect examples of such emasculated egos.

In the [Mainland] Chinese film *The Second Handshake*, there's a scene where the male protagonist single-handedly takes on four hooligans; he's a regular Paul Newman—type hero. However, when his father demands that he end his relationship with the female lead and marry another woman, the hero weeps bitterly and ultimately gives in to his father's will. . . .

In China, "tragedy" inevitably consists of the inability of a weak individual to make his own decisions and resist external pressure; in the end he can only submit to the fiats of fate, whimpering all the while. Tragedy Chinese-style is incomplete unless accompanied by the tears of the weak. . . .

Yet in Chinese culture, it is the person who displays an emasculated self who is always regarded as well-behaved, obedient, and dependable. Not only do parents and teachers think this, but a weakened ego is also a quality that both men and women look for in choosing a mate.

—*Lung-kee Sun*

Chinese intellectuals are moral and intellectual failures. They are mud-dled, woolly-headed, and just plain stupid. They're professional thinkers, but they can't think straight and their writing is no good. This makes it impossible for them to do anything right and leads them unwittingly to support evil. Out of touch with the masses, they are unable to influence them with their ideas. The only thing they achieve with their writing is self-intoxication and the creation of mutual admiration societies. In fact, none of it is any good. All I have ever seen in the vast majority of writings by Chinese intellectuals is "bound feet." . . . To look at it from the out-side, their writings are at best polished and finely honed; they add a touch of airiness here, profundity there. In other words, they have been bound by traditional thinking, mores, and ideology, by the coarse and superficial aspects of the past. . . . Bandaged again and again in tight foot bindings, Chinese writers can but hobble along. No matter how you try to wriggle your toes initially, as soon as they're out in the open they'll be broken and rebound.

1979

"Yellow Cloth, People, Environment: II," performance art by Zhang Guoliang, Ding Yi, and Qin Yifeng *(Fine Arts in China)*

Other Bindings

The Patriarchy

In the May Fourth period many intellectuals attacked the family for being the basic unit of Confucian control. They claimed its binding commitments and demands had to be overthrown for individual potential to be realized. One of the most famous works of literature on this theme was Ba Jin's novel The Family *(1933), in which he describes the destructive power of the patriarchal Confucian family and the struggle of the young to escape its suffocating confines.*

"I've had enough, enough of this life and everything that goes with it." Juehui became more agitated as he spoke, his face flushing. "Elder Brother spends his days sighing. Isn't it because he can't stand the lifestyle of the gentry, the oppressive atmosphere of this household anymore? I'm not telling you anything you don't know. . . . This family of ours may not have reached the ideal of having 'five generations living under one roof,' but there are four generations here, and just look at the state we're in. There's not a day that goes by without open disagreements and secret plots. . . ."

—from The Family

But the patriarchal hierarchy extended well beyond the home. The late Ming dynasty philosopher Li Zhi (sixteenth century) summed up his frustration in a letter to a friend:

People today all live under someone else, although at first they do not realize it. At home they live in the shadow of their parents; in public life they live in the shadow of their superiors; at court they are in the shadow of the ministers; if they are on military duty at the borders they are under the sway of central officials; even saints and sages live in the shadow of Confucius and Mencius; and all writers are under the sway of [the historians] Ban Gu and Sima Qian. Everyone thinks of themselves as grown men. In fact, though they are not aware of this, they are nothing more than children.

—*Li Zhi*

The Unit

After 1949 the family and the Confucian order were gradually supplanted as society's main binding forces by a new extended patriarchal organization under the aegis of the Communist Party, that of the "unit." During the 1950s, the work unit, or danwei *in Chinese, became the locus for the organization, regulation, and gratification of the individual. The unit, which could be a school or neighborhood committee as well as an office or a factory, assumed the functions of community, family, and Big Brother. While the assignment of everyone to a unit initially liberated people from family bonds and allayed fears of unemployment and exploitation, its discipline proved strict and demanding. Unlike the family, from which Ba Jin's hero Juehui finally escapes, the work unit cannot readily be abandoned, for the unit determines the individual's legal status and controls access to many things from housing and grain ration coupons to plane tickets and passports.*

Lu Feng, a cadre in his early thirties, was one of the first scholars in Mainland China to make a study of the unit and its social significance. The following quotation is from an article he published in early 1989 entitled "The Unit: A Unique Form of Social Organization."

Due to the specific social environment of our nation, the unit has evolved into a familylike group. In traditional Chinese society the family functioned as the basic organizational element in society. In modern China, especially in urban China, the family has lost many of its functions, not to the society as a whole, but to the unit. Even in form the unit has much in common with the traditional clan: It enforces a paternalistic style of authority over its members. The individual's duties toward the group take precedence over his rights; in turn the group is bound to take complete care of all those in its charge. This transformation has taken place within the official state structure. The control of the state over the individual and the reliance of the individual on the state has been realized in the form of a paternalistic unit.

—*Lu Feng*

The Personnel File

Within the unit, the personnel office, which has direct control over the secret files of all its employees or dependents, has the most pervasive control over a person's life. The personnel file contains records of the individual's public life and private conversations—including secret depositions made against him or her by colleagues and even family members.

Many Chinese scholars equate the power of the unit (and thus the state) today with that of the family in the past and see few differences in the style and nature of control between the "feudal" past and the social-

"H.I.A.C.S." ["He Is A Chinese Stalin"], Zhang Hongtu, Chairmen Mao Series

ist present. The debate over what exactly are the "feudal remnants" of the past and which elements of social and political control are unique to Soviet-style societies continues. Michael Dutton, an Australian scholar, has made a careful study of the subject in his recent work Policing and Punishment in China: From Patriarchy to "the People."

. . . is it not true that the brandings, whippings, castrations and decapitations inflicted upon the body in the classical period have given way to far more subtle and far less physical forms of punishment? Have we not moved away from regimes which physically mark (or obliterate) the body to ones which mark the subject in a different way? That is to say, have we not moved from regimes of coercion based on a marking of the body to regimes of policing based on a marking of the file? Have we not seen that within this communist regime it is the file which now marks the disciplinary subject out, plots his movements and makes him "visible," and not the mark of the iron?

—*Michael Dutton*

Guanxi

The strict state hierarchy and its organizational modes—the unit, the household register, the personnel file—limit and direct individual activity and regulate access to many goods and services. As a result, people must rely for many things on an alternative network of interpersonal relations known as guanxi, *literally "connections." Guanxi form the basis of an alternative social structure and value system, a "black market" trading in influence. The currency can vary from favors to goods, and the rates of exchange are both subtle and complex. Bartering in* guanxi *forms a secondary locus of social activity, especially since the advent of the economic reforms of the 1980s. While many have found the bonds of the unit loosened by the reforms, the pervasive ties of* guanxi *are not so easily broken. The skein of responsibilities ties the individual up in a net as restricting and all-pervasive as any aspect of Proledic, the dictatorship of the proletariat.*

The "privatization" of economic and political power in contemporary China has given a small group of people the power of life and death over others. As a result a network of personalized, dependent relationships has developed. This network of *guanxi* revolves around various centers of power, expressing itself through a hierarchy of profit, binding people into voluntary and involuntary relationships of dependence. It is like a massive and invisible mafialike organization enmeshing the whole of China.

—He Xin

The unit and guanxi *perform not only as negative mechanisms. During a political movement, the unit can protect its employees, just as the powerful may protect their weaker friends in the* guanxi *network. As the Chinese saying goes: "The authorities may have their policies, but we have our remedies"* (Shang you zhengce, xia you duice). *It is the complexities of* guanxi *that did, for example, make it so difficult for the party to carry out its post-massacre purge as effectively as it wished.*

A Pavilion for Sick Plum Trees

GONG ZIZHEN

Longpan in Jiangsu, Dengwei in Suzhou, and Xixi in Hangzhou are known for their fine plum trees. It is the accepted wisdom that the plum is at its most beautiful when its branches grow in writhen forms; for to be straight is to be graceless. The beauty and spirit of the plum manifest themselves only when the tree grows at an angle and when its branches are sparse; this is unquestioned.

Yet these requisite virtues of the plum are, in fact, no more than the fancy of scholar-painters. Naturally, it is not for them to demand publicly that all plum trees be cultivated in such a fashion; nor have they been able to impose their will so that all plums are maltreated, crippled, and savaged. After all, the common man has not the cunning to fashion plums in such a manner for profit.

Still, there are those who have told nursery owners of the clandestine passion of the scholars, and thus it has come about that gardeners will cut off the hale and straight branches of the plum, encouraging deformed and twisted limbs in their place. They have cropped the thick foliage and growth of the trees, killing their tender sprays and shoots. They have crippled the life force of the plums so they may be sold for large sums. Now the plums throughout Jiangsu and Zhejiang are mutilated and sickly—such is the devastation wrought by the literati!

I bought three hundred plums in pots, and not one of them was whole. For many days I felt ill at heart, then I swore to cure them. I released them from their bondage, planting them in the earth, smashing their pots so they may grow as nature dictates. I will spend the next five years nursing these trees back to health; and, as I have never regarded myself as one of their number, I am prepared to suffer the derision of the scholar-painters for building my Pavilion for Sick Plums. Sad indeed is the fate of the plum! If only I had more time and land, I would devote my remaining days to the plums of Jiangsu, Suzhou, and Hangzhou.

Painting by Feng Zikai

Gong Zizhen (1790–1841) was an early advocate of dynastic reform and self-strengthening along with Lin Zexu and Wei Yuan.

At the time [when the Chinese court refused the entreaties of the West] only one man in China was thinking clearly. It is because of his clearheadedness that he suffered more than anyone else. He said that it was an age of spiritual confusion, that there were no talented ministers at court or courageous generals in the army, that schools lacked outstanding teachers, and the peasantry was hopeless, as were artisans, builders, and merchants. It was an age of decay in which not even the thieves were competent. He would cry out each day for Heaven to restore order, but his appeals went unanswered, so then every day he called for great disorder under Heaven. His name was Gong Zizhen.

—From *River Elegy,*
Episode One: "Inspiration"

River Elegy: TV Politics

Mise-en-scène

In mid-1988, the controversial miniseries River Elegy *attempted both to identify and to break the bondage of traditional culture. A group of academics, writers, and television directors and technicians had pooled their resources and ideas to create the six-part documentary* River Elegy. *It questioned the national fascination for such cultural icons as the Great Wall and the dragon, calling on the Chinese to break away from the cycles of disaster and fatalism that its authors linked to the cult of the Yellow River:*

Heirs of the dragon, everything that the Yellow River has had to give, it has given to our ancestors. They created a civilization, but the river cannot give birth a second time. We need to create a new civilization; this time it cannot pour forth from the Yellow River. Like the silt accumulated on the bed of the Yellow River, the old civilization has left a sediment in the veins of our nation. Only a deluge can purge us of its dregs.

Such a flood is industrial civilization, and it beckons us.,
— *Episode One: "Searching for Dreams"*

Neither the symbolism of nor the thinking behind the series was particularly new either in China or among foreign observers.* What was

---

* See, for example, the essay "The Rhythm of China: China the Wonderful," in *China News Analysis*, No. 1105, January 6, 1978, where the destructive flooding of the Yellow River is used to symbolize periodic renewal. The concepts of cyclical change and cultural stagnation, central to *River Elegy*, were common in early Western discussions of Chinese history, some of which are quoted in the series.

"Yellow River" (Wang Miao)

different was that it confronted a mass television audience with a highly controversial political and cultural debate. In a sense, it was a televised "struggle session" against Chinese cultural icons and feudal Marxism.

Although the series was originally intended by its sponsors at China Central Television (CCTV) to pay homage to the Yellow River, the twenty-six-year-old director Xia Jun, and the leading writers Su Xiaokang (an ex–Red Guard turned controversial reportage author) and Wang Luxiang, a university lecturer, subverted the series so that it became a declaration of social, economic, and political crisis.

According to the Chinese calendar, 1988 was the Year of the Dragon. The last Year of the Dragon, 1976, had been marked by the death of Zhou Enlai, the Tiananmen Incident, the Tangshan earthquake, the death of Mao Zedong, and the arrest of the Gang of Four, bringing an official end to the Cultural Revolution. Pessimists saw the rail and air disasters of 1988, the massive Daxing'anling forest fire in northeast China, and rampant inflation as similar portents marking the end of the Reform era. Su Xiaokang later said he wrote River Elegy *under a cloud of imminent disaster. As one commentator said, if you weren't aware of the crisis China was facing in 1988, you would be after you'd seen* River Elegy.

Among the people interviewed for the series were Jin Guantao, a leading reformist thinker,* and the political firebrand Wang Juntao, who later played a leading role in the 1989 Protest Movement. River Elegy also used documentary footage from the Great Leap Forward and the Cultural Revolution. The juxtaposition of images and statements created a subtext equating Maoist-Stalinist orthodoxy with state Confucianism and traditional culture—and both of these with disaster. The solution to China's problems, it suggested, was an abandonment of the traditional inland, earthbound world view for an outward-reaching one linked to the sea, commerce, and contact with the outside world. It endorsed the coastal development plan of Zhao Ziyang as China's main hope.

Unabashedly pro-Reform and pro-Zhao, River Elegy adopted a stridently didactic tone; while the level of intellectual sophistication was possibly greater than that of any comparable series previously aired on CCTV, its narrative content at times degenerated into a simplistic grab bag of quotations and theories from China and abroad, their sources ranging from the essays of Francis Bacon to the film Yellow Earth.† Despite the involvement of a number of Chinese academics, the series was scholastically shoddy and glib. However, if nothing else, its inordinate popularity has earned it a special place in Chinese television and cultural history.

According to CCTV statistics, over 200 million people saw the series. It was so popular that the scripts were printed in full in the major newspapers and then published in book form to satisfy the massive demand for them. The television studio received thousands of letters from viewers, one of whom asked for copies of the scripts to hand out "in order to help all Chinese understand themselves."

Some of the people involved with the series, like Jin Guantao, an adviser to the production, had at first been dubious about the suitability of television as a medium for intellectual debate. They were overwhelmed by the public response.

The success of *River Elegy* reminds me of a famous saying: "Never underestimate the wisdom of the masses." . . . Real cultural exploration means creating something that reverberates through the soul of the nation; thinkers must allow the people to think along with them.

—*Jin Guantao*

* See *Seeds of Fire*, pp. 131–33.
† See *Seeds of Fire*, pp. 251–70.

The six-part series became the focus of an intense, sometimes vitriolic cultural and political debate in 1988–89. River Elegy *had broken major taboos, for it had questioned the very cultural totems—the Yellow River, the dragon, and the Great Wall—that constitute a virtual Chinese national mythology and that the party had been using to shore up its own prestige and legitimacy since the Cultural Revolution. Participants in the debate ranged from ordinary viewers to the very top level of party and government leaders. Wang Zhen, China's vice president, who in 1983 reportedly suggested to Deng Xiaoping that if he were given a company of soldiers he could "eliminate spiritual pollution" in China, attacked the series for being "even more reactionary than Bo Yang." He accused it of calling for a "restoration of capitalism" and of threatening the existence of the Communist Party and the nation itself.*

> If you're working in television in China you've got to ensure that you satisfy the "two olds": the old comrades in the Central Committee and the "old one hundred names" [i.e., the masses]. If either of these groups is not satisfied then you're in for trouble.
> —*Chen Hanyuan, producer of* River Elegy

The debate spilled over into Hong Kong, Taiwan, and overseas Chinese communities. Interestingly, the same criticisms raised by party leaders, for example that the series was "culturally nihilistic," were echoed in the comments of conservatives in Taiwan and elsewhere.

Originally, the makers of River Elegy *were preparing another series for the seventieth anniversary of the May Fourth Movement in 1989. Although the scripts had been completed, filming was banned on orders from the Politburo, which had also proscribed sales of videos of* River Elegy. *The fact that* River Elegy *had taken such a strong stance in favor of political reform and Zhao Ziyang was one reason why, following the June massacre, it became the target of a vicious denunciation campaign that continued well into 1990. As part of the campaign against* River Elegy, *the party propaganda machine produced its own four-part television riposte,* On the Road: A Century of Marxism, *screened on Chinese television in August 1990. Among other things,* On the Road *lauds the party's achievements, the historical necessity of Marxist-Leninist socialism in China, and the genius of Deng Xiaoping.*

River Elegy *was written by five authors. The details of their involvement in* River Elegy *and their subsequent fate are listed on the next page.*

Su Xiaokang, author of Episode One: "Searching for Dreams" and Episode Five: "Anxiety," and co-author of Episode Four: "The New Era," was on one of the government's "most wanted" lists after June 4. He was smuggled out of China and went to France, where he became active in the newly formed Federation for a Democratic China in late 1989.

Wang Luxiang was the author of Episode Two: "Destiny" and Episode Three: "Inspiration." Wang was detained and subjected to intense police investigation before his release.

Zhang Gang was Su Xiaokang's co-author for Episode Four: "The New Era." A member first of the Institute for the Reform of the Economic Structure and then of the Young Theorists' Association, both closely allied with Zhao Ziyang, Zhang studied the "overall strategy" of Reform. After June he fled by boat to Taiwan and subsequently moved to the United States to work with former Zhao associates in a research organization.

Episode Six: "The Color Blue" was written by Xie Xuanjun and Yuan Zhiming. Xie was unable to leave China and was detained by police, questioned, and eventually released. Yuan fled China with Su Xiaokang and found refuge in France, where he edited, with Su, the dissident journal Minzhu Zhongguo (Democratic China).

Xia Jun, the young director of the series, was reportedly protected by people at China Central Television and avoided arrest. Jin Guantao and his wife, Liu Qingfeng, were in Hong Kong when the massacre occurred and did not return to China. Liu became editor of a new intellectual bimonthly, Twenty-first Century, which began publication in late 1990. Wang Juntao, who appears in the fourth episode of the series, was arrested in late 1989 as one of the major "behind-the-scenes manipulators" of the 1989 Protest Movement. He was tried for "counterrevolutionary sedition" in February 1991 and sentenced to thirteen years' imprisonment.

The misfortune that has befallen *River Elegy* is the misfortune that has befallen Reform itself.

—Su Xiaokang

The Title: Shameless Intellectuals

The Chinese title of River Elegy *is Heshang. He, or "river," indicates the Yellow River, while* shang *means literally "the soul of someone who has died young" or "a lonely spirit." In fact, it is an elegy for those sacrificed to the Yellow River, used here as a symbol of the ultrastable structure of China, the traditional Confucian state, and even totalitarianism itself. The river is also used as a metaphor for cycles of chaos and disaster. Nicknamed "China's sorrow," the river has a history of changing course suddenly and unpredictably, flooding fields and obliterating large populated areas. Since early times, the Chinese have made sacrifices to appease the Lord of the River, He Bo. He Xin, a writer who has proudly described himself as a "cultural conservative," was outraged by what he regarded as the true intentions of the series' makers. He took advantage of the wave of official denunciations of* River Elegy *in the second half of 1989 to voice his objections publicly.*

If the Yellow River is used as a symbol for the Chinese nation, then what does it mean to say we are *shang* [ghosts of the prematurely dead, or "lost spirits"]? Isn't this a most malicious form of curse on us? Let me ask each and every Chinese, do you want to be addressed in this fashion? If this is allowed, anything will be tolerated!

As any clearheaded person can see, the idea for the name *River Elegy* was taken from Qu Yuan's outstanding poem "Hymn to the Fallen" *("Guoshang"),* a heroic elegy for a young warrior killed on the battlefield in defense of his country.* To use the word *shang* in this context is both powerful and moving. The aim of *River Elegy,* however, is to curse the Chinese nation and civilization, to declare them null and void.

"Hymn to the Fallen" resounds with the melody of heroism and patriotism; even after two millennia it is overwhelmingly moving. As for *River Elegy,* it reverberates with theories about the collapse of the country, obliteration of our nation, humiliation, and the loss of sovereignty, as well as praise and worship for things foreign. It is outrageous, infuriating, and deeply depressing, for one is forced to confront the fact that the so-called "intellectual elite" of China in the 1980s are shameless and depraved!

—He Xin, August 1989

* For Qu Yuan, see the footnote on p. 35.

The autumn floods came and the hundred streams poured into the Yellow River. The racing current swelled so that looking from one bank to the other, or from one island to another, it was impossible to tell horse from cow. He Bo, the Lord of the Yellow River, was delighted, thinking all the wondrous things of the world were in his possession. He followed the current east until at last he reached the North Sea. Looking eastward, he could see no end to the expanse of water.

The Lord of the River shook his head and rolled his eyes. Looking at Ruo, the God of the Sea, he sighed and said, "There is a saying: 'He heard one hundred things about the Way and thought he was equaled by none.' . . . But today I have seen your vastness, and it would be foolhardy not to take heed of you."

The God of the Sea said, "You can't discuss the sea with a frog in the bottom of a well, for he knows only that tiny space. You can't talk about ice with summer insects, for they know only their own season. Nor can you discuss the Way with twisted scholars, for they are bound by their doctrines. Now that you have left your banks and seen the vast ocean, and realize your meanness, I can talk to you about the Grand Design."

—*Zhuangzi, "Autumn Waters"*

History*

There is a blind spot in our national psyche, a vague belief that all of the shame of the past century is the result of a break in our glorious history. Ever since 1840, there have been people who have used the splendors and greatness of the past to conceal the feebleness and backwardness of our present state. It is as though we crave this ancient and timeworn poultice to salve the painful realities of the past century. We seem to find great solace in every earthshaking archaeological discovery. Yet the fact remains that our civilization is moribund.

* The illustrations used in this section are from Ernst Boerschmann's *Picturesque China, Architecture and Landscape: A Journey Through Twelve Provinces*, London: T. Fisher Unwin Ltd. None of these illustrations appeared in the original television series, and the section headings have been added by the editors.

The richness of the past, the length of China's civilization, do, after all, belong to yesteryear.

No matter how rich our archaeological discoveries, how venerable the origins of our civilization, don't they mean that our ancestors must be laughing at us in scorn? Don't they add weight to our sense of loss, regret, and shame?

—*Episode One: "Searching for Dreams"*

The Yellow River

The clear waters turned muddy, their peaceful flow was transformed into a raging torrent, their nurturing now wanton violence: The mother had become a tyrant.

The first time in recorded history that the Yellow River overflowed its banks was in 602 B.C., the fifth year of the reign of King Ding of Zhou. In the 2,540 years from then up to 1938, when the Nationalists broke the dikes at Huayuankou, the Yellow River overflowed its banks 1,590 times and changed course twenty-six times. That's an average of two large floods every three years and a major change of course every century. The Yellow River is probably the cruelest of all rivers on the earth. . . . What other nation on earth has experienced such cyclical destruction as the Chinese?

More terrible yet is that this cyclical destruction does not only occur in nature: It is also a social and historical phenomenon in China. Looking at the grand sweep of Chinese history, we can see that each feudal dynasty followed a pattern of establishment, prosperity, crisis, turmoil, and finally collapse in a violent upheaval, the whole process taking two to three hundred years. One dynasty disappeared only to have another arise to take its place in a clear cycle; as the traditional novelists put it, "separation at length leads to unity, unity at length to separation"—just like the continual flooding of the Yellow River.

Despite what some theorists might tell us, this kind of collapse of the social structure has no "revolutionary" significance. No—it is merely the expression of a frightening, vicious destructiveness. . . .

Periodic turmoil invariably leads to the pitiless destruction of accumulated productive forces. Inevitably it is the most economically developed and prosperous regions that suffer the greatest devastation. . . .

—Episode Five: "Anxiety"

The Yellow River has always been "China's sorrow." Yet today the Chinese have more reason than ever before to sigh: Why has our feudal age lasted so long—as long, it seems, as the ceaseless torrent of the Yellow River itself? This is an even greater nightmare. It has been oozing forth from the tomb of Qin Shihuang, the first Qin emperor, at the foot of Mount Li, filling space and time for two millennia. Over the past century, how many times have we thought of burying it once and for all? Yet it refuses to die.

History moves so slowly, its weight heavy within the rut of the mill. The Yellow River courses slowly and ponderously along its silt-laden bed.

Will there be yet another deluge?

Has the turmoil really passed forever?

We ask both the Yellow River and history.

—Episode Five: "Anxiety"

Peasant Mentality

Due to the ever-increasing population—and particularly thanks to [Mao Zedong's] muddled theories that "people are our greatest treasure" and "the more manpower the better"—the already limited amount of arable land has become even more precious and other resources even scarcer. There is too much healthy muscle power for this barren land, and the young have become increasingly expendable. Today, overpopulation is the greatest of all of China's woes. How many generations will have to taste the bitter fruit that we have sown?

Overinvestment of manpower in the countryside has made it difficult to develop modern, large-scale agricultural production, for that would result in massive unemployment. It has also meant that society has come to view hard physical labor by the majority of people as the norm. Any innovations that could save labor and increase efficiency or wealth are denigrated as schemes by get-rich-quick merchants on the make. Isn't this why jealousy of success is so very hard to overcome today?

—*Episode Four: "The New Era"*

The monopolies enjoyed by officials and the privileged classes over both the production and distribution of goods can result in the wanton undermining of the principles of socialist ownership. They also corrupt the state and party, poison the society as a whole, and make it easy for

anyone with the slightest power to convert the right to use and manage into private possession. State ownership becomes ownership by official organizations or individuals. The shocking cases of official corruption and misuse of power are surely evidence of this.

Small-scale agricultural production has given rise to a series of self-balancing value systems with modest aims. Satisfaction with one's lot, acceptance of whatever fate deals out to you, a lack of adventurousness, and the personal philosophy that it is better to live in ignominy than to die a righteous death—isn't this how the majority of Chinese live today? When we asked a young man in the countryside of northern Shaanxi why he preferred the tough, impoverished life at home to trying his luck in the world outside, he said, "Mom and Dad just didn't give me that type of courage."

—*Episode Four: "The New Era"*

An Ultrastable System

What powerful force has bound this nation together for over two thousand years? The enigma of the Great Unity has taxed the minds of Chinese and foreign scholars alike. . . . In ancient China small agricultural producers were as numerous as the stars in the summer firmament; they were like a plate of loose sand. The Confucian intellectuals, who created a coherent social structure with their unified belief system, were able to bring these disparate farmers together effectively to form a society.

This unique social structure once created great prosperity for China. However, within the miracle of the Great Unity, under the dazzling surface of its glorious culture, behind the swirling mists of incense burning on ancestral altars, and despite the homage paid to the emperor, the sages, and the elderly, the social system was slowly rotting away at the core—just as the pillars of the dikes along the Yellow River were being slowly gnawed away by rats and termites! The Confucian bureaucracy lurched irrevocably toward decay; power itself was a corrosive. The prosperity of each dynasty presaged its collapse.

The end of one dynasty would quickly lead to the establishment of another; the social structure would soon regain its original contours and start on a fresh path to collapse. So too it has been with the Yellow

River, the dikes bursting only to be restored by human labor, then bursting again. Why are we condemned to this cycle of fate?

The mysterious ultrastable system has controlled us for two thousand years. Today the Golden Phoenix Throne in the Forbidden City is nothing more than an antique; the massive network of Confucian bureaucracy has turned to dust. However, the specter of the Great Unity still prowls our land. The nightmare of social tremors still haunts our waking hours. And bureaucracy, the mentality of privilege, and corruption are undermining our grand plans for the "Four Modernizations." * These chronic, ancient ailments are not unlike the daily accumulation of silt in the Yellow River, forever building up to a new crisis. . . .

Perhaps we should be concerned by our eternally ultrastable system, just as we feel unsettled by the ever-increasing height of the dikes along the river. Hasn't history provided us with more than adequate lessons? . . .

One reassuring thing is that following the inception of economic re-

* The "Four Modernizations" are the modernization of agriculture, industry, defense, and science and technology. While the image of the specter prowling the land is inspired by Sun Jingxuan's poem of 1980 (see *Seeds of Fire*, pp. 121–28), this last line is taken from General Secretary Zhao Ziyang's speech to the Thirteenth Party Congress in October 1987.

form, we are now finally beginning to experiment with political reform
... no matter what type of resistance and threats this reform may face,
we have no choice but to move ahead. For behind us are surging floodwaters and ceaseless turmoil. We must move on and break out of the
vicious cycle of history.

—Episode Five: "Anxiety"

The Great Wall

Our ancestors were never able to transcend the soil or agriculture. For
them the most startlingly imaginative and daring act they were capable
of was merely this: the building of a Great Wall!

—Episode Two: "Destiny"

If the Great Wall could speak, surely it would tell the descendants of the
Yellow Emperor in all honesty that it is but a monument to tragedy, cast
in its present form by historical destiny. The Great Wall can in no way
represent strength, enterprise, and glory; it is a symbol of confinement,
conservatism, impotent defense, and timidity in the face of invasion.
Because of its massive scale and venerable history, it has left the imprint
of its grand conceit and self-deception on the very soul of the Chinese.
Ah, Great Wall, why do we still sing your praises?

—Episode Two: "Destiny"

When they tired of the Chinese-style pavilions and artificial pastoral
scenery, the emperor and his empress would remove themselves to the
western section of the [Old Summer] Palace.* In the spray of the foun-
tains shaped like dogs hunting deer, the Chinese emperor would never
deny himself Western-style pleasures. It's the same today: The very people who most hysterically denounce Western life-styles and values mer-
rily indulge in luxury cars and consumer goods from the West.

Worst of all, the Qing emperors built a large stone wall around the

---

* The Xiyanglou in Yuanming Yuan, a fantastic European-style palace in northwest
Peking designed by Jesuits.

palace. Soldiers armed with broadswords and halberds protected their dream world. Similarly, the emperors hoped to lock up China against the outside world, closing off all ports and the entire coastline. . . .

Some take the Great Wall to be a symbol of might and prosperity; when they climb the wall they feel proud, and the world shrinks beneath them. In contrast, they gnash their teeth in agony when facing the broken ruins of the Old Summer Palace [destroyed by British troops in 1860]. Of course they are angry, they want to wipe out this shame. But, dear compatriots, have you ever considered the causal relationship between these two monuments?

—*Episode Three: "Inspiration"*

The Dragon

Some say there is an element in Chinese culture that tolerates evil; others say the fatal weaknesses of the Chinese national character are worldly wisdom, fatalism, and a docile acceptance of suffering. This is no accident. . . . Water is the lifeblood of agriculture, and it is the dragon king who rules over water. For this reason, this nation both loves and hates the dragon, worships him and curses him. It is a complex combination of emotions, as twisted as the form of the dragon itself. In turn, it has made the Chinese a complex people.

—*Episode One: "Searching for Dreams"*

Hou Dejian's song "Heirs of the Dragon" became a kind of unofficial national anthem for Chinese in Taiwan and Hong Kong, and even on the mainland, during the 1980s.

Jimmy Ngai Siu-yan reports in "Tiananmen Days" (page 86) how very moved he was to hear "Heirs of the Dragon" sung on Tiananmen Square by the protesters. It appeals to the sense of a tragic national destiny shared by most Chinese today, though not everyone is aware that the author also intended it to express his profound frustration with the tradition it romanticizes: His lyrics describe growing up not in the embrace of the dragon, but under its mighty claws.

Hou, one of the last hunger strikers in Tiananmen Square in early June, changed the final verse of the song just before the Peking Massacre. The students and their supporters were singing "Heirs of the Dragon" as Tiananmen Square was surrounded on the morning of June 4.

HEIRS OF THE DRAGON
Hou Dejian

In the far-off East flows a river called the Yangtze.
In the far-off East flows the Yellow River, too.
I've never seen the beauty of the Yangtze
Though often have I sailed it in my dreams.
And while I've never heard the roar of the Yellow River,
It pounds against its shores in my dreams.

In the ancient East there is a dragon;
China is its name.
In the ancient East there lives a people,
The dragon's heirs every one.
Under the claws of this mighty dragon I grew up
And its heir I have become.
Like it or not—
Once and forever, an heir of the dragon.

It was a hundred years ago on a quiet night,
The deep dark night before the great changes,
A quiet night shattered by gunfire,
Enemies on all sides, the sword of the dictator.
For how many years did those gunshots resound?
So many years and so many years more.
Mighty dragon, open your eyes
For now and evermore, open your eyes.

Is there any Chinese who does not know this song?
Can you hear the deep sigh within the song?
But what's the use of sighing?

This ancient icon, both respected and feared, gave our ancestors end-less nightmares. Do we really think it has the power today to unite us in our current state of desolation and nostalgia?

Our dragon worship seems to show that in the depths of our national psyche we long for the ancient cultural ambience of the Yellow River, which nurtured us, and even now we hesitate in the shadow of our ancestral history. It is as though our souls still live in a dream world. But it is time that we woke up once and for all.

—Episode One: "Searching for Dreams"

You could say that [the dragon] is the symbol of our nation. But has anyone ever considered why the Chinese adore this terrifying monster?
—Episode One: "Searching for Dreams"

> I really don't know why the Chinese people have chosen the grim, hideous figure of the dragon to symbolize our nation! In fact, the dragon can symbolize only the hardships of our people! Whenever anyone mentions "The Heirs of the Dragon," my hair stands on end.
>
> *—Bo Yang*

Intellectuals

The Confucian world view expressed the life-style and ideals of China's landlocked civilization. Although clearly suited to Oriental feudalism in full flourish, its monopoly on intellectual life crippled the development of pluralism. The abundant, outward-looking, sea-oriented aspects of traditional life disappeared without trace, nothing more than a trickle from a clear spring on the surface of the yellow earth. . . .

Confucian culture may contain all sorts of venerable and perfected "treasures," but for some two thousand years it has completely failed to create a spirit of progress among the Chinese or any mechanism for the renewal of the state's legal system and culture. On the contrary, in its progress toward collapse it has evolved a suicidal mechanism: It constantly thwarts and destroys talent, murders the life-giving elements within itself, and asphyxiates the best and brightest of every generation.

History shows that although a landlocked culture can modernize and allow some modern scientific achievements, even the launching of satellites into space or the detonation of atom bombs, it is ultimately incapable of providing its people with a powerful living culture.
—Episode Six: "The Color Blue"

Chinese history never created a middle class to advance the progress of science and democracy; Chinese culture has never given birth to a civil consciousness. On the contrary, it has created a ruler-minister mentality that produces either an attitude of unquestioning compliance or mad risk

taking. However, history has also given China one very special group: its intellectuals.

It has been extremely difficult for them to consolidate their economic interests or hold independent political opinions; for thousands of years they have been no more than appendages. . . . Their talents have been manipulated, their wills twisted, their souls castrated, their backbones bent. They have even been murdered. Nonetheless, they hold in their hands the weapon that can destroy ignorance and superstition, for they are the ones who can communicate directly with the civilization of the sea, who can irrigate the yellow earth with the blue waters of the spring of science and democracy.

—Episode Six: "The Color Blue"

Entrepreneurs

Perhaps the new entrepreneurs, people of average appearance who have nothing surprising to say, are the ones with the real power [to change things]. Small shopkeepers, businessmen on the move, even peasants who travel around looking for work: Perhaps among them a new force is gathering, an energy that can be directed toward social change. We must not underestimate them.

—Episode Six: "The Color Blue"

The May Fourth Movement

The May Fourth Movement of 1919 was the first time that "science" and "democracy" were championed in China. Western thought, including Marxism, was widely propagated at the time. However, this radical intellectual climate did not manage to erode the feudal crust covering Chinese politics or economics or the Chinese character itself. Over the past seven decades the dregs of feudalism have sometimes risen to the surface; at other times they've clogged everything up.

It is as though so many things in China must start all over again from the May Fourth Movement.

—Episode Six: "The Color Blue"

Reform

The greatest obstacle to Reform seems to be that we're always worrying whether the Chinese will remain Chinese. Nobody seems to realize that in the West, no one ever agonized over whether the Renaissance, Reformation, or Enlightenment would make them any less Italian, German, or French. But in China this is the greatest taboo of all.

Perhaps this is both the weightiest and most shallow aspect of our Yellow Civilization.

—Episode Six: "The Color Blue"

The traits of authoritarian politics are inscrutability, dictatorship, and arbitrariness; those of democratic government should be transparency, popular will, and the scientific spirit.

We are leaving behind chaotic murkiness and progressing toward clarity; we have already abandoned the closed door for openness.

The Yellow River must pass through the loess plateau, but in the end it will flow into the great blue sea.

—*Episode Six: "The Color Blue"*

When visiting Taiwan in early 1990, Su Xiaokang, now a dissident in exile and mindful of the prestige traditional culture has on the island, sang a different song:

[In *River Elegy*] we attributed our suffering on the mainland to culture. We completely ignored the fact that the [Communist] system is the main reason for the mainland's backwardness. But my standards are different now. I think there are some positive values in our tradition.

The Debate

The nature of the Chinese polity is such that while intellectuals can flog our ancestors with impunity, they must be careful to circumnavigate the reef of direct criticism.

—*Wang Xiaodong and Qiu Tiancao, critics*

Following is a small selection from the volumes of letters, articles, and commentaries inspired by River Elegy.

I SAID IT FIRST

There are some things in *River Elegy* that I said two years ago [in 1986]. . . .

What, for instance? Well, that imperialism might not be the final stage of capitalism. That peasant rebellions are not the only progressive force in the history of China. That the Great Wall is like a massive enclosing wall and that the Yellow River is like a bandage for the breasts, squashing them so flat that they are incapable of providing nourishment. . . . I said that the dragon is a symbol of feudal autarchy and that the heirs of the dragon are but descendants of the dinosaur, massive, useless, and mutually destructive creatures. These ancestors have been extinct for ages, but the descendants don't care, they are still inordinately proud of them. I said that the Chinese people possess a strange combination of wisdom and stupidity, morality and depravity. The Cultural Revolution gives us reason enough to reflect on the quality of the nation. . . . China's only hope is for this generation to produce heirs of the dragon who are both "unloyal and unfilial." . . .

But I spoke out too soon. I got no kudos for it. In fact, I got myself into a hell of a lot of trouble. . . .

—*Wei Minglun, Sichuan playwright*

IT SHOULDN'T HAVE BEEN SAID AT ALL

You've made a forced connection between exploration of the Yellow River and the decay of our civilization. Are you saying that just because our civilization is in decay we should have no patriotic spirit? It's only right that we agonize over the loss of a sports match or the failure to win the championship; in my opinion, that's the natural reaction of every Chinese of conscience. Our Olympic gold medals are proof that China is a strong country. How many U.S. dollars or British pounds sterling did they pay you to heap so much praise on industrial Western civilization? What I want to know is, how could such a program have been produced following a major campaign to wipe out Bourgelib?

—*A university student*

THE ENEMY WITHIN

People complain about things, and that's understandable. There are more than enough reasons for people to be fed up with the way things are. So you attack our ancestors, blame the environment, and complain about the population problem; these are the conditions history has bequeathed to us. . . . There are both historical reasons and immediate causes for our present predicament, but the most important responsibility for it lies with us.

— *Gao Wangling and Wu Xin*

A CRITICAL OVERSIGHT

River Elegy blames China's backwardness on the fact that the quality of the population [judged by education and other standards] is so low. This infers a politically conservative attitude that I doubt the writers intended; it relieves the politicians of responsibility for the results of their erroneous policies.

— *Lin Yü-sheng, intellectual historian*
resident in the United States

A REACTIONARY REFORM

Following the institution of the Open Door and Reform policies, the economic infrastructure of the mainland has undergone tremendous change, resulting in concomitant changes in the superstructure. Since the new policies were introduced, there has been a thirst for profits and commodities, a collapse of political and social morality, an inferiority complex concerning the Chinese nation and culture, excessive idealization and worship of Western capitalist civilization, a loss of confidence in the future of socialism in China, and widespread skepticism about Marxism. Over the past five years or so, many mainland thinkers and intellectuals have tended to search for answers outside the framework of the party and socialism. From the Taiwanese point of view, Fang Lizhi —an absurdly Westernized intellectual—is the most extreme example. Even more shocking is that this basically immature intellectual current was encouraged by the leading state organizations most directly involved in the Reform program. The ideology and promotion of *River Elegy* was clearly in the service of the Deng-Zhao revisionist Open Door and Reform line.

— *Chen Ying-chen, Taiwan novelist*

A VIEWER'S LETTER

I was very small during the Cultural Revolution, too young to remember anything about it. After seeing images from that time in television shows like *River Elegy*, I'm dying to know what China was really like then. I've done some reading about it and know some of the basic facts, like who the Gang of Four were, and about the Red Guards and Big Character Posters, but I want to know more. I just can't understand it at all: those images of young people screaming "Long live [Chairman Mao]!" and waving their Little Red Books when they saw Chairman Mao, weeping with excitement; the "enthusiastic" struggle sessions; and also the scenes from the Great Leap Forward. I just don't understand how it could have happened.

—Diao Xiaoli, People's University
Middle School, Peking

SU XIAOKANG'S RESPONSE

This letter shook me far more than those criticisms of *River Elegy* as representing "historical nihilism." It's only been a little over twenty years since the Cultural Revolution began, and already we have a generation of young people who find it incomprehensible, as though it happened in another, completely foreign place. The letter scared me. I remember how it was when I was a Red Guard. How can we say for sure that young people will never again rush wildly into the streets, incited by revolutionary slogans? Nobody is telling the next generation what the Cultural Revolution was all about; what's worse is that no one is seriously studying the deep-seated social reasons and motivating forces behind this national catastrophe. Quite the opposite—it's as though there is a concerted effort to make everyone forget all about it. I fear that this is real "historical nihilism."

In fact, Dai Qing and other people in Peking, Shanghai, Hangzhou, and Canton had been working for several years on studies of the Cultural Revolution that included oral histories, dictionaries, and other projects. See "Publishing License" in Part III, "Red Noise."

HIDDEN AGENDAS

River Elegy has gone as far as anybody can on Chinese TV. Although I don't think it went nearly far enough, for China, it's a good thing. But if you apply higher standards, then I'd have to say that there's very little in it. I particularly dislike the commentary and the style of delivery used by the narrator. It reeks of Maoist language and hype, and it's messianic in tone. I'll give Mao this: His language has left its mark on all writers in China today.

Behind the commentary and the images of *River Elegy* lies the age-old vanity of the Chinese. It does not completely admit that China lags far behind the rest of the world. It raises the question of Westernization, but its point seems to be that one day China will convert the rest of the world. The Chinese think that although the Chinese have behaved like slaves while the West was strong, once China is strong Westerners will be our slaves. This is the hidden agenda of *River Elegy;* it's in keeping with the ideas of the late-Qing reformers who advocated "using the strengths of the barbarians to conquer the barbarians." Why is there always this need to conquer others? The Chinese denounce others as imperialists when in fact we're the most imperialistic of all. The Chinese may admit that we're materially backward, that our technology and clothing aren't as good as other people's, but spiritually and morally we still insist we're number one. . . .

The first dragon dance sequence [in the first episode] is very energetic and enthusiastic. Now, if I had made the series, I'd have shown how shriveled up, feeble, and bloody hopeless the Chinese really are. No commentary would be required. But the thinking behind *River Elegy* is that the Chinese are a mighty nation: What we are shown on the screen is a very long way from the crippled reality. As I've said elsewhere, the Chinese today are physically and spiritually impotent.

—Liu Xiaobo

A NEW CULTURAL REVOLUTION

Ever since the beginning of the twentieth century, the decline of Chinese civilization and an abnormal national psychology, plus the devastation wrought on our ancient culture and elite by the elite's anticivilized behavior, has brought Chinese civilization to the brink of disaster more than once.

The recent hullabaloo about the so-called "death of the Yellow River civilization" is a typical expression of this hysterical antitraditionalism. While it may seem different from the antitraditionalism of the Cultural Revolution, from a certain perspective the two have much in common.

What's truly tragic is that today the Chinese live suspended in a traditionless void. In my opinion, the thing that's pushing China toward oblivion is not the weight of tradition but the absence of it.

NO BIG DEAL

LEE YEE: Do you agree with Einstein's theory that nationalism is a kind of infantile malaise?

FANG LIZHI: I think every civilization on earth has a period in which it flourishes, and then it goes into decline. If a culture finds itself facing complete collapse, that's just the way things are. I approve of Einstein's desire to be a "global citizen." He said you shouldn't worry too much about which country you belong to; instead, you should look at things from an international perspective. The world is moving forward, and in the process it's possible that many of the cultures that are unable to adapt themselves to new developments are going to become obsolete, dead and buried. The two great riverine cultures of ancient times are no more, and Mayan culture is extinct as well. The death of a civilization is not necessarily a bad thing—there's no need to object too loudly. Most scientists have come to accept the view that science has no national boundaries. I am not, of course, denying the value of a good national culture. But if it really is that good, then you've got nothing to worry about; nothing anybody says can hurt it.

The trendy philosophers take their cues from Nietszche in telling us that God is dead and all tradition may be overthrown. But I really don't know. Who are you, anyway? Aren't you new prophets standing on the ruins of tradition? Aren't you strategists proclaiming the new creed of antitraditionalism?

Must we go along with you? One must ask: In promoting this kind of cultural nihilism, are you leading us toward greater happiness or greater misfortune?

—He Xin

Crisis Consciousness:
"China Problem Studies"

In the past, people [i.e., Deng Xiaoping] have talked about
Reform as being a process of "crossing the river by feeling
for the stones." The real worry now is that in all too many
situations we simply can't find any stones.
>   —*Xu Yinong, editor of* In the Hills of China,
>   *July 1988*

*In 1988–89, a number of books appeared that were devoted to the
discussion of crisis, or what some dubbed the "China illness." In early
1989 the* World Economic Herald *published a series of articles written
the year before in a book entitled* World Citizenship. *The articles debated
how long the crisis could continue before China actually lost its place in
the international community. The book was banned in mid-1989. Other
works that shared similar concerns appeared in Shanghai and Tianjin.*

*"Crisis" was a word on everyone's lips. Even articles written to com-
memorate the fortieth anniversary of Peking's "liberation" in early 1989
focused on the question of whether the nation's historic capital would
survive into the next century. Among other disasters facing the city
are a chronic and worsening water shortage, the encroaching desert, a
burgeoning population, and the related and nearly insurmountable
problems of housing and transportation.*

While some carried on from where River Elegy *left off, others chroni-
cled the gruesome details of the enormous political, social, economic,
cultural, and environmental problems China is facing today.*

In the Hills of China, *a book of over five hundred pages, is a typical
example of such a study. It was written by He Bochuan, a scholar of the
philosophy of science from Canton who was involved in the development
of China's first computer in the 1960s.* In the Hills of China *was the
subject of serious discussion among reformist intellectuals in early 1989.*

The book concludes with a proposal to found a new field of research, "China problem studies."

Following is the table of contents and a brief quotation from each chapter of He's book.

IN THE HILLS OF CHINA:
PROBLEMS, DILEMMAS, AND PAINFUL CHOICES

by He Bochuan

Introduction:
Contemporary Crisis Studies and the China Problem

Chapter 1. The Economic Earthquake

"In the past we often said, 'The Chinese are as good as their word.' In certain areas that is true. But anyone who studies the problems of China will discover that in China, theory and practice, what is said and what is done are often two completely different things."

Chapter 2. Industrial Difficulties and the Hidden Dangers in Agriculture

"The biggest problem [facing industry] is that the core of our heavy industry has sealed itself off; it is caught up in its own internal cycles and serves only itself. . . .

"We've always been very proud of the fact that we are 'rich in resources.' However, at least as far as agriculture goes, this claim is far from the truth."

Chapter 3. The Labor Pains of the Service Industry

"Certain 'proletarian revolutionaries' never stop nattering on about 'serving the people,' but somehow they cannot bring themselves to say 'serve the customers.' 'Service' is a 'duty,' and in their eyes it can have only a 'revolutionary' character, never a commercial one."

Chapter 4. Debates over New Windows

"Most of the large-scale delegations that are sent abroad to study foreign technology can be divided into two categories: the sightseers and the shoppers. The shoppers spend huge amounts of foreign currency on their purchases. They buy doorknobs, screws, and desk lamps, whatever bargains they can get. But when all this stuff gets back home, they won't provide another cent for absorbing the new technology, its assimilation or development, and they certainly won't provide for any increase in personnel. They'd rather see imported equipment rot or get stolen; then they can go abroad to buy some more."

Chapter 5. Speed and Regional Strategies

"As a result of our long-term blind optimism, we can never see that trying to achieve [economic progress] at exceptional speeds brings on true catastrophe."

Chapter 6. Weak Links in the Chain

"The most problematic aspect of [the party's official] goal of quadrupling economic and agricultural production by the year 2000 is that we must support a quadrupling of production with only twice as many energy resources."

Chapter 7. The Most Terrifying Shock Wave

"China can boast of having broken quite a few world records, but the biggest record breaker of all is its population. China is the most populous nation in the world. And the population increase is eating up every other aspect of our development in a frightful fashion."

Chapter 8. The Environmental Crisis: A Legacy for Our Grandchildren

"Long years of wanton destruction of forests and the despoliation of land, combined with the slash-and-burn agriculture practiced in some parts of the country, have created the worst [environmental] disaster in our nation's history."

Chapter 9. The Sins of Ingratitude

"It's a real shame that today most Chinese fail to grasp a very important fact: The chief threat to China's national security doesn't come from the outside—the possibility of foreign military invasion—but rather from the inside. It is the drying up of our natural resources, the dramatic rise in our population, the destruction of the ecological balance, and the pollution of our environment."

Chapter 10. China's Cadres: How Do They Rank Internationally?

"In the West there is an attempt to create an atmosphere and environment that allows individuals to realize their potential and actively develop their creative abilities. In China, on the other hand, the system is geared toward elevating cadres so they can lord it over everyone else. As a result, people become accustomed to waiting around passively for instructions and orders."

Chapter 11. A "Black Hole"

"Deng Xiaoping has said, 'Bureaucracy is still a major and widespread problem within the political life of our party and the state. Its harmful manifestations include the following: an attitude of superiority in regard to the masses, abuse of power, divorcing oneself from reality and the masses, the expenditure of time and effort to keep up appearances, the tendency to speak in empty phrases, fossilization of thought, being hidebound by convention, overstaffing administrative organs, being dilatory, inattention to efficiency, having irresponsible attitudes, unreliability, junketing on public funds, evading responsibility and even putting on the grand airs of a mandarin, constantly attacking others, being vindictive, suppressing democracy, deceiving superiors and subordinates, acting in an imperious and despotic fashion, favoritism, bribery, graft, violating the law, and so on. Whether in the management of our own domestic affairs or in our relations with other countries, this phenomenon has already reached an intolerable level.' He's right."

Chapter 12. Dilemmas in Education

"It's most unfortunate that for many years we have seen education solely as a tool in the service of politics. Today, if we face the facts, we have to admit that as far as education is concerned, we are losers."

Chapter 13. The Revenge of the Ten Great Crises

"Whereas one out of every four Americans is a university graduate, one out of every four Chinese today is illiterate or semiliterate. According to the calculations of Professor Qian Jiaju,* in 1983, 70 percent of school-age children in China were illiterate or semiliterate. . . . We ought to stress Professor Qian's warning that if we fail to improve the extremely backward state of China's education very soon, the consequences will be no less serious than those caused by the lack of attention paid to population growth in the 1950s."

Chapter 14. False Gods of the Poor

"At present, people have a great, superstitious faith in modern scientific technology, and most of all they are infatuated with computers."

Chapter 15. Anxiety Within Hope

"Looking at things from a negative angle, the biggest practical worry about microcomputers in China concerns their effect on employment. This is a very controversial issue abroad as well."

Chapter 16. Our Doubts

"Every day we carry on about how the Chinese nation is going through its most dangerous period. Yet, in fact, the Chinese people lack a sense of urgency about the crises and dangers we face. Our overweening sense of self-importance, conservatism and complacency, blind optimism, propensity for idle boasting, flattery, unscrupulous behavior, self-deceit, and trickery have the most serious consequences for the nation and our people."

* A veteran economist; see pp. 178–79.

Chapter 17. A Great Wall

"The essence of China's biggest problems today does not lie in poverty and weakness, but in the failure to fully utilize and develop human and material resources."

Chapter 18. The Challenge of the Future

"At the very core of the massive changes being wrought in China at the moment lies the need to change the way we think. Explorers aren't daunted by the weeds growing over the path to truth. The wheels of history cannot be stopped; anyone who would try to maintain old ideas and ways of thinking has no place in the future."

Reactions to *In the Hills of China*

In the April 1989 issue of Reading, *a number of prominent intellectuals commented on He Bochuan's work. The following quotations are a sample of their remarks:*

The Chinese have invariably lacked an awareness of crisis. This is due to our small-peasant mentality and the Confucian influence, which encourages "satisfaction with your lot and contentment in endurance." Our propaganda always claims the situation is excellent, every year is better than the one before, and so on. Perhaps it is as [He Bochuan] believes: Our policy makers are simply not interested in the crisis mentality. As he says, "Their only interest is in figuring out whether propagating the concept of crisis serves any ideological purpose. Will it reflect on the managers, will they be held responsible? Will it affect their power and prestige, and will it make the public panic?"

—*Su Shaozhi*

What is the scariest crisis of all? The inability to find the source of all the other crises. The author provides an analysis hidden between the lines. . . . But I think more work is required. The ultimate origin of all of China's crises is to be found in the system itself. Unless the system is dealt with, all other measures will fail. Without revolutionizing the meta-system, there's nothing you can do with the subsystems; you don't have the slightest chance of reforming them.

—*Yuan Zhiming*

It's Their Crisis, Not Ours

In late 1990, the People's Daily *published excerpts from a lengthy attack on the first major crisis book of 1989,* World Citizenship, *which had been edited by the* World Economic Herald.

There are those who in their "explorations" employ a frame of reference that is completely out of concert with that of our party and the broad masses of theoretical workers. Breaking with us, they have set themselves on an entirely different course. They blame socialism for all the errors resulting from the imperfections and deficiencies of our socialist system. They regard their own sense of "doom" as evidence of the "bankruptcy" of socialism itself; they see the disparity between our economy and those of the developed countries as proof of the "defeat" of socialism. For them the appearance of socialism in China was not a historical necessity but a "historical mistake," the outcome of "political interference," the product of human volition. They believe that the natural course of history dictated that China develop capitalism, a system they regard as being the fulfillment of human nature.

They call for the "rebirth" of humanity. But what stands in the way of such a "rebirth"? The Four Basic Principles of the Communist Party. In the final analysis, this is the true root of the "anxiety of the nation," the crisis consciousness of these people—men and women who have transformed themselves overnight into the "elite" of bourgeois liberalization. But there's more. To their way of thinking the outstanding national culture and fine traditions developed by the sons and daughters of China over thousands of years amount to little more than a "hidden danger." As they "sink into hopelessness," they squawk: "What can be done? There is only one way out: to create a new life no matter how painful that may be." What exactly is the "new life" they want? It is all about going for a swim in the sea of the "blue civilization," * even if it means becoming a colony for three hundred years.† This is their fervent hope; this is their ideal.

—Wu Jianguo, November 26, 1990

---

* The theme of the last episode of *River Elegy*.
† A reference to a remark made by Liu Xiaobo concerning Hong Kong and the benefits of colonial administration.

A Gallery of Reformers

There's a famous saying, "Reformers come to no good end." It may seem exaggerated, but it's the way things work in China.

—Li Honglin

China has produced many would-be reformers over the past century, men and women hopeful of salvaging a bankrupt system be it dynastic, republican, or socialist. Occasionally appreciated but often violently rejected by the rulers, many have been rewarded for their efforts with persecution, even execution. Their dogged sense of duty to state and ruler has often been likened to that of the faithful but honest court minister, what Liu Binyan has dubbed "the second kind of loyalty."* Whether their generally cautious, constrained approach can actually achieve results when the nation is in crisis is another question. At a welcoming banquet held for Liu by his Hong Kong fans in August 1988, Dai Qing publicly stated her opinion: "I don't care what Binyan says about the second kind of loyalty; even the third, fourth, or fifth kind of loyalty won't save China."

Many of those purged after June 1989 had helped provide the party with the theoretical basis for its reforms over the past decade. They also worked hard to come up with both practical and theoretical solutions to the myriad economic, political, and social problems in which Reform had become mired. Some even participated in "think tanks" giving advice to top leaders.

While they are adopting the slogans of democracy and freedom, their concrete understanding of these terms is informed by an elitist, hierar-

---

* The first kind of loyalty is unquestioning, the second is critical.

chical mentality, a Communist culture, an abiding loyalty to "social-ism," and a Marxist view of history. They also have something in com-mon with the Neo-Confucian "liberals" of the past.* We don't include Fang Lizhi among their number because his proposals for democracy and his claim that there is no such thing as "Western" or "Chinese" variants of it went far beyond what most of the reformers were initially advocating. To return to our metaphor of bound feet, they were until the massacre, at least, like the women with "liberated" feet (fangzu) who, while released from their footcloths, hobble cautiously and may secretly long for the security of their erstwhile bindings. Liu Xiaobo, in his critique of the stance of intellectuals after the death of Hu Yaobang, was to a great extent talking about these very people.

Still, to their conservative opponents, even their restricted gait hinted at unfettered, wild individualism, dangerous heterodoxy, the collapse of party authority, and social chaos. Some of the reformers had first fallen victim to official hostility in 1956–57 during the Anti-Rightist Cam-paign. Others were attacked in one way or another during the fitful 1983–84 purge of Spiritual Pollution and the attack on Bourgelib in 1987.†

But by the end of the eighties, it once again seemed that people had been freed from the need to "wear small shoes" and that further Reform was not only a practicable aim but an urgent necessity. The events of 1988—in particular the country's growing economic chaos and instabil-ity, further backsliding on the party's commitment to political reform, and signs that Party General Secretary Zhao Ziyang would soon fall—forced the reformers into revolt by the end of the year. Many among them are now officially regarded by the party as "instigators of turmoil" whose Bourgelib crimes helped bring on the "counterrevolutionary dis-turbances" of April–June 1989. Indeed, most of the reformers gathered in the small, and by no means all-inclusive, gallery below were de-nounced in the official government report presented to the Chinese Na-tional Congress in June 1989 by Peking Mayor Chen Xitong.

Following are some of the best known of China's reformers and quo-tations from statements they made before the massacre. Many of their writings have reportedly been banned in China.

---

* William Theodore de Bary's lectures on this subject are particularly relevant here. See de Bary, *The Liberal Tradition in China*, Hong Kong: Chinese University Press, 1983, in particular the epilogue, "China and the Limits of Liberalism," pp. 91–108.
† For a simple chronology of these purges, see *Seeds of Fire*, pp. 343–54.

BAO ZUNXIN (born 1937): *A member of the History Research Institute of the Academy of Social Sciences and former editor of the monthly* Reading *magazine, China's most controversial intellectual journal and a major forum for reformists since it was founded in 1979. Bao was also, along with Jin Guantao, editor in chief of the* Toward the Future *series of books, which included Jin's* Behind the Phenomena of History.* *A leading activist in the Protest Movement and a fiery critic of Deng Xiaoping, Bao was arrested shortly after the massacre and sentenced in early 1991 to five years' imprisonment.*

The democratic spirit and the scientific spirit are the things our nation most obviously lacks. Without these, however, modernization for China is unimaginable. A nation's uniqueness cannot be founded solely on advertising tradition or returning to the past. Now that we are open to the world and confronted in the course of our modernization with a clash between Chinese and foreign cultures, it is also a matter of historical creativity and choice. Even when the Yellow River flows into the sea, it cannot change its murky yellow color. The sea remains the sea; the Yellow River also remains unchanged. Only when the traditional cultural structure is broken up and replaced by one suited to the needs of socialist construction will Chinese culture itself have a future.

—*From* River Elegy, *1988*

DAI QING (born 1941): *The pen name of Fu Ning. The daughter of a party martyr, she was raised in the family of Ye Jianying, one of the ten marshals of the People's Liberation Army. Trained as a missile engineer, she was a Red Guard activist in the early days of the Cultural Revolution and underwent secret service training in the army. The victim of a security leak, she was forced to end her career as a spy. She then found a job at the* Guangming Daily *as a journalist in the early 1980s. She went quickly from penning short reports and stories to investigating the intellectual history of twentieth-century China, looking into controversial and often highly sensitive cases. Dai's connections and understanding of the party's mafialike inner workings convinced her of the danger of the continued student occupation of Tiananmen Square in May 1989, and she tried in vain to negotiate an end to the protests in the square. Ironically, she was detained after the massacre and denounced in her own newspaper as an "instigator of turmoil." Her outspoken calls for press freedom and the formation of an environmental lobby group (she said in*

---

* See *Seeds of Fire*, pp. 131–33.

May 1989: "If I weren't in the Communist Party and I had to choose some other organization to belong to, I'd become a Green"), as well as her dangerous revelations of party history, had made her a logical target for the purge. Eventually released in May 1990, Dai published a controversial account of her confinement, "My Imprisonment," in Hong Kong and Taiwan. She was still being attacked in the Mainland media in late 1990.

The Chinese people's understanding of the world is still infantile. They are like children who put all their hope and trust in their parents. They want a clean and efficient government, one which is united and in which there is no factionalism; a government that is concerned with the welfare of the people and not just its own personal interests. . . .

The [present] situation demands that people grow up. Intellectuals are the key group, yet they're immature, a mess. What they really need is "thought remolding." The thought remolding they went through in the past wiped out all their finest characteristics, and now their evil side has become inflated. They betray each other to the government, form factions, despise the talented, and so on. . . . It's not a question of how technically competent they are at their jobs; the first standard by which intellectuals should be judged is whether they have an independent soul, ideas of their own, an independent mind. What they have to do is struggle for freedom of expression.

—September 1988

GE YANG (born 1916): *A veteran reporter and editor in chief of* New Observer, *a leading Peking bimonthly and a vehicle for reformists, which was closed down after the Peking Massacre. A staunch party member, Ge Yang was denounced in the mainland press when the purge began. She went into exile in the United States.*

In 1988 Ge Yang made an official trip to Bulgaria, an unlikely source of inspiration at the time. However, on her return to China she wrote an article describing a chilling documentary she had seen there, People without Footsteps. *Her article was entitled "Black Dream."*

The film starts with a scene of people digging up skeletons in a barren field. It is hard work. They check the remains carefully and put them into crates, after which we see crate after crate of skulls and bones, all washed clean. . . . It had happened in 1923. Though the king had been relatively enlightened, the contradictions between the ruling class and the people had reached the point of no return. Someone suggested during a session of Parliament that the peasants be crushed; others suggested that the workers should be suppressed. Finally, the king decided to annihilate the intellectuals, because they were the thinkers. If they were beheaded, he reasoned, the workers and peasants wouldn't make any more trouble. A bloody massacre began immediately. These patriots, the greatest talents of the nation, were arrested at street corners on the way home, or sitting in their studies. Long, thick ropes were thrown around their necks, and they were garroted. One old intellectual pleaded bravely in court but maintained silence in prison. They wrote pleas to the king to be shot rather than strangled; their petitions were rejected. In the end they all went courageously to their death. . . .

That's all in the past now, a historical nightmare. But aren't we worried that in another country they may not kill you with ropes but strangle your soul?

—June 1988

HU JIWEI (born 1916): *Former editor of the* People's Daily, *purged in 1983 and later put in charge of drafting China's first press law. He led the National People's Congress push in May 1989 to have Li Peng dismissed as premier. After June he was subjected to intensive investigation and, among other things, denounced for advocating the legalization of oppositionist groups within the party.*

If the freedom of the press that is stipulated in the Constitution is truly respected in practice, then the people will believe that the Constitution is more than just a piece of paper, indeed, that it is an effective basic law. If freedom of the press is guaranteed, the people will have a greater faith in the Constitution, respect it, act according to it, and support it. This is the basic guarantee of social stability. However, if the principles and rights stipulated in the Constitution go unrealized, the people will feel they are unprotected by it, politically insecure. How then can true unity and stability be realized? The decade of the Cultural Revolution was the most serious period of instability in our history. It began with the public desecration of the Constitution and the total elimination of the freedoms of speech, publication, and the press. Everyone knows this; wasn't that enough of a lesson for us?

—May 1989

JIN GUANTAO (born 1947): *A research fellow in the Science Policy and Management Research Institute of the Chinese Academy of Social Sciences and an editor with Bao Zunxin of the* Toward the Future *series of books. Jin has been named by the Hong Kong press as one of China's Four Great Contemporary Thinkers along with Li Zehou, Fang Lizhi, and Wen Yuankai. He made significant attempts to introduce contemporary Western scientific theories, such as chaos theory, to Chinese so-*

cial science. Both he and his wife, Liu Qingfeng, were in Hong Kong in June 1989 and stayed there after being denounced by party authorities. Jin was quoted in Peking Mayor Chen Xitong's speech as having said at a conference held at Peking University in December 1988 that "Socialism and its failure are one of the great lessons of the twentieth century." Ge Yang reportedly supported this statement by commenting, "Jin Guantao hasn't been too tough on socialism; he's been too soft."

When the society is well ordered, people can keep themselves bound [by moral] standards. Only when everyone's thoughts and actions adhere strictly to these standards can the society enjoy order and operate normally. The moment the proposition is raised that people can pursue the liberation of the self and personal profit, the banks of the dam of morality will burst, social order will collapse into chaos, and people will turn into wild beasts. This is the drawback of a cultural structure based on morality. Quite simply, in order to undertake cultural reconstruction we must overcome our panmoralism. Morality is necessary, but we mustn't rely on external moral pressure to maintain social order....

—*May 1989*

LI HONGLIN (born 1927): *An expert in Marxism-Leninism and a former assistant chief of the theoretical bureau of the party Ministry of Propaganda, Li has been an active theorist of Reform since the 1970s. He was purged from his position in Peking in 1983 and appointed director of the Fujian Academy of Social Sciences. He was relieved of that post in 1987 following Hu Yaobang's fall and subsequently concentrated on research work. After the massacre he was detained; he was released in May 1990, along with Dai Qing and more than two hundred other prisoners.*

At present Chinese society is caught between the old and the new. The old system has not entirely quit the stage of history, while the new has yet to take over completely. Numerous problems surface in such periods of transition. For example, when a new market-oriented economy exists at the same time as a planned economy, widespread economic crime is inevitable ...

In order to hasten Reform it is essential to bring political democratization into line with economic modernization. It is essential that they not be divorced from each other or develop in opposing directions. This is the key to the success of Reform; history stands as a demonstration of the validity of this fact.

—*December 1988*

LI ZEHOU (born 1938): *A leading philosopher and intellectual historian attached to the Chinese Academy of Social Sciences. Liu Xiaobo once wrote a sharply worded, book-length attack on Li for his supposed defense of the "Confucian personality." Li was put under intensive investigation after June and urged to repudiate his writings for their "corrupting" influence. By the end of the year he had been named in internal documents along with the former Minister of Culture Wang Meng (see pp. 284–85) as a main target of official denunciation.*

The tragedy of China's liberal intellectuals is that they never had a popular base. They never came to occupy a position on the political stage, and so China never had a chance to experience freedom and democracy as it is known in the West. These are the facts of post–May Fourth history, and there's no use imagining how things might have been otherwise. The thing to do now is to draw some lessons from that history. The problem is that since 1949 we've given it so little thought. Instead, we've upheld the "Yan'an spirit," which was born of armed struggle, as our "precious revolutionary heirloom," to be preserved at all costs. Of course, there are positive aspects to the Yan'an spirit, such as the spirit of self-sacrifice for the sake of the state and the nation, the need for continuity. But something that was useful in wartime is not necessarily suited to peace; it needs to be reformed.

—March 1989

LIU BINYAN (born 1925): *One of China's best-known writers, famed for his exposés of corruption and the abuse of power by party functionaries. But he is also one of the most paradoxical figures in contemporary Chinese culture and has been criticized by both Liu Xiaobo and Dai Qing. Although purged from the party in 1987,* he acted as a "loyal dissident" remaining faithful to its creed and the belief that the "good people within the party" will be victorious. In 1988 Liu, a former People's* Daily *reporter, was given permission to visit the United States for a year. He joined the chorus of condemnation of Deng and the massacre in 1989–90 and has made a break with his past, less certain that the party can reform itself. Denounced again in the Mainland Chinese press from mid-1989, he remained in exile in the United States.*

To my understanding the word "totalitarian" is used to describe a government or a type of political system, not a political party. Originally, the Communist Party was a revolutionary party, having come to power through armed revolution. Of course, it has made many mistakes, but it

---

* See *Seeds of Fire*, pp. 354–60.

is changing. Although I have been expelled from it, I can neither condemn nor support it, for it is in the process of transformation. . . .

I have therefore repeatedly said that the most pressing thing in China today is reform of the political system, increased democracy, so that citizens can truly participate in the decision-making process. In this respect our progress is slower than that of the Soviets, far behind that of Gorbachev. This is cause for anxiety and concern.

—August 1988

LIU ZAIFU (born 1941): *A leading literary theorist and head of the Modern Chinese Literature Research Institute of the Chinese Academy of Social Sciences and a friend of Li Zehou. Much of his writing deals with the history of modern Chinese intellectuals, although he understands the milieu of the middle-aged intellectuals far better than that of their younger peers. A staunch party member, Liu used a vague and abstract style of discussion to expound what were, in fact, fairly controversial ideas in the 1980s. Liu Zaifu supported the Protest Movement and fled into exile after the June massacre, after which he took up residence in Chicago.*

Intellectuals have rediscovered themselves, the spirit of individualism first sparked in the May Fourth period, intellectual independence, and concern for absolute humanitarian social values. No longer requiring the approval of some external power, they have found self-affirmation, they have become their own masters. They have come to realize that they are the product of their own choices, not of somebody else's restrictions.

—April 1989

QIAN JIAJU (born 1909): *A banker and economist. Formerly an adviser to the People's Bank of China, Qian was also an outspoken critic of party economic policy. He was a staunch advocate of radical price reform and rejected Li Peng's remedies for the economy in 1988–89 as ineffective. Like other reformers, he had high praise for the "new thinking" propounded by Soviet leader Mikhail Gorbachev. Qian went into exile and, at the end of 1989, took up residence in the Buddhist Xilai Temple in the United States.*

The Boxer Rebellion of 1900 and the Great Cultural Revolution of 1966 were in their nature ignorant and retrogressive. Who would have ever thought that an anti-foreign movement with its origins in the late nineteenth century would replay itself more than fifty years later on such a large scale and in such a different form? If China fails to go through the baptism of "democracy" and "science," there is no telling whether another Cultural Revolution in some new form will not explode in the decades to come.

—May 1989

QIN BENLI (1918–1991): *A veteran editor and leading journalist in the 1950s, he was purged in the 1957 Anti-Rightist Campaign for giving prominence to opinions critical of monolithic Communist Party rule (what Mao dubbed "reactionary editing"). In 1979 he founded the* World Economic Herald, *a weekly newspaper that, under the protection of high-level party officials, became China's most open, even radical, forum for reformist debate. The banning of an April 1989 issue of the paper by Shanghai Party Secretary Jiang Zemin for articles positively reevaluating Hu Yaobang led to a general call for press freedom (see p. 39). Qin was eventually purged, Jiang was promoted to the position of party general secretary, and the paper closed down.*

Editing [a newspaper] is like playing Ping-Pong. If the ball doesn't hit the table, you lose a point, but hitting the middle of the table is too easy; the really difficult thing is just to graze the edge.

Qin developed cancer and died on April 15, 1991—exactly two years to the day after the death of Hu Yaobang.

SU SHAOZHI (born 1923): *An economist by training, Su was one of China's leading Marxist theorists and reformist thinkers until his flight from China in June 1989. As head of the Marxist-Leninist Research Institute of the Chinese Academy of Social Sciences, he became one of the first establishment thinkers to argue for the need for political pluralism and major theoretical reform in 1986.*

*In December 1988, Su Shaozhi attended a seminar in Peking held to commemorate the first decade of Reform. Su took advantage of the occasion to defend the much-abused Marxist thinker Wang Ruoshui and make a withering attack on party ideologues such as Hu Qiaomu.**

Ten years ago I participated in a seminar on party theory. It was the most intellectually liberated and stimulating meeting of its kind held since 1949. Many ideas that are now generally accepted, such as the need to abolish life tenure for government positions, were first raised at that meeting. Today, however, we are supposed to avoid the theoretical, emphasize the practical, and above all "not get entangled in questions of

* See *Seeds of Fire*, pp. 151, 271, 370–71.

the past." But there is no reason to cut ourselves off from the past; that would be a futile endeavor. If we can't sum up our past experiences, how can we learn from them and face the future with confidence? . . . What happens, for example, if people don't agree with the Anti–Spiritual Pollution Campaign [of 1983] or the Anti-Bourgelib Campaign [of 1987]? Of course, we're not supposed to tie ourselves into knots over the past, but I think those two events were the most important issues in the theoretical world in the last decade. Many comrades are demanding that things be cleared up, especially because [these two campaigns] touched on many theoretical and academic issues such as humanism, alienation, [the reevaluation of] Bukharin, the stages of socialism, how to oppose the residual poison of feudalism, and so on. These are all matters open to scholarly debate, yet during those campaigns only one group or sometimes only one person was given the final say. Furthermore, some people were politically persecuted for expressing academic opinions, and many scholars were unjustly punished. It simply isn't good enough to say that we should "not get entangled in questions of the past."

—December 1988

SU XIAOKANG (born 1949): *A member of the Cultural Revolution generation and formerly a Red Guard factional leader in Jiangxi Province. He avoided being purged for his past activism and became a lecturer at the Peking Broadcasting Institute. His first work of reportage appeared in 1983; within a few years he became, after Liu Binyan, the most popular author of this type of "faction" in China. His most controversial pieces have explored issues of Chinese law, education, and marriage. He was one of the main authors of* River Elegy. *An active organizer during the Protest Movement, Su fled China after the massacre and was granted asylum in France.*

My generation, the one born the year the republic was founded, grew up in the relatively politically sane era of the 1950s. We had a highly idealistic education, and we were brought up to believe in Marxism and socialism. The Cultural Revolution brought us face-to-face with ugliness, and this led us to adopt a highly critical attitude. The heavy cultural dross of thousands of years [of Chinese tradition] reveals evil phenomena that devour humanity, twist people's souls, and strangle the life force of the individual. In fact, what lies hidden behind it all is a fearful mechanism for national self-destruction. It is deeply disturbing. Now that we have awoken from fanaticism and ignorance, we cannot suppress our desire to discuss our fate and call on the nation to save itself.

—July 1988

WANG RUOSHUI (born 1926): *A Marxist philosopher who was for a period the editor of the* People's Daily. *Purged for his theoretical discussions of the individual and alienation in socialist society,* Wang remained a controversial although stalwart Marxist.*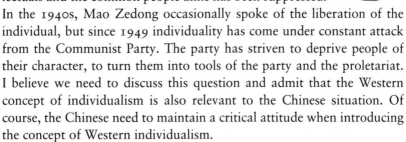

For a long time now the individuality of Chinese intellectuals and the common people alike has been suppressed. In the 1940s, Mao Zedong occasionally spoke of the liberation of the individual, but since 1949 individuality has come under constant attack from the Communist Party. The party has striven to deprive people of their character, to turn them into tools of the party and the proletariat. I believe we need to discuss this question and admit that the Western concept of individualism is also relevant to the Chinese situation. Of course, the Chinese need to maintain a critical attitude when introducing the concept of Western individualism.

—April 1989

WEN YUANKAI (born 1947): *Named in the Hong Kong press as one of China's Four Great Contemporary Thinkers along with Jin Guantao, Li Zehou, and Fang Lizhi, Wen was a radical and outspoken proponent of Reform in the 1980s. A prolific writer and translator, he has been an advocate of a Toffleresque "third wave" revolution in China and a transformation of the national character. He was purged from his position at the Chinese University of Science and Technology in Anhui in late 1989.*

I'm sure that people will increasingly come to see that the tide of Reform and the Open Door cannot be turned back. It's not a matter of propaganda or official statements. It is something we can see from the profound changes in the economic structure of China; we can observe this to be true in particular among businesspeople. . . .

We must show more people that modernization is a totalistic process. It requires holistic, thoroughgoing reform. If we pursue only economic reform, we will end up in a dead end.

—January 1989

YAN JIAQI (born 1942): *A philosopher and political scientist, former head of the Political Science Research Institute of the Chinese Academy of Social Sciences and a leading member of the now disbanded Party Institute for Political Reform. He was active during the Democracy Wall*

---

* See *Seeds of Fire*, pp. 150–51.

Movement and an early advocate of political reform. With his wife, Gao Gao, a medical doctor, Yan authored the first history of the Cultural Revolution published for general distribution on the mainland. It was a poorly written and scantily researched tome that basically panders to the views of orthodox party opinion. Previously an enthusiastic supporter of Deng Xiaoping and an advocate of political pluralism, Yan was forced into exile in mid-1989 and later in the year became one of the founders of the Federation for a Democratic China. In late 1990 he decided to devote his energies to political theorizing.

There are people overseas who have made a big thing of the Anti–Spiritual Pollution and Anti-Bourgelib campaigns, as well as the recent debate over *River Elegy*, but the really perceptive observers know full well that these are merely minor annoyances. The general trend is healthy and positive, and moving in the direction of Reform and the Open Door. China is getting closer to the goals of achieving a market economy and democratization all the time. Of course, you can't solve all the problems in one go. In such a large country you can't expect to change things overnight.

—November 1988

Yu Haocheng (born 1925): *A Manchu born in Peking. Formerly the head of the Masses Publishing House run by the Ministry of Public Security. A controversial figure throughout the 1980s, he was officially regarded as one of China's leading legal and constitutional experts until he was detained by police in June 1989 and reportedly released in early 1991.*

The general tendency at present is to seek stability and shy away from disorder. The party underestimates the level of public awareness and fears that the introduction of democracy will bring disunity and instability. Such concern is unnecessary, for the opposite is the case: If you allow democracy and freedom and permit the people to express different opinions, you supply society with a safety valve; to suppress differences of opinion among the people and to forbid freedom of speech, on the other hand, will result in unrest and turmoil. As Deng Xiaoping has said, "A revolutionary party fears above all not being able to hear the voice of the people; the most terrifying thing of all is complete silence." The Tiananmen Incident of 1976 should be a lesson to us all.

—February 1989

If you think about it carefully, the fanatical belief people have in Marxism is no longer a matter of faith in an ideology or religion; rather, it is a fascination with and subjugation to absolute power. Eastern Marxism is no longer an ideology or religion but an integral part of dictatorship itself; it is a means whereby Eastern autocrats can enforce their rule. Thus, a critique of Marxism can be converted into an attack on Eastern autocracy; to defend Marxism is to defend autocracy. This is particularly true in the case of both China and the Soviet Union; as long as the rulers persevere in using Marxism to cloak their power, truly awake individuals cannot let up in their criticism of it.

—*Liu Xiaobo, from*
"At the Gateway to Hell"

From Lin Zexu to Chiang Ching-kuo

DAI QING

The American academic Samuel P. Huntington's controversial theory that it may be necessary for certain nations to go through a period of authoritarian rule if they are to develop economically, and that such a regime does not preclude progress toward democracy, was hotly debated in Chinese intellectual circles in 1988–89. Some people argued that "new authoritarianism," as the theory is known, was just what China needed: the establishment of a powerful autocrat who could introduce democratic change while maintaining strong, stable rule and guiding the nation toward prosperity. Other reformist intellectuals, having actively advocated democratization and rule by law for many years, were outraged by the suggestion. Dai Qing gave the following speech at a meeting in September 1988 in Peking to commemorate the ninetieth anniversary of the "Hundred Days" Reform Movement of 1898. The 1898 Reform Movement (also known as the Wuxu or 1898 Renewal) was the first radical attempt to modernize the Chinese polity. It was stymied by the aged Dowager Empress Cixi, and the Guangxu emperor, the leader of the movement, was put under house arrest until his death in 1908. Its failure has featured in the debates surrounding political reform in China ever since, and is also a central element of River Elegy.

Although condemned as a supporter of "new authoritarianism" by some, Dai Qing was actually bewailing the fact that Mainland China had produced no enlightened autocrat like Taiwan's Chiang Ching-kuo who could put the country on the road to political modernization. In fact, her view is not dissimilar to that of Liu Xiaobo: They both concede the positive role that autocrats, including Deng, Hu, and Zhao have played in post-Mao China. But they had different opinions about the future: Liu thought it was time for people to write their own history, for a civil society; Dai, despairing of finding a suitably enlightened new authoritarian, advocated slow, patient, and painful change under party

Dai Qing *(The Nineties Monthly)*

rule. Neither saw their vision fulfilled in 1989, when both fell victim to what Yu Haocheng called, during the debate, the vicious cycle of totalitarianism and anarchy. In late 1990, a number of progovernment "intellectuals" revived the theory in the guise of "neoconservatism." Even a number of formerly radical activists began to advocate political stability and gradual reform.

We are here to commemorate the martyrdom of the "six gentlemen" executed [in 1898] for "treason and heresy." Their heresy was to call for reform. Yes, that's what they called it then, too. What did they want to reform? The decrees proposed by Kang Youwei during the 103 days of the Reform touched on everything from politics and economics to culture. The reforms infuriated the diehards, who, as usual, were the only ones to profit from the affair in the end. . . . Reform failed, and the grand plans of those noble-minded men melted into thin air. . . .

In trying to pinpoint when China made the transition from a traditional to a modern society, we ought to put aside for a moment the notion that this happened when the People's Republic was founded and look instead at the indications, both formalistic and substantial, that characterize modern society. In that case, 1898 occupies no less important a position than the 1919 May Fourth Movement or the founding of the Communist Party in 1921. The Westernizing faction, the reformers, and the revolutionaries of 1911 were all beacons along the long path of social development.

In my opinion, no matter how arduous and dangerous revolution may be, it is essentially an exhilarating business. Revolution appeals to large numbers of people; the excitement, the righteousness of its cause, idealism, and the call to sacrifice attract enthusiastic youths, courageous men and women, and people who want to change the world. While victory will bring blessings to their families, even defeat promises a place in history. And, above all, while engaging in revolution you're not obligated to stop and consider the tremendous damage you're wreaking on society.

Reform is altogether different. Every little thing counts. Each failure, the consequence of every action, matters. Each new move must be weighed and considered. You have to inch forward whenever an opportunity presents itself, even if the effect is minuscule. No matter how much you may fantasize about your goals, you can't afford to act hastily or lose your temper; you must remain levelheaded as you face the enemy. You have to negotiate with them, make allies, compromise, make concessions, and even be prepared to sell out your principles for a good bargain or to grab your opponent by the throat and patiently, firmly, squeeze the life out of him bit by bit.

Tan Sitong [1865–1898, a young leader of the "Hundred Days" Reform Movement and one of the six martyrs executed after Cixi's palace coup] had a choice. He was only eight years younger than the revolutionary Xu Xilin.* Tan despised and reviled autocracy no less than Xu Xilin, and his hopes for human rights, freedom, and democracy were no less fervent. As we grow older, as we are gradually exhausted by endless, daily difficulties and frustrations we come to appreciate even more the courage of Tan Sitong. His courage was revealed not only in the way he faced death, for in this sense he was no different from Xu Xilin and Qiu Jin. I mean, rather, that not only was he able to overcome the limitations of his background, he also managed to keep the flood of his emotions under control, emotions that had a rational dimension, including compassion for the common people, hatred of the foreign invaders, and admiration for the French Revolution. How mortifying it must have been for a truly awakened individual such as Tan to sport a shaved head and long queue and perform the kowtow ceremony every day, among other things.

Yet Tan Sitong and his fellows didn't engage in assassination, nor did

---

* Xu Xilin (1873–1907) plotted an anti-Qing rebellion with the woman revolutionary Qiu Jin (1875–1907). Xu successfully assassinated a provincial governor, but both he and Qiu were finally captured and executed.

> Other Reformers fled to Japan, Macao, and America, but some did not attempt to escape. On September 26 [1898], six of them were summarily executed without trial. The most notable of these was Tan Sitong, a promising official of about thirty-three years of age. A native of Hunan and son of a former governor of Hubei, he had been recommended by several officials and given a position as one of the undersecretaries of the Grand Council. He was instrumental with Kang Youwei in drawing up the emperor's famous edicts . . . As they were being led to the execution ground . . . Tan Sitong . . . boldly spoke out, ignoring permission, that he had heard how many Reformers in other lands had died for their country's good. "I am willing to shed my blood, if thereby my country may be saved. But," he cried to the judges, "for every one that perishes today a thousand will rise up to carry on the work of Reform, and uphold loyalty against usurpation." Thus died the martyrs of Reform.
>
> —*Timothy Richard*

they plot an uprising. Racking their brains for a solution, they decided to use the emperor to create a new polity: "Only with accumulated power and the use of autocratic authority can things be carried out with dispatch." It would be unfair to say that these establishment figures felt they could remain secure because of their position; equally, it would be too simplistic and uncompromising to say that in terms of their thinking they were more conservative or weaker than the revolutionaries of 1911 [who overthrew the Qing dynasty]. They were deeply thoughtful activists whose actions were determined by the unpredictable situation of their time: If it hadn't been for the [relatively open-minded] Guangxu emperor, they might never have worked together. Some of them might well have edited newspapers or set up translation centers or tried their hand at industry. But instead they took advantage of Guangxu's presence to propose a complete set of reforms in a series of memorials to the throne. These reforms are not necessarily much inferior, either, to today's policy of "crossing the river by feeling the stones." *

But they failed. The reasons for their failure are numerous. Here too, however, the most crucial factor was Guangxu.

If only Guangxu had not been so extreme, so precipitous, so weak. If

---

* This is Deng Xiaoping's maxim, which encapsulated the party's trial-and-error approach to economic reform in the 1980s.

only they could have convinced Guangxu to be more patient; to wait until the Dowager Empress Cixi was older, until nongovernmental enterprises were more developed, until some real communication had been established with the pro-Westernizing faction. If only he could have been persuaded to wait until he had gradually accumulated military power into his own hands. If the emperor had only been a little more calculating and had more followers, things could have been completely different. But Guangxu was the emperor Heaven had bestowed on the Chinese along with his adoptive mother, Cixi, a manipulative, vicious, and outstandingly energetic woman. And so it was that the six reformers were executed at Caishikou; and this is what we are commemorating here today.

"Only with accumulated power and the use of autocratic authority can things be carried out with dispatch." That seemed to have been the pattern followed by [the late president of Taiwan] Chiang Ching-kuo for the last ten or twenty years of his life; it may well be the only model we

PROS AND CONS

What is "new" about new authoritarianism? What's new is that it does not deprive people of their individual rights; rather, the ruler uses his authority to clear away the obstacles to the development of personal freedoms and to protect those freedoms.
—Wu Jiaxiang, January 16, 1989

Wu Jiaxiang, one of the champions of new authoritarianism, was an assistant research fellow in the Investigation and Research Department of the Office of the Central Committee of the Communist Party of China. He was detained after the Peking Massacre.

The experience of the past twenty years shows that in the political, as in the economic, sphere, control means death and relaxation results in chaos. It is like the pendulum of a grandfather clock that alternates between totalitarianism and anarchy. We have never had any real democracy or rule by law. Only by breaking out of this vicious cycle can democracy and a full legal system be realized. That is to say, we must establish the authority of democracy and law, not the authority of any one individual or autocracy.

—Yu Haocheng

have to follow today. When Chiang died, mourners lined the streets in their thousands, wailing as his coffin went past. All the fresh flowers on an island renowned for its abundance of flowers were sold out. Why? He arranged for an end to the rule of his own family and lifted the bans on opposition parties and restrictions on the press. "All right, I am an autocrat, but I am the last. I am using my power to ensure the introduction of democracy." If we admit that there is a transition from traditional society to modern society, I believe it began with Lin Zexu and Wei Yuan, men who established translation bureaus and thought to "utilize the strengths of the barbarians." And it concluded with Chiang Ching-kuo, a man who accepted authoritarian power [from his father] but denied it to his children.

Given our unique situation, only an enlightened autocrat can bring an end to autocracy in China. Following the Revolution of 1911, Yuan Shikai, an autocrat with no modern sensibilities, came to power. After him there was a period of chaos in which there was no single political authority. Sun Yat-sen may have been the embodiment of morality and justice, but once the problem of national sovereignty was resolved, he was unable to assert his authority. Following him we had Mao Zedong and Chiang Kai-shek. Both were authoritarian enough but lacked enlightenment; they didn't use their authority to protect freedom, maintain social stability, hasten the democratization of the society, or further economic development. Suffering from bloodlust, they were blinded by their desire to destroy each other. For this reason, they may both be classified as traditional autocrats. They could lead China only to death, turmoil, and stagnation.

From the time Mao was too feeble to look after political affairs in 1976, indeed from April 5, 1976, up to 1988 . . . we can see for ourselves that every step of progress, as well as every regression, has been the result of authoritarian decision making, not popular movements. Of course, this is not to underestimate the way that popular movements have inspired or restrained the actions of the authorities, especially when they have been reasonable and had public support.

People have used popular movements for the past seventy years to call for democracy and science, but the Chinese have yet to achieve a democratic government. No matter how enthusiastic a popular movement may be, if half of the population in a country can't get enough to eat, if half of them are illiterate, it is nothing more than empty posturing. We are witness to a repeated cycle of autocracy, decay, and turmoil. Apart from sacrificing themselves in order to arouse the people, each generation [of intellectuals] has been powerless to do anything about it.

No one is calling for new authoritarians; that is not something you can agitate for. If you were to create one, or establish one, it is doubtful that things would work out as you wished. But without one we have no choice but to fight on inch by inch, seeing the repetition of the same old cycles, taking comfort from the hope that there is such a thing as a cyclical progression. Only then will there be any hope that the transition [to a modern society] can be completed.

It is still too early to evaluate the authoritarians who are ruling us at the moment. But history surely demands of an autocrat whose task is to bring an end to autocracy far greater scholarship, courage, ability, and personality than it does of an elected president in a modern democracy.

Portraits of Individualists

These are the unfettered, eccentric, and temperamental figures of China's past and present, people infected with a dangerous spirit of individuality. He Xin, clearly alarmed by them, has likened some of them to hippies (see Part III, "Red Noise"). For these individualists the bindings of Confucian propriety, the cast-iron mentality of Communism, the swaddling clothes of social acceptability, even the threats of the dictatorial state have no power. Their number may be small, but they have existed throughout Chinese history, often reviled, occasionally revered. In the 1930s, a number of writers, including Zhou Zuoren and Lin Yutang, saw in the individualist tradition within Chinese letters an alternative to the straitjacketed orthodoxy of imperial Confucianism.* The individualists are most often appreciated after they are safely dead and gone. They may even attract followers who adorn themselves with the affectations of quirky individuality but wouldn't dream of tempting the fates by actually rebelling in thought or deed.

The individualists are a chaotic element in a world ordered by orthodoxy; they are the "unbound feet" of society. Their very existence is a threat, their free and unrestrained gait a mote in the eye of both those whose minds have been crippled by convention and those who themselves wish to run but who either cannot or dare not. They are dreaded by all, for they hold up a mirror to their fellows that displays an insipid, weak, and shallow image. As far as many people are concerned, they are better forgotten, dismissed as unrepresentative, or shunted aside.

Some Western observers compared the 1989 protests to the 1968 concert at Woodstock, and for many people in Peking they also marked a coming of age, a means of finding release from the bonds of both

---

* Zhou Zuoren propounded this theory in a series of lectures given at Furen University in Peking in 1932.

tradition and Communist rule. For a while, many reveled in the feeling of independence that the individualists below and their fellows either understood from birth or won through painful struggle.

The following is not a random or arbitrary selection of "individualists." The Shanghai critic Zhu Dake, the Taiwan academic Chen Guying, and He Xin, for example, are among those who have grouped many of these names together in writings and interviews.

ZHUANGZI (369?–286? B.C.): *A philosopher of the pre-imperial period when there was free intellectual debate. His writings, along with those of Laozi, are regarded as the basis of philosophical Taoism. A number of the anecdotes in the book* Zhuangzi *ridicule Confucius.*

On his way to the capital of Chu, Confucius stopped at Yiqiu. Next door to where he was staying, a husband and wife and their servants had climbed onto the rooftop. [Confucius's disciple] Zilu asked, "What are they all up to?"

"They are the followers of a sage who has concealed himself among the people, hidden himself in the fields. . . . He is a recluse who refuses to be part of the age. He has truly drowned on dry land [disappeared].* His name, I believe, is Yiliao of Shinan."

Zilu proposed that they meet him.

"Forget it," Confucius replied. "He knows I am better known than he is; he also knows I am on my way to Chu and probably assumes I will advise the king to invite him to serve at court. He will think me a toady of princes. Just to hear the name of a flatterer makes him feel ashamed, and he'd certainly not want to meet one in person! Is he even at home?"

Zilu went to see, but found the house empty.

RUAN JI (A.D. 210–263): *One of the "Seven Sages of the Bamboo Grove." The Seven Sages were friends united by their interest in wine, the Taoist works of Laozi and Zhuangzi, a dissolute spirit, and their desire to preserve their sanity in a period of chaos and violence. Ruan Ji's satirical portrait of the Confucian gentlemen in his "Biography of the Great Man" is a quintessential expression of the Seven Sages' irreverent attitude toward social convention.*

---

* In her essay "The Cloak of Invisibility" (see pp. 443–48), Yang Jiang comments that she admires Zhuangzi when he speaks of the sage who "drowned on dry land."

Zhuangzi, by Ren Weichang

Someone wrote to the Great Man: "By far the most precious thing in the world is the gentleman. He wears clothing of a fixed color and his expression is of a fixed nature. He chooses his words with great care, and his actions are of a set pattern. His back is bent humbly in the shape of a bow; when he greets people his arms join as if embracing a drum. Every movement has a rhythm, every step he takes is in time with [an inaudible] music. In all he utters and all his comings and goings he follows propriety meticulously. He trembles constantly in consternation as if he has a block of ice in his heart, ever trepidatious. He keeps himself well bound and cultivates virtue, becoming more restrained with each passing day. He takes such care for he is terrified of committing even the slightest transgression. He memorizes the teachings of the Duke of Zhou and Confucius; he sighs in praise of the virtues of the sage emperors Yao and Shun. . . . He serves his lord and rules the people, and in retirement he manages his household, supporting his wife and children. But this is not all, for he also chooses the most propitious of spots for his residence, so that it will benefit his descendants for myriad generations. He strains to keep disaster at a distance and attract good fortune, preserving forever his wealth and achievements. All of this shows the superior quality of the gentleman, the immutable morality of antiquity . . ."

The Great Man let out a carefree sigh and replied from amid the clouds: "Haven't you seen the way fleas nestle in a person's pants? They hide in the deepest seams and the rotten old cotton wadding of one's clothing. They think they have found the most propitious abode. In nothing they do would they dare leave those seams or those pants. They think that they are acting most properly and correctly. They bite people when they're hungry and consider themselves well provided for. But when the searing heat of the south comes, when the cities and towns swelter, the fleas remain hiding in the seams of those pants, and that's where they die. The gentleman you speak of, how different, then, is he from these fleas?"

JI KANG (A.D. 223–262): *Another one of the Seven Sages, Ji refused to cooperate with the rulers of the time. His spirit is best represented in a letter to his friend Shan Juyuan, also a member of the Seven Sages. In the letter he cuts off his friendship with Shan because the latter had proposed that Ji replace him in his official position. It is said that this letter led directly to Ji Kang's execution.*

It is easiest to train animals when they are young, for they will submit to control. When mature they bolt at the sight of the harness. You may decorate them with golden trappings and feed them the finest fodder, but they will merely pine for the forests and wild grasses.

There are seven things about serving the court that I could never tolerate, and two things I do that would not be permitted.

The seven things are: I like to stay in bed late and ignore calls to rise. I enjoy playing the lute and singing, fishing, and wandering in the countryside. How could I feel at ease with government attendants always at

Ji Kang, by Ren Weichang

hand? I would have to sit still respectfully for long periods although I am by nature restless, and I like scratching when bitten by lice. But how would this be possible when wrapped in official robes and paying my respects to my superiors? I hate writing letters and ignore my correspondence. Fifth, I detest attending funerals, although they are treated with the utmost seriousness by the worldly. I could not help offending people and they might want revenge. I could make a show of weeping but would be unconvincing and be disparaged for it. Then, too, I despise common men and could not tolerate working with them or socializing with them at banquets, having to listen to their prattle and observe their carryings-on. And finally, I have no patience for official tasks and could not tolerate the cares and worries that go with office.

The two things that would never be permitted are: I criticize Confucius and the sage kings he praises. I would be found severely wanting by "proper" society for this. I am also given to saying whatever I think. This, too, is forbidden.

Li Ao, himself one of Taiwan's most prickly individualists, discussed the problem of independence in his introduction to A Monologue on Tradition *in 1979:*

Chinese intellectuals lack a very important quality: independence . . . the result being that there is no difference between A and B, or C and D. They say the same things, write the same bullshit, and lick the same asses. A, B, C, and D might look a little different, but they're united in their lack of character and originality. . . .

The tradition is unforgiving when it comes to nonconformity. In other respects Chinese society may be completely inefficient, but when it comes to dealing with the true talents and people of conscience who won't conform, China is number one; it has a real genius for banning and killing. Individualists share a congenital disinclination to longevity. Most of them die young, and if they're lucky to live they still find it difficult to escape calamity. Li Zhi, the great prophetic writer of the Ming dynasty, died in prison at the age of seventy-six. It's an example written in blood. The path of the individualist is the path of the martyr.

So, theoretically, independent intellects have great difficulty existing in China. When they do appear, they rarely grow to maturity. If they do grow up, it's hard for them to flourish. Even if they do flourish, they can't keep going for long, and if they do, they're likely to come to no good end.

LIU LING (third century A.D.): *Yet another one of the Seven Sages of the Bamboo Grove. Most of what is known about him comes from anecdotes, although he is famous for a poem entitled "In Praise of the Virtues of Wine." In 1985, He Xin condemned the modern "superfluous people" of China for being "the disciples of Liu Ling, people who treat the universe as their pants and life as one big drinking session." In late 1989, he dismissed Liu Xiaobo for being nothing more than a "modern-day Liu Ling."*

In Liu Yiqing's New Sayings of the World *(fifth century A.D.), a collection of Jin dynasty bons mots and anecdotes, the following story about Liu Ling is recorded:*

Liu Ling was often uninhibited when drunk and sometimes sat at home naked. When someone visited him and upbraided him for it, he replied: "The universe is my home, this room my pants and robes. What, sir, are you doing in my pants?"

HAN SHAN, OR COLD MOUNTAIN (seventh or eighth century A.D.): *A Tang dynasty Buddhist monk famed for his carefree and unworldly poetry. The mainland playwright Wu Zuguang began work on a film scenario of Han Shan's life immediately after the Peking Massacre. Han Shan was popular in the West during the 1950s and '60s, known as Cold Mountain from Gary Snyder's translations. Jack Kerouac dedicated* The Dharma Bums *to Han Shan as the idol of the Beat Generation, and the Chinese poet makes a fleeting and suitably irreverent appearance at the end of the book.*

> When men see Han Shan
> They all say he's crazy
> And not much to look at—
> Dressed in rags and hides.
> They don't get what I say
> And I don't talk their language.
> All I can say to those I meet:
> "Try and make it to Cold Mountain."

In 1983, Li Zhenjie, a Chinese literary critic, commented on the fascination for Han Shan in the West. In fact, his comments could be seen to apply to some of China's own youths in the late 1980s.

Contemporary Western youth have a lot in common with Han Shan. With the advanced development of capitalism, people have become the adjuncts of machinery, their lives monotonous and empty. They seek motivation and meaning in the accumulation of money and material possessions. The young people in such societies experience spiritual torment, they sense that life is meaningless. They deride and rebel against the status quo or drift toward religion and mysticism. There is a real sympathy between themselves and Han Shan.

LI ZHI (1527–1602): *Fiercely individualistic, Li was renowned for his attacks on the hypocrisy of Confucian orthodoxy and his support for self-expression in literature. He abandoned his family to become a monk, and was finally indicted for "daring to promote the rebellious way and deluding the world." He died in prison. The twentieth-century essayist Lin Yutang thought of him as a mild psychopath for his inability to get on with others, although Lin admired his genius and ruthless honesty. Li Zhi's most famous collections of writings are* Books to Be Burnt *and* Books to Be Hidden Away, *titles indicating their subversive nature. They were listed in the Qing imperial index of forbidden books. Li's writings were made available in the last years of the Cultural Revolution and used in the campaign to criticize Confucius.*

In his testament, from which the following is taken, he explained to his disciples why he "left the world" and became a monk:

I've never liked being controlled by others. The moment you come into the world you're under other people's control: In childhood it is obvious, as are your first years under a tutor. But even later on there are always teachers and masters who are in charge; when you become an official you are controlled by other officials. Even when you give up a post to retire to your home, the district and county magistrates are in charge of you, as are your parents and grandparents. . . . So I'd rather wander free than return home. Of course, I would dearly like to have a good friend to talk to, but there are none who understand me. One thing is certain, however, and that is I do not want to be under the thumb of others . . . this is why I finally cut off my hair and became a monk.

YUAN HONGDAO (1568–1610): *With his brothers, Zhongdao and Zongdao, Yuan Hongdao developed a literary style labeled the "literature of self-expression" by twentieth-century admirers. Reacting against the artistic conformity of the late Ming dynasty, they pursued a simple, clear style in both poetry and prose to express their own feelings and personalities. As they came from Gongan County in Hupei Province, theirs was called the "Gongan school." Yuan Hongdao was an admirer and friend of Li Zhi. He was condemned by his contemporaries as being "heterodox and a wild fox," and his writings were deemed vulgar and superficial. The works of the Gongan school were banned in the Qing dynasty and not generally made available until Lin Yutang republished them in the 1930s. Zhou Zuoren said of these works that they "are so old but at the same time so fresh."*

Like Li Zhi, Yuan hated the life of an official and finally abandoned it. In a letter to Qiu Changru, another writer of the Gongan school, he said:

What a vile appearance I must affect as a magistrate! It beggars my powers of description. Basically, in front of a superior I must play the slave; when entertaining officials who pass through my district I must be as a courtesan. In dealing with the granary I have to act like an old watchman, yet when instructing the people I must display the talents of a wily matchmaker. From warm to cold, kind to harsh, a hundred times a day. I have indeed tasted all the foul flavors of mankind. How bitter and how despicable!

ZHENG BANQIAO (1693–1765): *One of the "Eight Eccentrics of Yang-zhou." This loosely related group active in and around Yangzhou in the early and middle Qing dynasty included the painters and calligraphers Jin Nong, Luo Pin, and Gao Xiang. They were famous for disdaining convention, emphasizing originality and creativity, and rejecting the prevailing trend of emulating the past.*

Zheng was dismissed from office as a local official in Shandong for supporting the impoverished people of his district against the wealthy. He then moved to Yangzhou in Jiangsu, a thriving center of commerce, where he lived as a painter. He is famous for his quirky "stone slab" style calligraphy and his paintings of bamboo. His letters to his younger brother Mo, written when he was an official, reveal a kind and thoughtful character. The following quotation is taken from one of these:

I was fifty-two when my first son was born, so of course I love him dearly. But there is a right way to love. Even while playing games, he should be taught care and sympathy, and to avoid cruelty. I've always detested the practice of keeping birds in cages. I think of them imprisoned there whenever I am enjoying myself; it would be so cruel and unreasonable to make another creature suffer so as to please me. I feel the same way about tying a dragonfly with a hair or a crab with a piece of string so they can serve briefly as toys for children before they lie broken and dead. . . .

P.S. As to what I have said about birds in cages, I don't mean I don't love them, but again, there is a better way to keep them. If you really love birds, then plant hundreds of trees around your house, and the shady foliage will become their kingdom, their home. Awakening at dawn, you will hear their song while still cozy in your quilt. . . . Getting up to wash and take your tea, you may observe their colorful plumage as they hop and flit in the trees. How could the pleasures of keeping a caged bird possibly compare with this?

CHEN DUXIU (1880–1942): *Participated in the 1911 revolution against the Qing dynasty after studying in Japan. In 1915 he became the founding editor of* La Jeunesse, *the most influential radical magazine of its time. He took a job at Peking University in 1916 and was prominent as a radical iconoclast, particularly in his attacks on Confucianism during the May Fourth period. He became the first general secretary of the Communist Party of China but was purged in 1927 and subsequently expelled from the party in 1929 as a Trotskyite. One of his most famous May Fourth essays was "On Iconoclasm."*

Destroy! Destroy the idols! Destroy the idols of hypocrisy! My beliefs are based on true and reasonable standards. The religious, political, and moral beliefs transmitted from ancient times are vain, deceptive, and unreasonable. They are all idols and must be destroyed! If we do not destroy them, universal truth and our own heartfelt beliefs will never be united.

LU XUN (the pen name of Zhou Shuren, 1881–1936): *One of the greatest and most irascible cultural figures of twentieth-century China. Many people have speculated what might have happened to him had he lived on to experience Communism in China.* In his later years much of his time was devoted to literary dogfighting with intellectuals of both the left and right, and producing volumes of brilliant and acerbic essays. In the following excerpt taken from an essay written in 1925, Lu Xun notes why so few individualists survive in Chinese society.*

Our forefathers, however dumb, managed after a few thousand years of reflection to elaborate a subtle recipe to control people: crush all those whom you can crush; as for others, put them on a pedestal. By putting them on a pedestal, you can also control them—you merely need to whisper constantly in their ears, "Do as I tell you, otherwise I shall bring you down."

ZHOU ZUOREN (1885–1967): *One of Lu Xun's two younger brothers. Zhou was one of China's greatest Japanologists; he was also a major*

---

* See, for example, Zhang Yu'an's "If Lu Xun Were Still Alive" and Yau Ma Tei's "One Autumn Night," in *Seeds of Fire*, pp. 314–21.

figure in the literary revolution of the May Fourth period who went on to become a leading advocate of individualism in literature. A translator of Greek, Japanese, and English literature, Zhou was a master of the modern Chinese casual essay. Although he wrote many satirical essays in the 1920s, he abandoned his vitriolic posture in favor of a gentler attitude, a transition he describes below. Lu Xun and Zhou became estranged for both personal and political reasons.

During the war, Zhou served under the Japanese invaders in Peking and as a result was jailed for treason by the Nationalists. He remained on the mainland after 1949, and although his name was never cleared, he was allowed to spend his latter years writing reminiscences and translating classical Greek and Japanese literature.

While Lu Xun has been claimed posthumously for the Communist cause, Zhou was treated as a nonperson—that is, until the 1980s, when his essays became available again, in particular as a result of the work of the editors Niu Han in Peking and Zhong Shuhe in Changsha, Hunan.* The revival of interest in him and Lin Yutang (see next entry) was identified in the second half of 1989 as an example of Bourgelib.

Two demons live within me. . . . One is a gentleman, the other a hooligan, a *liumang*. . . . † I am like a pendulum swinging between them. Sometimes the *liumang* gets the upper hand, and I go wandering off with him, learning every secret of the town, getting drunk, fighting, and swearing—I am capable of all of these, of becoming a spiritual cripple. But just when the *liumang* is about to take over, the gentleman calls him to order and oddly enough he takes to his heels, though he never flees very far, and, standing in some alleyway, looks back surreptitiously. He sees the gentleman take me away to teach me how to present myself to young ladies, how to speak properly. But gradually I go from mouthing fine words to putting on airs. At this point the *liumang* rushes back to scream at me: "You bastard! Who are you kidding? You make me sick!" Then the tables are turned and the dictatorship of the *liumang* is gradually resumed.

Lin Yutang (1895–1976): *Essayist, critic, translator, and novelist. His father was a Christian minister and a supporter of reform in the late Qing dynasty. Lin studied English from a young age and was educated*

---

* Niu Han, poet, editor, and supporter of nonestablishment literary figures from Bei Dao to Liu Xiaobo, is the editor of a leading Peking journal on the history of twentieth-century Chinese literature that was the first to reassess Zhou's life and work. See *Seeds of Fire*, pp. 291–92. For Zhong Shuhe, see p. 452 herein.
† For more on the *liumang*, see pp. 247–50 herein.

in Europe. Known in the West for such books as My Country and My People *(1936) and* The Importance of Living *(1938), Lin was influenced by Hu Shi during the May Fourth period, and for a while was an ally of Lu Xun. With Zhou Zuoren he promoted the writings of such writers as Li Zhi and Yuan Hongdao, finding in their work a homegrown precedent of their own style of individualism. In the 1930s, he founded a number of literary journals that advocated humor and the casual or individual essay, of which he was a uniquely talented practitioner. Like Zhou Zuoren, Feng Zikai (see below), and other practitioners of the nonpolemical essay, Lin was attacked by the politically committed writers of both the left and the right. (His response to these attacks is succinctly stated in the following quotation from 1934.) In the late 1930s, there was little place in China for his urbane literary persona, and Lin went into voluntary exile.*

After many years in the United States, Lin spent time in Hong Kong, Singapore, and finally Taiwan. His works became available in Mainland China only in the late 1980s and his importance as a literary figure was then grudgingly recognized.

To the east lives a Prole, to the west a Fascist, but I don't care for any of this stuff. If I'm forced to state what "ism" I'm for, all I can say is that I want to be an individual.

FENG ZIKAI (1898–1975): *An artist, essayist, teacher, and translator who, along with Zhou Zuoren and Lin Yutang, was a leading essayist of the 1930s, often contributing articles and paintings to Lin's magazines. He became a Buddhist layman in the late 1920s. Depressed by the increasing politicization of education, he quit his teaching job in Shanghai and retired to his native home, where he lived by writing and painting. His home and possessions were destroyed in the Japanese invasion and he fled to safety with his family. After 1949 Feng stayed in Shanghai and lived in semiretirement, keeping in close touch with his Buddhist friends both in China and overseas.*

Although he is now known as a children's artist and writer, Feng in fact pursued the "childlike mind" advocated by Li Zhi as a way of preserving his purity and innocence as an adult.

I am painfully aware of the fact that I have a split personality. On the one hand, I am an old man, hypocritical, callous, pragmatic. . . . On the other hand, I am a naïve, enthusiastic, curious, and impractical child. . . . These two personalities often do battle within my heart. Although there are momentary victories for one and defeats for the other, a rise to prominence or a falling into abeyance, they are still both of equal

"An Old Man at 30,"
self-portrait by Feng Zikai
(1928)

strength; neither can claim the final victory, and they remain at a stand-off in my soul. The invasions and struggles of these two forces have caused me great spiritual anguish. . . .

There are too few children in China. Adults too readily concern them-selves with the pursuit of fame or economic gain; their minds are occu-pied with social, political, economic, and industrial problems . . . they have no time for the trivial things that are so close at hand; they have neither the time nor the energy truly to live; they have no right to be counted as children. . . . If things continue as they are, I fear China will have only adults and no children; even infants will be turned into prag-matic old men and women!

Li Ao (born 1935): *Spent his youth in Peking and moved to Taiwan with his family in 1948. The leading student of Hu Shi, he graduated with a degree from Taiwan University in history in 1959 and began publishing highly erudite satirical essays that are at the same time stylis-tic and very entertaining.*

Unashamedly egotistical and almost unbelievably prolific, Li Ao has declared himself to be a genius and has launched withering attacks on all of his opponents, cultural and political figures, and even some of his (former) friends, including the essayist Bo Yang. Jin Zhong, the editor of the Hong Kong journal Open Magazine *(formerly* Emancipation

Li Ao (1979)

Monthly), *once said of Liu Xiaobo that he was the Li Ao of the main-land. Li Ao's work has often been banned, and he has been jailed twice. His writings finally began to appear on the mainland in the late 1980s.*

In the last fifty years, and for the last five hundred,
The three greatest writers of vernacular prose in Chinese have been
Li Ao, Li Ao, Li Ao.
Even the people who disparage me for being boastful,
Actually kowtow to my ancestral tablet in their hearts.

LIU XIAOBO (born 1955): *Formerly a lecturer at Peking Normal University and literary critic, Liu is scathing in his evaluation of both conventional, establishment writers and the angst-ridden poets and novelists of the semiofficial underground and has made himself one of the most controversial figures in contemporary culture. Dismissive of all Chinese writers past and present as mere puppets of convention, Liu fails to realize that he, too, belongs to a Chinese tradition—that of individualism and rebellion. Although popular with students in public lectures, his manner—uncouth habits, foul language, and superciliousness—lead even many enlightened reformist thinkers to dislike him, and he has horrified a number of observers of the scene. In early 1991 he was convicted on charges of "counterrevolutionary propaganda" for his role in the Protest Movement but released for his role in getting the students to leave the square on June 4.*

In the Chinese literary scene factional cronyism is all too common. It is virtually impossible to make a move without the backing of a coterie

... in fact, coteries restrain individual artists; they encourage homogenization and lead to mutual admiration societies and therefore mutual deception. Constantly on the lookout for allies, coteries are the most typical expression of the absence of individuality among Chinese intellectuals. . . . The tragedy of it is that when people discover their individual weakness they make no sincere attempt to enrich themselves or seek genuine inspiration; rather, they strive to put themselves under the banner of some "famous person" and feel emboldened—even if only momentarily—by their affiliation with a coterie.

When passing through Hong Kong in November 1988, Liu said to the editor of Open Magazine, Jin Zhong:

There should be room for my extremism; I certainly don't demand of others that they be like me. . . .

I'm pessimistic about mankind in general, but my pessimism does not allow for escape. Even though I might be faced with nothing but a series of tragedies, I will still struggle, still show my opposition. This is why I like Nietzsche and dislike Schopenhauer.

ZHU DAKE (born 1957): *A Shanghai writer, Zhu came to prominence in 1985 when he published the first in a series of articles analyzing the "Confucian paradigm" in the films of Xie Jin, China's most important and long-serving official director. As a result, Zhu became the object of numerous internal attacks by the cultural establishment. His literary criticism, in particular such essays as "Heartless Literature" (1988) and "The Burning Labyrinth" (1989), although not as flamboyantly iconoclastic as the writings of his friend Liu Xiaobo, reveals with devastating accuracy what lies beneath the modish surface shine of contemporary Chinese literature.*

During the 1989 Protest Movement, Zhu was involved with a major petition of literary figures in Shanghai (see pp. 60–61). Many of the poets in his circle were detained after the massacre, and he was put under intensive investigation. In 1988 he wrote:

The people are slaves. The people's role within the state structure is to accept both the overlordship and largesse of their rulers; they provide the constituency for the autocrats to betray. You could also say that the people are the autocrats who have already been deposed by history. From the day they are born they are tightly bound by labor and duty. They are the group deprived of autonomy by the social contract.

The people, as the icon of the weak, gain the pity and arouse the vigilance of the scholar-official. His mission is to play mediator, maintaining the political balance between the people and rulers, finessing the state of "democracy." "Democracy" shouldn't be a "People's" dictatorship, but an equitable dialogue between the People and the rulers.

People usually see the disruption of this balance of power as the result of the king's isolation in his palace and lack of support. They blame him for refusing to enact the People—while, in fact, this is precisely the ruler's grand design.

The People are the most blind and powerful will in history. For thousands of years, the People have lorded it over this suffering planet and are the source of all collective sin. The People are a vile assassin; on the one hand they kill the king, on the other they force the individual into anonymity. The People expel the individual from intellectual profundity and obliterate the reality of his existence, putting in its place an entirely illusory form and silhouette.

There are no witnesses to this "massacre," because no pure or vigilant observer can escape it. Others who could have been witnesses now join the execution squad. The murderers have no accusers, no judges. The People are more eternal than God. Nietzsche could kill God, but he was impotent to sentence the hideous People to death along with history.

All I can do is to declare that I am withdrawing from my relationship with the People. I will use enigmatic language to discuss solitude and its consequences, to describe the great fortune of the loner. For fortune will be mine, so long as I withdraw.

HOU DEJIAN (born 1956): *Born in Taiwan, the singer-songwriter Hou Dejian achieved fame with his 1979 song "Heirs of the Dragon." On June 4, 1983, Hou became the first young cultural figure from Taiwan to defect to Communist China. But while his move was a propaganda windfall for Peking, Hou's independent political stance, quirky individuality, and inclination to speak his mind increasingly alienated and sometimes embarrassed the Chinese government.*

During the Protest Movement, Hou joined his friend Liu Xiaobo in advising student leaders and took part in the four-man hunger strike with Liu on June 2. When troops surrounded Tiananmen Square early on the morning of June 4, Hou negotiated with the army to allow the students to leave the square. On June 6, Hou took refuge in the Australian embassy, returning to his Peking apartment some two months later. With his music already banned, subsequent interviews given to the international press in which he was highly critical of the government led to

Hou Dejian (Forrest Anderson)

visits from the police. He became the only Chinese dissident who was not in jail or exile and who continued to go public with his beliefs. Hou made the following statement to an Australian reporter in February 1990:

Sometimes it does seem hopeless, but I'm happier as an amateur dissident than as a professional musician.

I'm alone now; I can never talk about this to my Chinese friends because it would get them into trouble. As a Taiwan-born Chinese I can say things that would land them in jail. I could leave, but I love China and I can't escape from what I know.

In June 1990, the Chinese authorities decided they'd had enough of Hou's individualism and put him on a boat back to Taiwan.

On Solitude

LIU XIAOBO

It's become very fashionable for intellectuals to talk about self-negation. Renewal of knowledge, methodology, ideas, life-style, standards: Chinese intellectuals are drowning in myriad, much-needed renewals. Some people are scared; then there are extremists, conservatives, and, of course, the apathetic. But no matter how you feel about it, the general ambience forces you to make a choice. To my mind the question at the heart of this intellectual self-negation and self-examination, which is also the self-negation of Chinese traditional culture itself, is the need for the individual to extricate himself from the collective consciousness and break free of all external bonds so as to enter a liberating state of solitude.

Solitude often frightens people. But fear breeds pain and of that pain is born a desire to struggle, a struggle that can lead to salvation. All geniuses throughout human history have experienced solitude. Even Freud was isolated in his early years: No one understood or accepted his ideas. Only six hundred copies were printed of the first edition of *The Interpretation of Dreams,* and it took eight years before they were all sold. Solitude is a prerequisite for genius.

Solitude implies independence, self-reliance; it means not following the crowd.... While many intellectuals, especially undergraduate and postgraduate university students, like to put on the mask of nonconformist isolation, they are in fact united by their collective consciousness. In the words of a friend, they're only "playing at being individualists." But you can't fake character; you'll end up not knowing who you are. An intellectual's singularity must be something innate, an integral part of the personality. For Chinese intellectuals, solitude must start with a complete negation of the self, because throughout our long feudal history, Chinese intellectuals were never independent thinkers, they were but

> I would like to remind my compatriots that behind the cries
> of radical antitraditionalists and iconoclasts so popular today
> there is a hidden agenda that calls for another Cultural Revolution
> (the next time, won't it come from below rather than the top?). . . .
>   If we sit back and consider things calmly and rationally, we can
> discern many familiar shadows of the past in the miasma of cul-
> tural nihilism and radical antitraditionalism, as well as among the
> warped attitudes and extremism of some young intellectuals. The
> difference is that the antitraditionalism and cultural nihilism of
> those years marched under the banner of Marx and Mao Zedong;
> today it is hidden under the cloak of Freud and Nietzsche. The
> thing [the two currents of thought] have in common is their zeal-
> otry, their absurd theoretical framework, and their wrongheaded
> and distorted analysis of Eastern and Western cultures. (I strongly
> suggest people examine and reevaluate Mr. Liu Xiaobo's theories
> in this light.)
>
> —He Xin

"court literati." The establishment of the imperial examination system assured the rulers of a means of depriving intellectuals of their independence. People studied not to become independent thinkers but to win a career in the bureaucracy, in the hope of serving an enlightened ruler. This predetermined political goal restricted the development of the personality and limited the range, depth, and perspective of knowledge. By the Ming and Qing dynasties there was virtually no school of thought apart from Confucianism.

Perhaps the first appearance of literati with no independent character was in the Warring States Period [fifth to third centuries B.C.]. The historian Sima Qian [second century B.C.] bewailed the fact that his status was somewhere between that of prostitutes and actors, evidence that he was vaguely aware of the sorry truth that intellectuals had already lost their independence. And the Tang poet Li Bo lamented having to serve those in power. But no matter how they might despise the imperial examination system, the patriotism of Chinese intellectuals and their devotion to their rulers have since ancient times led them to sacrifice their independence. Thus, to emphasize the need for intellectuals to be independent of society boils down to calling for a rebellion against and negation of traditional culture. . . .

I am myself, nothing more. I worship no one and am no one's lackey;

I'm a perpetual loner. This [creed] is the basis of true pluralism. . . . In feudal society, people believed their fate depended on a savior, an emperor; what we need in China today is the attitude that whether you go to heaven or hell is all up to you.

Whoever wants to possess the universe must first possess an independent self.

The Chinese Cursed

BO YANG

In April 1987, at the height of the Anti-Bourgelib Campaign, Bo Yang, author of "The Ugly Chinaman," * *commented to Lee Yee, chief editor of* The Nineties Monthly *of Hong Kong:*

The Chinese people are under a most foul curse. I believe this to be the truth. Otherwise, how could we have become as we are? There's no way we can preserve any of the extraordinary achievements of our ancestors.†

In September of the same year, Bo Yang published a short story in The Nineties Monthly, *"Slaughter at Tashkent," in which he provided his own fictional account of how the Chinese had come under a curse.*

The story is based on an incident recorded in the Song dynasty Mirror to Aid the Art of Government, *an eleventh-century history of China that Bo Yang has been translating into modern Chinese. In 750 General Gao Xianzhi led an expedition to Tashkent (then known to the Chinese as Shiguo) to conclude a peace treaty with the king. He was so overwhelmed by the wealth of the distant western kingdom, however, that he betrayed the alliance and ransacked the city for its riches. He was subsequently executed. In "Slaughter at Tashkent" Bo Yang embellishes the story. Now, after killing the king of Tashkent, Gao tries to capture his widow, the queen Malinna, who flees to the top of a pagoda. Gao's archers fire their arrows at her, but they are repelled by her magic aura.*

---

* See *Seeds of Fire*, pp. 168–76.
† See *Seeds of Fire*, p. 377.

Finally they set fire to the tower and Malinna perishes in the flames, but not before she has condemned the Chinese to over a millennium of despair with the following curse:

I curse you, cried Queen Malinna of Tashkent to the Chinese general. . . .

I curse you to behave forever like barbarians; your souls will be corrupted, and your greatest pleasure will be to see your own people suffer. The high morals that you transmitted from generation to generation in the past will be despoiled.

I curse you. China will turn from being a country of great vitality to a vast and muddy marshland in which the Chinese will sink, writhe, and be eternally befuddled.

I curse you. Henceforth you will lose yourselves in reveries of past glories, but you will never again enjoy the prosperity for which your neighbors admired you.

I curse you. May you be dispirited, slow-witted, and uninspired. The wings of the phoenix, that symbol of hope, will break when it traverses your skies and it will fall dead to the earth; the magical *qilin,* that symbol of love, will be killed by the arrow of a hidden archer the moment it treads on your soil. Wells now full will dry up; the warm winds will cease to caress you; and nowhere will you find redemption.

I curse you. May you forever slaughter one another. The left hand will be the sworn enemy of the right. Your poisonous evil will pollute the very river that has given you birth, making its yellow silt build up to cause floods. But your poison will afflict only yourselves. When you confront foreigners, you will appear to be no more intimidating than a pitiful insect.

I curse you. May you be incapable of distinguishing right from wrong, black from white. You will confuse night and day. The Chinese will never again hear the strains of heavenly music, and will know only the cries of rage.

I curse you. Chinese men will never enjoy the warmth and comfort of women, and your children will be branded with the mark of death. Your doors will be flecked with the blood of your babies.

I curse you. The best and brightest of your race will evaporate at once, like drops of water in the desert. Your greatest achievements will be mere castles of sand to be trodden underfoot.

O spirit of the curse, I beseech you: Cling tenaciously to the Chinese, so they will fall down every few steps they take, and each time they lift themselves up they will fall once more, and so on without end. No matter what wars, starvation, disaster, evil, corruption, or cowardly betrayals you suffer, you will not even know to cry out, nor will you dare to scream. The Chinese will be unable to find their souls, just as it is impossible to see one's reflection in a rushing stream. . . .

This curse will not lift until the time the Chinese awaken to the fact that they have been so cursed.

Bo Yang's fictional curse and the comments it makes on the Chinese national character are to a great extent a repetition or continuation of what many Chinese writers said in the 1920s. Like Bo Yang, Liu Xiaobo, and many others more than sixty years later, Lu Xun and his brother Zhou Zuoren felt the Chinese had to face the curse they were living under and admit it to themselves before there would be any hope of change. They saw the bindings of the past, of convention, tradition, and society, as originating with the socialized Chinese self. Change, too, they argued, had to begin with the individual. In 1925, Zhou Zuoren wrote:

If China is to improve, the first thing we must do is wake up, be aware that we don't qualify as human beings, to the extent that we must suffer the humiliation of being insulted. After this we need the courage to confront our own repulsiveness, to repent sincerely for the past, to re-form our traditional erroneous way of thinking and evil habits so as to achieve some independence. Herein lie the seeds of hope. In short, be-cause the Chinese don't have the courage to slap themselves in the face, all reforms are illusory, for all true reform and renewal must be born of repentance.

PART III

Red Noise

The Cultural Revolution of Communist China not only failed to usher in an era of Great Harmony but was probably more calamitous to human ecology than Chernobyl, for it released venom, bile, spite, misanthropy, and simple insanity on an unprecedented scale. China today is still living under its fallout.

LUNG-KEE SUN, 1989

The religion of the Chinese today is cheating, deceit, blackmail, and theft, eating, drinking, whoring, gambling, and smoking. . . . We think any honest, humble gentleman a fool and regard any good person who works hard and demands little in return as an idiot. Crooks are our sages; thieves and swindlers our supermen. . . . There are no greater cynics than the Chinese people.

HE XIN, 1988

The title of this section was inspired by Don DeLillo's novel *White Noise*. "White noise" can be taken as the background music of urban life, social static, the atmospheric blur of signs and sounds against which people, relationships, and events stand out in relief.

"Red noise" is urban social static with contemporary Chinese characteristics. It is the steady hum of sloganizing and "spiritual civilization" campaigns clashing with the harsher buzz of social fragmentation, political and economic decentralization, anarchy, even national decomposition: China no longer reconstructing, but deconstructing. The red noise of the late 1980s was a cacophony arising from decades of erratic party rule and ten years of economic reform. Its keynote is the concerns of urban people as opposed to the rural-centered world of Mao and his cohorts. Its strains included the angry voice of the punk, the hard-sell pitch of both entrepreneur and black marketeer, and the smooth, cynical patter of the streetwise *liumang* as well as the self-expressive murmurings and cries of the poets, artists, maverick philosophers, and rock 'n' rollers.

The red noise grated on the ears of China's gerontocratic leaders. Sometimes they just turned down their hearing aids and ignored the rumbling, but in more alert moments they tried to drown it out with stern and deadly declamations against Bourgelib, renewed attacks on the publishing industry, purges of intellectuals, or gentler campaigns for courtesy and civil consciousness. In their view and that of younger theorists like He Xin, social and intellectual discord has been prevalent since the beginning of the Cultural Revolution in 1966. They yearn after the relative order and stability of the 1950s with a nostalgia backed by military might and a huge, repressive state apparatus.

The *fin de siècle* ambience of China in the late 1980s was to many observers reminiscent of the decadent last years of an imperial dynasty. It was felt that morality had fallen by the wayside, while mendacity and

"70% Red, 25% Black, 5% White," installation art by Wu Shanzhuan
(*Fine Arts in China*)

corruption, both material and spiritual, had become the norm for both
the rulers and their subjects. It is particularly in such times that the
individualists of yesteryear would shun official careers and accept the
Buddhist view of worldly success and splendor as but "red dust," es-
chewing them for a carefree life of art, wine, and conversation; today
they might, like the protagonist of "Variations without a Theme,"
choose to live in a dream world rather than pursue any practical ambitions.

The sampling of red noise presented in this chapter both reflects the
unsettled atmosphere of urban China in the late 1980s—what could be
called the ambience of anarchy—and tells us something about how student-led demonstrations for democracy and against corruption could
swell into the far more broadly based Protest Movement of 1989, and
why the government was so fearful of that peaceful rebellion. After all,
in some ways the Reform era epitomized what was known in traditional
times as an Age of Prosperity *(shengshi)*. It was in another period of
unsettling transformations in the late nineteenth century that the indus-
trialist and reformer Zheng Guanying wrote his famous *Words of Warning for an Age of Prosperity (Shengshi weiyan)* in which he argued,
among other things, that long-term economic well-being was impossible
without political reform.

Between April and June 1989, the jumble of solipsistic voices, the red
noise of Peking, gave way to a chorus of dissatisfaction and concern for
the nation. But political activism called down death and violence, so that
once again many people turned to self-gratification, material, sexual, or
artistic. Since the Peking Massacre, the red noise has continued, though
it is less audible than before. To many in Peking, the new threnody of
red noise seemed to foretell the inevitable collapse of the regime.

A Portrait of the Novelist as a Young Man

ZUO SHULA

Wang Shuo was one of the most interesting writers to emerge in the late 1980s and certainly among the most popular. In 1988–89 no less than four of his stories were made into films. In his writing Wang captures the crude vitality of the entrepreneur unbound, the loose world of the modern criminal, and the boredom and amorality that occasionally lead good girls into the arms of bad men.

Zuo Shula, a Peking film critic born in 1954, is a practitioner of a Chinese style of new journalism. He spent a great deal of time interviewing and socializing with Wang Shuo before writing this piece, a portrait of both the writer and his time. Zuo's flippant tone captures the mood of the other Cultural Revolution generation, not the idealistic and disillusioned Red Guards but their younger brothers and sisters who witnessed it all but never believed in it—a generation to which both Zuo and Wang belong. This younger generation, people who are now in their twenties and early to mid thirties, were either just born or still in primary school at the inception of the Cultural Revolution. They grew up in a world both chaotic and mendacious and came of age in the materialistic 1980s, part of a consumer culture in which everything is up for sale.

The style of this portrait is as playful as Wang Shuo's fiction. The irreverent use of party jargon and political slogans is typical of the unofficial discourse of Zuo's generation.

Wang Shuo presents a challenge to other writers. While older establishment figures actually have to make an effort to "engage in life" by going on planned research trips for their new novels, Wang Shuo just lives. Not an official state writer with a fixed wage, he makes a living from his writing and enjoys an unfettered existence, spending his spare time playing mah-jongg with his friends. Wang Shuo is an individualist of the Reform era, an "unbound foot" of independent means.

Wang Shuo

Wang Shuo—Manchu Bannerman—is nothing much to look at. When the "historically unprecedented" Cultural Revolution broke out in 1966, he was in his second year of primary school. As Mao said, in those days every man was a law unto himself. Everything and everybody except for the Red Sun had been overthrown. Wherever you looked there were Big Character Posters spilling the dirt on central leaders and other famous people, turning all their private indiscretions into public knowledge. The spell had been broken, and all the leaders, bosses, stars, and writers, demigods in the past, came tumbling down from their lofty heights. Now people could see that they had the same foibles and were just as degenerate and shameless as everyone else, and were even prone, on occasion, to falling flat on their faces. Everyone except for the Supreme Commander—the Great Leader, Great Commander, Great Teacher, Great Helmsman Mao Zedong—was stripped of authority overnight. Now anybody could joke about the height of Party General Secretary Deng Xiaoping or take potshots at the august Premier Zhou Enlai or the head of the National People's Congress. . . .

Given this state of affairs, it didn't take much effort for little Wang Shuo to learn that his father, a military officer who'd boasted about fighting the Japs in the war, had actually worked for them as a policeman.

As the Cultural Revolution grew and took hold, so did the tendency among the kids of Peking to become delinquents. The Red Guards who had so solemnly taken part in the review of the revolutionary troops by Chairman Mao in Tiananmen Square on August 18, 1966, were becoming bored with Revolutionary Action. Drinking, gang warfare, chasing girls, and stealing army caps proved to be much more fun. Gangs sprang up throughout Peking with names like "The Three Schools United Front," "Village of One Million," and "State Economic Commission." Young toughs set out from their home turf, creating havoc and looking for thrills. Peking boys and girls from twelve to twenty lived for kicks and sex. In 1969, when the senior high school kids were all banished to the countryside, the city settled down a little.

"The prairie fires cannot burn all the grass; when the spring winds blow, it is reborn." * Wang Shuo's generation grew up in the 1970s, and there was nothing the older kids could do that they couldn't do even better. They let loose with a vengeance and took the town over again, though not on the same scale as the Red Guards.

Wang Shuo's parents subscribed to the theory "spare the rod and spoil the child." Every time he acted up, his father beat the shit out of him. This went on until the old boy was physically too feeble to get away with it. Apart from toughening Wang Shuo's hide, the beatings succeeded only in making him hate his old man. And given his father's dubious past, it was only natural that Wang Shuo's rebellion began at home.

One day, a big official from his father's hometown was purged. It had been this guy who'd led Wang's father's home district to join the Communists. The man's relations asked Wang's father to hide some of his belongings in their apartment, but he was so scared he surrendered them to the authorities. This act of disloyalty toward his former patron made Wang despise his father even more. Needless to say, by the time Wang Shuo was big enough to take on the old man, he could neither be talked nor beaten into compliance.

"You're nothing but a hooligan, a *liumang*!" his father shouted.

"Chairman Mao teaches us to distinguish between big and small problems. So-and-so's father was penalized for hooliganism, and still they let him have a position in the leadership. My case is insignificant compared with his," Wang Shuo retorted.

"You've got a real attitude problem, young man."

"Everyone makes mistakes. I'm just like you: a good person who's made mistakes."

The father exploded. "Get the hell out of here!"

* A line from the Tang poet Li Bo.

"Where to?" the son responded, not fazed in the slightest. "I wouldn't stay here if I had anywhere else to go. I'm a 'blossom' of the motherland, and it's your patriotic duty to raise me. Part of the wages and the apartment you get from the state are intended for me."

(Much of the dialogue in Wang Shuo's story "The Operators" * is taken from such exchanges.)

Wang Shuo was always looking for trouble, but he's neither strong nor quick on his feet. In fact, he's physically very ordinary. Whenever he gets into a fix, he hesitates; since he's unwilling to put his life on the line, he's not a good fighter. As hierarchy was gradually restored to the capital in the last years of the Cultural Revolution, with the army at the top of the heap, kids started comparing their fathers' ranks, and Wang ended up a loser.

Wang Shuo got himself thrown in the can twice while he was in high school. Jail was even worse than home: all dictatorship and no democracy. The "Uncle Policemen" had foul tempers and liked to keep in shape by using prisoners as punching bags. Wang swallowed his pride and pretended to accept it with good grace. It was a bum deal. The first time he was up for brawling. No courage was involved: thirty against six. And he'd thought there was safety in numbers. The second time was because of the Tiananmen Incident in 1976. Wang got carried away like everyone else in the mourning for Zhou Enlai, coupled, in his case, with a hatred for the police. He grabbed the cap off one of the cops who'd come to crush the protest and threw it into the air. What a feeling! He got three months. Every day he was given old Mao's "Call to Du Yuming to Surrender" to study.

Wang's got a sweet face, a quick wit, and a fast tongue, and the girls really fall for him. He knows it's not on account of his family background either. He's proud of his history of amorous conquests, though the goddess of love has not always smiled on him. On occasion he's come across older women with a lot of experience and his talents in bed failed to impress. True misery.

He'd always been a clever lad. He knew just how far his family could protect him, just how much he could get away with. Unlike the scions of other army families, he never stepped out of line, joining in gang-bangs or live-in orgies. At most he was guilty of noncriminal offenses like

---

* The film version of *The Operators (Wanzhu)*, directed by Mi Jiashan of Sichuan, was released under the English title *Three T Company* in 1989. It was one of the most popular films of the year. A particularly memorable scene satirizes the "misty" poets.

underage love or premarital sex. But these were enough to keep his parents in a state of constant anxiety. So his old man packed Wang Shuo off to the army the moment he graduated from high school in 1976, without bothering even to ask what *he* wanted to do. Let's be charitable and say Wang Shuo "followed in his father's footsteps."

Having been inducted into the "imperial navy," Wang Shuo at first felt quite proud. He was a medic on a degaussing boat stationed at Qingdao in Shandong, part of the North Sea Fleet. His ship rarely went to sea, and the complement was only about eighty all told, although for some mysterious reason over a hundred people always turned up at mealtimes. In those days the daily food allowance was 45 fen: that meant corn bread and pickled vegetables every meal. Wang Shuo had no trouble coping with this, it was the hierarchy that really got up his nose. Two incidents entirely destroyed the idealized image he had held of the armed forces as a grand school of Mao Zedong Thought.

The first was the time he stood watch on a freezing cold night. Everything was dark, except for a light in the kitchen. Shivering and curious, Wang went over and peered into the kitchen window. What did he see but a senior officer gorging himself at a table weighed down with food and drink. Beads of sweat had appeared on the top of the officer's head, and his face was shining and oily. Stuck with his measly diet, Wang was mightily pissed off. "The bastard's living off our blood! 'No distinction between officers and enlisted men,' my ass!"

The second occasion was on a national holiday when they were given a rare treat: a banquet. Wang and his mates were looking forward to a royal pig-out. But just as they sat down several top brass appeared out of thin air, making even the commander jittery. The mess didn't have time to prepare anything special for them, so Wang and two of his mates were made to give up their places at the table to the VIPs. The sailors' faces turned sour, and their commissar, after having got his fill of food and wine, thought he'd better give them an ideological pep talk. "It's the same as if you had unexpected guests at home one day. Naturally, the kids have to leave the table. You're like our kids; the top brass are our guests. That's why you've had to make a bit of a sacrifice. But it's only one meal: no big deal." They didn't dare answer back, but they were bloody well unimpressed by his logic.

After this disillusioning experience, Wang Shuo's depression blossomed into open rebellion. One minute he was out chasing women, the next swimming and mucking around on the beach. He did as he pleased and became a sailor of leisure. He took no notice of rules and regulations. A serviceman who doesn't have the slightest interest in joining the party or getting a commission and doesn't break the law can get away with a hell of a lot. At worst he'd be booted out. So what was there to be scared of? Besides, it was pretty cool to be a navy man who didn't return to his barracks at night and was often seen strolling along the beach with a woman on his arm. "Let our thinking break free of all restraints, the Internationale will be realized!" was Wang Shuo's theme song.

He began writing fiction. His first story, "Waiting," was published in the monthly *PLA Arts* in 1978. The "story of a girl who freed herself of her family," it impressed the editors so much that they had him transferred to the magazine, the armed forces' most prestigious literary journal, as an editor. His commander was stunned. "Incredible! Looks like fools have all the luck!" And he concluded from this unexpected train of events that Wang had some heavy connections. Wang let him believe what he wanted. Watching the others torture themselves with speculation, he couldn't help grinning to himself in wicked delight under his covers at night.

Wang was too much of a live wire for the editing job. . . . The Third Plenum of 1978 had just been held, and everyone was carrying on about the Open Door and Reform. Wang was bored with editing. He saw an opening in the party's "strategic decision" to emphasize economic construction over politics. So he joined up with some old friends to become the boss of a smuggling operation. People were much simpler back then; the Chinese hadn't become as sly and calculating as they are today. It was easy to swindle dopes with money, they were everywhere you looked. Trading in contraband color TVs and tape recorders alone, the gang made a clear 100 to 200 percent profit. Wang Shuo took to trade effortlessly and, with the protection of his uniform, traveled all over the place, doing the milk run from Shenzhen to Peking via Guangzhou, Shanghai, Suzhou, and Hangzhou. One moment he'd be buying a color TV for some army unit, the next picking up a tape recorder for someone else, using other people's money to make a neat profit on the side for himself. Everyone was happy with the results, and people liked doing business with someone who could deliver the goods. With money in his pocket, Wang Shuo took on a new air of confidence, and it became even easier for him to make it with women. He lived for the moment, didn't miss home, and didn't give a damn for his reputation or future. He was happy and content.

In no time at all it was 1979. One day, while taking a stroll in Guangzhou, he overheard the news on the radio that China had begun a self-defensive war against Vietnam. Wang was, after all, the son of an army man and he responded as one. Drawing a tight rein on his feral mind, he gave in to an overwhelming sense of duty. Somewhat hysterically, he bade farewell to his gang and headed for his base to await orders. He bumped into some bad luck on the way, though: His pocket was picked at the train station. Even when the fellows seeing him off put all the money they had together it came to only 7 yuan, not nearly enough for a ticket. It wasn't the money that mattered: To be away from his post at a time of war was unforgivable. Wang Shuo started swearing his head off. Luckily for him, there are some decent people in the world as well, and a genuine Labor Hero generously bought him a ticket. This wiped the smirk right off Wang's face. "I can't just take this from you," he said sincerely, yanking the watch off the wrist of one of his friends and shoving it gratefully into the Labor Hero's hands. "Keep this till he pays you back!" And thus the "living Lei Feng," * Wang Shuo, rushed back to Qingdao with his head full of thoughts of protecting the motherland.

On the train Wang's head was filled with images of the intensive war training he imagined his comrades would surely be undergoing, and he expected to find them straining for a fight. Reality came as a bit of a shock: The usual placid state of affairs reigned; and no one was giving a thought to the front. It was as though the war was in another country, nothing to do with the North Sea Fleet in any case. Amazed by Wang's excited state, people looked at him as though he was off his head. "What are you doing back here?" the new commander said. Thinking Wang Shuo had been transferred to some cushy job elsewhere, the commander had struck him from the record long ago. No one knew what to do with him.

The cool reception brought him to his senses, and he went back to cruising the streets, getting up to his old tricks. Since he wasn't on the books in the first place, none of the commanders felt compelled to do anything about him. In 1980 he was demobilized. When he said he wanted to go, the leadership hesitated, grateful to him for all those TVs. "Shouldn't we at least help you get into the party?" Wang Shuo didn't balk at the suggestion: "All right, then, sign me up!" "Not so fast—I'm afraid we'll have to see how you do for another year." That was enough to send Wang packing, though he put on a show of high-mindedness: "Give the opening to some other comrade. Anyway, now that the party's

---

* Lei Feng was a model PLA soldier of the 1960s. Said to be something of a Red Samaritan and general do-gooder, he became a model for emulation after being killed in an accident. "Learn from Lei Feng" campaigns have been used by the party for a quarter of a century in times of army dominance or social and political disunity. Predictably, the party launched a major "Learn from Lei Feng" campaign in late 1989.

emphasizing economic construction, I'd better get home to do my bit for the Four Modernizations."

Back in Peking he got work as a salesman for the Peking Pharmaceutical Company, which meant he now spent all his time with a pack of small businessmen whose shops had been nationalized in the 1950s. He had nothing to do but smoke, drink tea, read the papers, and chat all day. The greasy little bosses sat around talking about the sexual dalliances of their youth with great nostalgia, competing with one another in exaggerating their past conquests and boasting of their sexual prowess. Around this time the minister of commerce was criticized in the press for getting free meals at a high-class restaurant, the Fengzeyuan. One of the fellows showered him with scorn: "What a pathetic no-hoper. When a Nationalist official went out to eat in the old days, he'd pay three times the amount on the check. Now that's what I call style." As the son of an old party cadre, Wang Shuo was deeply shocked; things had turned full circle, all right, and here was some petit bourgeois businessman taking the piss out of a Communist Party member. A sorry state of affairs, indeed.

Three years with the company passed quickly. He clocked in every day and chatted for a while before going to Xisi [in central Peking] to see if he could pick up a ticket for the movies. Then there was lunch, after which he'd have a rave about life in general with the female Youth League secretary, then he'd clock off and go home. It was dead boring.

He mucked around like this until 1982, when Party Central began a campaign to "strike hard" against economic criminals. His army friends who'd been trading illegally in electrical goods landed themselves in jail for "hooliganism" and Wang Shuo was named as an accomplice. He was called into the local cop shop a number of times and had no choice but to plead guilty to having made 1,000 yuan in illegal earnings. The police ordered it docked from his wages. They took 30 yuan from his monthly wage packet of 36 yuan. He figured it wasn't worth going to work for a measly 6 yuan, so he stopped going to the office. Everyone else was concentrating on "economic construction," and he figured he'd try his hand at starting a company or a restaurant. But things were different now. Everyone and his dog were into business and they were pretty damn clever at it, too. The good old days of easy money were over. Of every hundred deals, only one ever came good. When he got a warning from his company that if he didn't get back to work within three days he'd be fired, he took the hint and quit. It was 1983. His application to resign took a very high-minded tone: "There are countless young people waiting for employment at the moment; in consider-

> It's fashionable nowadays to talk about personal autonomy,
> though most people who do so live their lives bound to their work-
> place, never making a move without considering the reaction of
> others. So where's the autonomy? It's the same when you get
> involved in any literary or film clique. The minute you're "in," you
> feel oppressed. The parasites head straight for you, the new hot
> property, and watch out if you're not one to look up to them. It's so
> alienating, you might as well steer clear of the scene altogether.
> You'll have more peace of mind that way. . . .
>
> Once you are emotionally and materially independent, you can
> live a free and easy life. We are tormented and bound by the ex-
> cessive emphasis we put on our personal desires. But if you're not
> after anything, you can't lose out. I don't think this attitude can be
> dismissed as mere cynicism or world-weariness. It represents a
> different attitude toward the goals of life. These people are more
> relaxed, more at peace with themselves. Most of the rest of us are
> too greedy for that.
>
> —*Zuo Shula*

ation of the needs of the state, I've decided to give up my job to a needy comrade."

Although he knew he was not cut out for business, Wang Shuo had no choice but to try his hand. Luckily, he came across a young fellow who was a fiend in business but also a real coward. He was a bagman; but he always shook with fear when the crucial moment came to hand over the goods and collect the money. Offering to do the job, Wang Shuo said he led a charmed life; the fact was that he needed the money. So he became a professional bagman, like the hero of the film *Samsara*,* some-times handling as much as tens of thousands of yuan. Carrying all that money never worried him, and he got what for the time was very decent pay. He kept at this for a while, planning to use his savings to buy a secondhand taxi. But he'd learned his lesson: He knew these greedy characters would make themselves a pile and then let him take the flak for it. He decided to make a clean break with the lot of them.

But his savings didn't last, and with nothing coming in it wasn't long before Wang Shuo was flat broke and living off borrowed money. His

---

* A film made by Huang Jianxin of the Xi'an Film Studio, released in 1989. *Samsara* (*Lunhui*), also known as *Wheel of Life*, is based roughly on Wang's story "Flotsam" ("*Xiangpiren*").

first victim was the Youth League secretary from the pharmaceutical company. She wasn't too bad-looking, and she'd enjoyed their heartfelt talks. "Well," Wang argued, "she was always going on about her proletarian ideals. I gave her a chance to save a wayward youth; to make some brownie points for herself." If she hadn't turned up on his doorstep a few years later to demand repayment, she would probably never have seen that 100 yuan again.

Soon he headed south for Guangzhou. With only seven cents in his pocket, he managed to latch on to an air hostess in Air China. He became her kept man. . . .

Wang Shuo began writing fiction again. That's how he came to publish the story "Air Hostess" in 1984. It was purely autobiographical, not much imagination involved. Though I haven't read it, they tell me it's quite a sweet and romantic little piece. If that's the case, then I know it's fake: Don't believe a word of it. When he was living off the hostess, Wang Shuo was already having it on with the woman who was to become his wife. . . . He wrote that into a story as well, and Huang Jianxin turned it into the movie *Samsara*. According to Wang Shuo it's more honest.

But he was upfront with the air hostess. He told her he was in love with someone else and he wanted to break up with her. She had a crying fit, and while trying to comfort her he felt he'd been a real shit and started weeping, too. After this drama they made a clean break; he still hasn't paid her back. After living with his wife (a dancer) illegally for two years, they got married. They now have a daughter.

In 1989 Wang Shuo published two new stories, the first a merciless parody of the Peking literary scene that even poked fun at Bei Dao's petition for the release of Wei Jingsheng, and the second, which appeared after the massacre, a devastatingly funny and perceptive political and social satire. In August 1990, Wang and his friends opened a kara-oke club in central Peking. A visitor to the club—which advertised itself as a gathering spot for famous cultural figures—reportedly witnessed a brawl during which all the kara-oke television screens were broken. The floor manager that night commented to one stunned observer: "This sort of thing always happens when writers get together."

Wang's fiction and the films based on it have been attacked fitfully in the Chinese media for their flippancy.

Hot and Cold,
Measure for Measure

WANG SHUO

I

"Two couples have just gone into 927 and 1208. Oh yeah, and there's some slut in 1713 as well."

"Right."

I put down the receiver, threw on my suit jacket, and grabbed my bag. I told Fangfang, who lay sprawled in front of the television, to get his act together. We ran downstairs and headed for the old Peugeot I'd managed to pick up for only 4,000 yuan. It was parked on the corner. We jumped in and took off in the direction of the Yandu Hotel, by now ablaze with lights. I found a place to park behind a row of cars in a shady street at the back of the hotel. Hopping out, we raced to catch up with a group of Japanese tourists who'd just descended from a tour bus, our ticket to the magnificent foyer that lay within.

Weining was manning the reception desk, a model of courtesy. He gave us an almost imperceptible wink. So far, so good. We went into the Gents and I pulled two police uniforms out of the bag. I handed one to Fangfang. We changed into them and took the back stairs to the ninth floor. After pausing a moment to recover our breath, we strode over to the service desk. The attendant looked up at us in surprise.

"Police. Kindly open room 927."

Picking up a set of keys, he obediently led us to a room at the end of the long corridor. Seeing the "Do Not Disturb" sign, he turned and said, "But the guest is in the room."

"We know. Open it!"

He did as he was told and stood to one side.

"Now get out of here," Fangfang said with a dismissive wave of the hand. As soon as the attendant disappeared down the corridor, we stormed into the room.

"A Young Friend," Tong Hongsheng (*Fine Arts in China*)

We left with Yahong in tow and several thousand yuan in crisp new bills in the bag. Our expressions were deadly serious when we passed the attendant, but as soon as we entered the lift Fangfang and Yahong burst out laughing.

"What's so goddamn funny?" I said, then started laughing myself. "Wait for us in the bar downstairs," I told Yahong. "We still have a guy on the twelfth floor to deal with." We dropped Yahong off on the ground floor and took the lift back up.

Fifteen minutes later we were back in our street clothes and in the bar with Yahong and the other tart. We had a drink together and Fangfang left with Yahong on his arm. I gave Weining a call at the desk to let him know the job was done. As for the hooker on the seventeenth floor, I told him to let her have a good night's sleep. He could call the police the next morning. I left the hotel in a calm mood, arm in arm with the other girl. By this stage Fangfang had already brought the car around; we hopped in and sped off.

I was woken the next morning by the telephone. Yahong, who lay sleeping by my side, answered it and said it was Weining. He'd called to say that the two suckers had left that morning after paying the bill, while the other girl had been picked up by the police as she left. Yahong rolled over and went back to sleep. I lay there chain-smoking. Sunlight streamed in through the heavy curtains. I crept over to the window to gaze out through the narrow crack at the bright and busy street below. I drew the curtains shut. I hate sunny mornings; the sight of all those people happily toddling off to work and school makes me feel lonely. I've nothing to do in the daytime; no business to conduct and no one to see. All my friends are asleep. I smoked another five cigarettes, then checked the date on the calendar before finally throwing on some clothes and having a quick wash. I left the apartment building and walked to the bus stop, passing my car, which I'd left parked at the corner.

It was past rush hour, but the passengers were still packed in like sardines. A middle-aged man had just got off the bus and I was about to grab his seat when I saw a young woman with a child in her arms. I gave her my seat.

"Thank you." Smiling, she turned to her child. "Say, 'Thank you, Uncle.' "

"Thank you, Uncle," the child obliged, and I smiled back at him. Reaching into his pocket, he extracted a bar of chocolate in a brightly colored wrapper. He tore off the paper and was at the point of putting it into his mouth when he noticed I was watching him. He held it up to me.

"No, thanks. Uncle doesn't want any."

"Go on, it's okay."

"No, really. Uncle's got to get off the bus now."

I squeezed off the bus. From there I made my way to the clinic attached to my work unit and asked for the sick leave form in triplicate. Then I phoned a buddy of mine who has liver problems and asked him to go take my blood test for me. My next stop was the business district, where I deposited last night's earnings in accounts at two different banks. Both accounts are in the names of my late parents. My final call was at the post office, where I remitted the registration fee and a year's tuition to a correspondence school. It's the type of school where you can pick up a university degree without ever taking an exam. I'd chosen law for my major.

Having completed the day's tasks, I went to lunch at an upmarket but quiet restaurant. The food at this place is tops. I started getting into the red wine, picking a bottle for its pretty label, and rounded the meal off with an ice cream sundae drenched in chocolate syrup. I didn't leave till well into the afternoon. At the newsstand I bought the morning and evening papers, then went to the Telephone and Telegraph Building. There I grabbed a seat in the waiting room for long-distance calls and read the papers at a leisurely pace. At dusk I called home and spoke to Fangfang. He'd spent the day playing chess with Weining, who'd been there since morning. By now Fangfang had won four games, drawn three, and lost five. They were planning a mah-jongg session for the evening. I told him I'd be home late and hung up.

It was late spring. Everywhere the trees and grass provided a dense green cover and the flowers were in full bloom. An evening concert was being held in the park, so I stood in front of the box office waiting for someone to return a ticket. Eventually some old guy gave me his, but there was a couple with only one ticket so I gave it to them, refusing their offer to pay double for it.

I wandered along a long causeway with tall pillars the paint of which had grown dry and was crusty and peeling. It was then that I saw this attractive young girl sitting on a white marble platform, reading. She sat there with her legs crossed and dangling, swinging back and forth over the side. She held her book in one hand while the other was engaged in extracting melon seeds from a small bag by her side. The discarded shells had been placed in a tidy pile. She sat there softly humming, turning a page from time to time. She seemed so laid-back, she looked cool. I stole up behind her and tried to see what book could be so engrossing. I skimmed the page over her shoulder—it was a heavy, abstract tome on literary theory, too dull for words. I was at the point of walking away when I heard her say, "Over your head?" She was grinning at me.

I felt myself blushing. I didn't know I could still blush. Amazing. Getting a hold of myself, I responded, "Right, so you're a student. But isn't this business of reading in the park at night a bit of a put-on?"

"Actually, I've been here all afternoon. Look how much I've read!"

I flicked through the pages she'd said she'd read. Impressive. But considering the subject matter, I was dubious, so I asked, "How can you possibly read this so quickly?"

"Because I don't understand it either, that's why."

We laughed.

"I'm not going to read any more tonight," she put the book down. "What are you up to?"

"Nothing."

"Stay and talk for a bit, then."

"Sure." I sat down beside her. She gave me a handful of melon seeds. I've never been able to crack them open with my teeth, they sort of just disintegrate in my mouth.

"Here. I'll show you." She demonstrated how to crack a seed with your teeth, her white teeth gleaming as she did so. Somewhat self-consciously, I closed my mouth to hide my nicotine-stained teeth. She didn't seem to notice, gazing around as she swung her legs.

"Which university are you at?" I'd noticed the university badge on her sweater.

"I suppose this is your pickup line. Then you'll tell me where you study, how close our campuses are, and how easy it would be to see a lot of each other . . ."

"Do I look like a student?" was my reply. "I'm an ex-con from a labor camp. At the moment I'm trying my hand at blackmail."

"I don't give a damn what you are." She smiled down at her toes as if they were terribly amusing. "I really couldn't care less."

We sat there in silence for what seemed an eternity, gazing contentedly at the setting sun and the rapidly approaching darkness. The clouds were still visible and quite magnificent.

"Look, that cloud looks like Marx, and that one over there looks a bit like a pirate, don't you think?"

"How old are you?"

She turned and studied me. "You haven't had much experience with women, have you?"

"No, I haven't." I delivered this line totally poker-faced.

"I knew it the moment I saw you. You're just a kid. I could tell from the way you hovered there in the distance, trying to pluck up the courage to come over and talk to me. You were afraid I was going to say something to embarrass you, weren't you?"

"Actually, I've slept with more than a hundred girls."

She shrieked with laughter.

"You have a moronic laugh," I told her.

She stopped laughing and threw me a resentful look. "Look, I'm not dumping on you, so lay off me, okay? To tell you the truth, I've been going out with someone for over a year." She smiled smugly.

"Who is he? Some fuckwit classmate of yours?"

"He's definitely no fuckwit! He's a cadre in the Student Union!"

"Doesn't that prove my point? You can't get much worse than that."

"Hmph. You should talk. Your mother is the only woman who's ever kissed you, that's for sure."

"If I were him, at least I'd be man enough to sleep with you," I said with a smirk. "Tell me, does he?" Although it was already dark, I could see she had turned bright red.

"He respects me!"

I sniggered. "Respect? Bullshit! Give me a break. You don't really think I was born yesterday, do you?"

This got her. She sat there for ages without a word. I whistled to myself. Then I pulled out a pack of cigarettes, put one into my mouth, and offered one to her. She shook her head.

"So that's it? You'll read in a park, but you don't smoke. You're not really as trendy as you look."

"Cut the crap." She wasn't one to accept defeat. "Give me one."

I gave her the one from my lips. She took one puff and started coughing. I put my arm around her shoulders, and although she trembled, she didn't object. I drew her toward me and she examined me closely. Then she threw off my arm and burst out laughing.

"I'm beginning to believe this business about the hundred girls."

"Hey, it's the gospel truth. You know what they call me? 'Shotgun.' "

She gathered up her books. My laughter had a malicious tinge. "I've frightened you."

"No, you haven't." She stood up. "But . . . I've got to be going."

"How about a little name and address action before you go?"

Her eyes flashed, and she hopped off the platform. "So! At first I really did think you were different from the rest. But you're as crass as they come."

"Okay, so I'm crass. I'm not going to hold you up if you want to go. But," I called out to her as she walked away, "if we meet again we're friends, right?"

"Sure." She walked away laughing.

I sat there grinning to myself for a while, then I split, too.

II

Fangfang and I were cruising down one of the main drags, keeping an eye out for the talent. When we found any, Fangfang would pull up alongside the curb and we'd try to chat her up. If she wouldn't take the bait, we'd just laugh and drive on, taking the piss out of her as we went. Suddenly we spotted two young women who'd just come out of a grocery store with some fruit juice, and they were laughing and talking as they strolled along. Fangfang pulled up beside them. Winding down the window, I called out "Hey!" The two girls stopped and turned around.

"Don't you recognize me?" I asked.

"Oh, it's you!" replied one of the girls, grinning. "What a coincidence. What're you doing?"

"Looking for you," I said. "I haven't stopped thinking about you since we met."

"Ha! What a come-on!"

"Do you know him?" the second girl whispered to her friend.

"No, not really," the girl I'd met in the park told her friend, "but he admits himself that he's a real *liumang*."*

We all laughed at this. Leaning across, I opened the back door. "Jump in, we'll take you for a spin." As the two girls climbed in, Fangfang put the car into gear and we took off.

"Oh, by the way, I'm Zhang Ming, and this is my friend Fangfang." Fangfang turned around and smiled.

It was my girl's turn. "This is my friend Chen Weiling, and I'm Wu Di."

"Di? Oh, right, that means 'terrific.' "

"Yeah." Wu Di nodded, smiling.

"Where are you headed?"

"To the auditorium just around the corner."

"What's the movie?" Fangfang kept his eyes on the road.

"Oh, it's not a movie. It's a lecture: 'Young Readers Discuss Spiritual Civilization.' "

"What the hell is that?"

"It's probably one of those student things." Fangfang pulled a face.

"You're studying arts subjects, aren't you?"

"How did you know?" Wu Di asked with curious delight.

"It's simple. Women who study science look like the back end of a bus."

"You're outrageous." She laughed uncontrollably, obviously pleased by the flattery. "We study English."

"And what are you? Taxi drivers?" Chen Weiling asked with all the warmth of an iceberg.

"I've already told Wu Di. We're two ex-cons from a labor reform camp."

Wu Di just smiled, but Chen Weiling frowned and gazed out the window. It was obvious she didn't believe me. She'd already decided we were nothing but a couple of bored playboys, beneath contempt. "He told me," Wu Di addressed her friend while looking straight at me, "that he's slept his way through the phone book."

Chen Weiling glared at me briefly. To say she didn't like me would be an understatement. She wasn't a bit like Wu Di. I couldn't really give a fuck what she thought. She didn't even vaguely interest me.

We managed to park right outside the auditorium. A great many

---

* Hooligan (see pp. 247–50).

students were milling around in groups of three and four, people were rushing to and fro. A real lively scene.

I motioned to Wu Di to come closer and whispered in her ear, "Meet me at the Monument to the People's Heroes tomorrow at four, okay?"

She smiled. Meanwhile, Fangfang was attempting to hold a conversation with Chen Weiling. She'd already rendered him completely speechless.

"Are you frightened your boyfriend will be jealous?"

"He doesn't care who I see. He's very open-minded."

"Then what are you frightened of?"

"Come in and listen to the speeches, and I'll tell you afterward whether I'm coming or not."

"I really can't bear the thought of listening to those wankers. Anyway, why bother listening to them when you've got me?"

"If you don't come, then tomorrow's definitely off."

"Hey, Fangfang, what do you think, shall we go in or not?"

"If we're going, let's go." Fangfang sounded completely indifferent. "Anyway, we've got nothing else on, so we might as well check it out."

"Okay, let's go." I turned to Wu Di. "You'd better come tomorrow."

"We'll talk about it later."

As she got out of the car, Chen Weiling asked Wu Di, "Where'd he ask you to go?"

"Nowhere in particular. He just asked me to go out with him, that's all."

"And you're going?" Chen Weiling's tone of voice was severe.

"I didn't say either way." Wu Di was deliberately vague.

Fangfang and I got out of the car and followed the two girls inside. They ran into some classmates and stopped to chat, so the two of us went on ahead and found some empty seats on the aisle. Soon they came looking for us. I tossed aside the bookbags on the two seats next to us, at which point the girl who'd been saving the seats for her friends mumbled something and threw me an angry look. When Wu Di settled herself, she proceeded to give a preview of what was to come, sort of a vaccination. She told us how good the speakers were, how what they had to say was jam-packed with educational value, truly earth-shattering stuff, and that you could never get bored no matter how many times you heard it.

The first speaker was a woman worker of some description. As soon as she took the stage Fangfang and I burst out laughing. The speakers ran the usual spectrum of workers, peasants, students, and businessmen. They all spoke very forcefully, dramatically waving their hands about and shouting so loudly that the veins in their necks and faces bulged. As for content, it was all the standard bullshit about how young people should study hard and love the motherland and such. I'd heard it all a million times before. They threw in all the usual historical anecdotes, so it sounded like a recitation from the *Popular Household Book of Historical Facts*. Then they recited a few poems of the "rabidly revolutionary" school. It was like all these people had popped out of the same boring mold. When some slick young man took the stage and started rabbiting on about how the young people of today should "cultivate the flowers of love," I laughed so hard I almost wet my pants. This was so different from the appreciative murmurs issuing from the rest of the audience that Chen Weiling glared at me angrily. Wu Di gave me a small but sharp nudge.

"You should pay a bit more attention." Chen Weiling was pissed off. "Someone as ignorant as you could do with a little education."

I replied in my best embarrassingly loud voice: "I was getting this sort of education when you were still a twinkle in your daddy's eye."

Chen Weiling turned bright red. Wu Di, at a loss for what else to do and wanting to avoid the burning looks coming from all directions, pretended to be totally absorbed by the lecture.

"Just look at you!" Fangfang said to Chen Weiling. "All this fuckin' education and you've still got shit for brains. What a joke." He turned to me. "Come on, don't waste your breath. We're outta here."

> I know just what I'm capable of. If you think I should be doing something for others, serving the people or whatnot, well, quite frankly, I reckon about the only thing I could manage in that department is to polish their shoes. I've got no other talents. I've gotten this far, and apart from my mouth, which has been overexercised, everything else is underdeveloped. I can't just go out and lie to people, can I? (Anyway, I've tried and it doesn't work.) It's no fun, either—you need to know just as much as you do to write fiction, and it doesn't have the same status. . . . Although writing isn't entirely the same as prostitution, you can get away with it as long as you're shameless enough. Even now I wouldn't say I'm a master of the technique of fiction writing. Buggered if I know all the ins and outs of it. And if you want me to natter on about intellectual content, philosophy, the grand sweep . . . well, give me a break.
>
> —Wang Shuo

We went out into the foyer and stood there smoking, laughing about the whole thing, when Fangfang suddenly nudged me. "Hey." I turned around and saw Wu Di coming in. She caught sight of us and approached somewhat timidly, her face reddening.

"Are you angry with us?"

"No. Should I be?"

"That classmate of yours is bloody rude," Fangfang commented.

Looking up at me, Wu Di said, "You really insulted her. Right now she's sitting there crying, you know."

"Well, say sorry for us, will you? We didn't mean to upset her. She a good friend of yours?" I added.

"Sort of. We're classmates, but I wouldn't say we're the greatest of friends."

"Wu Di!"

"Yeah?" Wu Di spun around to see the young student who'd just been speaking walking toward us.

"This is my friend" was her muttered introduction. She blushed when she saw the look of amusement in our eyes.

"Oh, so you're Wu Di's friends." He sounded quite enthusiastic. "My speech must have been really awful to make you laugh like that."

"Oh, no, no, no. It was really good," I said in my most courteous voice.

"A lot better than the others." Even Fangfang felt sorry for him.

"I was told to do it, and I hardly had any time to prepare, so—" He was a down-to-earth sort of guy.

"Han Jin!" By now the foyer was crammed with people and a group of guys were calling to Wu Di's boyfriend.

"Catch you later," said Han Jin, moving off to join them.

"Nice guy," I remarked appreciatively.

"I can tell you don't think much of him." Wu Di looked deeply distressed.

"What do you mean? We were just being assholes, don't take it so seriously! We're just working-class guys, about as low as they come," I said in all sincerity. "We wouldn't dare look down on anyone."

"Forget it, no need to put yourself down." Wu Di's sidelong glance showed her growing annoyance.

"Mr. Shi!" she suddenly called out to a man about thirty years of age.

"Oh, hello, Wu Di." The man stopped and chatted happily with Wu Di until he caught sight of Fangfang and me. His smile evaporated.

"Hello, *Mister* Shi," Fangfang addressed him with obvious sarcasm.

"Hello Zhang Ming, Fangfang." Shi Yide smiled unconvincingly. We all shook hands.

"A university cadre, are you? Will wonders never cease?" I kidded him. "A real Youth League cadre. Well, where there's a will there's a way." Then I explained to Wu Di, who was standing there really out of it, "We're old classmates. None of us ever graduated. He ended up working for the school's Youth League, while the two of us were expelled."

III

I sat on the stone steps of the Monument to the People's Heroes. I didn't know if she'd come. It didn't worry me—it was a lovely day and a warm wind was caressing me. A crowd of old folks and children were flying kites on Tiananmen Square. Phoenixes pranced, eagles soared, and swallows fluttered against the blue sky. But everyone, foreign tourists as well as the Chinese, was watching a brightly colored centipede over ten meters long that this old guy was flying. It was rising and falling in a leisurely, relaxed way, and the crowd was staring up at it, clapping and shouting.

Over to the west side of the square, in front of the Great Hall of the People, the premier was conducting a formal welcoming ceremony for some foreign dignitary. As the cannon was fired in salute, the immaculate army band played the two national anthems on their gleaming brass instruments. The two heads of state, accompanied by their retinues, strode along a red carpet, reviewing the combined services' guard of honor.

I looked at my watch. It was past four. I stood up and climbed to the base of the monument to look out over the square. In the distance I saw a girl in a cream-colored embroidered silk blouse and a short blue and white batik skirt running in my direction. She slowed down only when she reached the flower garden in front of the monument. She looked around. Her gaze passed over me, but I didn't call out to her. I watched patiently as she checked the time on her watch and moved the minute hand back. Slowly she ambled up the steps of the monument and over to where I was standing—and stopped abruptly. I burst out laughing. "I wanted to see if you could spot me or not. Am I that inconspicuous?"

She just laughed and looked at me without saying anything.

"You're ten minutes late."

"No, I'm not!" She raised her slender wrist to show me her watch.

"Give me a break." I had caught her little game. "I saw you move the watch hand."

She giggled with embarrassment. The guard of honor presented arms as the two heads of state watched solemnly from the reviewing stand.

"I didn't think you'd show."

"Why not?"

"I thought Shi Yide and Chen Weiling were bound to say all sorts of bad things about me."

She laughed and glanced at me: "Shi Yide didn't really put you down. He said that although you and he didn't hit it off very well then, he always thought you were a really clever person, just a bit self-destructive."

"And what did Chen Weiling say?"

She smiled.

"Go on."

"It's not nice."

"Oh, come on. What do I care what people say about me?"

"She said you were a shameless *liumang*, the dregs of society. But really, you did treat her awfully badly."

"Did she tell you not to have anything more to do with me?"

"Yes."

"But you came all the same."

"Well, who's she to tell me what to do?"

"Right on."

"Of course."

The ceremony in front of the Great Hall was over. The motorcade of black luxury sedans drove off in single file behind a police motorcycle escort. The spectators slowly dispersed.

Wu Di and I walked along Qianmen East Street toward Chongwenmen. To begin with, we walked slightly apart from each other, but there were so many people and vehicles about that we were either always being separated or we kept bumping into each other. So it was quite natural for her to take my arm. I didn't have any job planned for that evening, so I could spend it with her. To tell the truth, the only thing I had in mind was getting her into the sack.

Yesterday in the car, after the lecture, I'd said to Fangfang: "I can't stand that bitch. She's about as warm as a piece of cloisonné."

"Who? Chen Weiling?"

"Of course. Our little Wu Di isn't bad, though, is she?"

"Have you scored a date?"

"Mais oui!"

"Hey, foreigner, you'll go far."

"She's really quite cute. But a little too naïve for my taste. I don't feel right about putting the make on her."

"Don't make me barf. As if it'll be the first time she's done it." Fang-fang put his foot down on the accelerator and turned a corner sharply.

"No way. She's an innocent. Hit the books all during high school and then went straight to university." I recited the curriculum vitae as I smoked a cigarette. "It's all a novelty for her. She wants to try everything. She's at the age where she's attracted to danger, she'd run straight at the barrel of a gun. Give me the key to your apartment, will you?"

"I should warn you, I'm a dangerous friend to have. I get up to things you don't even know about."

We were having a meal at a very quiet restaurant. After the waiters served the meal, they retreated to a far corner. I know that the best way of chatting up a girl who despises everything conventional and fancies herself a noncomformist is to make yourself out to be a bastard. Not only will she think you're more interesting, she'll even like you better for it. It's just like if you describe someone as being really hideous when in fact they're not that ugly. A girl will then try to find your good points rather than being hypercritical and just look for faults.

"I'm greedy, a sex maniac, and a complete moral wipeout. Every day I dress up as a police officer in order to blackmail Hong Kong businessmen and foreigners. I'm a criminal at large. You'd be doing everyone a service if you reported me to the police."

"I could tell right from the beginning. I'm actually an undercover police officer, and I've got you under surveillance."

"You've got a tape recorder in your handbag, right?"

"You bet."

"Is that guy over there one of yours?" I pointed to a waiter standing at attention with his hands at his side, staring across from the other side of the room.

"Yes." Wu Di looked across at the waiter and then back at me. She laughed. "Our men are everywhere."

We had a good laugh and then chatted about other things.

"Did you think the lectures yesterday were really that unbearable?" Wu Di asked.

"Oh, they weren't that bad." I drank some wine. "To be able to go on and on about obvious things like that is a kind of talent in itself."

"You looked as if you totally despised the lot of us."

"I just felt that it was all a bit beneath you university students to like that kind of thing. If you want to find out about something, why don't you just read a few books? I got so fed up with the patronizing tone of those speakers. What do they take you for? Who's more stupid than whom around here? All this crap about how to study, even how to fall in love. It's none of their bloody business. They're all still wet behind the ears, but they're up there preaching at others."

"Does that mean Your Majesty reads and searches for the truth on his own?"

"Wrong!" I grinned at her cheekily. "I've not the type of person to get anything out of books. Why not live the way you want to? Enjoy yourself, go through a few hard times, cry a bit, laugh a bit, do what moves you. Better than burying yourself in a book and heaving sighs over someone else's life. You have to take control of your own life."

"But can't you learn from other people's experience and mistakes? Doesn't it help you to define your own aims more clearly?"

"I don't want to know how things are going to end up. Slogging along at something, bit by bit, step by step, that's too boring. The more vision, the less excitement. If I knew my next move and what I'd be up against each step of the way and what would happen each time, I'd immediately lose all interest in living."

"And so . . . ?"

"And so, as soon as I discovered that I'd earn only 56 yuan a month after graduation from university, I left school. And so, as soon as I discovered I was going to be a lowly clerk all my life, I stopped going to work."

"But you can't avoid death. . . ."

"So I don't waste my time. Eat, drink, and rage to the limit. As long as you have to live, you might as well try everything, right? Stick your chopsticks into every dish at the banquet."

"Aren't the hundred 'dishes' you've tasted enough for you? You can die happy!"

"Each is different. Even noodles can be the stuff of banquets. I mean, there's always something new to experience. For instance, a week ago, I never dreamed I'd meet you. And now, here we are having dinner together, an intimate tête-à-tête. Who knows where things will go from here? Could be quite exciting, couldn't it? It all depends on us. Don't you think this is fun, what life's all about?"

"Tell me," said Wu Di curiously. "What do you think could happen between us?"

"It's possible you'll fall in love with me." She was hooked. I was delighted. "And I might fall in love with you."

"But I already have a boyfriend."

"So what! Perhaps this boyfriend, this Han Jin, will turn into the person you most detest. Perhaps you'll even die at his hands. When you read a book, you flick over the first few pages and you know what's going to happen next. But life is revealed one step at a time. You can't even tell whether it's going to turn out as a comedy or a tragedy. Do you like sad movies or comedies?"

"Sad films! I love films that make me cry, they're the best."

"I'll definitely make you cry."

"Do you want to hurt me?"

"It depends what you mean by hurt. If, for instance, you fall in love with me and if, well . . ."

Wu Di smiled, nodding her head. "Go on."

". . . you fall in love with me, and after we finish dinner, you go home with me. I fall in love with you too—it's not impossible—let's say I fall deeply in love with you. Hey, don't laugh. But you're a fickle kind of girl and you fall in love with someone else. I'm grief-stricken, but, nobly, I let you go. Years pass by. We grow old. We meet again by chance in this restaurant. I'm all alone in this world. You're also unhappy in your old age. You feel sentimental about times past. You cry."

Wu Di laughed so hard she had to spit the mouthful of wine she had just drunk back into the glass. Opening her red, moist lips, she said, "It doesn't sound to me as if you don't read any books. It sounds to me as if you've read too many bad romances."

"Well, don't you think it's a possibility?"

"No way. The only possible scenario would be like this: I fall in love with you, but you don't love me at all. I die for you. You—"

"It sounds as if both of us could be novelists."

"It's always the man who's at fault."

"Okay. Let's see what happens next. The essential thing is to get this story moving. Now, Chapter One: I've already fallen in love with you."

"But I haven't fallen in love with you." Wu Di laughed and, blushing, looked straight into my amorous eyes.

When the waiter came with the bill, Wu Di insisted on paying. In order to preserve her dignity and to make this scheme of mine seem more innocent, I let her do as she wanted.

It was already dark outside. The streets were still crowded and the traffic quite heavy. But when Wu Di took my arm again, I knew I had succeeded. This wasn't just a technical maneuver, the normal response to walking in a crowd of people, but the touch of a lover, shy, bashful, and clinging.

Traditional morality being held in universal disdain these days, I didn't have to make much effort to help her shed the slight residual sense of responsibility she felt toward Han Jin.

Fangfang's apartment was the usual thing: thin walls and hot, stuffy rooms. It was very easy getting her to take her clothes off. So as to give her a bit more courage, I left the lights off. She really was quite cool and composed about the whole thing. Actually, when kissing her, I even thought she seemed quite experienced. Of course she told me it was her "first time" and I said it was my "first time" too. Afterward, she wept in silence. I didn't hear anything. The room was pitch-black, and I couldn't see anything either. But I could tell something was wrong. She hadn't lied to me after all. I touched her face; it was soaked in tears.

"It really was your first time?"

She didn't say anything. I felt a little alarmed. I knew what the first time would mean to her. Things didn't look too good for the future. She could make things complicated. I didn't love her. I didn't love anyone. "Love" is such a ridiculous word. Although I often use it, I say it in the same easy way I do a word like "shit."

I woke up feeling very groggy the next morning. I looked up at the girl sitting next to me. I didn't feel a thing for her. She hadn't slept all night. Her hair was all tousled and she leaned over, looking at me with her bright, teary eyes and kissing me.

"You're awake." She smiled at me, an ingratiating and self-deprecating smile.

I shut my eyes. My dissipated and irregular life-style had wrought havoc with my health. I felt weak and clapped-out. I didn't even feel up to giving her a smile in return. Anyway, there was no need for me to try to please her anymore.

"Do you love me?" she whispered as she stroked my face.

"Yeah." I was thinking of how I could get rid of her.

"I love you too, really. You don't know how much I love you."

"I know."

"Shall we get married?"

I chuckled a little, not wanting to dampen her spirits.

"The two of us'll be so happy," she daydreamed excitedly as she cuddled up to me. "I'll be really good to you, make you really comfortable. We'll never quarrel, never get cross with each other. Everyone'll be envious of us. Do you want a boy or a girl?"

"A neuter."

"You're horrible! Don't go back to sleep, I won't let you!"

I opened my eyes. "I'm really tired, okay?" I leaned over and looked at my watch on the table. "You should get going to class."

"I'm not going."

"Hey, come on. You really ought to go, it's not right for you to skip class."

"I don't want to go. I want to stay here and look at you."

"You'll see plenty of me soon enough. Now I just want to sleep. . . . Hey, what's wrong?"

She was biting her lip, and her eyes were filling with tears. She didn't say anything.

"Okay, okay." I patted her cheek. "Now you must go to class. I'll call you this afternoon. Don't be cross. I'm only thinking of you."

I brushed my lips against hers, and she looked a bit happier. She put her arms around me and kissed me. Then she got up and put her clothes on.

"Will you see me off?" She had dressed and was standing at the mirror tying up her hair with a rubber band.

"Listen, the neighbors are a bit of a nuisance," I said, a bit fed up by now. "If they see the two of us together, they're bound to talk."

"All right. I don't need you to see me out. What time will you call me this afternoon?"

"When I get up."

"Make it as soon as you can."

She walked over, cupped my face in her hands, and kissed me hard and long. I almost passed out from lack of oxygen.

"See you!" She left, radiant with joy.

"See you."

I stared stupidly around me for a few minutes and then turned over and went back to sleep.

Wu Di falls in love with Zhang Ming but becomes deeply disillusioned. She ends up a prostitute and commits suicide when their gang is busted by the police. Zhang Ming is sentenced again to labor reform camp.

When he's released, he meets a girl who reminds him very much of Wu Di. . . .

Wu Di, the slightly rebellious student seeking personal liberation, might, if she had lived, just as easily have joined the Protest Movement as been seduced by Wang's "hero."

A Primer for Sexual Criminals

This is a work that describes in dulcet tones the enjoyments of a licentious, treacherous, and boorish criminal world. It's as if the author is standing on a grassy knoll in the middle of a swamp, appealing affectionately to his young readers to gather around and hear his tale. But I despair for these young readers; I fear they will sink into the mire and be unable to extricate themselves. . . .

The writer's literary talent is undeniable. He cunningly sucks his readers, especially younger ones, into the thick of this tale of felony and vice. It's an excellent textbook on a host of subjects that range from how to seduce young girls to ways of concealing a crime. The first half of the story, in which the man is the focus, glorifies the seduction of women, unrestrained hooliganism, fraud, and crime. When a woman takes center stage in the second half, cock teasing and egotistical hedonism are championed. The two halves make a whole in which the bleached bones of the dissolute relations between young men and women, of an unbridled and "free" life-style, are laid bare. It's hard to believe these sorts of things are happening in China in the mid-eighties. Even if they are, they are surely rare and isolated phenomena. We must ask ourselves what possible benefit it is to anyone to exaggerate such unrepresentative, foul, and smutty things and put them on public display? . . .

If this isn't a primer for sexual crime, what is it?

Writers must be socially responsible. If they aren't, they will have a negative influence on society, and bitter lessons will be learned. Young people love to fantasize, and they are very prone to imitating things; although they are passionate in their emotions, they are also extremely malleable. Many young people (especially students) search for self-definition in literature. They simply don't understand that a work of fiction is not social reality, and that fiction can't help them work out their problems positively and rationally. Swept away on a tide of emotion, they forget themselves. We mustn't underestimate the social impact of "Hot and Cold, Measure for Measure."

China is a socialist country, and it is imperative that we maintain our Marxist view of art and esthetics and adhere to Marxist principles. Art and literature must serve the task of constructing socialist material and spiritual civilization. We must rectify our thinking on these matters.

> —*Chen Yishui*
> *Municipal Institute for Labor Reform*
> *Jinan, Shandong Province*

Wang Shuo doesn't care about what other people might say about him. To be quite honest, which of those leaders, famous men, or "scholars," including the people of his father's generation, have led completely blameless lives? You can't help laughing at all that crap they feed you about how "we 1950s people are so uncomplicated, so serious."

But just look at yourself. From the Anti-Rightist Movement [of 1957] up to the Cultural Revolution and right up to today, with due respect, sir, you've been out to protect yourself and your position, remaining perfectly silent in the face of all of those outrageous injustices. You never say what's on your mind, you take whatever shit they serve up, and you've done your share of their dirty work. You blindly support the directives of your superiors, and you happily worship at the altars of the leaders and the famous. When everything is going your way you're cocky and self-satisfied, acting as though you're God's gift to mankind. You won't tolerate even the slightest disagreement. But when your political stock is low you whine endlessly, feel sorry for yourself, and, having nothing else to do, fake illness, right down to the moans and groans. You produce nothing but act as though the whole world owes you a living. And when it comes to power play, you're up there with the greediest of them fighting for better housing, a higher rank, more money. That respectable mien falls away and you're as grasping, jealous, and shameless as the next guy—not to mention despicable and callous. In the final analysis all that stuff about how uncomplicated and serious people were in the past doesn't impress the Wang Shuos of this world one bit; they think you're pathetic.

> —*Zuo Shula*

It is perhaps no coincidence that, like Wang Shuo, many of China's controversial cultural figures have had an army background. Their number includes many writers mentioned in this book, for example, Liu Yiran, Wang Peigong, Dai Qing, Luo Ke, and Zhang Zhenglong. Except perhaps for the scions of the revolutionary elite, few other groups in the society are so sorely aware of the contradiction between official propaganda and the drab reality. They are a natural fifth column in the move toward cultural dismemberment that is called "modernism." As Paul Fussell says in another context:

To the degree that conscripts become alienated from official culture, with its rationalizations and heroic fictions, they enact one of cultural modernism's main gestures. . . .

A disillusion resembling that of soldiers who have fought is one of the most noticeable motifs in modern culture, and so is the war between the generations—the older clinging to myths of idealism, the younger practiced in skepticism and proficient in rude plain-speaking.*

---

* From Paul Fussell's introduction to *The Norton Book of Modern War*, New York: W. W. Norton, 1991.

Liumang: Observations on Chinese "Hooliganism"

Wang Shuo and his opus represent a phenomenon that not only hor-rifies the Jinan Municipal Institute for Labor Reform but also frightens "decent" society in general: the rise to social prominence of the liumang, the hooligan or alienated youth. Reform encouraged entrepreneurial ini-tiative, but reformists were often appalled by the sorts of people who took the initiative, and what they did with it.

During the Protest Movement, the epithet liumang was applied freely both by the authorities, who derided those who took part in protests in late May as liumang, and by the protesters, who denounced the leaders who put Peking under martial law, pitting the army against the people, as the ultimate liumang.

Among those who suffered most in the aftermath of the massacre were individual entrepreneurs. Throughout the movement members of this group had provided the students with money, food, drinks, and other support; some even formed a "Flying Tigers" motorcycle squadron to monitor military movements. On the night of June 3–4, the self-employed were the ones seen racing the wounded and dying to the hos-pital on the back of their bicycle carts. Ideological and social prejudice against the entrepreneurial classes combined with official fury led to these people being given the blanket label of liumang and dealt the harshest treatment of all.

But the expression liumang actually encompasses a wide range of things.

On *Liumang*

JOHN MINFORD

. . . [As] China approaches the year 2000 and faces uncertainty in economic growth, urban alienation, and industrial pollution, it must confront its own double failure: a failure to conserve, and a failure to modernize.

And yet on this post-Mao wasteland a strange new indigenous culture is evolving, which could, perhaps a little provocatively, be called the culture of the *liumang* (an untranslatable term loosely meaning loafer, hoodlum, hobo, bum, punk). The original *liumang* is to be seen cruising the inner city streets on his Flying Pigeon bicycle, looking (somewhat lethargically) for the action, reflective sunglasses flashing a sinister warning. *Liumang* in everyday speech is a harsh word. It is the word for antisocial behavior, a category of crime.

But the *liumang* generation as I see it is a wider concept. Rapist, whore, black-marketeer, unemployed youth, alienated intellectual, frustrated artist or poet—the spectrum has its dark satanic end, its long middle band of relentless gray, and, shining at the other end, a patch of visionary light. It is an embryonic alternative culture, similar in certain striking ways to that of the 1960s in the United States and Europe.

In one sense these are the lost generation. They are the victims of the "ten years of catastrophe," the children of the Chinese holocaust. But in another sense it is precisely this void that can give birth to an authentic sense of identity and culture—not the government directives to reprint classical texts, to restore bits of tourist antiquity, or to rehabilitate octogenarian intellectuals.

The May Fourth Movement tried without success to uproot traditional values and to drag China screaming into the modern world. The Cultural Revolution failed in its more extreme endeavor, to create a blank and then engineer and imprint upon it a new consciousness. One of the ironies of recent Chinese history is that these very failures have left behind them a generation capable of reconciling tradition and a true feeling for modernity. The trauma of disillusionment and the anarchy to which they were abandoned during the formative years of their adolescence have driven the more aware representatives of the *liumang* generation to a radical perspective, not only on the present but also on their own traditional culture.

Official policymakers struggle against the odds to instill an artificial

"My Dream," Xu Mangyao *(Fine Arts in China)*

sense of values, to create a socialist spiritual civilization for the unmotivated and underemployed. These for their part observe the hypocrisy and opportunism of their seniors and remain unmoved. It seems almost irrelevant whether Marxism or neo-Confucianism is being resorted to in the effort to galvanize people. The medicine in either case is ineffective.

The liumang/*punk*/*poet generation has already created its own legends. There's the* liumang *painter who lost his front teeth in a drunken brawl and the* liumang *poet who broke into another artist's home to steal a painting the artist had refused to give him. There are endless tales of drinking and boasts of prowess in both the sexual and martial arts.**

Bai Hua, one of the protagonists in the poet Bei Dao's novel Waves, *is a typical modern* liumang *figure, a heroic hobo with a touch of the knight-errant. He is said to be based on the poet Mang Ke,† who founded the Democracy Wall literary journal* Today *together with Bei Dao. Mang Ke, like Liu Xiaobo, the "liumang literary critic," is a native of the northeast, home of many of China's traditional knights-errant.*

* In Sue Townsend's *True Confessions of Adrian Albert Mole* (1989), the blank verse by Baz Kent, the Skinhead Poet, is very much akin to the literary and social spirit of the *liumang* poet. For Adrian Mole, see also *Seeds of Fire*, p. 29.
† See *Seeds of Fire*, p. 245.

Knights-errant, wandering chivalrous fighters for justice, formed a special and admired group in traditional China. They represent for many the free and unfettered spirit of the individual.* Their history is complex, but in many ways there are links between the traditional knights-errant and the feisty members of the liumang *generation of today.*

One of the central values of the liumang, *as of the knight-errant, is that of mateship, sticking up for your buddies—gemer in 1980s Peking parlance. There's even a special expression, "gemer solidarity," to describe this special loyalty. In an age of corruption and decay, when the party and state are generally perceived as morally bankrupt and the workplace as merely a microcosm of the state, it is increasingly the case that only strong* gemer *relationships can inspire people to acts of heroism or even decency. In an age of disorder, knights-errant,* liumang, *and individualists come together.*

Those who remain bound by convention and law seek their release vicariously. They read the novels of Wang Shuo, listen to tapes of "liumang music" featuring songs like "The Official Banquet Song" (see below), or, most commonly, become addicted to the most popular genre of Chinese literature, the martial arts novel. The modern master of the martial arts novel is the Hong Kong writer Jin Yong (the pen name of Louis Cha, former editor of Mingpao Daily *and brother of the poet Mu Dan),† arguably the most widely read living Chinese novelist.*

In early 1989, one Chinese analyst writing in the People's Daily *pondered the question of why so many top-ranking intellectuals were devotees of martial arts fiction.*

Kung-fu Kicks

Some Chinese intellectuals complain that "life is a bore." Hundreds of years soaked in blood and tears and lit up by the glint of knives and swords have passed into history. It seems that today, when people should be thanking their lucky stars that life is "peaceful and uneventful," there's this feeling that there aren't any real opportunities to give full expression to their talents. Meanwhile, the traditional sense of mission

---

* See James J. Y. Liu, *The Chinese Knight-Errant*, London: Routledge & Kegan Paul, 1967.
† See *Seeds of Fire*, pp. 166, 412.

and social responsibility of the Chinese intellectual binds them, makes them itch to do something with their life . . . which leaves them both frustrated and inactive. Their souls are unsettled and their minds restless, and they often feel unhappy with the lack of excitement in their lives. They can find an impassioned and forceful release within the great dramas of the martial arts novels, even if the actual fighting is fairly meaningless. . . . The heroes of these novels are untroubled by the problem of distinguishing good from evil, nor do they care one whit for convention, ceremony, or law; they do what they feel like doing, they have no regrets and no complaints. Although they endure incredible hardships, in the end poetic justice is always theirs. This clearly gives those intellectuals who are totally powerless to extricate themselves from the Way of the Golden Mean a certain kind of spiritual comfort.

—*Wang Zheng*

In early 1989, the Economics Weekly, *a Peking paper run by Wang Juntao and Chen Ziming (among others), who were among the backstage leaders of the Protest Movement, published an article that also comments on the* liumang. *It pinpoints, however, a social and political malaise far more serious than that created by social misfits, cultural rowdies, and a few ex-cons. In fact, the article can be read as an attack on the salient* liumang *nature of party rule itself.*

The *Liumang* Society

YI SHUIHAN*

I'm afraid you can't simply blame everything that happens in China on the "bourgeoisie." Things like mixing dirt in with wool, passing rice soup off as honey or lumps of iron as aluminum ingots, putting DDT in mao-tai, and producing counterfeit medicines, cigarettes, and trademarks—the whole spectrum of immoral business activities. . . .

* The author of this article uses a pen name that itself has strong *liumang* knight-errant connotations, for it is the name of a song sung by Jing Ke, the would-be assassin of the ancient tyrant Qin Shihuang.

Feudalism is more to blame, for such nefarious activities are the specialties of the *liumang*, the rootless and the dregs of society. I'm afraid they have a lot more to do with the proletariat than with the bourgeoisie.

The lumpen or *liumang* proletariat despises labor; it is nonproductive and parasitical. Its members do not create wealth for the society; they only consume and destroy. During the years of the Revolution [before 1949], they were the ones responsible for random beatings and killing. They were into struggling the landlords and grabbing their wealth before the peasantry was even mobilized, and when they'd finished with the

THE OFFICIAL BANQUET SONG
Anonymous

I'm a Big Official, so I eat and drink, eat and drink,
Everyone says I'm a Big Official, so I eat and drink.
I can really eat, in I shove it,
And I've got the potbelly to prove it.
I can really drink, and boy do I love it:
Beer, spirits, rice wine, love potions, medicinal grog—
I drink it all.

Mongolian hot pot? Off to the Mongolian Restaurant we go!
Peking duck? To Quanjude with all in tow!
It's not my money we're spending, after all,
So eat and be merry and let's have a ball!

I'm a Big Official, so I eat and drink, eat and drink,
I'm a Big Official, so I eat and drink, that's me.

Want to eat chicken, let's go to Kentucky,
A Western meal, Maxim's if we're lucky.
Or to Fangshantang to eat like Empress Cixi.
Or Renren Restaurant for Cantonese,
So let's book a table or two or three.

I'm a Big Official, so I eat and drink, eat and drink,
I'm a Big Official, so I eat and drink, that's me.

When I eat and drink on your expense
Don't get worried, don't get tense,
When you want something done and don't know where to go,
I'm a useful chap to know.
                                    —*Peking pop song from 1988–89*

landlords they moved on to struggle well-off peasants, merchants, and industrialists. You could call them professional strugglers.

During the political campaigns after 1949, again it was such people who formed the vanguard of "heroic elements"; they were the most "revolutionary" of all. To them rebellion was justified. They showed no mercy and reveled in chaos.

In the age of Reform, they appear once more in the guise of the most unscrupulous [entrepreneurs], utterly without conscience and contemptuous of the law. They take what they can and squander what they get. Unlike the bourgeoisie, who reinvest their profits and expand production, the *liumang* proletariat eats and spends until there is nothing left. They are wasteful and extravagant in the extreme, and live as if there were no tomorrow.

This social stratum is adventurous, vengeful, opportunistic, and destructive.

This *liumang* mentality has already insinuated its way into some party and state organs, companies, and industries. Creaming off a percentage of whatever goes through their hands, they take every advantage of their position to eat and drink for free, exploit every bit of power they have, and use whatever resources available to them—be it land, means of transportation, even official seals—for their personal benefit. . . .

The bourgeoisie would be insulted by any inference that the *liumang* proletariat has been corrupted by bourgeois thought. What capitalist would run a business in such a fashion? What bourgeois government would act so recklessly? Or treat its people like this? Acting as though one's workplace is a piece of turf in some mafia network, doing whatever you please, and ignoring all laws and principles are all part of the *liumang* mentality.

The Ugliest Chinamen

As everyone knows, in many ways the Chinese have regressed to become the most uncivilized, ill-educated, quasi-barbaric nation on earth. . . .

We eat raw birds and beasts. We copulate in the wild and indiscriminately. Phallic worship is the highest aesthetic in our literature and art, and we take the release of pent-up frustrations through the use of vulgar language as the basic function of literature. Whether in politics, commerce, sports, or any other area of activity, we break as many rules as we can get away with. We steal what can be stolen and cheat the gullible, so as long as we don't get caught. The religion of the Chinese today is cheating, deceit, blackmail and theft, eating, drinking, whoring, gambling, and smoking. We make laws in order to evade them; our rules and regulations are a sham. Our tactics consist of carrying out policy; our strategy is to get people to fall into the traps they have set for others. We think any honest, humble gentleman a fool and regard any good person who works hard and demands little in return as an idiot. Crooks are our sages; thieves and swindlers our supermen. Thirty years ago people would sell out God, their own father, or friends for the sake of political advantage. There's been progress since then. Today we are like Judas and betray others only for money. There are no greater cynics than the Chinese people. We refuse to take on any responsibility that won't profit ourselves and show no respect for any values that transcend the utilitarian. Starting in 1966, China has fallen into repeated cycles in which all social norms and standards are obliterated.

If this situation is allowed to continue, we can say categorically that a massive new national disaster will be inevitable.

—He Xin

Nothing New

"The world is going to the dogs. Men are growing more degenerate every day. The country is faced with ruin!" Such laments have been heard in China since time immemorial. But "degeneracy" varies from age to age. It used to mean one thing, now it means another. Except in memorials to the throne and the like, in which no one dares make wild statements, this is the tone of all written and spoken pronouncements. For not only is such carping good for people; it removes the speaker from the ranks of the degenerate. That gentlemen sigh when they meet is only natural. But now even murderers, incendiaries, libertines, swindlers, and other scoundrels shake their heads in the intervals between their crimes and mutter, "Men are growing more degenerate every day!"

—Lu Xun, 1918

Disintegration Doesn't Have to Be the End. . . .

LEE YEE: Do you think that China's youth are generally turning toward nihilism?

FANG LIZHI: I think that people feel at a loss, they don't think the country has any future. In China, one's personal future and the future of the nation are closely intertwined; politics directly affects the way people live. It's not like here [in Hong Kong], or the United States— in the United States a change of presidents doesn't directly affect people's lives. But it's different in China. Now things are more relaxed than in Mao's day, at least in the Pearl River Delta [in Guangdong], though in Peking things are still tense. The current situation sometimes makes me feel as though China needs dissolution, not liberation. It feels like it's breaking up, nothing's holding it together. In fact, lots of people subscribe to this theory: If a certain culture is no longer viable, then why not just dump it?

—October 1988

"The Dove Hidden in Shadow and the Lost Rubik's Cube," Yang Yingsheng *(Fine Arts in China)*

Variations Without a Theme

XU XING

The story from which these excerpts are taken was published in 1985.

. . . Maybe I'm just a loser. It's possible.

It's just that I can't work out what else I should want from life besides what I've already got. Who the hell am I, anyway? I have no expectations.

Maybe everyone else is sitting around waiting in this incredible way, waiting for something to happen that'll change their whole life. But what that something will be, well, they don't have a clue.

But I mean it. I'm not waiting for anything. And I'm not just saying that to let you know I'm different from the rest. On another level, I know exactly what I need in life. I need to eat and I need to work.

As far as I'm concerned, the rest has nothing to do with me.

If I suddenly dropped dead, would it change anything? It'd probably have the same impact on the world as the death of an ant. Maybe Q. would be upset for a day or two, but she'd soon get over it. She'd probably end up marrying someone else. She'd go on enjoying life, working on her career. She'd just rededicate all those smiles and affectionate looks to some other guy.

If the person I care about the most is going to act like this, then why should anyone else give a damn? . . .

What would be wanting? There'd be pain aplenty, but, damn it, there'd be joy as well.

She wanted me to have a "career" like her. So everything's been done before, you still have to cultivate your own garden properly, she said. Pity. She just couldn't understand that everyone has his own place in this world. As long as a person likes what he's doing you could say he's got a career. Actually, you could even say that, like Q. [who is a musician], I too am "in the arts." I'm not talking about the stories that I write and no one else understands and that even I find completely irrelevant. No, I mean my job.

First I put the snow-white, stiffly starched tablecloths on the tables. Then I place the crystal-clear, long-stemmed glasses of different sizes in a row and fill them with the multihued wines for the diners. I always stand back for a moment to appreciate the masterpieces created by those guys in the wineries—they look so bright and translucent against the white of the tablecloth under the lavish chandeliers. They say one master oil painter spent his life trying to achieve this effect; he died without seeing the colors of my wines under the chandeliers.

I pad softly over the plush and giving carpet, holding my stainless steel tray. The light reflects off it, bouncing on the ceiling, a bright and mobile patch. Before the guests arrive, the large vault of the restaurant is so silent that this patch of light becomes an ideal companion, its furtive whisperings keeping me from feeling lonely. At such moments I quite sincerely feel that life is refined, glamorous, and beautiful.

But, of course, all good things come to an end.

Once the guests have taken their seats, even before they've touched their chopsticks, my work of art has been completely destroyed. It's quite unlike Q.'s art, which continues to resonate for so damn long after a concert, even putting you off your meat for three days or whatever.*

I really do like my work. That's to say I enjoy the tensions and strains, the way we really have to bustle at the hotel. I enjoy doing the bidding of the guests, men and women who come from every corner of the globe. It makes me feel as though there's some need for me in this world, that somebody actually requires my presence, at least a little. It gives me a sense of worth. It's so liberating to give yourself over to someone else. I don't have to think about what I ought to do; I don't have to make any decisions. The day we have off every week is a terrible burden for me.

As I walk home on the evening before my day off, I make all these plans: I'll go out onto the balcony of my apartment and count the number of cars that go by in an hour and note the different makes; or I'll go downstairs and count the number of windows in the building, how many

---

* In the *Analects* Confucius says, "After hearing the music of Shao, I did not feel like eating meat for three months." This is taken to mean that he could think of nothing but the music.

are shut or whatever. But every week my plans are destroyed by Q.'s ambitious schemes for me. She holes me up in her place and keeps me all to herself. That's all right, but she takes the fun out of things. How could I be like her, studying so hard and all? I couldn't embrace Debussy or Verdi or whatever the way she does. . . .

It looked as though Q. was determined to drag me up to her own level. She wanted me to be like all of those other career-minded people who pay attention to how they dress, act very refined, speak in a cultivated manner, wear glasses, that type of thing. It wasn't that I didn't understand what they were doing; I just didn't like it. You could say that whatever I understood I disliked. . . .

"You're downwardly mobile," Q. once said to me.

I beg to differ. I may look as if I'm sinking slowly and ever so softly into the mire. But all the while there's something in my soul that is rising to some higher plane. And there are quite a few things in life that actually excite me. For instance, going to the foothills in the outlying suburbs at twilight to gaze at the mountains, trying to guess what lies beyond the farthest one, the one bathed in the glow of the setting sun. The sea? Grasslands? An orchard filled with apricot trees?

What is on the other side of the mountains?

One day I asked Q., and she came out with this radically unpoetic response: "More mountains, of course." Maybe she's right, but I don't want to believe it. I'm still excited by imagining, even though her answer is etched deeply in my brain. "But as long as there are mountains, there will always be people who climb them," I said.

Or like when you do something for someone else and they are really grateful. That makes me feel good, too, and excited.

Q. introduced me to lots of famous people to help me with my writing. Most of them were middle-aged celebrities.

"If you want to be a successful novelist, you have to belong to a coterie," she told me. "You read one another's works. You can make quicker progress that way."

"Now the thing about writing fiction . . ." Each of them had his or her particular forte.

"Mmmm." I usually avoided giving an opinion.

"How old are you?"

"Twenty."

"The Psychiatrist and His Patient Friends," Fan Hancheng *(Fine Arts in China)*

"Where do you work?"

"In such-and-such a hotel." It was like I was reciting my identity papers.

"Is that so?" The climax was always the same. Suddenly the dull and beady little eyes of the famous would sparkle. The rest was predictable.

"Last time I went there for lunch I had to stand in line all morning. Now that I know you, things'll be much easier."

"At your service," I'd say, feeling fucking insulted.

Xu Xing supported the Protest Movement. He later left Peking and went into exile in Germany, where he found a job in a factory.

On Superfluous People

HE XIN

This essay was published as the lead article of the influential intellectual monthly Reading *in November 1985, having been revised by party ideologue Hu Qiaomu.*

"Superfluous people" is an old expression; it's also foreign, so we can't just take it at face value. Some people translate the concept as "outsiders." But whatever you call it, like so many philosophical or aesthetic terms, it's difficult to define precisely. It seems to encompass the following approach to life: indifference, passivity, even a philosophical sense of noninvolvement, an attitude of cynicism, superiority, one that finds everything risible and therefore takes life as just one big game. To put it simply, superfluous people are those who feel they don't have a place in life.

Readers of European literature will be familiar with the concept of "superfluous people." The famous personalities of Rameau's nephew, Julien Sorel, Rudin, Onegin, Oblomov, Karamazov, and many others all have something of the superfluous in them. . . .

What is important to note is that the "superfluous people" in contemporary Chinese literature are quite different from their European counterparts. European authors adopted a critical attitude toward their "superfluous" characters, and this was true regardless of whether they thought but did not act or had no positive significance at all. They satirized them, or at least sympathized with them as some sort of tragic phenomenon. Yet we are hard-pressed to find such a critical attitude in our literature today. Indeed, you'll have difficulty finding any distance between writers and their characters at all.* . . .

* He Xin's reading of Western literature is obviously somewhat limited, for there are numerous examples of a far more ambiguous, even positive, attitude toward "super-

It's too easy to be critical of such "superfluous people" and this story ["Variations without a Theme"]. The difficulty lies in trying to understand their appearance in contemporary Chinese literature. This is complicated by the fact that the advent of "superfluous people" is a social as well as a cultural phenomenon.

Let's put it in a historical context. Post-1949 Chinese literature took heroism as its starting point; later characters were inflated into superheroes (the Outstanding, Great, and Perfect Heroes of the Cultural Revolution); and then the whole thing collapsed. Since the crushing of the Gang of Four, "scar literature," "humane literature," and even more recently "Reform literature" have all appeared in turn. But now we also have this new genre, the literature of absurdity and superfluousness. . . . There has been a sort of progress, a type of development, but the paradox is that it's an advance that appears to be a regression, it's a development that expresses itself as a return to the past. (Indeed, aren't some of our writers now identifying with certain literary genres of the 1930s?) In the characters now appearing in fiction we see that the sacred has given way to the mediocre; heroic ideals have descended into nihilism.

The result is that recent literature champions nonheroes. A new quest has been undertaken, not for the "sublime" (a word made obsolete, perhaps, through overuse), but for the commonplace. It is a search for silent and unknown people, a search for the everyday and trivial. . . .

"Variations Without a Theme" is not a vulgar story; indeed, it adopts an elevated tone. The protagonist is an aloof loner. He is above it all, unmoved by such worldly things as money and beautiful women. His introverted and melancholic persona is the reification of elegance and refinement. On one level his melancholia is an expression of the aesthetic of sickness. Perhaps this is why the story is so readable and some people have lavished praise on it.

But I don't like the protagonist at all (and my reaction is shared by many other readers). I neither sympathize with him nor like him. . . .

The protagonist is right when he says: "People say your experiences in youth can influence your whole life." The prepubescent experiences of this whole generation have turned them into what they are today—they were children in an age of displacement and obliteration, when all

---

fluousness" in nineteenth-century Western fiction. This is even more so the case in twentieth-century literature in the works of the existentialist novelists Jack Kerouac and, most recently, Brett Easton Ellis and Jay McInerney, to name some of the most obvious examples. In literary temper, however, He Xin strikes a more contemporary note. In mid-eighties China He Xin was in a sense playing Norman Podhoretz to Xu Xing's Jack Kerouac.

He Xin

civilization and values were destroyed and defiled. The whole nation lost its concept of self-worth; that is to say, it lost its ideas, rationality, and soul. Equally thought-provoking is the following passage in Liu Xinwu's "Zooming In on May 19": *

> We should point out that the Cultural Revolution broke out in 1966. . . . The majority of Red Guards were in senior middle school or university at the time, that is, from 17 to 23 years of age. By 1985 they were 36 to 41. Yet the eldest of the 127 May 19 Incident detainees was 35 . . . the majority were young people from 15 to 25. At the start of the Cultural Revolution they were infants or hadn't even been born.

From the psychological point of view, the fascinating thing about this is that Hua Zhiming, the "troublemaker" Liu Xinwu creates in his depiction of the May 19 Incident, is a typical "superfluous person."

It seems as though Liu Xinwu is trying to say that you can't blame the Cultural Revolution for the appearance of people like Hua Zhiming. But I'm afraid our author has overlooked the continuity of things, the

* On May 19, 1985, there was a major soccer riot in Peking. An excerpt from Liu Xinwu's "factional" report of the incident follows this piece.

> *Elsewhere, in response to a criticism of this passage, He Xin wrote:*
>
> When approaching deconstruction, collapse, or transformation, virtually every culture throws up different types of anticultural elements. Chinese history is no exception: For example, there are the wandering scholars and knights-errant of the Warring States Period who used their writings to confound authority or broke taboos with their fighting. And the wanton literati of the Wei-Jin Period, represented by the totally uninhibited Sages of the Bamboo Grove. . . . It is in just such antisocial attitudes that we can see common elements between the superfluous man and the outsider (or hippie). This is the very point at which we are drawn to deep reflection by certain phenomena in our contemporary literary trends.

broader cultural background of the childhood experiences of this generation. As one historian said shortly before his death, the Cultural Revolution represented a pernicious break in China's history. The full extent of its effects will be felt in China for many decades to come. . . .

In fact, the "hippies" that appeared in the West in the 1970s [sic] were also a kind of "superfluous people." In historical terms, whenever traditional values break down, or when a culture goes through a period of crisis, an attitude surfaces that casts doubt on, satirizes, and calls for a reevaluation of basic values, culture, and even life itself. "Superfluous people" evince just such a temper. China has had these types since ancient times, there's nothing new or different about them today: for example, the obfuscating Zhuangzi, Liezi, Yang Zhu, and of course the disciples of Liu Ling, the man who took the world for the inside of his pants and life for a bout of drinking. There's also the Mad Monk Master Ji, who defamed the Buddha and swore at the patriarchs, and the like.* All of them share the same cynical "hippie" spirit. Nietzsche summed up the intellectual crisis of the Western value system in one sentence: "God is dead!"

---

* Master Ji is a vagabond monk whose adventures are supposedly based on the life of the twelfth-century monk Daoji. Dressed in rags, Master Ji breaks Buddhist precepts by eating meat and getting drunk, as well as frequenting brothels. But he is also a chivalric hero who cures the sick, confounds government officials, and chases away evil. Above all, he is disrespectful and humorous. Master Ji was the object of a traditional cult that underwent a revival in the mid-1980s, when a popular TV miniseries on his life was made. For more on Yang Zhu, see p. 342.

A GRAND TRADITION

Another close relative of the liumang *is the vagabond. A vaga-bond can be literally a wanderer or just a spiritual hobo.*

The playful vagabond belongs to a grand tradition. . . . The tradition is one of posing an alternative, spurious goal outside the usual utilitarian ones in order to distract people's attention from their anxieties. The achievement of this false goal gives the impression that complex desires have been fulfilled in a fashion impossible in the real world.
    Playing games may be a pseudophilosophy of life, but it has inspired countless artists with a desire to really live. Zhuangzi, Tao Yuanming, Liu Ling, Ruan Ji, Ji Kang . . . They represent a playful spirit that has always excited people: They play games as a strategy of presenting a false self to the world while preserving their real selves. This tradition tells us: The real game players are those who play false games.

—Zhu Dake

For over a century China has experienced tumultuous change. A traditional culture with a lineage that dates back thousands of years to the Yellow Emperor and Confucius has been rent apart by the violent impact of Western culture. This was followed by the unprecedented holocaust of the Cultural Revolution twenty years ago, which obliterated what little remained of the traditional value system and cultural essence. None of this can be recovered merely by allocating funds for the restoration or rebuilding of cultural relics. On one level this ambience of absurdity, the superfluous people who are appearing in our literature, represent in negative terms the break that has taken place with traditional cultural values. What they are saying to the reader is: We are lost.

We can understand this, certainly, but such a literary trend does not deserve encouragement or support. The reasons for this should be all too obvious. Anyone with the slightest sense of reality or responsibility will appreciate that China's youth do not have the right to be cynical.

A Riot

LIU XINWU

On *May 19, 1985, a soccer riot occurred in Peking that made head-lines around the world. The Peking novelist Liu Xinwu wrote a semific-tional account of the incident in "Zooming In on May 19" from which the following excerpts are taken.**

Liu, an interested bystander and supporter of the 1989 Protest Move-ment, was collecting material on popular reactions to the protests before the massacre. Following June, Liu's official stock suffered a sudden fall. But this was not the first time Liu has been the victim of the party's political fiats; in many ways his writing career reflects the turbulent ideological climate of contemporary China.

Many of the issues touched on or discussed even cursorily in the story, such as inflation and corruption, helped feed the public dissatisfaction with the government that surfaced in the Protest Movement of 1989. Four years to the day of the soccer riot, on May 19, 1989, Chinese Premier Li Peng was to declare peaceful student-led protests in Peking to have created a state of "turmoil" that had led to near anarchy in the city. He announced along with President Yang Shangkun that the gov-ernment was deploying troops to enter the city to "restore order." Then as before, the government proved itself incapable of addressing the real issues behind the popular foment.

One particular interjection by Liu Xinwu near the end of "Zooming In on May 19" remains relevant in light of the party's decision to crush the Protest Movement:

> We need to be more rational in our responses; more notice should
> be taken of local reactions, in particular those of our own people, of

---

* See *Seeds of Fire*, pp. 19–29, for "Black Walls," another story by Liu. The Chinese term for soccer hooligan, incidentally, is *qiumang*, a shortened form of *zuqiu liumang* —literally, "soccer *liumang*."

our young people, regardless of whether they are direct or indirect, pleasing or offensive. If a country is constantly annoyed by its youth, concerned solely with lecturing them and never bothering to listen to them, that country is suffering from senility. . . .

Originally, Hua Zhiming hadn't been particularly interested in the match that night.

On the afternoon of the eighteenth he had been in a great mood. He finished his daily production quota in the morning, and after hanging around the workshop for a while in the afternoon he told his foreman he was "splitting" early. The foreman had wanted to give him a hard time, but he knew Hua had a short fuse. So in the end he let him go. Hua sped out of the factory on his bike like greased lightning, heading for the public bathhouse. They had one in the factory, too, but he didn't want to let on to any busybodies that he'd got off early. After a good wash he changed into clean clothes and set out for Zhengyi Road, just over from Wangfujing, the street that had been planted with trees earlier than any other part of Peking. The green strip down the center of the street with its trees, shrubs, and lawn, divided by a path, made for a restful scene.

Hua had arranged to meet his girlfriend there at six that evening. It was still early: five past five.

He was twenty-six, yet in all those years he'd never taken a stroll by himself. He had no idea why anyone would go for a walk alone. He could have taken the opportunity that now presented itself to wander down the path. But that was beyond his ken. He carelessly parked his bike and found himself a bench to sit on, where he proceeded to smoke his way through a packet of cigarettes.

Three sculptures had been put up on the green strip that ran through Zhengyi Road during the run-up to the 1984 National Day celebrations. One of them—a woman street sweeper made out of imitation bronze entitled *Cleaning the Street*—had been toppled in early May and broken into three pieces. Another one, *Tuning the Zither,* of a woman playing the Chinese horizontal harp, had had her middle finger broken off, and someone had colored her cheeks with red ink and painted a necklace around her neck. *Study,* the third sculpture, was of a girl reading. Her lips had been painted bright red. Hua was sitting near the comical figure of this girl, but as he never took much notice of the things around him he wasn't aware of what had happened to the statue. . . . The only girl he was thinking of was Yingzi.

They'd met at the movies three months ago. He'd put on a show of being a real live wire. It was a method he'd used to make lots of friends, though as far as girls went, whether on the free market of love or going through a matchmaker, he'd never been much of a success. . . .

Yingzi had taken more care than usual over her appearance, though it was wasted on Hua Zhiming. She noticed his khaki safari jacket, his light blue shirt, and the gold-and-red-striped tie that she'd never seen him in before. As she coquettishly sidled up to him, Hua caught the faint smell of milk about her. She cleaned bottles in a dairy. No matter what camouflaging perfumes she used on her hair or skin, there was always a whiff of the dairy about her. Hua Zhiming actually liked the smell; but he never told her. . . .

They walked down the street pushing their bikes and went for dinner at the Songzhu Restaurant on the southern corner of East Qianmen Avenue. As usual, Hua Zhiming wanted to order enough dishes to cover the table, but Yingzi kept him in check. It was her way of showing that she was already thinking of "his money" as "our money"; Hua could only conceive of it as being proof that she was "a true pal." As they were about to set off to his place, Hua Zhiming told her, "I want to give you a real good time. I'm going to show you a video."

Hua's father had noticed something was wrong the moment he set foot in the door after work that day. He shouted out to his wife, who was in the kitchen preparing dinner, "Where'd that thing next to the TV come from?"

Hua's mom came rushing out of the kitchen with a bottle of oil in her hand. She knew her husband could explode at the drop of a hat, and she splurted out, "Zhiming brought it back at lunchtime. Said he borrowed it from his classmate Mengzi. His father worked in Japan for a while. He brought this back with him. It's a machine for showing videos. I told Zhiming not to borrow things like that. We could never pay for it if we broke it. But he—"

"The nerve! That son of yours has gotten out of hand. But go on, go right ahead, keep on spoiling him. . . ."

The oil in the wok was beginning to splutter, so Hua's mother had to rush back to the kitchen. His father plopped himself down on their newly acquired "Italian" settee and lit up a cigarette with a quivering hand. French-, Belgian-, and Italian-style imitation leather sofas were all the rage—there was even one in the dairy—so he took no exception to this type of innovation. Video recorders were not so common, and Hua's father fixed his gaze on the shiny new piece of equipment with disgust, like a shepherd confronted by some ungainly new creature in his paddock.

As he sat glaring at the video machine, his mind was ticking over: The very strangeness of the machine—both its physical appearance and the nature of its function—made him think of recent porn video cases. Then there was Mengzi's dad. He was one of those technician types who had been let into the party, promoted, then sent on an overseas junket. He'd used the chance to buy a few things for himself. To Hua's father, a cadre who had never helped himself to the perks of office, there was little difference between Mengzi's educated father and the self-satisfied and cocky profiteers out on the streets. His head filled with images of what he saw as the confusion and spiritual pollution created by the Open Door and Economic Revitalization policies. . . . Complex and contradictory emotions and thoughts mingled, clashed, and exploded in his brain, sending his blood pressure soaring and leaving him so edgy that just about anything could have set him off. So when Hua Zhiming strode breezily into the room in the company of a woman who was just as alien to his father as the video machine, the old man went right off the handle.

I'll leave the details of the ensuing scene to your imagination. Hua's mother was an indispensable lubricant in the machinery of conciliation, and despite the emotional scene Yingzi stayed for a while out of respect for "auntie." But she was deeply hurt. It was her first visit, and she couldn't understand why Hua Zhiming hadn't told his parents beforehand. She couldn't remember what Hua's father had been going on about, though it shocked her very much: At home Hua was a nobody. The mother finally herded her son and his girlfriend into Hua's small bedroom, shutting the door anxiously on them while she tried her best to calm the old man down: She told him dinner would soon be ready and coaxed him off to their room for a short rest. She made him tea, heated some water so he could wash his feet, and did all she could to humor him. Finally she slipped in a few words on her son's behalf: "We should be happy that the boy's finally got himself a girl, and she seems a

Just look at how fanatical the Chinese are about sports. Whenever the flag of the People's Republic of China is raised, everyone stamps loudly and yells.

But if the Chinese team loses? Everyone swears, breaks the place up, and creates a disturbance.

We are a nation that can't accept losing.

—*Su Xiaokang*, River Elegy

decent sort . . . considering his education, job, looks, and personality, well, it's a good thing he found someone. . . ."

Meanwhile Hua was sitting on the other side of the cramped room from Yingzi, smoking silently. Yingzi leafed through a shoddy pirated edition of a martial arts novel, *Wonder Woman from Snow River*. Hua was hopeless at expressing his feelings, though he was not even aware that the situation demanded some sort of explanation. Yingzi left fairly soon. Only long after the lingering scent of milk had vanished entirely did it occur to Hua Zhiming that they hadn't fixed a time and place for their next date.

An uneasy silence finally settled on the household. In the normal course of events the mother would watch television; tonight she knew better. Some time after nine, a disheveled Hua Zhiming slunk out of his room. He'd decided to cheer himself up with a video. It was the first time he'd operated one of those things by himself, and he couldn't remember which button to press first. No matter how much he fiddled around, there was no trace of the Hong Kong martial arts movie Mengzi had loaned him on the blizzard-stricken screen. "Fuck this. What a rip-off!" Angry with Mengzi, he gave up trying.

The next day, Sunday, May 19, was one he would never forget. He went over to Mengzi's place first thing to return the video player and cassette. Naturally, he started out by complaining, but Mengzi lost his head when he discovered that Zhiming had managed to erase the whole tape, which he'd borrowed from someone else. Hua Zhiming was dumbfounded. He couldn't remember what buttons he'd pressed, so he was in no position to defend himself. Just his luck; everything was going against him. But he didn't take it out on Mengzi. "How much will it take to make it up to you?" he asked. Mengzi told him 150 yuan. Hua went straight home without another word, took 180 yuan out of his room, and went back. He handed over the 150 without a shudder. With the other 30 in his pocket he cycled around aimlessly. . . .

He didn't think of going to the park; as we've observed, he was oblivious to the attractions of nature. There were a few exhibitions on at the China Art Gallery, but he passed by it without so much as a glance. He vaguely felt like dancing (a stray impulse, for he knew full well he was too short to look good on a dance floor). But where could you dance? Ordering a tableful of food and a few pints of beer at a restaurant and leaving it all half eaten was Hua's normal mode of self-indulgence. But since he'd known Yingzi that all seemed dumb. All that was left was the movies. He'd seen the American 3-D movie *Gunner Hart* twice already; as for the latest local product *Code Name 213*, he wasn't sure it was worth the 30 fen for a ticket. He'd have preferred to find a place with video games, but the only spot he could think of was in Zhongshan Park, and here he was all the way off in Dongdan. The last thing he wanted to do was ride back. This was the capital, and there was nowhere for Hua Zhiming to go to let off steam! As he rode on out to Jianguomen, where all the foreigners live, passing the International Club, the Friendship Store, then the Jianguo Hotel and the Hotel Beijing-Toronto, it occurred to him: Chinese like him weren't allowed into any of those places. . . . Then he thought about the Great Wall Hotel, which he'd seen on TV, and what Mengzi had said; "In Guangzhou you can get into any place you want so long as you have dough. . . ."

These ruminations ended with his arrival at the eastern end of town. Around Dabeiyao there were so many entrepreneurs' stalls on the footpath that the languorous pedestrians were forced to walk in the bicycle lane. Somehow Hua's front wheel hit a man in his late forties. The fellow swung around with a mean look on his face and spat out, "Clean up your act, slob."

He didn't light into the guy. Sure, Hua got off his bike without a word of apology, but wasn't his silence enough? Then someone else's bike struck his back wheel and he turned around without even looking clearly and shouted, "Are you blind?"

The fellow he'd yelled at was about his age and they started arguing loudly, each exchange getting nastier, although not out of control. Hua couldn't recall whether anyone tried to stop them, or what they said to each other. But by the time he turned into the Third Ring Road, he couldn't have been in a fouler mood.

The May 21 edition of the London *Daily Mirror* had a commentary on the May 19 Incident entitled "Throwing Stones." In a speculative tone it concluded that there may have been among these Chinese soccer fans some disaffected ex–Red Guards who had committed acts of violence during the Cultural Revolution period.

This was typical of the overseas responses [to the riot].

We should point out that the Cultural Revolution broke out in 1966 and the first three years were the most violent. The majority of Red Guards were in senior middle school or university at the time, that is, from 17 to 23 years of age. By 1985 they were 36 to 41. Yet the oldest of the 127 May 19 Incident detainees was 35 and the majority were young people from 15 to 25. At the start of the Cultural Revolution they were infants or hadn't even been born. No, they were not "disaffected ex–Red Guards."

There was also no lack of speculation about the rioters within China, first and foremost in Peking itself, not among other soccer fans but among middle-aged and elderly people, including many cadres. "Is it all linked to price increases?" they wondered. As everyone knows, starting on May 10 some consumer items had been subject to "upward price adjustment." Naturally, this had had quite an impact on consumers, although it hurt older people more. Of the people detained during the incident, few were married, most were unattached and still living with their families. They had never had to do any shopping for things like meat, fish, or vegetables. Although their wages and bonuses were low, they had a reasonable disposable income. Their spending patterns were also different from their elders': They judged goods on the basis of taste and whim rather than merely on price. All in all, it's hard to provide convincing evidence that the incident was a protest against state economic policy.

It wasn't entirely accidental that Hua Zhiming ended up at the stadium that night. In the first place, he enjoyed spectator sports. One reason he wasn't as caught up in the regional competition for the Eleventh World Cup as he would have been in the past was Yingzi. She didn't like sports. The second was that he thought there was no real competition.

After a meal at the Phoenix Restaurant on Guanghua Road, he rushed over to the Workers' Stadium and bought himself a 60-fen ticket from a scalper for 2 yuan. By this stage he was in a pretty good mood again. So long as it's a draw, he thought to himself, China wins this heat. Anyway, Hong Kong had never beaten China, and tonight China would have everything going for it. Hong Kong's fans were sure to be disappointed.

Hua squeezed his way into the stands, found himself a place, and looked around at the crowd. People were holding up homemade banners with legends like "China Can't Lose! On to Mexico!," "Fans from Tianjin Support the Team," "Score some for us, Gu Boy" (the meaning of this escaped Hua for a moment until he realized they were talking about Gu Guangming). Suddenly the stadium exploded: Some people in stand number two had held up a banner reading "China: 2—Hong Kong: 0." Hua felt elated, and he waited impatiently for the Chinese team to appear. Every one of their goals would help him get rid of his pent-up frustration. . . .

The old fellow on Hua's right had come well prepared: transistor radio, high-powered binoculars, push-button umbrella, and the latest edition of the tabloid *Soccer*. Once the match began he sat there listening to his radio and talking to himself while he watched the game. On Hua's left was someone who looked like a high school student. He acted as if he were sitting on a pin: Every few minutes he jumped up from his seat, and even when seated he kept swaying from side to side. Every once in a while he would pick up a colorful toy horn and blow it in support of the home team. But none of this annoyed Hua Zhiming because he let him use his binoculars. The lad sitting in front of Hua was holding two pigeons wrapped in a handkerchief; he was just waiting for China to win so he could release them.

Hua Zhiming behaved himself during the game. He was like a drop of water that followed the ebb and flow of the crowd's emotions. The mood changed suddenly because everyone was completely unprepared for what was happening on the field: China was losing. The shock had an extraordinary effect on the collective unconscious: There was ceaseless hooting and shouting, and then, without any prompting, the stadium echoed with tens of thousands of people stamping their feet in unison. When the Hong Kong team scored a goal eighteen minutes into the game, there was a momentary silence, as though the entire place had entered the eye of a typhoon; but when the Chinese team won a goal in the thirty-second minute of the game, the wild tide of rejoicing reached a peak. . . . Even the police who were there to maintain order were wildly cheering for the home team. Defeat was unthinkable and the crowd wouldn't countenance a draw—they wanted nothing less than a decisive victory. So even when the Hong Kong team gained momentary control over the ball, there was mass outrage, as if it were an unconscionable insult. This attitude can, in part, be attributed to the excessive emphasis on national dignity in Chinese reports of sports competitions. If there is a victory or a record is broken, it is spoken of as "China Taking Off"; defeat or mediocre results are construed as nothing less than "National Shame." . . . When the Hong Kong side scored another goal in the sixtieth minute of the second half, the fans, who had all been anticipating a frenzied celebration at the end of the match, lost control altogether. The atmosphere in the stadium became hysterical. The heavens added to the maelstrom by sending along a sudden downpour. Some spectators without umbrellas moved under the cover of the stands, but the majority stood out in the wet in furious defiance. Some even stripped off and danced around in the rain, screaming until they went hoarse. In the last quarter the national team fell about itself and lost two to one. At the end of the match, the spectators stood up as one, a sullen wall of fury. The face of the old boy next to Hua was awash with tears; the student on the left had long before trampled his horn underfoot; the lad in front ripped off the tails of the pigeons and let them go. They flew away dripping blood, some of the feathers landing on Hua's face. That's when he noticed plastic drink containers flying overhead onto the playing field. . . .

The whole incident was both simple and complex. On the one hand, it was an explosion of mass hysteria born of a frustrated competitive spirit, something that transcends nationality, race, politics, and morality. The complex side of it includes psychological elements peculiar to the Chinese people: Thirty years of political and economic instability have cast a shadow over everyone; the Cultural Revolution left China with a generation of young people who are culturally and educationally deprived in the extreme; and Chinese society lacks channels for people to let off their pent-up frustrations. Then there is the energy of individual liberation released by the present Open Door Policy, as well as its repression—all phenomena that have been little studied. . . .

Hua Zhiming went along with the mob, caterwauling all the way out of the stadium. The cool evening air brought him somewhat to his senses. He heard the sound of breaking glass; the police were running toward it. But the strangest thing was what he heard next: From somewhere around the north gate of the stadium came the sound of an emotional voice singing "The Internationale" and "We Workers Are Powerful"! *

Those songs and the extraordinary energy of their singers somehow set Hua Zhiming off: Everything came rushing out at once: the video tape, the 150 yuan he'd forfeited, Mengzi's pettiness, his father's glare, Yingzi's discomfort. Then there were the white teardrop earrings she had been wearing last night. This reminded him of milk and its soft fragrance. He felt he'd really been done over. Then he thought of the cock-up the Chinese team had made tonight. All Li Huajun and Zhao Dayu could do was pass the ball and break through the Hong Kong defense; even "Gu Boy" had seemed weak-kneed. And the Hong Kong team was so up itself; they'd have Foreign Exchange Certificates for sure. Then Hua recalled that black marketeer at the Xidan market; that the Jianguo and Beijing-Toronto wouldn't have let him in; that you could see the

---

* Both songs were again very popular with demonstrators in the 1989 Protest Movement.

> Over the past century we have continually been losers. First
> we lost to England, then to the Eight Powers during the Boxer
> Rebellion, then to the Japanese. Having finally gotten rid of the
> Japanese, New China enjoyed a short period of pride and
> achievement. Who was to guess that when we finally woke up
> from the thirty-odd years of internal turmoil we had created, we
> would find ourselves in the company of nations like Tanzania and
> Zambia? Even South Korea and Singapore were ahead of us. And
> as for the Japanese, they were the ones laughing, now that they
> were back with their Toshibas, Hitachis, Toyotas, Crowns, Yama-
> has, and Casios.
>   When the Chinese snap up imported color TVs and refrigera-
> tors, they probably never consider that it is proof that we have lost
> yet again. That's because everyone is so proud that the Chinese
> women's volleyball team has won all the international awards,
> that our Ping-Pong players are the world's best and the go cham-
> pion Nie Weiping has routed all comers from Japan. . . . We relish
> the sight of our women's volleyball team beating the Japanese on
> color TV sets imported from Japan; we feel great. If in such a
> hyped-up atmosphere they actually lost, we'd all jump up and
> scream, "Fuck your ancestors' ancestors' ancestors!"

ritzy chandeliers and restaurant through the window and the waitresses
in their revealing cheongsam dresses. He tried to imagine himself and
Yingzi sitting there but then wiped the vision from his mind. Without
thinking, he was already outside the metal fence around the stadium,
and he hardly noticed he'd crossed the street and was approaching the
intersection at North Sanlitun. . . .

He realized he'd forgotten his bike. He also found he was walking in
the wrong direction. This only made him feel worse. Just then a group
of rowdies appeared at the T intersection up ahead. Their fury perfectly
matched Hua's own frustrated anger. He ran over and joined them without so much as a second thought.

There were about thirty people in the group, most of them Hua's age.
They wanted to see some action, or at least create some. They stopped
every passing taxi, shouting and jeering at the drivers. Later, under
repeated questioning from the investigating officer, Hua was, with difficulty, able to recall that there was a tall, skinny fellow who had been

particularly vociferous, shouting: "Fuck it, while I spend my hard-earned money to go to some lousy game, these guys are sitting in their cars pulling in a coupla hundred bucks a night. Get the bastards!" From this we may conclude that the "collective unconscious" of the mob was fired more by jealousy of those who had been making a lot of money than by concerted antiforeign sentiment.

The mob waylaid a taxi and the driver jumped out with his hands clasped in supplication. "Come on, fellas, let me go. I've got to make my quota, can't stop . . ."

They let him go on his way.

Another taxi was stopped. This time the driver stuck his head out of the window to plead with them: "Hey guys, can't you just leave me out of this? I've got a passenger here, you know, and if anything happens I'll be in the shit . . ."

They beat the car doors, some kicked the trunk, others spat on the vehicle. Hua Zhiming just stood by hooting. After a while they let this car go as well.

From what he could remember, Hua said, it didn't seem like they were picking on cars holding foreigners or Hong Kong people [as reported by the foreign press]. He and the others were not, after all, the same as the Boxers who had appeared in Peking eighty-five years earlier. Now *they* were xenophobes. Remember their oath?

Heavenly spirits, earthly wraiths
We beg all masters to answer our call:
First, Tripitaka and Pigsy,
Second, Sandy and Monkey,
Third, Erlang, show your might,
Fourth, Ma Chao and Huang Hansheng,
Fifth, our ancestor Mad Monk Ji,
Sixth, Liu Shuqing the knight-errant,
Seventh, Flying Dart Huang Santai,
Eighth, Leng Yubing of the past dynasty,
Ninth, the Doctor Hua Tuo to cure all ills,
Tenth, Pagoda Bearer Devarâja and the three princes Jintuo, Mutuo,
*   and Nata*
To lead 100,000 heavenly troops. . . .

This chant is proof that in their own unlettered fashion the Boxers wanted to evoke the force of every symbol in traditional Chinese culture. Hua Zhiming and these rioters, however, had no leadership, plan of action, organization, or aim. They were simply a mob excited by football fever. If they were to have a chant, it would probably go like this:

Heavenly spirits, earthly wraiths
We all want to have a good time,
Let's evoke Xi Xiulan, Zhang Mingmin,
*Wang Mingquan, Xu Xiaoming;**
Let's watch [the TV series] Huo Yuanjia *and* Love Ties Together
   the Rivers and Mountains
We want jeans,
We want discos and Washi cosmetics,
We want Sharp, Toshiba, and Hitachi electrical appliances,
We want Suzuki, Yamaha, plus Seiko and Citizen. . . .

They are the most ardent consumers of popular Hong Kong culture and Japanese products. The real reason they targeted foreigners and Hong Kong people during the incident was that they dislike the way these people enjoy special privileges in Peking and flaunt their superiority. What the mob was expressing was a long-repressed resentment and jealousy.

Another taxi appeared. It was a beige Citroën. Again they surrounded it and forced it to stop. The driver jumped out and told them off in no uncertain terms: "What do you think you're up to? What's all this fuss about?"

"Get the bastard!" someone shouted. They went for the driver, and he took flight. . . .

Hua Zhiming was still hooting mindlessly, though he was feeling much better now.

"Let's flip this fuckin' car over!" someone yelled. Hua Zhiming applied himself to the task enthusiastically, taking up a position by the rear wheel. Hands that should have been embracing Yingzi clasped the rear mudguard instead. Someone shouted out directions as they began to turn the car over. Their first attempt failed; the second time they had it on its side.

A policeman came running over, and the mob dispersed. Hua put no particular effort into making a getaway; in fact, he walked over to the other side of the road at a calm, lackadaisical pace. He felt as though all

---

* Names of mainland and Hong Kong pop singers.

that built-up tension had disappeared. His conscience certainly wasn't bothering him: He'd never been in trouble with the police before, so he wasn't scared of them now. This was the best he'd felt all day. . . .

By the time the policeman appeared, most of the mob had disappeared into the crowd of bystanders, although one large fellow grabbed hold of Hua Zhiming's wrist and shouted at the approaching policeman, "Here's one of them, no doubt about it!"

Hua Zhiming was shocked to his senses. But he went quietly. The fellow who had grabbed hold of him had been looking on as the mob had done its work. He hadn't been at the game, he was a government cadre who had been passing by on his bike. He'd waited until the police were in range before taking action in case Hua tried to run away, although Hua hadn't given escape a thought. His outraged captor overestimated Hua's desire and ability to resist, for he took off his leather belt and bound the young man's hands behind his back. Hua was taken to a temporary enclosure. The police didn't have time to take down all the details of the stream of detainees. As morning approached, however, they were divided up and shipped off to detention centers. Only then did they discover that Hua still had his hands bound. Hua had made no attempt to resist, nor did he deny his participation in the incident involving the car.

Two days later he was officially notified that he'd been arrested. As

POLITICAL FALLOUT

The Cultural Revolution of Communist China not only failed to usher in an era of Great Harmony but was probably more calamitous to human ecology than Chernobyl, for it released venom, bile, spite, misanthropy, and simple insanity on an unprecedented scale. Today China is still living under its fallout. The sad fact is, even in its unchanneled and amorphous emotional dissipation, Chinese individuality lacks salience. Chinese emotional muzzling and irrational eruptions both testify to a fragile ego structure. A bifocalized personality development that programs people to live for one another is more likely to end up decentering both and weakening an individual's rationality. Confucianism confuses! The Communists compound the confusion further by their commandment, "Thou shalt not work in thine own interest, even a bit, only in the interest of the Other."

—*Lung-kee Sun*

there was a clear-cut case against him, he was charged under articles 157 and 160 of the Criminal Code of the People's Republic of China. . . .

Yingzi had been waiting for a call from Hua Zhiming since May 20. On May 25, a Saturday, she couldn't stand it any longer: She phoned his factory. The person who took the call was extremely off-putting: "What's he to you? Come on, are you playing dumb or don't you know? Hua was nabbed by the cops . . . 'cause of the May 19 Incident. It's a national disgrace—yeah, he's really in the shit this time. We think it's great. 'Bout time he got his."

Yingzi felt faint. She was calling from a public phone booth, and she leaned against the glass wall and closed her eyes just long enough for her heartbeat to slow down a little. Then she phoned her workplace and asked for the day off, saying she had a doctor's appointment. It was the first time she'd ever lied to them. Still in a daze, she went for a long, aimless walk. Somehow or other she ended up at the green strip where Hua Zhiming usually waited for her. She sat on a stone seat. A group of Young Pioneers was cleaning the statue of the girl reading. Yingzi started crying, and as the tears rolled down her face she took off her white teardrop earrings and grasped them tightly in her hand. . . .

—*From "Zooming In on May 19"*

An Exhibition of Anarchy:
Postmodern Art in Peking

In 1979 the Stars, a group of dissident avant-garde artists, held their first exhibition outside the China Art Gallery, China's most prestigious venue for artistic events. Their overtly political works influenced many younger artists and set the tone for much post-Mao unofficial art. Some ten years later, in February 1989, the China Art Gallery hosted a retrospective exhibition of post-1978 art. Many of the works displayed were well known and in the relatively staid tradition of the post-Stars modernism, which had reached its apogee in China in 1985. Chinese postmodernism, represented by the works of a younger generation, however, also raised its fearful head in the 1989 exhibition. One artist sold prawns, another scattered condoms on the floor, and a third fired a gun at her work. Even in the wildly "liberal" atmosphere of the time, the official reaction was one of disbelief and outrage. The exhibition was closed a number of times and the organizers were eventually fined for allowing the hallowed halls of the proletarian palace of people's art to be so abused. During the demonstrations in May, however, artists once again raised the trademark banner of the exhibition—a "U-turns Prohibited" sign—in the protest marches. In late 1989, one of the key organizing

On the morning of February 5, Wu Shanzhuan took up the position assigned to his work in the exhibition hall on the first floor and sold prawns. Many people crowded around to buy. After approximately half an hour two men in plainclothes ordered him to stop, tore up his sign, and forced Wu to go with them. Shortly after this Wu reappeared in the hall and wrote on a blackboard: "Closed temporarily for stocktaking."
—The editors of Fine Arts in China

bodies of the exhibition, the controversial art weekly Fine Arts in China, *was forced to stop publication, and in 1990 the gallery itself was closed for two years of "renovations." Since the organizers were also banned from participating in China Art Gallery exhibitions for two years, it will presumably open just in time for them to try again.*

Big Business

Anyone can make a name for himself doing business. Anyone can make himself rich.

Selling prawns in the China Art Gallery was a protest against the gallery itself, that law court at which works of art are put on trial. Art, like an innocent, sacrificial lamb, is subjected to a quasi-legal process by the authority of the gallery. Artists, as eyewitnesses, are forced to give evidence. It is a waste of good space.

Selling prawns in the China Art Gallery was a protest against art theorists. Works of art that start out as signifying nothing suffer the tragedy of being made to signify everything by the power of the theorists. The artist as producer of the "goods" is forced to go around hawking his wares. It's a waste of good money.

On the morning of February 5, 1989, the China Art Gallery became the black market it has always been; art theory, the profiteer it really is.*

It's big business. You've got something, but you can't go out and sell it directly; or you want something, but you can't just go and buy it. There's a middleman with his black briefcase who intercedes to maintain our mythic tradition.

—*Wu Shanzhuan*

---

* Although the exhibition officially opened on Sunday, February 5, there was a preview on February 4. The reports translated here were inconsistent regarding the date of the exhibition's opening, some saying the fourth and others the fifth. For convenience we have changed all references to February 5.

"Dialogue," installation/performance art by Tang Song and Xiao Lu

Action Art: Shooting at the Telephone Booth

At approximately 11:20 on the morning of February 5, 1989, on the first floor of the China Art Gallery, in the hall holding the exhibition of "Modern Chinese Art," Tang Song and Xiao Lu,* participants in the exhibition from the Zhejiang Art Academy, shot two rounds at their own art work, a sculpture entitled *Dialogue*.

The artists were both detained by members of the Public Security Bureau and the gallery was closed down. They were released unharmed three days later, marking the completion of their creation.

—*Li Xianting* †

---

* Tang Song was active in the Protest Movement. After the massacre both he and Xiao Lu, his girlfriend, left China.
† See the comments by Li Xianting, one of the editors of *Fine Arts in China*, in *Seeds of Fire*, p. 416. After the massacre, Li was put under intense investigation for his activities during and prior to the Protest Movement.

A Notice

On February 13, 1989, the China Art Gallery sent an official notice to the seven organizations that sponsored the "Modern Chinese Art" exhibition. . . .

The notice said that on the morning of February 5, when the "Modern Chinese Art" exhibition opened at the China Art Gallery, a number of incidents occurred that were in contravention of the exhibition agreement with the gallery and in clear violation of other regulations in force at the gallery:

The plaza outside the entrance to the gallery was covered in black cloth on which was displayed the symbol of the exhibition ["U-turns Prohibited" or "There's No Going Back"];

A framed plaque in the form of an award was hung outside both the men's and women's toilets. It was decorated with red silk bunting and was inscribed with the words "No water this afternoon";

Inside the gallery three people made an appearance wrapped entirely in white cloth;

"*The History of Chinese Art* and *A Short History of Modern Art* after Two Minutes in a Washing Machine, December 1987," by Huang Yongping

In the eastern hall of the first floor of the gallery there were people variously selling fish and prawns, washing their feet, and scattering condoms and coins on the floor; and

In the exhibition hall on the second floor there was a person who claimed he was trying to hatch eggs by sitting on them.

In light of these incidents the responsible people of our gallery made representations to the exhibition's organizers who were present in an attempt to put an end to the violations of our agreement. These efforts met with only partial success. As a result, the gallery had no choice but to remove the aforesaid "award" [from the toilets].

At approximately 11 A.M., a most serious shooting incident occurred in the eastern exhibition hall on the first floor. This incident was instigated by participants in the exhibition. This led to the Public Security Bureau taking emergency action to close the exhibition and stop the sale of tickets.

In view of the disruptive influence this had on other exhibitions and the serious harm caused thereby to the reputation of the China Art Gallery, it has been decided to fine the organizers of the "Modern Chinese Art" exhibition 2,000 yuan and ban them from participating in all activities at the gallery for a period of two years.

—*The editors of* Fine Arts in China

Following an incident in December 1990 in which several Peking artists were banned from exhibiting their work, the People's Daily *published a fresh attack on the 1989 "Modern Chinese Art" exhibition, mentioning the shooting incident in particular.*

On the great stage of Chinese culture in the eighties, the "new wave" was certainly the most socially explosive art form of all. Welling up in the late seventies, surging in the mid-eighties, it reached a peak in the 1989 "Modern Art Exhibition," accompanied by gunshots and the cries of a prawn seller. Theoreticians for "new wave" art have in recent years blustered that it stands at the avant-garde of artistic reform in China. Even now there are those who write articles declaring that it is in keeping with the direction of Chinese modernization and the tide of international art. They go so far as to predict that the tide will invariably "come back in.". . .

—*Wang Zhong, December 13, 1990*

Publishing License

During *the Cultural Revolution, magazines and books were closely scrutinized for political rectitude before publication by cadres of at least provincial level and sometimes the top leadership itself. In the 1980s, ideological vigilance flagged despite recurring campaigns against Spiritual Pollution and Bourgelib. People could once more read for pleasure, or at least diversion, as the publishing industry flourished, producing a plethora of books and magazines for eager consumers. Economic reforms made it necessary for publishers to profit or perish, and competition for readers led to a scramble for thrilling, even salacious, new works. Bookstores and newsstands could now offer readers a selection that ran the gamut from magazines dedicated to film star gossip to martial arts novels to experimental fiction and a wide variety of foreign works in translation.*

Wang Meng, novelist and then minister of culture,* wondered whether things had gotten a little out of control. From 1987, writing under the pen name Yang Yu ("Sun Shower"), he attempted both to delineate the healthy anarchy of the cultural scene and to provide avuncular party counsel. In an article in the Literary Gazette, *he described the arts scene as follows:*

Take a look around: there are the advocates of realism, those who go straight for surrealism, and the avant-gardists. What would have been considered heresy in the past is now all the rage. Some go for on-the-

---

* See *Seeds of Fire,* p. 408. Wang was obliged to retire from his government post after the massacre. Essays he wrote under the pen name Yang Yu were attacked in the press throughout 1990 for having encouraged Bourgelib. Following a lengthy attack on Wang published in February 1991, during the Gulf War, he is reported to have remarked wryly to friends, "They Scudded me so suddenly, I had no time to send up a Patriot." ("Scud" in Chinese is *feimaotui daodan*—"flying hairy leg missile.")

spot reporting and new journalism, others are into the absurd, the gro-
tesque, or the magical. There are those who are elegant and sentimental,
and others who champion the aesthetic of vulgarity. Some still insist on
the search for truth, goodness, and beauty, of course, while others pursue
the repulsive, claiming that even falsehood, evil, and ugliness, when
creatively "processed," can be the stuff of art. Some seek harmony,
balance, and clarity, while others do things that fall under the headings
of disharmony, imbalance, and obscurity. There are those who try for
best-sellers or good "box office"; others take a more highbrow approach; and still others try to please everyone with middlebrow art.
There are those who would be content if only one person understood
their work, while some writers would be satisfied only if they got a
national award. There are those who crave foreign awards, and some
are caught up in what's mockingly referred to as the Chinese writers'
"Nobel Prize Obsession" and film directors' "Oscar Obsession." Some
are critical of themselves, others seek new directions or lash out at the
current state of the arts. There are those who disdain such critics, devot-
ing themselves instead to violating taboos, making further breakthroughs, then breaking through the breakthroughs. Some madly aim to
"go international," others assert categorically that the new focus of the
arts is "cruelty." Some advocate making art embrace life, to keep "in
step" with life. Others promote the lyrical and shun reality. Some strive
sedulously to be innovative, only to make the painful discovery that
foreigners did whatever they're doing ages ago, and they become para-
lyzed by their fear of being repetitious. Others upbraid anyone who tries
something new as a heretic and call in the heavy artillery. There are even
those who say that innovation is like a rabid dog in mad pursuit
of artists and writers. Some proclaim they've devised new theoretical
paradigms, ontologies, and methodologies. Others denounce all systems.
And others call on everyone to preserve traditional schema. What a
scene! . . .

Can or has our culture entered a phase of weightlessness? Have we
lost our goals, lost all gravitational pull? . . . Surely, the end result will
be that we lose the distinction between art and nonart, lose art itself, and
thereby lose that very thing that makes the artist.

—*Yang Yu, April 1988*

*The array of experimentation may have left the minister of culture
breathless. However, he was constant in his advice to writers to accept*

the social responsibility that went with creative license. Many writers in their late forties or fifties, such as Liu Xinwu, Feng Jicai, and Zhang Xianliang,* subscribed to this aspect of the party line on culture. They were, after all, state employees, and their position as public servants circumscribed their independence. As Miklós Haraszti, the Hungarian critic of civilian (as opposed to military) socialist culture, wrote in his classic Velvet Prison: Artists Under State Socialism:

The professional writer knows that the right to speak carries with it responsibility. His writing must be not only beautiful but also useful; his care with these two aspects is what makes him a writer. . . .

Long gone are the days when artists waited, in happy or frightened ignorance, for successive instructions concerning speedy fulfillment of the Five-Year Plan! Today every artist is a minor politician of culture. We prepare our innovations so as to bid competitively for the creation of an official aesthetic.†

While after June 1989 the Chinese Velvet Prison would have appeared to have been replaced by something of a Bastille, Haraszti's work is useful when reflecting on culture in the 1980s and remains relevant even in the 1990s.

As the eighties wore on, the reading public proved eager for ever more titillating material. One old genre of popular literature, that which focused on court intrigue, was revived and given a contemporary twist as everyone from Mao's bodyguards and dance partners to former Nationalist assassins published their memoirs. Even the woman widely understood to have been Mao's concubine in his final years, Zhang Yufeng, wrote up her reminiscences, albeit highly guarded, in 1988.

The publishing authorities issued repeated directives forbidding the publication of works that dealt with the Cultural Revolution, the Anti-Rightist Campaign, sex, and pacifism. Although these were strongly in force during ideological purges such as in 1983–84 and 1987, the moment there was a relaxation in the political atmosphere, writers and publishers encroached on these forbidden territories once again. A number of writers had been more or less discreetly collecting oral histories,

* For more on Zhang Xianliang, see Seeds of Fire, pp. 218–25.
† For more on the Chinese Velvet Prison, see Seeds of Fire, pp. 385–408.

> The Cultural Revolution was a great catastrophe for the people of our nation. It is important to study this period, learn lessons from it, and draw conclusions in a scientific manner. . . . In fact, research into this period has been carried out continuously for the last ten years. The task of collecting and organizing materials on the Cultural Revolution is an important one. Books and articles that are of high quality and of value in helping people come to a correct understanding of history may be published.
>
> The problem today, however, is that there are many works on the Cultural Revolution that delight in revealing "anecdotes," "inside stories," and "behind-the-scenes information" about Lin Biao, Jiang Qing, and other people, thus vulgarizing what was in fact a very serious political struggle. Some of these works lack sufficient or accurate factual evidence and indulge in farfetched interpretations leading to incorrect and facile conclusions. This way of doing things has a negative impact on society.
>
> —*Spokesman for the National Publishing Administration, April 1989*

compiling dictionaries, and writing about the Cultural Revolution and other related topics from the mid-eighties onward. Dai Qing authored a series of articles probing into some of the most sensitive areas of party history. Yan Jiaqi and his wife, Gao Gao, wrote a potted history of the Cultural Revolution that attracted an inordinate amount of publicity and was subsequently banned from public distribution. But the memoirs, which proliferated in 1988–89, were undoubtedly the most popular with the masses.

The blatant corruption of party and government leaders in the 1980s fueled a nostalgia for the Mao era, and many of the things written about Mao himself were adulatory. Other major figures were given less courteous treatment: Jiang Qing and Mao's "close comrade-in-arms" Lin Biao are the subjects of many titillating exposés of varying authenticity. While the Cultural Revolution is generally viewed in the West as a period of austere, asexual political fanaticism, many Chinese tend to regard it as a time of anarchy and extreme corruption. These exposés of the leadership's luxurious life-styles, decadence, and intramural intrigues are as riveting as any episode of Dynasty or Dallas. They have also naturally fueled speculation about how the present leadership lives, adding to the general dissatisfaction with party and government that coalesced in the Protest Movement of 1989.

The following excerpt is from a book titled Secrets of the Lin Family: The Memoirs of Lin Biao's Secretary. *It is set in Maojiawan, Lin Biao's Peking headquarters, during the Cultural Revolution, when Lin Biao was at the height of his power. Its subject, Ye Qun, was Lin's wife and a veteran Yan'an cadre in her own right. It claims to be a true story.*

Ye Qun's Love Affair

A chief secretary was needed in Lin Biao's office [which was run by his wife, Ye Qun]. But who was to fill the position?

Ye Qun discussed the matter several times with [staff member] He Yiwei, who proposed several candidates. But she rejected each one on the pretext that Lin Biao hadn't given his approval. In fact, she was after more than a secretary. . . .

She was after He Yiwei himself. Sidling up to him on the sofa after calling him in to speak with her one day, Ye Qun confided to He that she and Lin Biao hadn't slept together for ages. Disconcerted by her "hot, hungry gaze," He Yiwei bolted out the door the minute his colleague Wang Lianjun came in to tell Ye Qun that she had a phone call.

"You're joking," Wang Lianjun responded dubiously to He's story.

"I swear before Chairman Mao."

"Well, if it's true, the old bag's quite a mover. This is goddamn absurd, an offense to public decency. I think you should report her!"

"Report her? To whom? All she'd have to say is that she was playing a joke. What proof is there, anyway? She could say I was the one who was putting the make on her, and then I'd never be able to clear myself. My head would roll before I even knew what hit me."

"You're right. Actually, people have been saying she's not exactly the prim and proper type for some time now. You'd better watch out."

"But she's all over me like a rash!"

"Take it easy, I've got a plan. If she calls you in for some more funny business, I'll think of some excuse to interrupt you every ten minutes or so. Anyway, I've never heard of a woman raping a man!"

Ye Qun *(left)* (*People's Pictorial,* October 1971)

Heavens! A secretary for Lin Biao's family had to prepare for all sorts of contingencies!

He Yiwei was called in again the next day.

Ye Qun was sitting casually on the sofa, dressed to kill. Her perfume rent the air, and she smiled at him bashfully.

A wave of revulsion swept over him, and he tensed up.

"I think of you all the time," murmured Ye Qun. "I never dared tell you, but two years ago I became a prisoner of love. I've tried to control my emotions. Whenever I went anywhere with the Leader [Lin Biao], I wanted to get you to come along as well, but I restrained myself for fear of what people might say. But I can't stand this torment anymore. When I criticize you or blame you for something, it's my way of letting off steam. It's tearing me apart; I can't live with you, and I can't live without you. I once thought of having you transferred, but I couldn't bring myself to do it."

He Yiwei felt sullied. He blushed.

He wanted to go, but she forbade him with a wave of her hand. "Sit down. There's so much to tell you." Just at this moment, Wang Lianjun burst in. Ye Qun cast a quick glance at Wang. "We're discussing business. You'll have to wait." Just after Wang Lianjun retreated, the phone in the bathroom rang.

Ye Qun was forced to get up and answer it. Standing there with one hand cradling the receiver and the other on her hip, she cast a reproachful glance at He Yiwei, a look that was rich in meaning, for it encompassed dissatisfaction, blame, and coquetry.

He Yiwei, his heart pounding, took a few steps back in fright, then dashed out of the room, mumbling as he went, "Madam Director, you must be terribly tired, you should get some rest."

As he slipped out the door, Ye Qun shouted, "Hold it right there! Don't leave!"

—*Mei Xinsheng and Gao Xiaoling*

The Chinese government claims that Ye Qun died with her husband and son when their plane crashed in Outer Mongolia in September 1971 while they were fleeing the country after Lin Biao's alleged plot to assassinate Mao Zedong had been uncovered. In 1990, Outer Mongolian authorities said there was in fact no evidence that the Lin family had been in the crashed plane. Their fate remains a mystery.

ONLY THEIR SECRETARIES KNOW FOR SURE

LEE YEE: In your opinion, are the privileged classes China's biggest problem? How corrupt are they?

FANG LIZHI: The problem is power plus corruption. I can't say what the degree of corruption is for sure, but people tell me it's getting worse all the time. It's terrifying. For example, not only is the army involved in smuggling, it's even dealing in contraband drugs. That's about as corrupt as you can get. Everything is done for power and money.

In a roundabout way, I find a correlation curve: The less people know about China, the more optimistic they are. For example, foreigners are the most optimistic, babbling on about how much housing has improved and so on; overseas Chinese are a little less optimistic because they have access to more information; Chinese studying abroad are more pessimistic—it wasn't easy for them to leave the country, and they have their personal experience to go by; the Chinese in China, people like us, are even less optimistic. But there's one category of people who are the most pessimistic of all. Who are they? Those close to the top leaders, their attendants and secretaries. They say you can't believe anything at all.

In late 1989, Zhang Zhenglong, an army officer-turned-writer in his early forties, published White Snow, Red Blood. *It is a long and scarifying historical account of the War of Liberation in northeast China at the end of the 1940s, the civil war that finally brought the Communist Party to power on the mainland. Overtly humanist and pacifist, the book describes in harrowing detail the cruel and cold-blooded strategies of People's Liberation Army leaders, including Lin Biao, and reveals, among other things, that officers of the PLA had been engaged in opium smuggling. Zhang uses memoirs and eyewitness accounts to reconstruct the events surrounding the fall of Changchun in 1948: while hardly sympathizing with Chiang Kai-shek's Nationalist forces, he records how in order to "liberate" Changchun the Communists decided to starve the provincial capital into submission, killing some 150,000 civilians in the process. "Changchun and Hiroshima: roughly the same number of people died," Zhang writes. "What took only nine seconds in Hiroshima took five months in Changchun."*

After repeatedly commenting on the political struggles and infighting that have characterized life in the People's Republic, Zhang says:

At the start of the twentieth century, the Father of the Nation, Sun Yat-sen, asked bitterly: Why must China, a nation with such a brilliant and ancient culture, suffer such ignominy and poverty?

Now, at the end of the twentieth century, do we not find ourselves confronted by the same question?

The bold measures that Gorbachev has taken since assuming office have had an extremely profound and subtle effect on China. Nearly all the reforming socialist nations are presently reexamining their own histories, including the great Stalinist purges. Every day new details are revealed, not only in the Soviet Union but in other countries as well, including China. This has made China reflect deeply on its own past. In fact, the recent flood of nonfiction publications about the Cultural Revolution is a part of this phenomenon. Through them people can see that policies that meant life or death for millions of people were decided by the workings of an absurd, palace-style political machine. How could China be anything but backward? Our Reform must be aimed at changing the workings of the machine itself.
—Wen Yuankai, January 1989

Starting in mid-1989 a number of controversial works about the party's history were banned. White Snow, Red Blood, *however, enjoyed considerable popularity after its appearance. In mid-1990 it was suddenly denounced and the author was detained for a short time. An inconclusive purge of the army publishing industry ensued.*

Only a few months before June 4, 1989, Zhang Zhenglong had written in his preface to White Snow, Red Blood:

A historian friend of mine once remarked: "History's like a whore: anyone in power can screw her!"

A Sexy Lady

DAI QING AND LUO KE

Sex, *an artistic theme condemned by Confucian and Communist culture alike, also suddenly found its place in public letters in the late 1980s.* In some ways this period was similar to the late Ming dynasty (sixteenth and seventeenth centuries), when the imperial house was in decay and a new literary movement emphasizing self-expression developed, and some of China's best pornographic literature was written— some notable examples of which are still not openly available on the mainland. However, modern pornography did flourish in the late eighties, much to the concern of officials, teachers, and parents. At the same time, China's cities seemed to be undergoing a sexual revolution of sorts, and numerous studies of the phenomenon began appearing under titles such as* Twenty-four People and Their Sexual World *and* A Sexually "Liberated" Woman. *The latter is a collection of reportage on sex-related topics. The title piece, of which a major excerpt appears below, was written by Dai Qing together with Qiu Ming, a woman editor in her forties. Writing under the pen name Luo Ke, she worked for an army literary journal and is the author of a handbook on family law. (Qiu subsequently moved to the United States.)*

Old China was the home of a highly sophisticated erotic culture. Even New China has never been the rigidly puritanical society it pretended to be and many foreigners imagined it to be. But as Dai Qing and Luo Ke note in their introduction to A Sexually "Liberated" Woman, *in the eyes of China's moral guardians, the incidence of premarital sex, extramarital relations, and, for students, extracurricular "activities" had reached almost epidemic proportions by the late 1980s. While the orthodox may have read in this signs of a dangerous, even apocalyptic, moral decay, the authors were less perturbed. They concluded that "Chinese views on*

---

* For some remarks on sex and literature in the early eighties, see *Seeds of Fire*, pp. 199–231.

"Snow, Sea, Woman," Chai
Xu (from a 1988 exhibition
of Chinese nude paintings in
Peking's China Art Gallery)

*sex are becoming like the views of other people in the world who under-
stand sex as something quite normal, correct, and proper (just like
human rights, democracy, freedom, the sanctity of private property, and
so on)."*

*The authors also point out, however, that in China it is still "extremely
rare" to find a woman who "looks at sex as a matter of pleasure—not
something done for a living, or to produce babies, or to fulfill her marital
duties, or to secure a promotion or wrap up a business deal, or, even
more pitifully, to solve her housing problems or save a family member
from persecution."*

*Any woman who actually admits to sexual desire is considered "bad"
—the archetypal "bad woman" being the character Pan Jinlian of the
late Ming pornographic classic* Jin Ping Mei. *Seductive women have
frequently been portrayed in popular Chinese literature as harmful "fox
spirits." Feminine lust is seen as not just morally undesirable but physically dangerous, as too much sex is believed to sap a man of his vital
principle (yang). Indeed, in the particularly memorable chapter 79 of* Jin
Ping Mei, *Pan Jinlian's unquenchable lust actually kills her lover.*

*Chinese society today may choose to overlook the sexual indiscretions
of a poet or party leader—indeed, tales of Mao Zedong's sexual prowess*

> In what way do unchaste women injure the country? It is only too
> clear today that "the country is faced with ruin." There is no end to
> the dastardly crimes committed, and war, banditry, famine, flood,
> and drought follow one after the other. But this is owing to the fact
> that we have no new morality or new science and all our thoughts
> and actions are out of date. That is why these benighted times
> resemble the old dark ages. Besides, all government, army, aca-
> demic, and business posts are filled by men, not by unchaste
> women. And it can hardly be because the men in power have been
> bewitched by such women that they lose all sense of right and
> wrong and plunge into dissipation. As for flood, drought, and
> famine, they result from a lack of modern knowledge, from wor-
> shiping dragons and snakes, cutting down forests, and neglecting
> water conservancy—they have even less to do with women. War
> and banditry, it is true, often produce a crop of unchaste women;
> but the war and banditry come first, and the unchaste women fol-
> low. It is not women's wantonness that causes such troubles.
> —Lu Xun, 1918

*and appetite constitute the informal side of his ongoing personality cult.
Yet it still tends to regard with horror any woman who would dare to
sleep with more than one man. Unbridled sex is associated not merely
with the collapse of morals and defiance of authority (as in George
Orwell's 1984) but on a deeper level with dynastic collapse; unchaste
women are seen as presaging the fall of the state itself. Lu Xun ridiculed
this idea in a 1918 essay, but seventy years later, it is still current, as can
be seen in Zhang Mingduo's critique of "A Sexy Lady," in which he
expresses the conviction that unchecked sexual license will lead to political and social destabilization.* (Zhang also frets that the "heroine" of
the piece, a PLA nurse, could bring the army into disrepute. Little did
he know that violence, not sex, would be the undoing of the PLA's
reputation.)*

Slightly taller than average, with a round, babyish face, she was the
sort of girl that everyone takes to at first sight. Her eyes weren't very
big, but they shone with vivacity. Full, red lips. A tiny waist, though her

---

* It is interesting to note that an unexpurgated edition of *Jin Ping Mei*, erotic wood-
block illustrations and all, appeared on the mainland in June 1989.

figure was far from willowy—round neck, round shoulders, round arms, and round, taut little buttocks. Even her fingers were smooth and rounded.

When she heard that we wanted to write about a sexually liberated woman, she didn't think she'd fit the bill at all; indeed, she didn't even know what the term meant. She'd never discussed this sort of thing with anyone, including her various lovers. But her acquaintances and her colleagues in the army generally thought of her as a "bad woman." . . . She's married now, but she's never told her husband about her past. . . .

This is her story.*

I joined the army when I was sixteen. After enlisting I went to nursing school. When I graduated in 1981, I was assigned as a nurse to an air force hospital. I was only nineteen and terribly innocent. My parents were technicians in a factory in Tianjin, and I was their pride and joy.

At first I had no idea that I had such a strong sex drive, though I often daydreamed about marrying some tall, well-built macho man. I believed that marriage was the be-all and end-all for a woman, and I still do. That's not to say I didn't take my job seriously: I worked hard at it and did well. I've always been very competitive in everything I do, including the search for a good husband from a good family.

At first I worked in the surgical ward. One of my patients, Zhao, was only a machinist, but he was the son of a divisional political commissar. Zhao wasn't exactly a knockout in the looks department, being neither tall nor handsome. But he was a real smooth talker. He always spoke to me in such a nice, considerate way, and he would never let me do dirty or exhausting tasks for him. He thanked me ever so politely for whatever I did. I felt he had class. I thought how wonderful it would be to go out with him. Quite honestly, he was the first man in my life, and marriage was the only thing on my mind.

We grew closer. When we spoke, our eyes told another story, and I couldn't get him out of my mind. One day, he put his hand on my arm. His palm was rough, but the touch of his skin made my heart beat faster. I'd had a lot of contact with men in the course of my work: wiping down their bodies, helping them go to the toilet, and all that, but nothing like this had ever happened before. It felt good, and I began to long for his touch.

---

* In fact, it was Big Boy and not the protagonist herself who told the story to Luo Ke, who wrote it up as a first-person narrative.

After a while, when no one else was around, we'd embrace and kiss. He was always touching me. At that time it was okay; it suited me fine. I believed he truly loved me and that we'd get married someday. And since his father was a high-ranking army officer, his was a good family to marry into.

Zhao was discharged from the hospital soon afterward. We couldn't bear to be apart, and I wanted to see him all the time. One day when we were out for a stroll he led me to an air raid shelter. He embraced me and said how much he longed for me. I felt we were really in love. Then he said, "Let's be like a real husband and wife." I had my reservations, but we'd been so close for such a long time already, and I was very aroused; in any case, I felt I'd be his woman sooner or later, and so I said yes.

It was my first sexual experience. It wasn't so good. In fact, it hurt like hell. The moment we finished, I was terrified I'd become pregnant. Zhao asked me when my last period was, and when I told him, he said not to worry.

We met frequently after this and did it whenever we could. I'd become so dependent on him that if I went without seeing him for even a few days I'd feel completely empty; I was always reliving our moments together in my mind. I was very happy.

But before long I sensed that Zhao had changed. He was cooling off, and when we made love his mind often wandered. He'd go through the motions, but I was left unsatisfied. Eventually I discovered that he had another woman, a worker, and that she had already had two abortions on his account. I loathed him! At the time I really believed that a man had to marry a woman who had given him her virginity. It never occurred to me that Zhao was just playing around. Now I found him to be extremely unattractive, disgusting, a creep. But I wasn't just going to stand by while that worker took him from me. If I couldn't have him, neither would she. I gave him hell for a very long time, fighting with him till he broke off with her as well. Soon afterward, Zhao married a woman two years his senior.

I was devastated. About this time a peasant boy, a soldier, was admitted to the ward. He was company quartermaster in a guided missile unit. In the normal course of events, I'd never have considered getting it on with him; I certainly didn't want to marry into a peasant family. But he was real cute, with fine features and a bashful smile. Just being near him made me excited. I hadn't lost control of myself, but I was stuck on him. I wondered whether I was too loose; but I hadn't had any sex since breaking up with Zhao several months before, and I was dying for a man. Though I knew it wouldn't do my reputation any good, the moment I clapped eyes on this guy I forgot everything and couldn't control myself. Finally, I made my move and we did it. He was so very uptight and didn't have the first idea what to say to a girl. After all of Zhao's tenderness, I felt this guy was just a good-looking lay; sex with him was as flat as a glass of water. There was no magnetism between us; still, we screwed around for about two months.

Qian's appearance on the scene brought an end to my tepid relationship with the peasant.

Qian was short, ugly, and thickset, a real tough. He was also a pain in the ass, always ringing his bell to get attention; when you went to check on him, there was never anything wrong. I gave him a piece of my mind, but he was so thick-skinned he just laughed. When he was well enough to get out of bed, he constantly made a nuisance of himself at the nurses' station. He was so pushy he was driving us all nuts. A few days before he was to leave, the fellow sharing his ward was discharged. Qian rang his bell, but when I saw who it was, I ignored it. Another nurse answered the call but returned to say he only wanted me. In the end I went just to shut him up.

He jumped on me the minute I entered the ward. I was disgusted, but I didn't scream, and he took this to mean I wanted him. It was summer, and we nurses wore only an unlined white gown over our undies. He lifted up the gown and pulled down my underpants. I don't know why, but suddenly I decided I liked his crude, forceful approach. Zhao and the cute soldier had both been quite tender, careful. But Qian's roughness somehow made him seem more like a real man. So after a feeble show of resistance on my part, we had a quickie in the ward.

I saw Qian in his ward over the next few days, during the lunch break or when I was on night shift. I was quite taken by his manhandling. He left the hospital a few days later, and we never saw each other again.

I started wondering what sort of person I'd become. Why was I such an easy lay? If anyone knew what I'd been doing, they'd call me a slut. On the other hand, I couldn't deny my need for sex. I couldn't go without a man, I needed a sex life. What could I do? The only way to save myself, it seemed, was to get married. Then I could have sex without having to mess around. I decided to be a good girl and find myself a fiancé.

I had a classmate in nursing school who came from Peking. After graduation we were assigned to the same hospital and even lived in the same dorm. Her boyfriend was the son of high-level army cadres, and he wasn't doing badly himself, winning honors and awards every year. Since I don't want to get him into trouble, I won't use his real name.

He's 1.85 meters tall, dark-skinned, and real spunky. We all called him Big Boy, so that's what I'll do here.

My roommate's family was moving back to Peking and she was preparing to take the university entrance exams. She and Big Boy quarreled, and they stopped seeing each other. When I asked her about it, she said they'd split up. I didn't think they'd get back together again. Around this time I developed TB, and the hospital sent me off to a sanatorium in Shijiazhuang. I went to say good-bye to Big Boy. He was very depressed. He said that now that her family had moved to Peking and she was going to university, she'd never come back to him. I didn't know what to say, I'm not very good at that sort of thing, so I kept quiet. Oh well, he said, guess I'll have to find someone else.

"Just a moment ago you were so miserable. Now you're ready for someone new!" I exclaimed.

"What am I supposed to do, hang myself from the nearest tree?"

"Well, then, how about me?"

He looked me over and said, "Sure!" Then he added, "But you're joking, aren't you?"

I didn't say anything. Why should I? I had been joking, trying to comfort him and lighten things up a bit. But now that he'd asked me, I thought, why not?

I thought about Big Boy all the time I was in the sanatorium. Zhao, Qian, and the peasant boy had been nothing more than strangers in the night, but Big Boy was someone I'd known for ages. In the past he'd often come to the dorm and we'd hang out and get together for meals on Sundays and holidays. Because he'd been my friend's boyfriend, I'd never even thought of him as a possibility. But now I couldn't stop thinking about him, and soon I felt I was in love. I wrote to tell him I missed him very much, and asked him to visit me over the Spring Festival —and he did.

I met him at the railway station. He was taller by a head than most people getting off the train and looked strikingly handsome. "Did you miss me too?" I kept asking him. I was so happy to see him.

He smiled but didn't say anything. Such style. Now I knew I really loved him. We stayed in town till very late, so late that we missed the last bus back to the hospital. Big Boy called a pal to send a car to pick us up and take us to his home. Big Boy told his friend's parents that I was his fiancée. I thought he really meant it, and I was thrilled to bits.

I returned to the sanatorium the following day and asked to be released. The doctor said that I hadn't fully recovered yet, but I told him my boyfriend had come to take me home. They let me out, though I wasn't completely cured. I was still coughing, but as long as I had Big Boy I felt nothing else mattered. We left immediately for Tianjin with some medicine in tow.

My parents were thrilled with Big Boy. Later, my grandparents and uncle all said how pleased they were that I'd found such a good-looking fellow.

The following morning, my parents went off to work and my brother and sister went to school, leaving only me and Big Boy at home. It had been an exhausting trip, and I woke up late. Big Boy came into my bedroom and said, "Can you believe it, we've never even talked about it and here we are, engaged for real."

I told him I really loved him. He said, "It's not like we just met. On the other hand, although she said she'd never come back, we still care for each other and it's likely we'll get back together again."

"So you don't want me after all?"

"Let's not jump to conclusions. Tell me—are you a virgin? If you are, I want you. If you're not, forget it."

My heart stopped. I held my breath and then began coughing fiercely. To my surprise, when I looked up again he was completely naked. I lowered my eyes and heard him say, "You've got to let me check you out." What could I do but take off my clothes, too? It felt like taking an exam, not making love. He kissed me all over my body. I didn't dare open my eyes, I was so scared. Then he couldn't find the place to stick it in and was panting desperately. Finally, he said, "Give us a hand, won't you?" I did, and things went pretty smoothly from then on. He asked distractedly, "Are you going to bleed?"

I was very upset. He'd been going with my classmate for two years, but they'd never had sex—this was obviously his first time. We'd been together only a short time, and he'd already made his move. One moment I felt I owed him an apology because I wasn't a virgin; the next I felt upset that he didn't respect me as much as her. But what it boiled down to was that he was tall and a real man; he was neither overly gentle nor too rough; no matter how you looked at it, he was just right. Sure, he came too quickly, but I knew it was his first time; he'd certainly improve with practice. All in all, I was very satisfied with him, and I felt I'd never love anyone else.

When it was over, I went straight to the toilet. It was the wrong time of the month, and I was terrified I'd become pregnant, so I wanted to get rid of all his semen. He came to the bathroom door and asked, "Did you bleed?"

"Yes."

"Let's see."

"No way!"

He insisted. I had no choice but to open the door.

"So where's the blood?" I said nothing. His expression hardened and he stared at me. Finally he burst out, "Liar!"

I thought the game was up, it was hopeless. I went back to my room and lay down, extremely depressed. I didn't know if it was me that was no good, or him. It was ages before he finally came in again. He had undergone a complete transformation, and he showered me with sweet nothings. That's when he said he needed a sweater: Could I knit one for him? We went out and bought some wool, and I immediately set to it. As soon as I began I stitched his name into the sweater as a symbol of my love.

After a few days we both went back to work. He didn't come to see me. I worked on his sweater every day. Then I found out I was pregnant. He came immediately after I wrote to him. "Are you sure it's mine?" was the first thing he said. I said I was. Although he only half believed me, he arranged for an abortion.

Looking back on it, I realize I was in a terrible mess. Since I was in the army, I'd have been in big trouble if they found out. The operation was on a Saturday morning. I took some leave, rested for a day and a half afterward, and went back to work on Monday.

The operation was at 8:30 A.M. He was waiting for me when I came out at ten. I leaned on him. He said he'd take me back, but I didn't want to say good-bye so quickly. "What's the hurry?" I asked. "We may never see each other again. Anyway, I've almost finished the sweater. If you wait a minute you can wear it away." Believe it or not, I'd actually taken the unfinished sweater along to my abortion. Sitting on a bench in the corridor, I quickly did the final stitches as he watched, his arm around my waist. I wished time could have frozen at that moment. That's how I finished the sweater. Although he's married, with a two-year-old child, he still wears it. It was already afternoon by the time he took me home. I watched him go, wearing my sweater, and I knew it was over between us.

The news that he was getting married still came as a terrible blow. My ex-roommate had followed her parents to Peking after their transfer to the capital and then arranged for Big Boy to be posted there too. They had put aside their past misunderstandings. I refused to believe it till he showed me their marriage certificate. Actually, it wasn't that unexpected; what came as a shock was that I took it so badly. I embraced him and cried my eyes out. "Were you just playing with me? Were you ever serious about us?" I asked.

He replied, "You're not like other women. A guy only has to take one look at you to want to get you into bed. Really. I'm not kidding. But that's also why very few men would want to marry you."

It took a while for his transfer to come through. During that time, Big Boy became my de facto husband. We spent every moment we could together. I didn't even look at another man; I was wholly devoted to him. We were very happy together. We never quarreled. I asked him to divorce her and told him I couldn't live without him.

"Okay," he said, "but you'll have to wait for me, because I can't rush things. I have to wait for the right time."

I believed him. I waited for him devotedly. In November 1984 he finally managed the move to Peking, thanks to a bit of string-pulling by his father-in-law. His departure left me devastated—I missed him so much. I found an excuse to visit him. Although he was settled into his new home, he made no attempt to stop me; he even found a place for me to stay with one of his friends. We spent whole days in bed. I must say, his lovemaking had improved a lot. I knew we'd have to part sooner or later, but I refused to think about it, and neither of us mentioned it.

One time, when I was utterly "blissed out"—whenever we were making love, he'd always say, "You make a man feel completely blissed out!" —at that exact moment, he took my face in his hands and said, "You're such a sexy lady, a real temptress, how about me finding you someone to marry?"

I reminded him of his promise that he'd divorce his wife if I waited. I'd been waiting for more than two years, and now he was going back on his word again.

"I don't want to keep you hanging on, but it's not that easy to get a divorce. She's pregnant, and once we have the kid it'll be even harder. I can't get a divorce while she's pregnant, nor while she's breast-feeding. It'll be two years before all that's through, and the child will be a year old. I wouldn't have the heart to divorce her then."

While he was saying this I was thinking, "You liar! You've been screwing me around right from the start!" But I didn't say a word or shed a tear. I'd known this was coming all along. I'd imagined it a thousand times. He was still lying next to me, and I embraced him tightly. Secretly I hoped I'd get pregnant this time. But it was impossible, since I was already on the pill. I said to him, "If you want me to get married I will. But after I'm married, I must have your child."

"You can't go on loving me like this," he said as he embraced me. "I've treated you like a real bastard these past few years, and I feel dirty every time I think about it—not because of us sleeping together, but because ever since I realized you weren't a virgin, all I've wanted was to get some kicks. I've never been serious about you. Now I feel like I'm in a corner. You're too sexy, I can't even look at you without wanting it. I can't bear to leave you. But you've always been serious about me. If I go on stringing you along, I'll ruin your life. You ought to make a home for yourself. And don't even think of having my child, you can only have your husband's child. Get married as quickly as possible, and make a life for yourself."

Now I was really desperate. I had loved Big Boy, but he'd only been playing around with me. I really was a bit mixed up. I met a guy called Sun at a dance, a real playboy. Life was one big party for him. I'd been sharing a room with a young nurse, Xiao Li, a real innocent. After I met Sun he started coming to our room with a friend, Old Si.

One day Sun said he had some time off and wanted to take me up to Peking for some fun. A friend of his who lived in Haidian [district] loaned us his place. It was a room in a two-room flat; the other room was occupied by neighbors. The whole time we stayed there, I never met his friend. After a few days, Old Si came up as well. When I saw him I said, "But there's only one bed, how are we going to sleep three people in here?"

Old Si said, "No problem. I'll just sack out on the floor."

In fact, he ended up in the bed. At first I slept on one side, Sun in the middle, and Old Si on the other side. Sun didn't care what Old Si might think and began banging away as usual. When he finished he rolled off me and over to the side, leaving me in the middle. That is to say, he gave me over to Old Si.

Nothing shows the difference between men more than the way they act in bed. Old Si really knew how to make a girl feel good, he was very attentive. He couldn't really say much in front of Sun, but his hands, mouth, tongue, and other things never stopped for a moment, kneading, stroking, and kissing me until I was really turned on. From that evening on I began to go off Sun and became quite infatuated with Old Si.

The people in the next room eventually figured out what was going on and reported us to the police. So that's what they mean by the term "hooliganism"! It seems we'd broken the law, and I was scared stiff. I called Big Boy; he pulled some strings and they let me out. Later he arranged a meeting. "You really are a slut, aren't you?" he said. "You're absolutely shameless. I never want to speak to you again. The very thought of you makes me sick!"

I burst into tears. I knew I was bad, I'd known it for a long time, but I couldn't get along without a man and I'd never hurt anyone. As a nurse I was second to none. There were only two people in the whole hospital who could give infants their shots, and I was one of them. I was kind and considerate to all my patients, male and female, old and young alike. None of my patients ever got bedsores, and I'd never caused any accidents on account of negligence. It's just that I had to have a man. If it hadn't been for the fact that Big Boy had rejected me, I'd never have ended up with Sun and Old Si like that. Was Big Boy totally blameless for how things had turned out? One word and I'd have given up everything for him. Even though I'm married, I'd go to him right now if he wanted me. I love Big Boy, always have and always will.

I wept and clung to the front of his jacket: "No! I can't live without you!"

He stood there stiffly without moving but didn't push me away. I could tell he didn't really hate me, so I threw my arms about his waist. (He was too tall for me to put my hands around his neck comfortably.) I pressed my face to his chest and hugged tight. I could hear his heart beating; somehow this comforted me. Seeing I wouldn't let go, he finally caressed my shoulders. "It's all right, it's all right. Don't cry."

It was too much to expect him to forgive me. "So this is it. But after all those years as lovers, we can't part just like that, can we?" I asked. So we slept together one final time.

Thinking back on it, Big Boy really was my Mr. Right, the only person who ever really meant anything in my life. I don't know why, but as soon as I lay down next to him, my whole body went limp, as if it had no strength left whatsoever. *The Story of the Stone** often speaks of women appearing as if they have no bones; in Big Boy's arms I felt just like that. I've never been so infatuated with anyone.

All I ever wanted Big Boy to say was "I love you." He never did. Each time I was about to come, I'd hold him tight, call out his name, and cry out "I love you" again and again. His response was to use those great, gentle hands of his to knead my breasts. At most, he'd say, "You're

---

* The Qing dynasty novel *The Story of the Stone,* by Cao Xueqin (eighteenth century), also known as *A Dream of Red Mansions,* is generally considered to be the most outstanding Chinese novel ever written. About a great family in decline, it features many romantic subplots and intrigues. See *The Story of the Stone* (Vols. I–V), trans. David Hawkes and John Minford, London: Penguin Classics, 1973–1986.

great," "You're a little fox come to steal my soul," that sort of thing. The last time we had sex, I said to him, "All these years, you've never said that you loved me. Say it once, won't you?"

"I really am fond of you. But I've got a one-year-old daughter. I can't say I love you. Besides, I don't love you, you're no good."

I started crying again. "But I've loved you with all my heart. If you always want me but don't love me, how good does that make you?"

He became extremely serious and said, "I've told you before, our relationship makes me feel dirty and low. I've only been using you all along. But you are a very attractive woman, extremely sexy and seductive. And you're very kindhearted. Honestly, I can't go on like this. You really must get married, and quick!"

That's how Big Boy and I finally ended our affair. If he wants me to get married, I thought, I'll get married. On that trip to Peking, I hadn't used any contraceptives. It was possible I was carrying his child. So as soon as I got back home I set my sights on getting Old Si to marry me. We got a room in a military hostel using the name of Old Si's father. He was the assistant political commissar for a military subregion. Old Si often phoned me to go sleep with him in the hostel.

I wrote to Big Boy to tell him about my relationship with Old Si. I told him I was pregnant and had no idea whose it was. After all, I'd been with Sun, Old Si, and Big Boy. If fate was kind to me it would be Big Boy's son, and that would make me happy for the rest of my life.

He came as soon as he received my letter. I was thrilled to think he was jealous, it proved he loved me. But he didn't say a thing. He picked up Xiao Li, the young nurse who was my roommate, got a car and went straight to Old Si's home. Old Si and his father were both there. Big Boy took out two letters and showed them to Old Si's father. As it turned out, Old Si had been screwing Xiao Li at the hostel in the morning and me in the afternoon. It wasn't such a terrible blow for me. Old Si wasn't exactly the first man I'd ever slept with, after all. But Xiao Li had been a virgin, and Old Si had forced himself on her. As it turned out, Xiao Li had also written to Big Boy, saying that she was my good friend and she knew that Big Boy was my closest friend. There was no one else to whom she could turn and she thought of Big Boy as an elder brother. Although she wasn't in love with Old Si, she felt she was his since she'd slept with him. But she couldn't tell whether Old Si wanted to marry her or not, and besides, he was my boyfriend, too, and she wasn't willing to steal him from me, so she had asked Big Boy for advice.

I felt so sorry for her. I understood all too well how a woman feels about her first man. Old Si had treated her just as Zhao had treated me all those years ago. I made my position quite clear: "I don't want Old Si, and I hope he'll do the right thing by Xiao Li."

After a long silence, Xiao Li said, "I wouldn't marry a lout like him even if it meant never getting married."

Although I was pregnant, my hopes for marriage had been shattered. I couldn't have the child, not now. When we left Old Si's house, Big Boy held my hand and said, "Come to Peking with me."

I wept. I knew what he had in mind. But I really couldn't bear the thought of getting rid of this baby. I was certain it was Big Boy's and I knew if I had an abortion, there would never be another chance to have his child. But with no immediate prospect of marriage, I risked being kicked out of the army once my belly began to swell. At the very least, I'd be punished. I had to go with Big Boy. I had the operation the following morning. Big Boy bought a soft sleeper for me on the train, and I went straight from the hospital to the train and back to the unit. No one knew about the abortion, and within a few hours I was back on duty in the hospital. I cried my heart out on the train. Big Boy would never be mine, not in this life anyway. Fate would not even let me keep his child.

I became very depressed. I felt that life wasn't worth living, and I started hitting the bottle. If I had nothing else to do after work, I'd change out of my uniform and go find some small restaurant where I could drink. I often got drunk. One day, this guy sat down with me. He was a lab technician in a local hospital. We began drinking together, and soon we were both smashed. We stumbled over to his hospital, clutching each other, and screwed right there in the lab, on the examination table. Strangely enough, he actually fell in love with me and wouldn't leave me alone. I hadn't the slightest intention of marrying him. It took one hell of an effort to dump him.

Big Boy wrote to me: "You're not getting any younger, you know. You'd better get married. Now that you're picking up men, you'll be beyond saving if you don't get married soon." Who made me like this? I asked myself as I read the letter.

I wrote back to him: "You're the only one I want. If you'll have me, I'll never sleep with another man. Without you, who knows what I'll do?"

He replied. "Please, I beg of you, stop carrying on like this. Even if I acted disgracefully toward you, my daughter is already two years old. I refuse to let her or her mother down. Why can't you accept that in this life I can think of you only as a sister—isn't that good enough?"

So I'd become an emotional burden for him! He had absolutely no idea how much I loved him. "All right, all right. I'll find a husband," I replied.

At the time I had a patient called Wu, a radar platoon leader from Tianjin—my hometown. He was 1.80 meters tall and had a gentle disposition. I thought he wouldn't be a bad catch. If nothing else, we could go back to Tianjin together once we'd finished our terms of duty. So I began to treat him with an extra dose of tender loving care. I don't know what it was about me—once I set my sights on a man, he was like putty in my hands.

Once we began going together, I wrote to Big Boy to tell him. What followed was really a comedy of errors. For it to make sense, I have to begin with Big Boy's side of the story.

Big Boy set out as soon as he received my letter. It was 11 P.M. when he got off the train. He went straight to my dorm to look for me. When he knocked on the door, the person inside asked who he was looking for. Because he didn't want to make any trouble for me, he pretended to be passing on a message that I had a phone call. He was told I was on night shift. He went to the nurses' station, but they told him I was in the dorm. Big Boy hadn't a clue where to look next, so he decided to get himself a room for the night at the hostel. The attendant on duty looked through the room register and told him there was a spare bed in No. 5 —one of the nurses' boyfriends had the other. Big Boy registered and found No. 5. Seeing the door was locked, he knocked.

Wu and I were inside. The room had indeed been taken by another nurse's boyfriend, but he'd left that day. I'd asked her to keep the room and had given the boyfriend's registration card to Wu. We'd arranged to meet there to spend the night together. When Big Boy knocked on the door, Wu asked who it was. Big Boy replied, "Another guest for the room." I recognized his voice immediately and flew into a rage. You bastard, I thought, first you tell me to find a husband and then you come running here to catch me in the act. I was furious. Still wearing my nightdress—after all, I had nothing Big Boy hadn't seen before—I threw the door open and started screaming at him before he had even stepped into the room. "You bastard! You've ruined my life, and now you want to add insult to injury! You are the biggest son of a bitch I've ever met!"

Big Boy grabbed me under my arms and held me. Then, pushing me down into the armchair, he turned to close the door. "I had no idea you were here!"

I didn't believe him. I started punching him with my fists. "You liar!

You've always been a liar!" He tried to explain, but I wasn't having any of it. I wouldn't let him speak. I went on hitting and swearing at him. I hated him!

He paid no attention to me. He walked into the bedroom and stood in the doorway while Wu put on his clothes. Wu was scared shitless. He'd gone all pale, and his knees were knocking together. Looking at the pathetic spectacle of Wu and then at Big Boy, I grew even angrier. I don't know why, but despite the fact that I'd looked high and low, I'd never found another man to compare with Big Boy.

Wu stood there looking absolutely wretched. Big Boy asked his name and unit. Wu answered the questions obediently. I didn't say anything, though I felt like I was suffocating, and went on pummeling Big Boy's back. Ignoring me, he continued his "interrogation."

Then Big Boy reached out and dragged me over to Wu, saying to him, "Are you going to marry her or what?"

Having no idea what Big Boy's game was, Wu quickly shook his head no. At this, Big Boy threw me into the chair and grabbed a stool. Finally, Wu had a flash of machismo and said, "So you're looking for a fight?"

Big Boy replied, "Yes, you mongrel bastard!"

Wu said, "She's just a woman, don't blame her. If you want a fight, then fight me!"

I interjected, "Big Boy, this is none of your business! I want to be with him!"

Big Boy gave me a look full of hatred: "I just can't stand by as people use you!"

As soon as he spoke, he swung the stool at Wu. Luckily, Wu was a soldier too and his reactions were quick. He ducked, and the stool caught him on the shoulder, knocking him to the floor. After all, the poor guy was sick, shorter than Big Boy by six centimeters, and a pale, weak-looking thing. He was no match for Big Boy. As he sat there on the floor, Big Boy stood in front of him and asked again, "Well, are you going to marry her?"

Wu said, "I can't talk to you while I'm sitting on the floor!" Big Boy helped him up and they both sat on the sofa.

Wu asked, "What are you after?"

Big Boy said, "If you're just fooling around with her, you're not going to get out of here tonight in one piece. She's a good woman, intelligent and clever. A real jewel. If you intend to marry her, fine. Otherwise, you'd better watch out. If you dump her, I'll report you to your unit and then you'll be finished!"

This made me hopping mad. "Big Boy, you are a shit. Get out! I don't want you here. Stop interfering in my life. What right do you have to force us to marry?"

"I mean what I say," Big Boy continued to Wu without so much as a glance in my direction. "If you don't believe it, try me."

That's how Wu and I came to be married. But I was still furious with Big Boy. Before my wedding, I went to his parents' home and spilled out the entire story of our relationship in front of his wife. As a result, his wife nagged and ranted at him for nearly six months, demanding a divorce. Big Boy made a big show of repentance, and in the end they decided to stay together. I felt I'd had my revenge. I didn't hate him anymore. Later I learned that he didn't hate me either: He actually felt he'd behaved badly toward me and gotten what he deserved.

Moral Depravity and Animal Passion

ZHANG MINGDUO

"A Sexy Lady" by comrades Dai Qing and Luo Ke has left me shocked and apprehensive. It goes to great lengths to proclaim the uncontrollable nature of sexual passion and presents us with a picture of permissiveness, free sex, seduction, and promiscuity limned in unblushing detail. The detailed depiction of carnal desire and promiscuity reveals moral degradation and animal desire, a world in which man has degenerated into beast and modern civilization has fallen into barbarism. It is a story that reduces heterosexual love to its most primitive and basic form. Given the low educational standards of people today, the portrayal of sexual arousal and release, unrestrained by law and breaking all the rules of morality, threatens the sanctity of family life and flouts the demands of socialist spiritual construction. It may also lure our young men and women into crime in their quest for sexual gratification and contribute to the destabilization of the society.

We don't deny that love is one of literature's eternal themes. The problem lies, rather, in the aesthetic approach of the writer: Should the portrayal of love elevate the subject to a highly civilized plane and promote social stability or reduce it to primitive barbarism and create chaos? The answer, of course, is the former. Certainly, people are creatures with a complex emotional makeup that includes the sexual instinct, but in the final analysis there must be something that distinguishes us from animals. The human race requires normal, chaste, and faithful love; it will always despise "laid-back," "casual," "easy" attitudes toward sex.

To condemn giving free reign to carnal desire and dissipation is not to advocate asceticism. Nowhere in the world, not even in bourgeois societies, does sexual activity go unbounded by law and morality—socialist China cannot be an exception. Yet we are perplexed by the fact that contemporary love stories look increasingly as though they're turning into sex stories. This kind of writing quietly got under way when the fetters of "leftism" were smashed; since then it's torn off the veil of bashfulness and made a frontal assault on the literary sphere. Now sex brazenly exposes itself on the pages of certain books and periodicals. Titillation and descriptions of the sexual act are flagrantly used to attract readers, make money, and corrupt the healthy bodies and souls of our youth, thereby creating a man-made state of turmoil.

"A Sexy Lady" describes the dissolute love life of an air force hospital nurse and her male patients. This young lady . . . defines her personal worth in terms of sexual relations. . . . She will sleep with anyone, anywhere, and even has sex with two men in the same bed. Though she had tuberculosis, she couldn't wait until she was sufficiently recovered to have a dirty night with Big Boy. One can see, from these examples, the fearful lengths to which sexual frenzy may extend.

The image of the nurse projected here is not one of shining nobility but, rather, a composite of promiscuity and debauchery, and the male patients are portrayed as sex maniacs. We must make it quite clear that this blackens the name of the People's Liberation Army and befouls the reputation of army nurses and patients.

While we are opposed to the whitewashing of reality, we also condemn mudslinging.

If one evaluates "A Sexy Lady" in terms of contemporary Chinese and international standards, one cannot avoid the following conclusions:

1. This work stands in contradiction to the overall demands of socialist spiritual construction. Evidence from both China and abroad shows that a nation that has no ideals or spiritual standards lives in pathetic ignorance. In "Establish Socialism with Chinese Characteristics," Comrade Deng Xiaoping has pointed out: "The most important thing in establishing socialist spiritual civilization is to instill Communist ideals, morality, culture, and discipline in the broad masses of the people." Yet the ideals and goals of "A Sexy Lady" place sexual desire above all else.

2. The work is an insult to both the honor and good character of military personnel. The portrayal of moral depravity among military and

"Lock," sculpture by Wu Shaoxiang

medical workers undermines the people's trust in them. The army is the symbol of national dignity; it is a body formed of the nation's most outstanding sons and daughters, and it sets high standards of morality, idealism, and character for everyone. As the Sixth Plenum of the Twelfth Party Congress has pointed out with regard to the building of spiritual civilization, "The People's Liberation Army is the Great Wall of Iron protecting the motherland and the force making the strongest contribution toward the construction of the motherland, an army with a high degree of ideological awareness, excellent moral character, and strict organizational discipline, which has a great spiritual influence on the whole people." Where in "A Sexy Lady" can you find the People's Army Hospital of the 1980s, the true image of today's soldiers and hospital workers?

One must ask, do the authors have any conscience at all? Where is their sense of responsibility toward society, their sense of historical mission?

—December 1988

The book containing "A Sexy Lady" was banned in Mainland China around the time of Dai Qing's imprisonment in July 1989.

Sounds of the City

Another strain of poetic red noise is that of the "urban poets," whose ironic examinations of alienation and self-gratification contributed a lighter note to the literary proceedings of the 1980s. Many of these writers, including Sun Xiaogang and Song Lin, were based in Shanghai.

The Black-Skinned City

SUN XIAOGANG

In this city
Five dance halls, five scattered shells
Forever
Luring the frothy sunlight and aerobics outfits

Black-skinned city
Black-skinned city.

The latest fashions in silk stockings on a row of milk-white
*   mannequins' feet*
Spinning
An impression of avenues
Tapping out the success of a commodity fair.
Very pretty—but the young girls are still practicing

Black-skinned city
Black-skinned city . . .

Life
Is a stadium in the South

Never enough
Seats
A blue advertisement announces the Swan
On a corner of the street is a pile of bras on sale. . . .

Prisoners of Work

SONG LIN

On holiday mornings the city plays "Pinocchio"
When did our group,
Mad for the night,
Learn to be as speechless as marionettes?
Someone whistles softly in the cold street
Like minks we playfully slide down night's fur coat
Hungry for exile
Thirsting for close encounters with the Muse
Irrepressible waves of emotion surge past the Adam's apple
Extravagant brush strokes describe the form of the soul
Until the exhausted stallions pass through the damp wall
To come trampling on my forehead
The goose quill tumbles into the abyss beneath my arm
The loud nasal snoring of the simple sofa
Strikes up the holiday prelude
Our gang
      prisoners of work . . .

Urban Poetry

ZHU DAKE

The dancing, festive crowds, as well as every type of romantic crowd, assemble within the tradition of poetry recital, marching around the sacred fire of racial images. This does, after all, offend the brittle sensitivities of the so-called "neoindividualists." But they are in all truth born of the small clans and mah-jongg players of the semi-industrialized city. They establish claques of warm camaraderie on the basis of poetry and play, begetting the gray sentimentality of the little man. Doubting all the while the national myths and the heroic aesthetic, they are compromised by all that is mediocre, forming a new stratum that joins in with the urban ideology. . . .

In the drama of everyday life they play the most debased roles with equanimity, determined to continue the deception of happiness and thereby giving succor to their timid souls. . . .

The victory of the urban mentality and the power displayed by the national ideology have melded to pose a real threat to the avant-garde poetry movement. They are powerful, yet elusive, as omnipresent as dust, while at the same time possessing an appearance of familiarity and ordinariness. The soft technology can confound even the most extreme attitudes of rebellion. Yet from another angle, the moment that passion, belief, and imagination have all been annihilated, leaving nothing but wretched everyday experience, these things themselves form into the new building blocks of urban poetry. This is misread by the critics, whom it takes by surprise; they mistakenly believe it augurs a new age for the avant-garde.

The Rites of Marx

SUN XIAOGANG

If
There really is an Asiatic mode of recreation
Marx, of course,
To this quiet Chinese lawn would come
To meet
With some of the East's more outstanding individuals.

Even if you're only a bust
Pull up a comfy chair anyway.

The sculptor
Calculating the surface area of a great man
Lets the fresh flowers of March create a contrast.
Today

We cannot help but add a note
To the history of the citizens of the world.

The works of Marx
Sit prominently in the National Library.
But can you reproduce his cranium?
Since time can't satisfy the demands of three-dimensional space
What can we in the East do about it?

. . . Eastern gracefulness lends the statue a white harmony
The weekend invented by Marx separates the weeks by a day.

A sea gull, deep in thought, decorates an advertisement.

A city dedicates a statue to Marx.
News from space: looks great from up here.

In the post-massacre purge, Zhu Dake was, for a time, put under inves-
tigation and a number of the young Shanghai poets, including Song Lin,
were detained. Yet in the spring of 1990, a new underground poetry
journal, Art Stranger, *appeared in Shanghai. In May of that year, Song*
Lin was released, and in April 1991 a new national, unofficial poetry
journal, Modern Chinese Poetry, *was produced in Peking.*

And the Beat Goes On

NICHOLAS JOSE

Nicholas Jose is an Australian novelist who taught in China and served as Cultural Counselor in the Australian Embassy in Peking from 1987 to 1990. Fluent in Chinese, he had an intimate knowledge of both the official and unofficial cultural scenes of the Chinese capital. He returned to Peking from Shanghai on the morning of June 4 and was evacuated with other Australian nationals on June 7, returning several months later to continue his work at the embassy. This excerpt is taken from an article written around the time of the October 1 National Day celebrations in 1989 and published in the Australian magazine The Independent Monthly.

The propaganda campaign continues on a massive scale, working its way into all areas of society. From senior officials and teachers to hotel employees and taxi drivers, people are spending days watching videos of the "peaceful quelling of the counter-revolutionary rebellion," studying texts, hearing speeches, and being asked to explain their behavior around June 3–4. Fortunately, if they can stay awake, they too can exploit the art of ambiguous interpretation. "I am clear now, I understand, I know what really happened," they say, and if they're lucky, they pass. Meanwhile, every night the television news lists half a dozen bumper harvests.

The single fact that leaves no doubt in my mind that what happened in Peking on June 3–4 was substantially as it was reported [overseas] is not a statistic, nor what I saw, nor another eyewitness report. It is the mood of the people of Peking, now, four months after the suppression: not quite as palpable as the stone with which Dr. Johnson refuted Bishop Berkeley, but almost. A city is not easily filled with a sense of moral anger and righteous hatred, not to mention shock, anguish, and despondency so profound as that existing in Peking today.

Autumn is the favored season in Peking, a time of brilliant blue skies and golden days, of festivals and abundance. The market stalls groan with grapes as big as plums, crisp Chinese pears, mountains of melons, and the mutton carcasses brought in for the Mongolian hotpot that is eaten as the weather gets colder. The quality of produce is dramatically better than five years ago, thanks to the Reforms and the increased use of chemicals in farming, but inflation has driven prices dramatically higher. People are buying still, but this year there is a sense of garnering in. The price offered by the moneychangers has dropped. There is a move away from imported goods. The demand for color television sets has eased (perhaps in revulsion at the propaganda campaign waged on TV, because shortwave radios are a hot item, for listening to the Voice of America and the BBC).

The government has ordered an austerity campaign, and the people have responded in their own way by battening down the hatches. Families are making long-term plans. There is a widespread but unspoken feeling that things could get worse before they get better. Economic collapse, famine, even civil war, are not impossible, and the specter of the latter has determined many people to get themselves out of China. The government distributes largesse—eggs and fish—to mark the festival period and then orders employees to buy government bonds to the value of two months' pay. He that giveth also taketh away.

But the real festival this autumn was the 100-days' anniversary of the Peking massacre, and the regime is reaping what it has sown in a harvest of popular alienation.

The students at Peking University, subjected to intensive reeducation and threatened with assignment to the countryside on graduation, bang their chopsticks on the canteen tables and hoot when the newly appointed hard-line president speaks. They slow-march around campus lugubriously singing. "Without the Communist Party there'd be no New China." A solitary old woman burns paper in a residential courtyard to mourn the death of her son on June 4, and the neighbors silently gather. A young man jumps to his death in front of the martial law troops, from the bridge where the tanks were stationed. On a streetside stall, the bookseller draws browsers' attention to an essay by one of the dissidents now organizing abroad, Yan Jiaqi, in a book on display. All night long, people are losing themselves in a purposeless frenzy of gambling, clicking the 144 mah-jongg pieces, which they satirically call "Reading the 144th Directive of Deng Xiaoping." Others respond in a more upbeat way, wearing smarter clothes, more makeup, wilder hairstyles—as if, in the sophistication born of the newfound clarity with which they regard their rulers, they are determined to indulge their "bourgeois liberalization" to the utmost.

The regime seems to be nervous, paying paranoid and counterproductive attention to detail in the measures taken to stop further unrest. How crass to erect the Styrofoam sculpture of united workers, peasants, intellectuals, and soldiers where the Goddess of Democracy had stood in Tiananmen Square. For Peking is a city that has not been permitted to grieve for its dead, and the festering grief and shock have produced a lasting defiance, which is the most threatening possible force in a society based on deference. The empty, cordoned-off square at the heart of the State remains haunted ground, an unavoidable reminder. And while this mood continues people are waiting, edgily, for the next explosion.

The determination of a people is not something that can be seen in an organized resistance or spelled out in manifestos, and for that reason it is impossible for the regime to dispel it. Whatever restrictions are imposed, the spirit of 1989 will find its way.

Everyone is just sitting around, whining and cursing, waiting for the authorities to make fools of themselves, for something to happen or someone to die. . . . We must do something before it's too late to do anything.

—Hou Dejian, November 1989

On the afternoon of June 4, Hou, who had been taken secretly from Tiananmen Square with Liu Xiaobo, took refuge with Australian friends. He was eventually smuggled into the Australian embassy, where he remained in hiding until the Chinese authorities gave assurances that he would not be arrested. After Australian nationals had been evacuated, he slept in Nicholas Jose's empty office in the embassy.

Although his fellow hunger strikers had all been arrested, Hou was presumably spared because of his special status as a Taiwan "defector." After his emergence from the embassy, he was free to travel the city in his "pajett red" Mercedes-Benz, though the authorities forbade him to leave Peking and the police called him in for "polite" questioning after he insisted on giving interviews to foreign reporters in which he said he believed at least one thousand people had died in the massacre and made other remarks critical of the government.

At Liubukou, outside the forbidden headquarters where China's leaders live, and where one of the bloodiest encounters took place on June 4 —like doubting Thomas I have seen the bullet hole in a friend's leg—a new nightclub has been opened, valiantly continuing the entrepreneurial spirit. A newly formed Chinese band was playing. They call themselves "1989, I Love You." The place was packed, jumping to versions of "Hey, Joe," "Get Back," and "Let It Bleed" only meters from where hundreds of people had been bleeding only weeks before, in one of the grimmest nights of recent Chinese history. The point was lost on no one. When the band concluded its gig with one of the obligatory patriotic songs, they turned "Without the Communist Party there'd be no New China" into a weird, cacophonous twenty-minute improvisation that could be interpreted as a musical reenactment of events still imprinted on everyone's mind. It was electrifying. Nothing was said, and nothing needed to be said.

There will be those who claim that the situation in Peking has returned to normal. There will be photographs of tourists going to the Great Wall, of old men exercising their birds, of children singing charming songs for the leaders, and of merchants signing deals. As the poet W. H. Auden observed, the farmers in the field don't even look up as Icarus falls from the sky, and "the torturer's horse scratches its innocent behind on a tree" even as the torturer goes about his work.

But look again. The dangerous liaisons and secret meetings go on, and people disappear in the middle of the night. Perhaps the civil war has already begun, in a clash of cultures and values, regions and generations. Let us hope that moderation and pragmatism prevail, and that a way forward is found before the armies line up to fight again. The process of struggle is under way. For that reason I dare to have hope for China.

Carry On

HOU DEJIAN

We must carry on.
Go on living.
Do it well.

What's the sound of life?
The melody of age?

I cannot sing an illness,
I'm not willing to die.

I'm afraid.
Is there really a God above?
I doubt it.
Does anybody believe in anything anymore?
Why is life so unfair?
Why can't things work out the way we'd like?

I'm sick of that ancient and boring game.
I love you, more than anyone else.
But there's just one thing—I love myself even more.
I can't help loving myself more.

What are the melodies of love?
The acoustics of anger?
I cannot sing my grief,
I forgot long ago what happiness is.

We played too many games these past few years
We only just discovered that someone else made up the rules.
I protest against the unfair rules;
I refuse to play a game I'll never win.

To carry on is my last remaining right.
Don't tell me to give it up.
No matter what others have to say,
We must carry on.

We must carry on,
And not bring grief upon ourselves again.
We must go on living,
We must carry on.
                    —August 1989, the Australian Embassy, Peking

In early 1990, Hou Dejian said he'd stopped trying to write songs with
messages and started playing the blues instead.

PART IV

Wheels

Revolution, counter-revolution, nonrevolution.

Revolutionaries are massacred by counter-revolutionaries. Counter-revolutionaries are massacred by revolutionaries. Non-revolutionaries are sometimes taken for revolutionaries, and then they are massacred by counter-revolutionaries, or again they are taken for counter-revolutionaries, and then they are massacred by revolutionaries. Sometimes, also, they are not taken for anything in particular, but they are still massacred by revolutionaries and by counter-revolutionaries.

Revolution. To revolutionize revolution; to revolutionize the revolution of revolution; to rev . . .

LU XUN, 1927

China's a massive thing, still hidden in the mists.

The Chinese don't understand China; all they know are "Chinese clichés." Foreigners don't understand China; all they know is "Chinese chop suey."

. . . to understand China, you must come to grips with the tradition.

LI AO, 1979

The traditional Chinese worldview saw history as a cyclical development: dynasties were founded, flourished, and then, growing corrupt, fell into decline, to be overthrown and replaced by a new imperial house that would then repeat the cycle. Although historians have shown this to be an overly simplistic, even fallacious, view, the notion of cycles still has a potent grip on the Chinese imagination, one further strengthened by the television series *River Elegy* and the "historical" writings of authors like Jin Guantao.

There are all kinds of cycles, or wheels. They can be found in the supposedly immutable alternation of order and chaos, in the traditional calendar, which represents time as a series of sixty-year cycles (with years of danger and calamity, such as the Year of the Dragon), and in the Buddhist doctrine of reincarnation within the Wheel of Life. (A common pre–May Fourth curse was "May you fall into the wheel!") In this chapter we attempt to illustrate several cycles related to the events of the late 1980s; cycles to which many of those involved in the 1989 Protest Movement felt themselves bound.

The wheel of protest, denunciation, and self-flagellation has been revolving in China since 1949. Each new political movement—and there have been dozens of them, as Wu Zuguang comments in his speech "On China's National Characteristics"—represents another turn of that wheel. Sometimes the similarities between one political movement and another are deeply unsettling, as illustrated in Chen Ruoxi's story "The Old Man," which is set just after the April 5 Tiananmen Incident of 1976 but which with a few minor changes could describe the aftermath of the Protest Movement of 1989. And the Protest Movement itself, as we saw in Part I, "The Cry," began with petitions to release Wei Jingsheng—the dissident whose activities symbolized the beginning of pro-democracy agitation in post-Mao China.

The continued relevance of the May Fourth Movement as an "old dream" has been a major theme of this book. In this section, the mainland scholar Xu Jilin analyzes what he calls the "vicious cycle of the May Fourth Movement." On the eve of the seventieth anniversary of the movement in 1989, he asked: Why were the cries for the introduction of democracy and the "liberation of thought" first heard in 1919 raised afresh sixty, and indeed seventy, years later, with equal passion and urgency?

The 1980s also saw the recycling of the old debate concerning China's "national characteristics" and the revival of interest in China's "national essence" as illustrated by the fad for *qigong,* that most mysterious form of Chinese kung fu. *Qigong* mania became widespread as the 1980s wore on, and its near-universal popularity seemed almost to be a reaction to the spiritual confusion and "foreignness" of the Reform era.

In applying the heavy hand of "order" to quell what it perceived as unbearable "chaos" in 1989, the party was itself following a pattern thousands of years old. Just as the first Qin emperor, Qin Shihuang, had

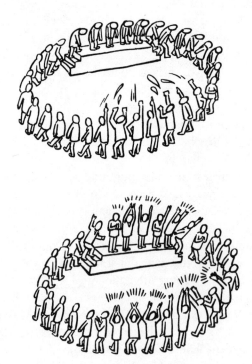

"Transmigration: Two Views," Xia Qingquan

responded to criticism by killing his critics and burning their books, so too did the government of Deng Xiaoping, Yang Shangkun, and Li Peng react to the petitions and pleas for dialogue with bloodshed and censorship. Here both Luo Beishan, an elderly Chinese writer in exile, and Lao She, a Peking novelist, comment on the patterns of control, both new and old, that are familiar to every Chinese.

In Part II, "Bindings," we saw how both reformers and individualists have tried to break free of the cycle of history, sometimes with fatal consequences. Often they have ended up "rediscovering the wheel": The essays and polemics of Li Ao, Bo Yang, Liu Xiaobo, and others repeat and reformulate the concerns of leaders of the 1898 Reform Movement and the May Fourth generation.

The journalist Dai Qing, however, embarked on her own course: She set out to undo the very mechanism of the wheel of modern Chinese history, hoping thereby to break its fatal charm. Her planned series of "historical reportage," which dealt first with such figures as Wang Shiwei (a victim of the party's first political and cultural purge in 1942) and then with Chu Anping (a prominent victim of the 1957 Anti-Rightist Campaign), would, if allowed to continue, have led to a collapse of the party's control over the past, thereby threatening the basis of the party's legitimacy itself. It was a danger the party clearly recognized.

The attraction of the wheel—these cycles of history—is both subtle and insidious. It causes people to think that change is impossible, that progress is a dream, and that the future is reflected in nothing so much as the past. After all, the traditional aim of each revolution, each turn of the dynastic wheel, was not to progress into the future but to pursue a dream of returning to the Golden Age of the past. The belief in the cycles of history itself is tyrannic, for it feeds a gloomy fatalism that serves the status quo.

The Mysterious Circle of Mao Zedong

LIU YAZHOU

It was three days before his death, and Mao Zedong could no longer talk. He put his thumb and forefinger together to form a circle and showed the doctors and nurses. Then, afraid they hadn't understood, he lifted his arm with great effort and traced a circle in the air.

But what did it mean? Was this some mysterious cipher? A prophecy? In the last days of his life, he bequeathed a riddle in the shape of a circle to his empire.

The doctors panicked. Hua Guofeng, Wang Dongxing,* and the rest rushed to his bedside. They tried to work out what he meant, like children playing a guessing game. Jiang Qing came as well, but not even she knew what her husband's gesture signified. . . .

I don't understand what he meant, either. No one will ever know for sure. But if you ask me, I'd say he was describing his own history.

History is circular.

Everything is circular.

Isn't that so?

He began in Tiananmen Square, and that's where he ended up. He had traveled in a big circle.

He returned to Tiananmen Square, never to leave again. He became the square's resident in perpetuity, its only resident. . . .

The largest tomb in the modern world was erected on Tiananmen Square. But it's not really a tomb. It's a spacious, resplendent villa. It has a white marble armchair inside. You can see it when you enter the main hall. There's a bed, too, and that's where you'll find him. The place is air-conditioned and has an elevator. In the morning the elevator takes him up to the hall where he works, and at night it lowers him to the depths where he sleeps.

* Hua was to be Mao's successor as party chairman, Wang was head of security.

Mao Zedong presides over Tiananmen Square. He is forever observing his people, and the people are forever watching him, ever mindful of his Thought. No matter how you look at it, he is immutable.

Mao Zedong, male, from Xiangtan County, Hunan Province, 1.78 meters tall, born of a rich peasant family.

This passage concludes the book The Square—Altar for an Idol *by Liu Yazhou, which was published in Hong Kong in early 1990. The thirty-seven-year-old novelist is the son-in-law of Li Xiannian, China's former state president.*

Another popular explanation for the "mysterious circle of Mao Zedong" is that the dying chairman was trying to tell those around him to work together and not to purge one another after he was gone. If so, no one paid any attention.

Tiananmen Revisited

Gone now those surging crowds, no more the chaotic and
discordant noise. Gone, too, that forest of pup tents, no
trace of that Styrofoam statue, either, the so-called
Goddess. The flag of the People's Republic of China flies
high in the center of the square, guarded closely by orderly
ranks of People's Liberation Army soldiers. "Restore the
noble mien of Tiananmen Square as soon as possible."
This, the repeated call of the people of Peking, has been
realized at last. The solemn vista of the square emerges
now as the massive portrait of Mao Zedong hanging on
Tiananmen Gate once more beams out a beatific smile.
        —*"A correspondent,"* Peking Daily,
        June 8, 1989

The Old Man

CHEN RUOXI

*Shortly after Tiananmen Square was taken away from the people and
returned to the People in June 1989, work units throughout Peking
ordered their employees to explain their involvement in the six-week
Protest Movement, in particular where they were on June 3–4, and to
write what was called an "understanding" of the movement, that is, how
they viewed it in retrospect. Such a widespread campaign to elicit confessions and self-criticisms had not been seen in the capital since the Cultural Revolution.*

*Chen Ruoxi's short story "The Old Man" describes a person who was
caught up in the Tiananmen Incident of April 5, 1976, when crowds
clashed with police over the removal of memorials to the recently de-
ceased Premier Zhou Enlai. For many people, this public mourning was
a pretext for expressing their profound dissatisfaction with the Cultural
Revolution. Many of the poems and posters made scathing references to
the Dowager Empress Cixi of the Qing dynasty and Qin Shihuang, one*

(Paul Slattery)

of the most ruthless rulers in Chinese history—barely disguised attacks on Jiang Qing and Mao himself.

In the following extract from "The Old Man," a local cadre comes to check on the old man's progress in writing his "confession."

The door of the courtyard opened with a squeak, and the old couple's eyes turned to the door of their room. Who could be coming in this late? The footsteps approached, moved up the steps, and stopped outside their door. Suddenly there was a knock. It gave the old woman a start, and she nearly jabbed her hand with her needle. She walked toward the door without even a glance at her husband, her heart pounding.

She opened the door, letting in a gust of cold wind and with it a leading cadre from the local party branch, the husband of the Neighborhood Committee leader. The old couple were somewhat relieved. This subgroup chief was a fellow party member and treated the old man with the respect due to an older cadre.

"Have you eaten?" the subgroup chief inquired politely, doing his best to conceal his feelings behind a poker face. He nodded his head and smiled a lot when he was with them; it must have taken a lot of self-control to maintain his equanimity.

"Yes, yes, we've eaten, please have a seat." The old woman offered the visitor her own chair and went to close the door. Rather than sitting down, he grasped the back of the chair with both hands. His posture implied that if he were to sit down and relax, he would soften. He thought it better to remain standing.

"Have you written your confession?" he asked, staring at the old man.

The old man hesitated a moment. "No, I haven't."

"Have you started it?"

"I haven't finished it." The old man avoided his gaze.

The subgroup chief's expression wavered, and the corners of his mouth trembled. He was about to go on but remembered that the old man had been in the party almost as long as he'd been alive, and he stopped himself.

"Listen." He leaned forward as he spoke. "The Neighborhood Committee believes you are being stubborn and procrastinating. I'm here to warn you to treat this matter more seriously. If everyone were as stubborn as you about writing their confessions, the committee would never get any work done! You're an old party member, you should be aware of the party's firm policy: leniency toward those who confess their crimes and severity toward those who refuse. Just tell the truth, don't beat around the bush. Your confession should be simple and clear—just describe what you saw—that's all there is to it. Actually, we don't believe you participated in the incident."

The subgroup chief offered them a toothy smile and looked at the old man's balding head and the few scattered, graying hairs that were left on it.

"You were out the entire day. Who were you with? What did you talk about? What did you do? Were you with someone who took part in the incident? You said you were drinking in a wine shop. What wine shop? Who can vouch for you? Chairman Mao says, 'We must have faith in the masses and in the party.' You're not the main object of our investigations. We're trying to ferret out the handful of counterrevolutionary elements who instigated the April 5 Incident. Were you in Tiananmen Square those mornings before the incident? Finally, you should examine your own actions in the light of the campaign to criticize Deng Xiaoping!"

When the subgroup chief said "in the light of the campaign to criticize Deng Xiaoping," the old man remembered how, not so long ago, the subgroup chief had been praising Deng Xiaoping. The old man smiled derisively at the way he was making a fool of himself.

The subgroup chief hesitated for a moment. Actually, he himself hadn't worked out the precise role Deng Xiaoping was playing in this affair.

"In short, what I'm saying is for your own good. If you can't write your confession and self-criticism in time, the Neighborhood Committee will have to deal with you as a special case and turn you over to your old work unit. That's all I've got to say. Now it's up to you."

The old woman, who had been sitting quietly all this time on the edge of the bed, spoke up. "He'll give it to you tomorrow," she said. "He'll write it tonight."

The old man turned toward his wife. When the subgroup chief mentioned the old man's former work unit, her face had paled in fright. The old man guessed that she had been reminded of the criticisms and grillings they had suffered in the 1960s.

"All right, I'll have it done first thing tomorrow morning," he said.

"Fine. Then we'll come early tomorrow to collect it."

The subgroup chief pushed his chair back to its original place next to the table to indicate the end of the conversation. By the time the old man managed to stand up to see him off, his wife had already opened the door. The couple watched him go down the steps before closing their door and bolting it. The old man stumbled back into his chair, his hands pressed against the small of his back. The pain was excruciating. His lower back felt as if it were about to shatter into little pieces. . . .

"Do you feel any better?" He had been lying completely still for a whole minute, and she thought that he had fallen asleep.

"Much better," he said, turning over and sitting up to put on his clothes. "At least there's some feeling there now. This afternoon I was so stiff I couldn't feel a thing."

"That's because you cleaned the toilet!" the old woman admonished him. "Next time, I'll do it for you."

"The doctor said that physical exercise is good for rheumatism."

"Yes, but you've got to think of your age too." His wife sighed. "Now you'd better write something so that you can hand in your confession tomorrow!"

The old woman cast an entreating and doleful glance at her husband, as if she were the object of criticism and not he. Under the dim yellow light, her short, graying hair, thin face, and protruding cheekbones made her look as though she had just recovered from a long illness.

"I'll do it now."

He couldn't bear to disappoint her. Every time he noticed her silent, imploring eyes, that lump of lead in the pit of his stomach received a jolt and melted into acquiescence. . . .

"I'll make you a pot of tea!" The thought of helping the old man write his confession so pleased her that she couldn't sit still.

"Don't bother, just put a little more water in my cup and go to bed. Don't wait up."

The old woman filled his cup and took it into the smaller room in silence. She switched on the table lamp and noticed that the pen and paper on the table hadn't been moved. She put the cup down on the table, returned to the larger room, sat down on the bed, and continued working on her shoe. She lowered her head and concentrated on her sewing, watching the study out of the corner of her eye. But the old man needed to be alone, and he gently closed the door.

"April 1. It was a fine day . . ."

Leaning back in the rattan chair, the old man gazed up at the floral curtains, resting the cup in his hands against his chest. There was no clock in the room, so he didn't know what time it was, but he guessed it was late. For a long while there had been no sounds of activity from any of the other households in the courtyard. His wife came in twice to fill his cup, but after that, there was silence. She had probably gone to sleep. The wind stopped and the night fell silent, strangely empty and cool.

He looked down at the sheet of white lined paper. He could hardly believe it had taken him such a long time to write those seven words: "April 1. It was a fine day."

The subgroup chief's threat to turn his case over to his old work unit was still ringing in his ears.

So what if he had to go back there, he said to himself defiantly, a detached smile passing momentarily over his face. Since he had already resolved the great questions of life and death for himself, these more mundane matters seemed as insignificant as dust.

"If the people fear not death, then death will not threaten them." It was because there were people who feared neither death nor punishment that the Tiananmen Incident, that expression of protest against twen-tieth-century tyranny, had occurred.

Opposition hadn't suddenly sprung up on April 5, either. In late March, people had already begun placing wreaths before the Monument to the People's Heroes. The Peking Municipal Committee became appre-hensive and sent out instructions to all of the city's schools and offices forbidding it. The old man learned this from the primary school teacher [who shared the courtyard]. As laying wreaths was prohibited, it natu-rally became difficult to buy them, but people found ways around it, and began making their own. In the teacher's school, students and teachers worked through the night and produced beautiful paper wreaths in a rainbow of colors.

The restrictions on laying wreaths at the monument only served to increase their numbers. At this time, the old man started taking a walk to Tiananmen Square after breakfast every day. On April 4, the wreaths were piled so high that they began spilling over the railings surrounding the monument. Some who were unable to make wreaths wrote elegiac poems instead, and attached them to other people's wreaths. There were so many poems that there wasn't enough room for them all around the monument, so they were hung from the trees in the grove of pines. Crowds of spectators came here too, both to read the poems and to copy them down. Leaflets containing the poems were quickly printed and distributed, but it was even more inspiring to watch as, tape-recorded by others, people recited the poems. When they came to the most moving parts of a poem, many people shed tears. "Wild ghosts jibber, cold dew covers the ground . . ." This line brought a sigh from the old man and many others who heard it and when the lines "Return to me my precious isle; Unite the Motherland" were read the old man's tears fell like rain.*

Though the old man hadn't copied down any poems, the Neighbor-hood Committee insisted that he had copies in his possession and de-manded that he hand them over. The primary school teacher had copied some but had turned his in when asked. The accountant's daughter had written some on her handkerchief, but this had been confiscated by a teacher while she was passing it around among her schoolmates.

As he stared at the white sheet of lined paper before him, he felt things to be at once familiar and strange. The old man couldn't believe that at his age he still had to grovel before authority. He knew that if he didn't

---

* The old man was originally from Taiwan, the "precious isle." Later, when he daydreams about being "reunited with his family," he is referring to the family he left behind on Taiwan.

write his confession, his wife would continue to fret; but what could he write? He looked at the date, April 1, and decided that this was too early. He put his cup down, took up his pen and changed the 1 to a 5.

Writing a confession about that one day would be enough, he thought to himself. He threw down his pen, clasped his hands together, and leaned back in the rattan chair. Again he began daydreaming. . . .

Outside, the wind had started up again, shattering the silence of the night. There was a lull, and he heard the clock on the chest in the main room striking clearly and insistently. The old man listened and became conscious of a feeling of great urgency. Why waste a peaceful night like this writing out boring political lies? It was a perfect time for reminiscing, for thinking of distant loved ones, and for reviving childhood dreams; for closing his eyes and letting his thoughts fly far across the sea; it was a perfect night to be reunited with his family again.

The old woman slept fitfully, and woke up in the middle of a dream. She turned on the light, wrapped some clothes around herself, and got out of bed. Ever so gently, she pushed open the door of the study and saw the old man's heavy head resting on his chest; he seemed to be fast asleep. The white paper lay on the desk, with the seven words:

"April 5. It was a fine day . . ."

Following the suppression of the protests on Tiananmen Square in 1976, Deng Xiaoping was accused of plotting the incident from behind the scenes and purged. After Mao died in September of that year, Jiang Qing and her fellows (the "Gang of Four") were arrested in a military coup. Deng returned to power in 1977, and at the time of the Democracy Wall Movement, the official verdict on the Tiananmen Incident as a "counterrevolutionary riot" was reversed.

When, thirteen years later, people seized the opportunity of Hu Yaobang's death in April 1989 to march to Tiananmen Square with wreaths, poems, and banners—many of which complained about corruption and the lack of political reform—they were self-consciously echoing the April 1976 protests. This time, however, they were disillusioned with Deng; after ten years in power, he was perceived as an obstacle to change. Now it was Deng, ruling the country from "behind the screen" of his semi-retirement, whom the people likened to the Dowager Empress, and soon it was his turn to call their protests a "counterrevolutionary riot."

During the purge that followed, the party was acutely aware of the association people were making between the two "Tiananmen incidents." Lest they prevaricate about writing their confessions because they believed that, as in the Tiananmen Incident of 1976, the verdict on the Protest Movement of 1989 would ultimately be reversed, the Peking Daily *attempted to demonstrate otherwise.*

August 3, 1989: After undergoing political study, cadres of the Peking No. 2 Light Industry Company recognized the true nature of the turmoil and now understand that—

This Verdict Will Not Be Reversed

(By our correspondent Fang Chuanming) "Will the verdict on the counterrevolutionary turmoil be reversed?" On the basis of repeated study of the documents produced by the Fourth Plenary Session of the Thirteenth Central Committee of the Chinese Communist Party, the leading cadres of the Peking No. 2 Light Industry Company have come to a clear understanding of the true nature of the counterrevolutionary turmoil, arriving at the correct answer to this question: "This verdict will not be reversed."

Even after the appalling counterrevolutionary tumult in the capital had subsided, some comrades failed to recognize its true nature. Fearing that the verdict on it would eventually be overturned, they balked at actively participating in the struggle to suppress it. An extremely small number of people with ulterior motives have stirred up confusion among the masses by encouraging the notion that the insurrection can be compared to the Tiananmen Incident of April 5, 1976. In the course of their political study, the leading cadres of the No. 2 Light Industry Company touched directly on this "thought button." Contrasting the recent counterrevolutionary turmoil with the Tiananmen Incident of 1976, they concluded that this time the verdict cannot be overturned. Ideological unity has bolstered their confidence to carry out the struggle against this counterrevolutionary insurrection to the end.

They noted five crucial differences between the counterrevolutionary turmoil and the Tiananmen Incident of 1976:

(1) *Core participants:* The force behind the 1976 "April 5 Movement" consisted of workers and the broad masses who love the party and socialism, whereas the chief insurrectionists in the counterrevolutionary turmoil were people who had undergone labor reform or labor reeducation and had failed to reform, evil liege men of the "Gang of Four," and so on. Behind the turmoil was an extremely small handful of people who had supported Bourgelib over a long period of time, had been involved in political plots, were colluding with hostile overseas powers, and so on.

(2) *Political orientation:* The "April 5 Movement" was a struggle

directed at the overthrow of the "Gang of Four," a goal with which all agreed in their hearts, whereas the aim of the present counterrevolutionary insurrection was to oppose the Communist Party of China and the socialist system and overthrow the People's Republic of China in order to establish a bourgeois republic. This is completely contrary to the wishes of the broad masses.

(3) *Form and method:* In 1976 people expressed their love for Premier Zhou Enlai and hatred of the "Gang of Four" through song and poetry, elegiac couplets, and speeches. This time, the insurrectionists held illegal parades, stormed party and government offices, went on hunger strikes, boycotted classes, disrupted social order, and carried out such crimes as beating, smashing, looting, burning, and killing.

(4) *The party and the society:* The "April 5 Movement" enjoyed the support of many cadres within the party and the broad masses of party members. At the time the country was in the grip of an extreme leftist line. Ten years of internal chaos had already left the national economy on the brink of bankruptcy. The people rose up, "yearning for stability in the midst of chaos." The counterrevolutionary turmoil, on the other hand, was opposed by the old comrades within the party as well as most party members—party members were very unified in their opposition. Moreover, the counterrevolutionary turmoil occurred at a time when the country had achieved great things as a result of the economic reforms and the Open Door; some people "yearned for chaos in the midst of stability." At its most basic level it violated both the wishes and ultimate interests of the people.

(5) *Background:* The "April 5 Movement" was a movement by the righteous forces within the party and the broad masses against a tiny handful of plotters and careerists whom they hated bitterly, whereas the counterrevolutionary insurrection broke out because a small number of plotters were unable to achieve their aims through peaceful methods.

Why is it that the Chinese government can only maintain its image through rehabilitation? Why can't it just make fewer mistakes? Why does rehabilitation bring out such feelings of gratitude among our citizens? Just as the right to consign daring people to hell is a special privilege, so is the power to rehabilitate. As long as the concept of rehabilitation exists, there's no chance for democracy and the rule of law in China.

—Liu Xiaobo, 1989

(Paul Slattery)

They worked in close concert with reactionary forces overseas in a vain attempt to overthrow the leadership of the party and the People's Republic of China.

Once they had achieved a clear understanding of the basic differences between the counterrevolutionary insurrection and the 1976 Tiananmen Incident, the leading political cadres of the No. 2 Light Industry Company strengthened their confidence in the party and the People's Liberation Army. They unanimously agreed that the wishful thinking and plots of an extremely small number of hostile elements to see the verdict on the insurrection reversed would come to naught. As long as the elder generation of proletarian revolutionaries is still alive, there will be no reversal of this verdict. In the future, our party will—as it has always done in the past—firmly uphold the Four Basic Principles and push forward with the task of socialist modernization, never permitting the verdict on the counterrevolutionary rebellion to be overturned.

The political workers of the company have already persuasively communicated the logic of this argument to meetings of management cadres, office workers, and party members, thus clearing up any fuzzy thinking on the issue and strengthening confidence.

Never Say Never

BO YANG

The violent suppression of the Protest Movement took many observers by surprise. For years, the Chinese had been assuring one another—and foreigners—that the Cultural Revolution, or any similar regime of repression and terror, could never recur in China. Bo Yang, however, thought differently, as is shown by what he wrote after his return to Taiwan from a trip to the mainland in 1988.

[When traveling on the mainland] we often heard people say that a violent upheaval like the Cultural Revolution could not occur again in China. They reasoned that people had suffered more than enough and would be on their guard in the future.

I hold precisely the opposite view. I believe that an upheaval could erupt at any moment, even though it might go against the trend of the times—indeed, against human nature itself—just like the Cultural Revolution. What people really mean when they say it "couldn't happen again" is that it's impossible for the old actors to take to the stage again: Madame Jiang Qing reappearing on the rostrum to harangue the crowds, Mao Zedong popping up on Tiananmen Gate to egg on the Red Guards. Of course that couldn't happen. History doesn't replay itself like that. But the crux of the matter is that any soil in which poisonous weeds have flourished in the past can surely produce more poisonous weeds; as long as the factories for manufacturing Cow Demons and Snake Spirits * still exist, they will be able to produce more Cow Demons and Snake Spirits. In Mainland China the soil and the factories are intact. It's just that they're temporarily out of order due to extreme overwork. But the moment ambitious men are once again inspired, disaster will revisit the land.

The government's policy has been to encourage forgetfulness, and, indeed, the people themselves have already pushed the Cultural Revolution out of their minds. The most chilling phrases one hears on the lips of Chinese people are "Just forget it!" and "Let bygones be bygones!" These sayings will be the downfall of the Chinese people. Superficially they would appear to be the voice of a generous spirit; in fact, they cloak

---

* An expression used in the Cultural Revolution to describe counterrevolutionaries and other political criminals.

profound fear. At the Nazi concentration camp at Dachau, there's a plaque on which is engraved the following warning [by George Santayana]: "Those who do not remember the past are condemned to relive it." * The same is true of Mainland China: As soon as people forget the calamity of the Cultural Revolution, it will be sure to happen again! We won't have to wait until the 1990s either—the eighties have already given us the Anti–Spiritual Pollution Campaign and the Anti-Bourgelib Campaign. Even the television newscasters felt compelled to put on Mao jackets during those movements. Those two campaigns petered out only because the leaders exercised some self-restraint, not because the people opposed them.

Ba Jin once proposed the establishment of a "Cultural Revolution Museum," † a suggestion that elicited an enthusiastic response from people around the country and energetic opposition from officialdom. In any standoff between the people and the officials, the people always lose. The goal of the authorities has been to make people forget the wounds they've received. This is just another example of the curious workings of the official mind.

What's even stranger is that right up to the present day, the People's Government still insists on upholding Mao Zedong Thought, but because even they have some sense of shame, they hasten to explain that "Mao Zedong Thought has nothing to do with Mao Zedong himself!" This is the sort of absurd logic to which only the Chinese dare resort— the officials who came up with this twisted logic, however, are probably convinced that other people are as stupid as they are.

* See *Seeds of Fire*, p. 121.
† See *Seeds of Fire*, pp. 381–84.

The May Fourth Spirit, Now and Then

Modern Chinese intellectuals, progressives and revolutionaries, have increasingly felt strangled by the seeming invincibility and deadly pervasiveness of tradition. The outstanding exponent of the struggle to get rid of the past was of course Lu Xun, who analyzed with unique clear-sightedness the desperate nature of the modernizers' predicament: they can never pin the enemy down, for the enemy is a formless, invisible ghost, an indestructible shadow.

—Pierre Ryckmans (Simon Leys)

On *May 4, 1919, more than three thousand students from thirteen universities in Peking gathered in the area in front of Tiananmen (at the time there was no square as such) to demonstrate against imperialist aggression toward China, in particular against the Versailles Peace Treaty, which gave the former German imperial concessions in China to Japan. Together with a concomitant, progressive movement to "modernize" Chinese culture, this became known as the May Fourth Movement.*

The May Fourth Movement grew out of the New Culture Movement, including the literary revolution of 1917 during which it was first proposed that the spoken language replace classical Chinese as the major written form. Liberal intellectuals such as Hu Shi, Chen Duxiu, Zhou Zuoren, and Lu Xun, as well as students, campaigned for an end to what they perceived as the stifling and antidemocratic influence of Confucianism on Chinese society. Many hoped that the New Culture Movement, which stressed the importance of democracy and science ("Mr. D. and Mr. S.") would allow people to liberate their thinking and free themselves from the past.* However, the pressing issue of national salvation

---

* Science, as a symbol of modern, rational thinking and methods, was seen by intellectuals of the May Fourth period—and has been ever since—as the partner of democracy. For a study of these attitudes toward science, see David Kwok, *Scientism in Chinese Thought, 1900–1950,* New Haven, Conn.: Yale University Press, 1965.

came to overshadow that earlier movement for cultural renewal and self-liberation.

Throughout the 1920s and '30s, Chinese intellectuals grew increasingly politicized, most of them aligned with the Communists or the Nationalists depending on which one they perceived as being more capable of "saving the nation." Inevitably, the May Fourth Movement became a symbol used by both the left and the right for their own purposes.

Floodwaters and Wild Beasts

CAI YUANPEI

Cai Yuanpei (1868–1940) was an educationalist and a revolutionary. He was the chancellor of Peking University from 1917 to 1919, forced to resign at the height of the May Fourth period. In 1932 he founded the China League for the Defense of Civil Rights with Lu Xun, Yang Quan, and Soong Ch'ing-ling (Madame Sun Yat-sen).

While head of Peking University, Cai, a leader of the intellectual revolution of the period, tried to turn the university into a school to train China's new intellectual leaders. He employed such controversial intellectuals as Chen Duxiu, Liu Shipei, and Hu Shi. He also encouraged scholars with markedly different views from his own, as well as traditional studies, and for a time both Gu Hongming and the philosopher Ma Yifu lectured at the university.* Cai's tenure fostered an atmosphere of intellectual variety and tolerance never seen before or since at a modern institution of learning in Mainland China.

In the following article, first published in 1920 in La Jeunesse, a leading journal of the May Fourth Movement, Cai describes a situation that would have familiar resonances in the late 1980s. The "floodwaters" of liberal thinking in the late eighties were in some ways remarkably— some would say depressingly—similar to those of Cai's time. Although there were no longer warlords to torment the people and live off the fat

---

* A young provincial from Hunan by the name of Mao Runzhi, better known as Mao Zedong, worked in the university library during the May Fourth period. The offhand manner with which some of the lecturers, including Hu Shi and Yu Pingbo, supposedly treated him is said to have made Mao distrust, if not despise, men with book learning. It has been argued that his post-1949 anti-intellectual policies were to an extent informed by his experiences at Peking University.

of the land, the Communist Party, widely perceived as corrupt and parasitic, would probably fit Cai's notion of "wild beasts"—it too sent an army to crush the students.

About 2,200 years ago there lived a Chinese philosopher called Mencius. He said that the history of a state often went in cycles of chaos and order. He named the great flood of 4,200 years ago as the first great chaos; the second occurred 3,000 years ago, when there was a plague of wild beasts. The next, he said, was in his own day, referring to the appearance of the theories of Yang Zhu and Mozi.* He likened his own attack on Yang and Mo to the taming of the floods by the Emperor Yu and the dispersing of the wild beasts by the Duke of Zhou. Thus the admirers of Mencius like to say that the threat posed by Yang Zhu and Mozi was "even greater than the floodwaters and wild beasts." †

As time passed, whenever a scholar wanted to attack another school of thought he would accuse its adherents of being "worse than floodwaters and wild beasts." The Confucians attacked the Buddhists and Taoists in those terms in the Tang and Song dynasties; such was also the case in the Qing dynasty, when the Cheng-Zhu school attacked the Lu-Wang school. Today the traditionalists say the new school [of the May Fourth Movement] is "worse than floodwaters and wild beasts."

I think there is something to be said for calling the tide of new thought a "great flood." It is, after all, like a deluge that has washed away the habits of the past, and naturally there are those who find this very painful. It's as if the flood tides are too strong, overwhelming the old riverbeds, and the waters are spilling out, devastating the surrounding fields. Yet if you try to block the waters as Yao did [in antiquity], it will only make the flood worse, the damage irreparable. That's why Yu instead channeled the floodwaters to the great rivers. Not only did this prevent destruction, it was also beneficial to irrigation. Similarly, in dealing with the tide of new thought one must allow it to develop freely; only then will it be beneficial and not destructive. Mencius said, "The way Yu controlled the waters was by doing it in a way that caused no trouble." This is the best way the old school can deal with the new.

---

* Mencius characterized his own time as a period when perverse doctrines and violent acts were rife. Yang Zhu propounded a philosophy of self-centeredness that excluded fealty to the ruler; Mozi spoke of universal love that militated against Confucius's teaching of respecting one's father above all others. Were these principles to gain currency, Mencius argued, there would be nothing to differentiate humans from beasts. It will be recalled that in Part III, "Red Noise," He Xin mentions Yang Zhu when commenting on China's traditional "hippie spirit."
† See *Mencius,* Book 3B: 9.

As for "wild beasts," that's a perfect description of the warlords. Mencius quoted Gongming Yi as saying, "You have fatty meat in your kitchens and fine horses in your stables, but on the faces of the people is the pallor of starvation, and in the wilderness there are the bodies of those who have died from famine. You give the wild beasts a lead by devouring your fellowman." Today the warlords possess immense personal wealth and enjoy unimaginable luxuries, while those who work for a living are starving to death in poverty. Isn't this like leading the beasts to eat other men? The armies in Peking and Tianjin have been instructed by their leaders to attack patriotic young people. Are they not acting like wild beasts?

The situation in China today could be described as one in which the floodwaters and the wild beasts are in competition. If the wild beasts can be quelled and the floodwaters run free, China will immediately find peace.

—April 1, 1920

A five-part television documentary entitled We Are Writing History *made by the Taiwan photographer Chang Chao-tang was screened in Taiwan and Hong Kong in early 1990. Filmed in Peking during the 1989 Protest Movement, the second part of the series, "Peking University," included an interview with Ding Shisun, then president of the university.*

Here at Peking University we have a very strong sense of our historical responsibility. The university is the product of the 1898 Reform Movement, and we have a tradition, especially after Mr. Cai Yuanpei's incumbency as president. That was a period of immense change in China. Our ninety-year history—ninety-one years this year—has been inextricably tied up with the modern history of China.

We say we breathe with the rhythm of history. So our teachers and students have always felt it imperative to make our contribution to the creation of a new and strong China and to push history forward. This is an intangible thing, an ambience if you will. . . .

—Ding Shisun

President Ding was relieved of his position in late 1989 for allowing the students and staff of Peking University to take part in the Protest Movement.

343

A High Price

LI AO

Unfortunately, after the May Fourth Movement, as both the Nationalists and the Communists adopted Soviet-style organizational methods and party discipline under the tutelage of the Soviet Union, the goal of "healthy individualism" was abandoned for that of collectivism. This foreign import brought disaster on China, for it stifled intellectual liberation. Hu Shi recalled, "The ironfisted discipline introduced from the Soviet Union was excessively intolerant; it outlawed heterodox opinion. It was diametrically opposed to the liberalism we had advocated from the inception of the May Fourth Movement." . . . And so it was that both the Bolsheviks and the fascists embarked on the path of collectivization, diverting China from the individual and intellectual liberation of the New Culture Movement.

The theme of the New Culture Movement was "enlightenment," intellectual and cultural self-renewal, and self-transformation. The call of the May Fourth Movement was for "national salvation," its thrust was primarily political, and it led people to join parties for self-benefit. Renewal and transformation became something to be imposed on others. The feeling that national collapse was imminent sent the whole country into a frenzy. It's understandable that since people felt time was running out they became quite desperate, and began aligning themselves with whichever faction seemed to benefit the cause of salvation. The question remains, however: If all those committed heroes hadn't come forth to save the nation, would China have been any worse off? Was it really a matter of such urgency?

Thirty years after the 1898 Reform Movement, Wang Zhao, a reformist colleague of Kang Youwei, the leading salvationist at the time, wrote the following in his memoirs:

> In 1898 I said to Old Kang, ". . . only by building more modern schools and expanding our [educational] base will the atmosphere gradually change. Only then will it be possible to establish a new polity." But Old Kang replied, "The nation is about to be sliced up like a melon [by the imperialist powers], there's no time to pursue your methods." That was thirty-two years ago. All talk of whether there was sufficient time or not is irrelevant.

Wang Zhao observed that thirty years later, China was still there. If, back in 1898, they'd concentrated on saving the children instead of saving the nation, and if that generation had gone on to save the next generation and the next, after three decades there would have been a large enlightened population with liberated attitudes and a sense of personal freedom. The second and third generations, no longer slaves, could have formed the basis for the establishment of a new China. Of course, no one was interested in listening to an old pedant like Wang Zhao.

Instead, people were busy declaring that China was finished and arguing with one another over what emergency action should be taken. It was this sense of urgency that led so many of the outstanding intellectuals of the New Culture Movement to throw themselves body and soul into the political agitation of the May Fourth Movement.

After thirty years of activism, we won back Taiwan and lost Outer Mongolia (a territory forty-four times larger than Taiwan). We invited the Soviet wolves right into our homes and repaid the cruelty of the Japanese with kindness. Then, with the nation covered in wounds [from the war], the right-wing fascists in the Nationalist Party fled to Taiwan and the left-wing Bolsheviks of the Communist Party took over the mainland.

The Chinese have paid dearly for those decades of "saving the nation." China may finally have have stood up, but the Chinese have fallen down.

—*April 1989*

The Vicious Cycle of the May Fourth Movement

XU JILIN

The political and cultural rebels of the May Fourth period encountered virulent opposition from conservatives who perceived themselves as guardians of Chinese tradition. In the River Elegy *debate (see pp. 158–64), we saw how even in the 1980s "totalistic iconoclasm,"* the radical*

* See Lin Yü-sheng's study of the significance of "totalistic iconoclasm" in *The Crisis of Chinese Consciousness: Radical Antitraditionalism in the May Fourth Era.* Madi-

reassessment of an entire culture, could still bring down the wrath of conservative forces. What is ironic is that the new self-appointed guardians of tradition are leaders of (or, in He Xin's case, advisers to) the Communist Party, a party that was conceived in the spirit of radical iconoclasm—and indeed, of the May Fourth Movement itself.

As a youthful organization in the 1920s and '30s, the Communist Party won the hearts and minds of many intellectuals with its antitraditionalist and anti-imperialist stance. It jettisoned Confucianism, however, only to put a new state ideology, a new tradition as it were, in its place, that of Marxism-Leninism and Mao Zedong Thought. Gradually, the party appropriated China's cultural symbols and traditions for its own use: The People's Liberation Army, for example, was officially dubbed the "Great Wall of Iron" and loyalty to the party's cause linked with the Yellow River (as, for example, in the Yellow River Concerto). When faced with an unprecedented crisis of belief in its ideology and a general collapse of confidence in the 1980s, the party increasingly relied on its identification with tradition and the redefined symbols of national pride to prop up its authority.

In a further irony, the May Fourth Movement itself has, over the years, become a tradition and a symbol. In China, the past often gains significance only when it can be used to serve the present; the icon of the May Fourth Movement is no exception.

In March 1989, Xu Jilin, a Shanghai-based academic, summed up his view of the dilemma of Chinese intellectuals in the twentieth century in an article entitled "The Vicious Cycle of the May Fourth Movement." Xu found that on virtually every tenth anniversary of the movement a new interpretation had been found for it. He also noted that in 1979, sixty years after the May Fourth Movement—in other words, a complete cycle in the traditional Chinese calendar—history appeared to have come full circle. The following is his summary with some additional information (in brackets) and an update by the editors to 1989:

[1919: The May Fourth Movement calls for national salvation, science, and democracy.]
1939: The [Communists] champion the idea of "superseding the May Fourth Movement" so as to establish speedily a new national

---

son: University of Wisconsin Press, 1979. A Chinese version of this book appeared in 1987 and has had a considerable, although not always acknowledged, influence in Mainland China. Lin's arguments are also relevant when considering radical antitraditionalism in China in the 1980s.

culture. [Renaming the holiday to commemorate the May Fourth "National Youth Day," they call on young people to join the war effort and unite with the workers and peasants "in the May Fourth spirit."]

1949: The Communists [close to victory in their war with the Nationalists] confirm Mao Zedong Thought as the nation's ideology. [They also declare that the participation of the intellectuals in the workers' movement had been the greatest achievement of the May Fourth Movement.]

1959: The May Fourth Movement is celebrated as part of the Great Leap Forward.

1969: The May Fourth spirit is completely negated by the Cultural Revolution [though still celebrated in name].

1979: On the sixtieth anniversary of the May Fourth Movement the Chinese set out from the same starting point and once more call for democracy and science. [There is also a renewed call for the "liberation of thought," this time in opposition not to Confucianism but to the modern dogma of Maoism; it is aimed at validating the rule of Deng Xiaoping and his fellows.]

[*1989:* The official government slogan to commemorate the seventieth anniversary of the movement is "Patriotism, Reform, Enterprise, Advancement." All mention of democracy and science is pointedly avoided. Meanwhile, students and intellectuals demonstrate in Peking and other cities for greater democracy, using the original slogans of the May Fourth Movement.]

May Fourth Demonstration, 1989. The banner reads: "It's been 70 years!" (Da Jun)

According to Xu Jilin (and many other writers), the half-digested and often misunderstood ideology of Marxism-Leninism combined after 1949 with powerful although often unrecognized traditional modes of thinking and action to create a self-ossifying mechanism within Chinese culture.

As China approaches the twentieth century, one wonders, Are we bound to repeat the vicious cycle of the May Fourth Movement? This question cannot but arouse our vigilance.

The post-1979 intellectual enlightenment seems to have repeated the patterns of the first May Fourth Movement. There are startling similarities between these two periods: general anxiety over the backwardness of the nation and deep-felt anguish over the premature demise of democracy. As people in both periods looked beyond the superficial aspects of the current system to delve into Chinese traditional culture, they discovered many elements there that were antagonistic to modernization. The

In mainland academic circles we can still find some young people who are continuing the May Fourth spirit of totalistic iconoclasm. Liu Xiaobo is an example. I've read some of his articles. The way he writes reminds me of Bo Yang in Taiwan, for they both argue their points in a casual, random style.

While the influence of "The Ugly Chinaman" has certainly been great, in terms of its antitraditionalism, there's nothing very new in it. Basically, Bo Yang is refrying Lu Xun's leftovers. He's far less profound than Lu Xun. Bo Yang's conviction that the Chinese have an odious national character is essentially a continuation of Lu Xun's line of thought. Indeed, while Lu Xun originated the expression the "soy sauce vat [of Chinese culture]," Bo Yang has played up its horrors and taken on the expression as if it were his own. Bo Yang says exactly what most Chinese people want to hear. His popularity is due not to the profundity of his ideas but to the fact that the antitraditionalist thinking and methods he represents have a wide audience. This is the tragedy of Chinese culture. This shows how the May Fourth method of "using philosophy and culture to resolve problems" has been preserved to the present day and, in a manner of speaking, has even been immensely enhanced.

*—The scholar Lin Yü-sheng in
conversation with Xu Jilin*

result in both cases was cultural reassessment. But as this reassessment was in itself inspired by a mood of political utilitarianism rather than a quest for knowledge, all cultural debates have invariably been tinged with an ideological hue and marked by a desire for immediate results.

In the initial phase [of both periods], intellectuals were drawn to Western thinking and denounced their own tradition, but when this led to a serious loss of cultural standards, they backed down.

Whenever the paradigms of the social and cultural systems are going through a period of renewal or change, there will inevitably be a period of disorientation. The West experienced such a phase in its own recent history. However, because the cultural transformation experienced by the West was by nature spontaneous and independent, it didn't lead to a chain reaction by which the whole social, political, and economic framework was destabilized. But in China's case, the cultural crisis is part and parcel of the crisis of the society as a whole. Cultural and moral models have lost their authority and are thus powerless to ameliorate the crisis.

At this critical juncture, people pin their hopes on the emergence of new, rational forces. But what they find instead is the appearance of countless disparate, irrational, and chaotic influences. Before rational elements have a chance to join into a coherent whole, the blind destructiveness of the chaotic forces may push the society toward total collapse.

[The Chinese] want to catch up with and even surpass the rest of the world. But this requires a spirit of national determination, a near-religious spirit of sacrifice, on the part of every citizen. China lacks the kind of consensus that can act as an ideological foundation for such an enterprise. The twofold sense of anxiety is then exacerbated by calls for a new authoritarianism in the political sphere* and an increasing demand for the speedy establishment of a national spirit in the cultural arena. Many intellectuals find themselves unable to tolerate the concomitant cultural disintegration and social disorder that comes with the loss of moral standards, and so, either consciously or unconsciously, they wish to reestablish or identify with a definite system of values and beliefs.† The above outline [of the 1980s] is similar to the situation that developed in the 1930s. The "vicious cycle of the May Fourth Movement" casts a long shadow not only over the past and present, but over the future as well.

---

* See Dai Qing, "From Lin Zexu to Chiang Ching-kuo" in Part II, "Bindings."
† Perhaps He Xin's writings can be seen as part of such an intellectual trend.

Xu suggested that history offered at least two ways for China to break out of this vicious circle: first, reducing the ideological aspect of cultural debates and working toward a system that could encompass both Chinese and Western culture and, second, maintaining openness to the outside world and encouraging an atmosphere of cultural pluralism. Putting the onus on intellectuals rather than the power holders, he concluded:

It depends entirely on the practical choices made by China's intellectuals whether the "Vicious Cycle of the May Fourth Movement" will repeat itself a second time.

Chinese Democracy: The View from the Peking Observatory

FANG LIZHI

With his relentless concern for science and democracy, the dissident astrophysicist Fang Lizhi is one of the Chinese intellectuals who embodies the May Fourth spirit today. This essay was written for the seventieth anniversary of the May Fourth Movement.

No one can deny that China's Reform has run into big trouble. Modernization and democratization have come to a halt. Advance and retreat are both impossible. All around us, we can see countries and territories with similar peoples or cultures racing ahead to join the ranks of the developed nations while on the Chinese mainland time is slipping away. Seventy years have been lost since the May Fourth Movement. How many more years must pass before there is a decisive change in China? It's a question that gives rise to anxiety, pain, and despair.

So as to avoid making this commemorative essay intolerably pessimistic, I won't dwell on the issue of democracy in China. Instead, I will review the history of the Peking Observatory over the last three hundred years.

The most valuable contribution of the May Fourth New Culture Movement was to promote the absorption of democracy and science into Chinese culture. Both were absent or in short supply in the Chinese tradition. The process of their absorption, however, began and ended with the May Fourth Movement. . . .

The history of the Peking Observatory is intimately linked with the introduction of Western science. Western science made its debut in China with the arrival of the Italian Jesuit Matteo Ricci in 1582. (Today Ricci's tomb can be found on the grounds of the Peking Municipal Party School.) But it ran into strong resistance from the very start. Leng Shouzhong and others in the late Ming dynasty opposed using Western methods to calculate the Chinese calendar; they insisted it had to be based on the Song dynasty neo-Confucianist text *Huangji jingshi*.* This marked the debut of the theory of "China's special characteristics" [see "On China's National Characteristics," pp. 363–73]. As a result, the court continued to use the obsolete Datong and Islamic calendars.

In 1610 and again in 1629, these traditional methods led to erroneous predictions of solar eclipses while [the Catholic mandarin] Paul Xu Guangqi made wholly accurate forecasts using Western methodology. Only then did the Ming Chongzhen emperor [reigned 1628–1644] accept these methods, and the *Chongzhen Treatise on the Calendar* was based on them. But because of conservative opposition, this text was never used. Indeed, the scientific treatise on which it was based wasn't published until the reign of the Qing Shunzhi emperor [reigned 1644–1661]. It was then used to calculate the official calendar. In all likelihood this was the first time contemporary Western science actually became a part of Chinese life.

But it was too good to last. As soon as Shunzhi died, the anti-science forces came back into power. The leading Confucian Yang Guangxian wrote a memorial to the throne: "It would be better for China to do without an accurate calendar than to tolerate the presence of Westerners." His antipathy to both Westerners and their techniques can be regarded as the second exposition of the theory of China's special characteristics. Once this became the prevailing attitude, Li Zubai and four others who had used the Western methods were put to death. They were the first martyrs of the Peking Observatory who died for the cause of China's modernization. (Throughout history, astronomers have often been punished or executed as a result of official intolerance.)

When Kangxi [reigned 1662–1722] came to power, the situation improved. Of all the emperors, Kangxi was the one most interested in

* The *Huangji jingshi* was itself influenced by the *Book of Changes*, a Confucian classic.

science, and the imperial calendar was again calculated according to Western methods. Even as a youth Kangxi had studied Western astronomy with the missionary Ferdinand Verbiest. The *Lixiang kaocheng* and the *Kangxi Perpetual Calendar* were for their time both scientific works of world standard, and they were representative of that enlightened period.

The ascent of the Yongzheng emperor to the throne [in 1723] marked the beginning of a period of more than a century during which science was rejected. China shut its doors to the outside world and cut off scientific exchange. The Qing school of textual criticism, which represented the intellectual mainstream, concerned itself solely with research in the [Confucian] classics and had no interest whatsoever in science based on observation. As late as the nineteenth century, Ruan Yuan, one of the leaders of that school, still refused to accept that the earth revolved around the sun. He wrote, "This theory, which turns things topsy-turvy and confuses movement and stasis, is heretical and transgresses the Way. It must not be taken as the standard." The only norm Ruan Yuan would accept was one based on the theory of "China's special characteristics."

It was only after the Opium Wars [in the mid-nineteenth century] that such views began to lose currency. The astronomer Li Shanlan refuted Ruan Yuan. As he put it, "It is totally meaningless to concoct preposterous theories by mindlessly dragging in the classics instead of making careful observations." In 1868 Li Shanlan took up the post of chief instructor in astronomy at the Institute for Scientific and Linguistic Studies in Peking, and Western astronomy was once again systematically introduced into China. But the calendar was not calculated scientifically again until after the Revolution of 1911 and the establishment of the Republic of China. Then the Imperial Directorate of Astronomy was renamed the Central Observatory and assigned the task of calculating a new calendar. Because it took time to make the calculations, the old calendar had to be used for the first two years of the republic. Only in the third year, 1914, was the calendar based completely on contemporary astronomy. This time the change stuck. Even during the Cultural Revolution, when "bourgeois science" was criticized, the calendar wasn't changed.

In their explanatory notes to the 1914 calendar, Gao Lu and Chang Fuyuan wrote, "This calendar has been calculated on the basis of methods used in both the East and West." The key expression is "methods used in both the East and West," for that signaled that Chinese society had finally recognized that the methods of calculation are universal, and that there is nothing unique about China when it comes to scientific laws. . . .

This chapter in the history of science in China can perhaps give us a better perspective on the problems facing democracy in China today. First of all, there's no need to be overly pessimistic about the progress of democracy. It's been seventy years since the May Fourth Movement, not a short time; but if we consider that it took three centuries for science to be accepted, there's no call for complete despair. Second, the basic principles and standards of modernization and democratization are, like those of science, universal. There's no such thing as "Eastern-style" or "Western-style"; there's only a difference between "backward" and "advanced," "correct" and "mistaken." Third, the chief obstacle to the modernization and democratization of Chinese culture lies in the same wrongheaded notion that kept science out of China for so many years: the theory of China's "special characteristics" and all its variations.

This year the Peking Observatory is celebrating its seven hundred and tenth birthday. From ancient times, China's emperors governed according to heavenly portents. After the Yuan dynasty moved its capital to Peking, the Peking Observatory served successive monarchs by determining the Will of Heaven. It fell into disuse only after the May Fourth Movement. But its long history can still teach us an important lesson, particularly those of us in power. The theory that we must not copy Western methods, the view that everything was being turned topsy-turvy, the notions about heresy and treason against the Way—all these have had their precursors. My hope is that this history will be a useful reference for our present rulers.

The Peking Observatory gives us a cosmic vantage point from which to observe the world of men. From here you can see the movement of the stars and the turning of the Wheel of the Law. The dharma wheel of science has already come rolling into China, and that of democracy is starting to turn as well. The problems we face today are merely the creaking sounds the wheel makes as it begins to revolve. This is the basis of my confidence and strength.

On the occasion of the seventy-first anniversary of the May Fourth Movement in 1990, Party General Secretary Jiang Zemin delivered a speech aimed at the younger members of China's intelligentsia. Entitled "Patriotism and the Mission of Our Intellectuals," it gave the party's (latest) view of the May Fourth tradition.

A group of progressive intellectuals stood at the forefront of the May Fourth Movement . . . some particularly enlightened individuals discovered in Marxism-Leninism a mighty ideological weapon for understanding and transforming China. . . . It was through their efforts that Marxism-Leninism was melded with the Chinese workers' movement, giving birth to the Communist Party of China. This was the greatest contribution of our intellectuals in modern history. . . .

In China today patriotism and people's democracy—that is to say, socialist democracy—are essentially identical. . . .

Inimical forces both inside and outside China have been plotting to use the tactic of peaceful evolution to overthrow our socialist system and thereby deprive the Chinese people of their right to determine the fate of their nation. They want to turn China into a vassal of the West. . . . The small minority of people who stirred up, planned, and orchestrated the turmoil and counterrevolutionary riot of 1989, as well as those rioters and louts who betrayed China to flee overseas, are not only the enemies of socialism, but allies of foreign aggressors. Their activities have harmed the motherland and the People, revealing an antipatriotic stance and spirit. They don't care a whit for national respect or even self-respect. What right do they have to talk about patriotism, democracy, and human rights! . . .

There was a time during which we were lax in ideological work and education in our fine party traditions. As a result some of our younger intellectuals fell prey to the influence of a Western bourgeois worldview and values, as well as national nihilism. We are confident that our younger comrades will be able to solve these problems through study and social practice, and by drawing lessons from their experience.

—*Jiang Zemin, May 3, 1990*

Under Observation

AH CHENG

*A**h** Cheng is a writer from Peking and a former member of the Stars. He lives in the United States and writes a regular column for* The Nineties Monthly *in Hong Kong. The following short story appeared in that magazine in February 1990.*

Old Zhang was as fit as a fiddle; his hair was still thick and black. He didn't look as though he'd reached retirement age. But the time had come, and there were plenty of documents and injunctions about sticking to the rules.

His colleagues really didn't want to see Old Zhang go, and the atmosphere at his farewell gathering was one of forced gaiety. In the end, it was Old Zhang who tried to cheer everyone up.

No banquet goes on forever, Old Zhang said. Not that the party's work is like a banquet. No, what I mean is, after everyone has worked together for a time, someone has to leave first. I'm not saying I'm just going off to die; you'll continue working for the party, but I may outlive you yet. And it's not as though I won't keep contributing to the party's work, there are still things I can do. Just a few days ago, you know, a research institute asked me to write something for them on psychology. Sure, I said. Now, I might not know much about that guy—what's his name?—Frood? Floyd? Fruitcake? Anyway, I do know where people's hearts are; and that's all you need to know: Understand how the body works, and you'll be able to cope with anyone. That's my parting advice to you all. Now, if anything comes up that's too hot to handle, feel free to call on me. I'm not saying I'm better than anyone or that I feel superior. Not at all. It's just that I have, after all, been at it for nearly fifty years.

And so Old Zhang retired. He didn't know anything about keeping songbirds or taking them for walks in a cage, and although he occasionally stopped to glance at the games of chess or cards being played on the street, he couldn't follow them.

Nor did he go in for *qigong* classes. I've got more *qi* in my gut than you can find in the "elixir fields" of two of those guys put together, he said.

Old Zhang spent most of his time at home, staring at the four walls. He also kept an eye on his son. In the jargon of his old unit, he had his son "under observation."

Because he'd often worked the night shift, Old Zhang had never spent much time with his family. It hadn't been easy for them. His son had been born relatively late, and Old Zhang hadn't spent much time with him in the past. Now they had all the time in the world.

It wasn't long before Old Zhang discovered that his son masturbated. Old Zhang brought it up with him.

So you jerk off, do you? Nothing to be embarrassed about, everybody does it. The old blunderbuss has to be kept busy somehow. Heaven knows, better to exercise it at home than go around breaking the law. If you got yourself into trouble, your old man really would lose face. You're not that young anymore, you know. Now, I know the party encourages late marriage, but you've reached the legal age. My advice is that if you meet a suitable match, marry her. Pocket pinball depletes your *yang;* you'll end up impotent. You'll be finished; though you may want to work for the Revolution, you won't be able to physically. If you're weak, you lose your revolutionary ardor. Don't you agree? Do you see what your old dad is trying to say? It's for your own good, I don't want to see you knock yourself out and get depressed by it, too. You're my only son. Masturbate if you like, it's no big deal, but don't make a habit of it.

Old Zhang knew that most problems, no matter how big, could be solved just by talking them over. He'd been like that all his life, he hated keeping things bottled up. It didn't help anyone and only complicated things.

One day someone from the old unit stopped by to see how Old Zhang was doing. As he poured the visitor some tea, Old Zhang told him he was doing fine. He appreciated the thoughtfulness of the organization and everyone there for asking after him.

Old Zhang, the visitor said, we'd really like your advice.

Shoot. I'll do what I can, Old Zhang replied.

It's this case we've got, his former colleague said, a new prisoner, a political. The people upstairs are very interested in this guy, so they're pressing us for results. We're getting worried.

Old Zhang laughed. What is it, some intellectual who won't talk?

What would you suggest? asked the visitor.

Observe him, said Old Zhang. Catch him playing pocket pinball.

Pocket pinball? the visitor asked.

I see you're a regular intellectual yourself, Old Zhang said. Pocket pinball means playing with yourself. The general rule is three times a day in the spring, four in the autumn, never stops in winter, and twice a day in summer. Everyone's made of flesh and blood, they all "play the cello" when they're locked up. You have to get them right after they've jerked off. They're completely exhausted then, prone, got no fighting spirit left. That's when you should do the interrogation. It'll get results, believe you me. Besides, intellectuals are easily shamed; if you tell him you were watching it'll take the air right out of his sails. He'll talk. Beating them up is a bad strategy: makes them cocky, just builds up their resistance. Then there's some who don't survive. So really, it's best just to keep them under observation.

"The Walls Have Ears," Chen Shizeng (early twentieth century)

The Case of Chu Anping

Chinese history has been completely perverted; it is a
history of deception.

—Dai Qing

Dai Qing, a member of the Guangming Daily *staff since the early
1980s, was intrigued by the glaring "memory holes" in the history of
the party and began investigating the concealed history and fate of some
of China's leading intellectual and literary figures. She hoped her studies
would help force party leaders to face up to their own ignominious
policies toward free thinkers. But the cumulative effect of her writings
has been to further deconstruct party history, thereby loosening the bindings of that history and its myths on the Chinese. As a member of the
party elite, she has an understanding of the inner workings of the party
mentality that is rare among Chinese writers. Her works of "historical
investigative journalism" were banned from being reprinted in China so
as to limit their availability. After the June massacre, they were indirectly
attacked in the pages of the* Guangming Daily *as attempts to "reverse
the verdict" on major party cases.*

*Dai Qing's study of the editor and publisher Chu Anping, entitled
"Chu Anping and the 'Party Empire,'" appeared in early 1989, first in
magazines in Hong Kong and the mainland, then as a book on the
mainland. Dai took advantage of the publication of the book to reprint
many of Chu's writings, thus introducing to modern readers unfamiliar
with Chu and his work an array of materials quite damaging to the
party.*

*Chu Anping (1909–1966) was educated in journalism in Shanghai,
where he came under the influence of Hu Shi, and in England, where he
was a student of Harold J. Laski. Back in China in the 1940s, Chu
became a leading editor and independent intellectual in the tradition of
the early May Fourth period. In 1946 he founded* The Observer, *a major
forum for independent political debate. In his publication announcement
he summed up his views in four words—"democracy, freedom, progress,*

and rationality"—which Dai Qing has called his "four basic principles." (Forty years later, from the mid-1980s, intellectuals in China, especially reformist and independent intellectuals, were to propound very similar ideas.)

The Observer, *which had been closed down by the Nationalists, was revived after 1949. The magazine lasted only until mid-1950, when it was taken over by the party and renamed* The New Observer *(the same magazine that, after a long and varied history, was denounced in 1989 for cosponsoring the memorial conference on Hu Yaobang with the* World Economic Herald *in April that year (See p. 39 of this book).*

Nationalists and Communists

In 1947 Chu wrote an article in The Observer *in which he reviewed the sorry state of the Nationalist government in the late 1940s. The Communists reprinted it in 1957 as part of their denunciation of Chu. Its continued relevance was certain to strike people when Dai quoted it again in 1989.*

In a nation where political parties come to power through armed violence, even if the ruling party has reached an impasse, it will struggle doggedly to maintain its hold on power. This is only natural. If it's a righteous struggle, its effort can be appreciated. However, if it has taken the wrong path and is merely battling to keep itself in power, in the end everything it does will be a waste and a criminal act. . . . The Nationalists today have become an organization for the protection of vested interests. We hope they will pay more attention to the needs of the common people on the lower rungs of society, and not treat them as meaningless. . . .

The Communist Party is presently making a big song and dance about "democracy." But if we consider the basic spirit of the Communists, we must realize that they are antidemocratic. In terms of the spirit in which they rule, there is no difference between them and the fascists. Both aim at using a strong organization to control people's thinking. The Communists are undoubtedly chanting "democracy" today in order to unite people to oppose the political monopoly of the Nationalists. But their real aim is their own political monopoly, not democracy. There is a prerequisite in the discussion of democracy, one that cannot be compromised: People must be allowed intellectual freedom. Only when they have such freedom, when they can freely express their ideas, will the spirit of democracy be realized. If only those who believe in Communism are allowed this freedom, there will be no [real] intellectual freedom or freedom of speech. . . . To be quite frank, our present struggle for freedom under Nationalist rule is really a matter of increasing the degree of our freedom. If the Communists were in power, the question would be whether we would have any freedom at all.

—Chu Anping, March 8, 1947

The Party Empire: Some Advice to Chairman Mao and Premier Zhou Enlai

Chu attempted to adjust to the new regime after 1949. He became a publishing official and was eventually given a prestigious position on the Guangming Daily, *a leading newspaper for "intellectuals" and the organ for the Chinese Democratic League. In the spring of 1957, under Chu's tutelage, the paper attempted to assert its independence from the Communist Party and set up a network of correspondents outside Peking. The* Guangming Daily *became a forum for dissident opinion. In June 1957, encouraged to speak out against the party by Mao's call to "let a hundred flowers bloom and a hundred schools of thought contend," Chu made a famous speech entitled "The Party Empire."*

The following is a short extract from that speech, which Dai Qing reprinted in full in her book.

The crux of the problem lies with what I call the "Party Empire." In my opinion the party's control of the state does not give it the right to treat the nation as its personal property. Everyone supports the party, but no one has forgotten that it is the master of the nation. The main concern of a political party that takes power should be the realization of its ideals and implementation of its policies. Certainly, a party needs to remain strong so that it can do this and maintain stability; it needs control over some crucial sectors of the state mechanism. This is quite natural. However, to put a party boss into every unit and organization throughout the nation, in every bureau and group, and to make everything, no matter how large or small, contingent on the reaction of the party man, to force people to rely on the party man's nod of approval to do anything, is surely somewhat extreme, isn't it?

—*Chu Anping, June 1, 1957*

Soon after, Mao turned the campaign for free speech into a witch-hunt for dissident opinion. Chu and many others connected with the Guangming Daily *were labeled rightists and denounced as conspirators who had made a "frenzied attack on the party and planned to turn China into a bourgeois country." Most of them were persuaded to "recognize" their errors and make self-criticisms. In these a number of people blamed the influence of the Soviet Twentieth Party Congress, at which Khrushchev began the process of de-Stalinization, as well as the Polish and Hungarian uprisings, for leading them astray.*

Chu Anping disappeared mysteriously in 1966, early in the Cultural Revolution.

In the late 1970s, the party officially reassessed the Anti-Rightist Campaign. It said the movement had been justified but criticized it for "excesses." Hundreds of thousands of its victims were finally freed from the stigma of "anti-party" or "rightist" labels (including such figures as Fang Lizhi, Liu Binyan, Wu Zuguang, and Qin Benli). Chu Anping, however, was one of five Peking-based rightists who was never "rehabilitated." Ninety other rightists outside Peking were not pardoned, and the alleged "crimes" of these ninety-five people were held up as justification for a savage political purge that touched the lives of millions of people. By not reversing the verdict on all the rightists, Deng Xiaoping, the party general secretary in the late 1950s who administered the purge, and his associates in the party leadership could save face and maintain a rationale for continued purges of dissident opinion.

There were echoes of the Anti-Rightist Campaign in the 1989 post-

The way I see it, even a hundred years from now we'll still have to crush unrepentant rightists.

—Mao Zedong, July 1957

In fact, Dai Qing is not a member of China's intellectual elite at all. She's nothing more than a pawn in the machinations of reactionary forces both in and outside China who have been plotting to turn our country into a bourgeois republic.

—Kuang Yan, September 13, 1989

massacre purge. Not only were a number of the victims—Qin Benli, Fang Lizhi, and so on—the same, they were also accused by Deng Xiaoping of trying to turn China into a "bourgeois republic," a refrain from 1957. Once again, Eastern Europe, particularly the Soviet Union, was seen to have had an influence on events. Though the most dramatic changes in the Eastern bloc occurred later in the year, Mikhail Gorbachev's policies of perestroika *and* glasnost *had inspired and encouraged many participants in and supporters of the Protest Movement.*

Dai Qing quit the party on the morning of the Peking massacre in protest against the government's action. Detained by police in July 1989, she was not released until May of the following year. She immediately published "My Imprisonment," an account of her time in custody, in the Hong Kong and Taiwan press. In it she had the following to say about party hacks like "Kuang Yan" (the joint pen name of a number of her colleagues at the Guangming Daily):

To my mind they are the most backward group in China today. Sure, they fly around in Boeing 747s and use "101 Hair-Oil Extract"* but intellectually and emotionally they're stuck in time in the Cultural Revolution, or even as far back as the Anti-Rightist Campaign.

* A reportedly miraculous Chinese treatment for baldness.

On China's National Characteristics

WU ZUGUANG

Wu Zuguang made the following speech on March 22, 1989, at the National People's Political Consultative Congress in Peking.* Wu had been forced to resign from the party in 1987 as part of the campaign against Bourgelib, although he retained his non-party posts such as the vice chairmanship of the China Dramatists' Association.† His outspoken criticism of censorship in the arts and political purges had for many years infuriated such leaders as Vice President Wang Zhen (see p. 141). After his resignation, Wu became even more critical of the government and began addressing such basic issues as the political system itself.

I wonder how many comrades attending this congress have ever really delved into the daily life of the nation? How many of you have ever come into close contact with the people, been jostled on public buses, for example, or elbowed your way into the shops and markets, squeezed up to the bookstalls, or crowded into restaurants—really tasted the whole range of flavors that makes up Chinese life? How much do you know about what concerns people today? Of course, the people have no end of concerns: inflation, students' lack of interest in their studies, the hardships suffered by teachers, the enviable fortunes made by official and private speculators alike. They are perturbed by the rapid decay of public morality and the ever-increasing corruption of the privileged class. . . . They are also concerned as to whether leaders in the Center are really capable of understanding popular sentiment. Popular sentiment is, in short, the sentiment of the nation.

---

* The NPPCC is a body composed of prominent non-party and "democratic personages" appointed to it by the party for the purpose of counseling the party on the concerns of the masses on the one hand, and communicating party policies to the masses on the other.
† For more on Wu Zuguang, see *Seeds of Fire*, pp. 368–72, 407.

But what I want to talk about today is the subject of *guoqing,* "national characteristics." This is because I have heard the expression used three times recently. The first was when Fei Xiaotong, the vice chairman of the National People's Political Consultative Conference [and a famous sociologist], used it a few months ago. The second time was last month in a comment by General Secretary Zhao Ziyang. Most recently it was used in mid-March by Yuan Mu, the spokesman for the State Council. On all three occasions the speakers were using the term "national characteristics" to deny that the Western multiparty system and parliamentary politics could be imported to China. They all gave the same reason: the Western political setup is not suited to China's national characteristics.

I was born after the elimination of feudal rule from China. I have lived through the internecine warfare of the warlords, the success of the Northern Expedition, the autocratic rule of the Nationalists, the eight years of the Anti-Japanese War, the three years of the War of Liberation, and the appearance of a liberated New China.

The birth of the People's Republic of China was the glorious achievement of the Communist Party of China. It saved the people of China from the distress and suffering of the past century, leading them into a new, peaceful, and happy world. During the exhilarating days that followed the establishment of the People's Republic, I was so intoxicated with joy that I would even wake up in the middle of the night laughing. The nation seemed the picture of prosperity, and I contemplated the future of our great motherland with boundless optimism. Comparing the past with the present, the people of China were so grateful to the party and Chairman Mao that we worshiped them to the point of fanaticism. . . .

The atmosphere of renewal and the energy and enthusiasm of those days made it possible to recover speedily from the wounds of war. The whole country was in a state of constant excitement; it was thriving. China even took upon itself the internationalist duty of supporting Korea in its war against American imperialism, forcing the world's mightiest war machine back to the Thirty-eighth Parallel. This stunning victory dispelled in one stroke the woeful impression that China was the Sick Old Man of Asia and won for China the praise of progressive people everywhere. It made every Chinese proud.

After this, however, Chairman Mao Zedong adopted an autocratic style of rule, and from the early 1950s on he launched continual political movements on every front as well as mass movements in industry and agriculture. These included:

1. The criticism of the film *The Life of Wu Xun*
2. The criticism of [Yu Pingbo's] *Researches on* The Story of the Stone
3. The criticism of the "Hu Feng Anti-Party Clique"
4. The Anti-Rightist Campaign
5. The Great Leap Forward, which began with communization, the mass movement to produce steel, and the insanity about entering [the final phase of] Communism
6. The Great Proletarian Cultural Revolution

There is no need for me to enumerate the numerous other minor political campaigns of these years. The campaign against Hu Feng initiated the odious practice of jailing and banning intellectuals and famous writers. In the Anti-Rightist Movement of 1957, nearly one million people were made into rightists; many died before being rehabilitated, and innumerable families were split up. The Great Leap Forward led to peasants falsifying production statistics to satisfy local bureaucrats, thereby deceiving themselves and everybody else. This led to the "three bad years" that left the countryside destitute. . . . In 1966 [Mao Zedong] personally initiated and led the Cultural Revolution, a disaster that blighted the country for ten long years. During that time the nation was so badly abused it nearly collapsed. It created the greatest tragedy and horror China, and indeed mankind, has ever known.

The facts show that none of these movements was justifiable. After the Cultural Revolution, the party was forced to clean up the mess, which it did with the utmost difficulty, correcting past errors and bringing order out of chaos. Yet it could do nothing about those who had been killed, the damaged environment, the economic waste, the cultural relics that had been destroyed, or the squandered wealth of the nation.

Then there is a question that clouds the future of our children and grandchildren: the population explosion. In the 1950s Chairman Mao Zedong not only ignored the specialists who wisely counseled that the population must be kept under control, he actually punished the scholar Ma Yinchu for his outspokenness on the issue. . . . This led to the situation today whereby even with population control in place, the number of people in China has increased wildly to eleven hundred million. What can possibly be done in the future, when things will only get worse?

The above are the actual national characteristics of China. Although we have made progress, the shadows and tragic consequences of the past four decades will stay with us forever. I'm sure many people would agree with me that if none of these disastrous political campaigns had taken place, China would be a very different country today.

In my opinion it is just because of China's national peculiarities—the stubborn persistence of feudal thinking—that a great effort must be made to study the democratic systems of the West.

In the half century since World War II, the capitalist countries have generally enjoyed prosperity and stability while the socialist nations have remained in a depression, the obvious losers on the economic front. The facts speak for themselves: The crux of the matter is the political system. Nothing could be clearer. With the fate of the nation at stake, we cannot allow ourselves false pride. We cannot permit the disasters of the past to be repeated, and for this reason we should in a spirit of humility and in all seriousness ponder the question of our political system.

The main reason for such endless suffering was the authoritarian rule of one party and one man; it was a lack of democracy. Those in power are still unrestrained by public opinion; they can do as they wish, they can even run wild.

"The Dinosaur," Huang Yongyu: "I'm the only reality in all your myths."

Guoqing

The term guoqing, *or "national characteristics," is used to describe China's supposed uniqueness or exclusivity. It implies that the Chinese reality is different from any other, and therefore standards that apply or methods that work elsewhere, or that may even be regarded as being universal, are irrelevant when imported to China. For more than a cen-*

tury, the question of Chinese exclusiveness has been a central element in the debates concerning modernization (associated here with Westernization) and political reform. For some, the crux of the debate is whether the "Chinese essence" can or ought to be retained in the process of modernization. If so, how? For others, there is doubt as to just what the "national essence" really is.

The hoary arguments of the past have been recast by the party for popular consumption in the modern age. Marxism-Leninism and Mao Zedong Thought, or the Four Basic Principles, are now presented as pristine elements of Chinese exclusiveness to which the nation must cling if it is to survive. The particular problems of China—its vast territory, overpopulation, massive agricultural sector, and widespread poverty— are all cited as crucial factors that make democracy or political liberalization anathema.

To appreciate China's gouqing is to understand China, or so the party would have it. People are criticized for failing to come to grips with it, students have to be reeducated by the army to grasp it, and even peasants

In early 1989 Dai Qing was instrumental in the formation of an environmental lobby group that included scientists, reporters, and writers. The group was opposed to the Three Gorges Project for further damming the Yangtze River, a plan first mooted in 1954. Investigations indicated that its environmental impact could be catastrophic and its actual usefulness quite limited. Dai Qing edited a volume of specialist commentary on the subject that was published in February 1989 entitled Yangtze, Yangtze—The Debate over the Three Gorges Project. In her postscript to the book, she commented on the dangers of accepting without question party interpretations of guoqing.

The reason China is in its present state after four decades of "peaceful reconstruction" is that there has always been silence when people should have taken a stand against the numerous serious policy errors that have been made. Everyone would whisper: You'd better keep your mouth shut, the people upstairs have made their decision. This was true thirty years ago and even twenty years ago. It remains true today. But should naked political force or science be our guide in policy decisions? It's a question everyone asks himself but no one ever wants to say out loud.

—Dai Qing

are expected to learn about it. Yet guoqing has no fixed definition, no abiding meaning. The usefulness of the term lies not in its content but in its interpretation. Guoqing, in short, is frequently a pretext for party fiats. To follow the ascendant party line is to be in tune with the mysteries of guoqing. Throughout the 1980s, Deng Xiaoping declared that the party's aim was to build "socialism with Chinese characteristics," that is, socialism that conformed to China's guoqing. In practice, that meant carrying out sweeping economic reform without concomitant political reform—just as in the past dynastic reformers hoped to strengthen China economically and militarily by introducing Western know-how while retaining the "national essence" (those things sanctioned by the power holders and conventional wisdom). In the China of the 1980s, policy failures are laid at the door of purged leaders and thinkers, jailed dissidents, or anyone else who gets out of line; they are guilty of one all-inclusive crime: Bourgelib, which also means they have failed to comprehend China's guoqing.

Recurring Nightmares

QIAN LIQUN

In my research into modern Chinese intellectual, cultural, and literary history, I find myself increasingly terrified by "historical cycles." I often have nightmares about the future.

I have found, for example, that on one level China's modern history is a record of intellectuals engaged in mutual destruction. I had a "dream" that in the not-too-distant future the famous intellectuals who are presently most active in the intellectual and cultural spheres, people who have differing "strategies for national salvation," will finally draw up battle lines and fight to the death. . . .

Of course, it's only a dream, perhaps a premonition. But it is based on historical precedent.

In their investigations of the history and conditions of Chinese intellectuals and writers, the brothers Zhou Zuoren and Lu Xun came to a similar conclusion: Zhou Zuoren lumped "intellectuals," "the emperor," and *liumang* together; Lu Xun said that in the Chinese intellectual world there were only "official souls" and "bandit souls."

> In fact, there is a definite mechanism within Chinese society that eliminates outstanding talents. That is to say, in our society, the most intellectually independent people in every field, the most enterprising and creative talents, are invariably and easily obliterated. The majority are destroyed while still in the formative stage; a few are wiped out as they are just coming to maturity. It's only an extremely small minority who can be accepted by the society, and that is only after they have altered or snuffed out their own creativity and individuality.
>
> —He Xin, March 1988

While contemplating today's famous intellectuals—regardless of whether they are my seniors, my peers, or my juniors—I always find in them something of the "imperial air" (hegemony) or a "touch of the *liumang*" (a breath of the bandit). It is there in all of them, be it to a greater or lesser extent, obvious or disguised, consciously recognized or unconscious.

Furthermore, I find the very same thing in myself.

There have always been intellectuals who have been the accomplices or handmaidens of the rulers. When feudal authoritarianism saturated the national spirit as a whole, intellectuals got a big dose of it. Thus, in China we have not only autocracy and the autocracy of the ignorant, we even have the autocracy of the intellectuals. People say the role of the ignorant is fearful because it means that an "unbridled mass" goes wild; but the terrifying thing about the dictatorship of intellectuals is that it is "scientific" and "legitimate," precise and exacting. In its respect for power and unity of thought, its opposition to individualism, freedom, the minority, heretics, dissonance, and pluralism . . . its purpose is at one with the rule of the kings or the ignorant. Be it the autocrats or the masses in control, their dictatorship invariably leads to bloody murder —China is a nation with a tradition of "killing heterodoxy."

—*May 20, 1989*

I Us' um Fork Now

LI AO

The question of Westernization has been central to Chinese debates on reform and modernization for over a century. In the May Fourth period, Hu Shi was a leading proponent of "wholesale Westernization," as was Li Ao in Taiwan in the early 1960s, when the debate raged once again. Again on the mainland in the late 1980s, Fang Lizhi and Wang Ruowang were bitterly denounced for advocating this approach.*

If we have any sense at all, first and foremost we must admit that we have never wholeheartedly attempted to modernize. We've always been opportunistic, taking whatever appeals to us but never trying to learn from the "spiritual civilization" of others, their scientific attitude or spirit, the fair play that goes with political democracy, the attitudes born of an economy of abundance, or dynamism. In fact, we've never even learned the easygoing sincerity that goes with the greeting "Hi!" We've only ever learned, ever wanted to learn, the most pathetically superficial stuff. When it comes to modernization, we're all still in kindergarten. And though we're at school, we can hardly boast that we've covered the whole curriculum.

A British explorer once came across a cannibal. He was astounded to discover that the cannibal was a graduate of an English university. "And you still eat human flesh?" he asked in surprise. The reply was brilliant: "I us' um fork now." †

This may be only a joke, but you don't know whether to laugh or cry. Just take a look at our own society. How many people with 1691 minds are driving around in 1961 model cars? How many people use the latest printing presses to produce paper money for the dead? How many modern plastics factories are churning out mah-jongg sets? How many people use their refrigerators to store the pork used in sacrifices to Confucius? How many people use microphones to spread the Buddhist dharma? Confucius's descendants done up in Western suits, and smoking the most expensive foreign cigarettes, sit in halls dedicated to the Sage Teacher, writing Chinese characters with a brush. . . .

* See *Seeds of Fire*, pp. 327, 365.
† Li Ao uses this English sentence in the original.

In our fetid "use of Chinese learning as the basis" and wondrous "adaptation of Western technology," are we any better than our cannibal friend? Isn't this the most superficial type of Westernization? It's pretty weird, if you ask me. Everything about it indicates a decay of both the national nervous system and digestive tract; it's all typical of a pack of sick-minded people who are satisfied with a smattering of knowledge.

—*1962*

Hu Yaobang was remarkable as the Chinese Communist leader who advocated replacing chopsticks with the knife and fork. He also reportedly thought the Chinese would grow strong and modern if they increased their intake of dairy products, chocolate, and wine. When dining at the Australian Press Club in Canberra on an official visit in 1985, he was seen to stab his breadroll with his fork, then nibble it around the edges as though it were an ice cream cone.

A Narrow Nationalism

LI XIAOSHAN

There's no doubt that in theory, at least, the concept of "modern Chinese art" is a step in the right direction, and it has been playing a leading role in artistic development. We have left behind the ossified conservatism of the closed door and come to a reluctant and embarrassed recognition of the realities of the modern world. . . . The problem is that the expression "modern Chinese art" in fact cloaks a dangerous parochialism. The moment external conditions change, this very expression will become the ally of conservatism, and people will be forced to return to the well-worn path of tradition. . . .

People invariably think in the following way: Chinese culture with its ancient traditions has fallen under the sway of expansionist modern Western culture because it is feeble and static; if we abandon all tradition and go in for wholesale Westernization, however, we will surely be set adrift. They think the best solution is to "amalgamate East and West," which certainly sounds both impressive and commonsensical. In fact, in practical terms, it is useless.

Desperate to keep up with the latest international trends, people nonetheless insist that we not lose our "special characteristics" in the process. This boils down to applying a modern Western approach . . . to mining the vein of traditional culture. The new look that they manufacture for tradition is then hailed as a sign of creativity. But let's face it, unless this reformed tradition has universal significance, the Chinese artist, as a mere reformer of tradition, will never achieve any real standing in world art. . . .

If you rely on local color to find a niche in the international art scene, all you'll ever be is a bit player. In the final analysis it is the most energetic proponents of "modern Chinese art" who are the most desperate to achieve international recognition. Lacking the courage to rely on imagination, passion, or creativity to compete on the basis of equality with others and win that recognition, they attempt to curry favor by proffering the exotic. Anxious for instant success, many Chinese artists strive not to establish an individual style but to create works that they think will satisfy foreigners' fascination for the exotic; they happily cast themselves in the role of "rustic painters." . . . Many people blame the paucity of modern Chinese art on economic, cultural, and social factors. Certainly, all of these have a bearing on the situation. But surely artists should also admit the influence of their own attitudes and cultural vision?

—April 1989

Li, an art critic in his thirties, came to prominence in 1985 when he declared traditional Chinese ink painting was best left dead and buried.* Like Liu Xiaobo, Zhu Dake, Zuo Shula, and other outspoken cultural critics, he has been penalized for his candor.

* See *Seeds of Fire*, p. 241.

The Common Cold

YI DIAN

The common cold's been here and back
We're used to the winds of the Han
And the air of the Qing as well
But the stimulating atmosphere of this new century
Makes us coughcoughcoughcough
The common cold is common once more
The only thing to do is to buy a sack
And stuff in the new air to the last drop
If even the tiniest bit leaks out
A few dry coughs will sound out a protest
In China, some people's dry coughs are as awesome as A-bombs

A pair of bell-bottoms can bring on the infection
As can a few lines of sympathetic, symbolic poetry
And even the jitterbug
Or an increase in businessmen
Once the cold starts doing the rounds
Everything else is banned
Nothing else
Is allowed to go around

The atom bomb makes Venice shake
The Muse shakes
The rich quake
Ugliness, barrenness, ignorance, and poverty rock and shake
The sound of one cough
China ponders
China wakes

Now they're giving away
Special prescriptions for the cold

Open those sacks
Let the stimulating air of the new century
Fill everyone's lungs
Fill all of China

Qigong:
The Ultimate Revolution

Qigong can enable one to overcome illness and disaster,
improve one's health, and add years to one's life; it can
also help expel spiritual angst. But there is far more to it
than that. The cosmic truths it reveals and explores will
overturn all existing scientific and philosophical systems.
Qigong will usher in the greatest revolution mankind has
ever known. It will enable all humanity to reach a higher
plane of intelligence. There is nothing with a more avant-
garde revolutionary significance than the study of *qigong*
and the special powers it bestows.

> —*From the author's introduction*
> *to* The Great *Qigong* Masters

*In the May Fourth era, as China's traditional world view crumbled,
many cultural conservatives and patriots reacted to the challenge of
foreign ideas by insisting that China had a spiritual culture superior to
that of the materially wealthy West. Similarly, by the late 1980s, when
faith in the trinity of Marxism, Leninism, and Mao Zedong Thought
had all but collapsed, large numbers of people in their desperate search
for self-affirmation turned to qigong (pronounced "tchee-goong") as an
alternative belief system—one that, unlike Marxism, was wholly, satis-
fyingly Chinese. For others like Liu Xiaobo, the popular fascination for
qigong signified nothing so much as a mechanism for further spiritual
and emotional binding.*

*In the 1980s, while many in the West became devotees of the New
Age vogue in which all manner of mysticism was recycled for a monied
middle class set on self-perfection and preservation, China, too, was
rediscovering the wisdom of the ancients. The study and practice of
qigong, a Taoist form of yoga that covers everything from breathing
exercises to spiritual healing and transcendental meditation, became the
most popular nonpolitical fad China had seen since 1949. Many Chinese
have, of course, practiced qigong all their lives. Even old Yan'an period*

(1930s and '40s) party cadres use it, not only for health and longevity but also in the hope that they can avail themselves of its philosophy to survive: "unpretentious like wood that has not been fashioned into anything; vacant like a valley, and dull like muddy water" as Laozi puts it in Chapter 15 of the Tao Te Ching, *the Taoist classic.*

The party's interest in qigong *both as a healing technique and for its presumed connection with other extraordinary powers dates back to the 1950s. Not only do many cadres practice it to keep themselves fit and alert well beyond their prime,* qigong *masters may be called on to help revive failing members of the elderly leadership. It is widely rumored that a gifted young* qigong *adept by the name of Zhang Baosheng has been employed to maintain the safety of China's space program and missile facilities, as well as the health of key members of the aged revolutionary elite.*

The qigong *masters themselves have become a new and captivating source of authority, and lectures by such adepts as Yan Xin (born 1950), a charismatic* qigong *doctor from Sichuan, have attracted large and devoted audiences throughout the country. At one point in the narrative of Ke Yunlu's* The Great Qigong Masters, *one of the characters exclaims on meeting a powerful* qigong *master: "My heart's beating so fast, I'm even more excited than when I saw Chairman Mao in the Cultural Revolution!" Although some* qigong *experts were said to have been involved in the 1989 Protest Movement, the more prominent of their number, conservatives in favor of "unity and stability" on an even more sublime level than the party bosses, seemed to steer well clear of the unbounded expressions of freedom during the Peking Spring.*

The Great *Qigong* Masters

KE YUNLU

Ke Yunlu is a novelist who wrote two of the most famous works of pulp fiction for the party's Reform policy, New Star *and* Night and Day. *As the Reform policies began to founder in the late 1980s and the limitations of literary works based on them became obvious, Ke turned to the highly popular topic of* qigong. *The result was the novel* The Great Qigong Masters, *which, serialized early in the year, appeared in Peking as a book in December 1989, published by the most prestigious party press, the People's Literature Publishing House. Ironically, Ke Yunlu had by then been detained for his role in leading writers to join the Protest Movement in May and was not released until 1990.*

The novel follows the researches of Ouyang Jue ("Ouyang the Enlightened"), a young scholar besotted with qigong. Ouyang's spiritual odyssey, what he calls a search for "universalistic thinking," touches on nearly every aspect of the "Wisdom of the East": the hexagrams of the Book of Changes, Laozi, Zhuangzi, *geomancy, acupuncture, Chinese herbal medicine, and Zen (Chan) Buddhism, with UFOs, astral travel, and the pyramids thrown in for good measure. At one point Ke Yunlu lists in Chinese the titles of the trendier Western books on mysticism and ESP from the 1960s and '70s. (There are a few glaring omissions: Shirley MacLaine, crystals, Tibetan Buddhism—including Lobsang Rampa's writings—and the notoriously salacious aspects of Taoist sexual alchemy.)*

To inspire the reader to plow through this detailed 500-page cut-and-paste tome on philosophy and special powers, Ke inserts a limp love story and an insidious campaign to discredit Ouyang, his valiant voyager through inner space.

Among the most curious sections of the book are discussions of the Book of Changes *as analyzed by an old professor named Weng Naishan, a character who seems to be based on Lao Naixuan (1843–1921), the conservative scholar-politician who helped Richard Wilhelm in his studies and translation of the classic text before and after World War I. As Helmut Wilhelm, Richard's son, noted in the 1960s, each loosening of political control in China has resulted in a debate involving both Confucius and the* Book of Changes. *This was certainly true in the 1980s, when a voluminous literature on both subjects appeared.* The fad for the Book of Changes *continued into the nineties. At the Baiyunguan Taoist temple in Peking, people could even buy Hexagram playing cards with which they could play poker and tell their own fortune at the same time. In late October 1990, the* Beijing Review, *an English propaganda weekly, reported that an athlete had developed "Book of Changes aerobics" (Yijing gong) combining "ancient Chinese philosophy with the scientific benefits of calisthenics."*

In early 1991, following his release, Ke published a second qigong opus, appropriately titled The New Age, *amid considerable controversy.*

---

* See Helmut Wilhelm's preface to *"I Ching" or Book of Changes*, trans. Richard Wilhelm, rendered into English by Cary F. Baynes, London: Routledge & Kegan Paul, 1970, pp. xiv, xvi–xvii.

In a long introductory essay, "The Great Qigong *Masters," Ke Yunlu claims that the book itself is* qigong-*empowered, and the very reading of it can cure the reader's illnesses.*

A DEMONSTRATION

In the novel, Yao Jiu, the disciple of a mysterious old master, is given the mission of spreading the teaching of qigong *throughout China. Ouyang Jue befriends him and takes him as his mentor.*

The character Yao Jiu (whose name means "receptacle [or mortar] of Sage Emperor Yao") seems to be based on Yan Xin, the disciple of Master Haideng. In 1987–1988, Yan's lectures in Peking attracted mass audiences and high-level party and scientific interest. Tapes of the lectures also sold widely as it was said that illnesses could be cured just by listening to him. In the 1989 protests, one banner held high during the mass marches in support of the students read: "Where are you now, Yan Xin?"

Ke Yunlu describes a lecture by Yao Jiu; it is a scene of mass hysteria. The audience "goes wild" in Yao Jiu's empowered stadium, finding momentary release from the depressing realities of everyday life. Yet none of Yao's devotees ever leaves his seat: In qigong-*style liberation, they are still bound by the necessity to maintain "good order."*

The famous *qigong* master Yao Jiu was giving a public lecture.

The Capital Stadium in Peking, which could seat ten thousand people, was packed to capacity. There were milling crowds outside, people waving fistfuls of yuan, offering 20, 30, or in some cases 100 yuan for 5-yuan tickets.

The meeting began. A number of famous people were seated up on the podium with the chairman. Yao Jiu, a man with delicate, clear features, was sitting bolt upright in front of the microphone. His penetrating gaze was directed at the dark mass of people packed in a huge circle around him. His soft, kindly voice was clear and pleasant; he had a southern accent.

Yao was very modest, repeatedly claiming that he possessed only an average ability; a great *qigong* master would possess the equivalent of his total *qigong* power in his little finger. He explained that the popular stories about him, although factual to some extent, were exaggerated. It was going a bit overboard to call him a "living [Mad Monk] Master Ji" or a "god incarnate." Many true *qigong* masters never go public, he

Yan Xin with Master Haideng (Ao Dalun)

said; there may even be some hidden in the audience today. Compared to them, he was like a primary school pupil. He was only an ordinary doctor with slight *qigong* abilities. His master had instructed him to "leave the mountains" and propagate *qigong,* and he had willingly acquiesced to this mission since *qigong* was one of China's national treasures.

Then he said he would be emanating *qigong* energy as he lectured. As he spoke he would empower the whole stadium and create a force field. He advised everyone to sit bolt upright with waist, chest, and neck forming a straight line, close both eyes slightly, relax the whole body, and shut out all random thoughts. In this way it would be possible to receive the positive thoughts, the external *qi,* that he was emanating. . . .

As he would be manipulating the *qi* of over ten thousand people, a very strong force field would develop in the stadium. The experience of past demonstrations led him to expect that some people would experience spontaneous activity: Their bodies might sway, or they might flail their arms or stamp their feet. People would also make all types of uncontrollable noises.

He advised his audience not to be afraid, for these are all normal and healthy phenomena. If you have any illnesses, he said, these spontaneous responses are the channel by which you release your diseased *qi*. If you're not ill but highly sensitive, you may be helping those around you adjust their biological mechanism: Their illness may be discharged through you. There is no danger to you; it's like being inoculated, it increases your own resistance to illness.

He told everyone to remain calm, regardless of what spontaneous actions occurred during the lecture; the moment he finished and stopped channeling power, everyone would cease moving and return to normal.

Some people, he pointed out, have already reacted to the empowerment. And he was right: Members of the audience were swaying uncontrollably left and right in their seats, some were waving their arms or moving back and forth, others were twisting. All had their eyes closed. There weren't that many of them, only a few hundred.

Do not be alarmed, he repeated. Shortly many more people will be moving, and their actions will grow more exaggerated. Please remain in your seats and maintain good order.

Now there were people crying out, calling, or screaming. Yao Jiu asked the comrade in charge of his microphone to turn up the volume, especially the high frequency. Then he began a calm, clear presentation of *qigong*: its history, major features, benefits, objective effects, the ten great mechanisms, its essence, its universal principles, the history of scientific research in *qigong* in the People's Republic, the principles of its practice, and social and political questions related to *qigong*.*

Ouyang Jue sat in the audience looking at the thousands of people, a dark, viscous crowd filling the great circle of the stadium. They were all listening with their eyes closed. It occurred to him: Who else could possibly give a public speech that could so enthrall such a large audience? There was probably no other speaker in the whole of China who could attract such a wide range of people. Surely, he thought, we can draw some sociological conclusions from this?

By now the force field in the stadium was quite strong. The moment he closed his eyes and relaxed, Ouyang could feel it come over him: a numb, dilated, floating feeling that wafted him into a trance. Many people were reacting by now: some swaying gracefully, others waving their arms or stomping their feet. Others were moving back and forth as they screamed or cried, some shouted hysterically. Others were beating

---

* This outline covers topics similar to those dealt with by Yan Xin in a nine-hour lecture on *qigong* given at Qinghua University—one of China's top science universities—in Peking on October 24–25, 1987. The lecture was published in book form as *The Spiritual Power of China: Yan Xin, Grand Disciple of Master Haideng, on Qigong*, Peking: Qinghua University Press, 1988.

their chests painfully, the sound of the pounding quite audible. Some were crying with relief or swearing angrily, frighteningly loud. It was obvious that these people were generally too repressed or too depressed, caught in violent contradictions they normally kept pent up. The instant they entered the *qigong* state, they found release, they let everything out. The energy released was like an explosion.

More people began moving, the energy surged through the audience like a wave, arms and bodies moving everywhere, the colors of people's clothing seeming to mix together. You could say the whole stadium was chaotic, wild, crazy! Cries and shouts melded with insane laughter and hysterical squeals. The stadium had been blown wide open, yet no one had even left his seat. Yao Jiu's voice was composed and leisurely and carried through the cacophony. He was in complete control. He was in charge.

Ouyang Jue counted the people who were doing the spontaneous *qigong*. A fifth of the audience—several thousand people activated together on this one *qigong* wave! . . .

A SKEPTICAL PARTY

The provincial leader in this excerpt seems to be based on Ye Xuanping, governor of Guangdong Province in the late 1980s and Dai Qing's adopted brother. (The Ye family is said to have been enamored of qigong *masters since the early 1980s; a* qigong *master is also credited with keeping the critically ill Marshal Ye Jianying, Ye Xuanping's father, alive for some time in the early 1980s.) This episode is interesting in that it reflects the conservative, pro-status-quo mentality of the* qigong *practitioner. Ke Yunlu is also attempting to justify the rules of social development as outlined in Marxist-Leninist materialist philosophy in terms of* qigong: to go against socialism would be to offend the Will of Heaven and call down punishment on oneself.*

Ouyang Jue found himself sitting next to a middle-aged man, the governor of a province in the south.

They knew each other, and Ouyang began to discuss with him the question of why the powers of *qigong* masters were so often ignored.

The governor was an extremely open-minded and amiable leading cadre, but he was not convinced by the *qigong* exhibition he had just seen. He said that while he could believe that *qigong* could be used to build up one's health and all that "hard *qigong*" could make people very strong, he could not take seriously all this business about using thought to generate electricity. Why, if that were possible, they could do without power stations altogether! In his province they were short of generating capacity. If the *qigong* masters really had such an ability, he'd be happy to invite a few over to generate power and pay them tens or even hundreds of thousands of yuan a month.

Ouyang Jue patiently explained that the *qigong* masters' extraordinary powers had their limits. If they used them to excess, they would weaken themselves. Thus they could use them only on occasion and within certain bounds.

But what's the use of that? the cadre asked.

In the first place, they provide us with a unique channel for understanding the mysteries of the universe and the human body. Second, in practical, everyday terms *qigong* is the best thing for building up one's strength, curing disease, increasing longevity, developing intelligence, and providing spiritual succor, Ouyang Jue told him, explaining the bare essentials in the simplest possible way.

Can they cure any illness?

Not necessarily. It also depends on the patient.

The cadre laughed indulgently, as if to say this was all terribly interesting. Then he turned his attention to what was happening onstage.

But Ouyang Jue persisted: Many of the supernatural beings in our legends, Mad Monk Ji, for example, are artistic representations of great *qigong* masters.

The leader turned to Ouyang with a smile. Do you really believe in supernatural beings? If so, how is it that none of them ever took political power or could control the development of society?

They must respect the Will of Heaven, Ouyang smiled in reply.

The Will of Heaven indeed.

In materialist terms there are fixed laws for the development of the universe and humanity. These laws are the Will of Heaven; nobody can transgress them. Even those with special powers must obey them. Defiance of the Will of Heaven will be punished. Even the most powerful *qigong* masters draw their power from the universe and must obey the rules of nature. They would not survive if they were to oppose nature.

So in the final analysis, we are the masters of our own affairs and they can't interfere. Right? The governor raised his eyebrows questioningly.

You could say that.

Then let's leave worldly affairs in our own hands. As for "supernatural beings," we can look into all of that when and if we have the time. . . .

EAST VERSUS WEST

Western science, long regarded as a threat to traditional Chinese cultural integrity (see "Chinese Democracy: The View from the Peking Observatory," pp. 350–54), is seen here as being no match for Chinese qigong. The parable of the elephant is of Buddhist origin and is used in the popular Chinese saying "[like] a blind man touching an elephant," which is used to describe someone who is ignorant of the whole picture.

Today's so-called "modern" scientific methods of research are in fact "traditional" methods; yet if one grasps the traditional culture of the East, especially the genius and wisdom of traditional China, it is possible to uncover a completely new and "modern" path.

The genius, intuitiveness, and unique mentality and philosophy of Eastern mysticism can be compared to an elephant. Modern science, which has grown out of the Western cultural tradition, is like any number of microscopes trained on many tiny parts of the elephant. People put immense effort into an exacting study of the minutiae of the elephant, but even then their conclusions about the whole creature are tenuous. Perhaps by continuing in this way for one or two thousand years they will be able to combine their results to produce an image of the whole elephant, one that is richer and more meaningful. Pity it will take so long. . . .

"Tai-chi Series," street art by the Pond Art Collective *(Fine Arts in China)*

A CRITICAL MASS

Ke Yunlu introduces a skeptical middle-aged cadre with heavy-framed spectacles; his ridiculous demeanor implies that his criticism of qigong *is less than credible.*

He was of the opinion that Ouyang Jue's entire theory was opposed to dialectical materialism. On the one hand, it spoke of thought and matter as being the same, which was typical of mechanistic or vulgar materialism; on the other, it overemphasized the power of thought, reducing the material world to nothing more than a pile of ciphers. That was out-and-out idealism. The speaker became quite agitated. Flipping through his prepared speech, his tongue flapped wildly and everyone felt the spray of spittle. He often departed from his text to hit some point home. Ouyang Jue's whole theory, he said, concealed the material nature of the world and was at loggerheads with the truth and philosophy. In practice, his philosophy would lose us in the abstruse darkness of mysticism so that we would not dare face the vital, complex, contradictory social realities of the Age of Reform. Such theories encourage people to delve into arcane books, to seek refuge in the religious nihilism of Confucianism and Taoism, to evade the mission presented to them by history, to abandon the historical opportunity we have to revive and uplift the Chinese nation. We can say that his theories are extremely dangerous and harmful. If we allow such thinking to spread, it will influence people throughout the country, in particular the younger generation. These theories look new, thus making them even more seductive for our youth, but the consequences will be disastrous. We now emphasize scholastic freedom. This not only allows the free expression of all manner of outrageous theories and doctrines, it also compels us to undertake a serious analysis and repudiation of those theories.

A Traditional Tool

LIU XIAOBO

One of the first articles Liu Xiaobo published independently overseas, in late 1988, was his critique of the qigong *fad on the mainland. His comments on the debate concerning Chinese spiritual values versus Western materialism parallel the sentiments of such pro-Western intellectuals as Hu Shi in the May Fourth Era and Li Ao on Taiwan in the 1960s.*

Although the Chinese have lost the spiritual crutch of Marxism-Leninism and Communism, the rulers use their power to enforce adherence to the Marxist-Leninist ideology, forbidding people from freely selecting a belief system of their own choice. They will not allow any other Western ideology to replace Communism. . . . As a result, people have taken to looking for a system that has nothing to do with politics and that can be condoned by the authorities. *Qigong* is the ideal choice. Not only is it officially protected, it is lauded for enhancing the national tradition. . . .

The popularity of *qigong* is the result of a nonofficial and spontaneous movement. It wouldn't be a bad thing in a pluralistic society—which could encompass *qigong*, Christianity, and Marxism-Leninism—but the present *qigong* fad has developed within the context of China's authori-

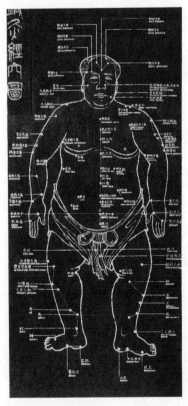

"Bilingual Chart of Acupuncture Points and Meridians," Zhang Hongtu, Chairmen Mao Series

tarian political monopoly. It shows that the state philosophy is powerless to help people, and this is a good thing. But I have my doubts about it. Given the general condition of the Chinese personality today, I doubt whether people are really capable of believing in anything. *Qigong* may be nothing more than a political tool in the hands of the bureaucrats. . . .

As politics pervades every aspect of life in China, it is not surprising that the moment something comes along that can free people from politics, something that will not irritate the powers that be, people go wild over it. . . .

Since the Cultural Revolution the Chinese have been searching for a way out. On the surface, or on the rational level, this has found expression in the desire to open up to the outside world. But deep down, emotionally, the Chinese remain closed off. In their heart of hearts they want to find some superior cultural tradition of their own that will help them create a unified system of belief. That is to say, from the beginning of the Opium Wars [of the nineteenth century], all Chinese reforms have been carried out in an atmosphere of admiration for and fear of the West. But the Chinese will never admit to themselves that they are hopelessly backward, that their culture is senile. Instead, they are constantly engaged in a quest to find some source of national pride with which to console themselves. When the Chinese admit the material superiority of the West, in the same breath they belittle Westerners for their lack of a spiritual life. At the same time that they recognize the West's scientific superiority, they opine that it is morally decadent. Thus the Chinese want, on the one hand, to enjoy the material comforts of the West, but on the other to use the national spirit to oppose total Westernization. Confronted with the powerful culture of the West, the Chinese search for a spiritual crutch in the ancient culture that once made them so proud. . . .

But *qigong* will provide no crutch for us on our journey toward modernization. It can only encourage us to be content with the status quo and hold up progress. To be a great *qigong* master, you have to go beyond the mundane, abandon the vulgar world, and take a path that leads away from reality. The *qigong* craze has taken off because the Chinese dare not oppose authoritarianism.

The New Regime—
An Old Tale

With each new dynasty and each new reign throughout
Chinese history, the throne has never changed, only the ass
that is on it.

—Bo Yang

Under Communism the Chinese have come to think of themselves as
being subjected to cycles of relaxation (fang, or release) and restriction
(shou, or restraint). During the former, the atmosphere is almost heady
with freedom, the "red noise" at its highest pitch; the latter are marked
by increased political study sessions, arrests, executions, restraints on
intellectual and cultural freedom, and a general feeling of repression.
The bindings are loosened and then put back on, only to be loosened
once more. Some people wonder if it will ever be possible to stop the
pendulum of history swinging one moment toward anarchy, the next
back toward authoritarianism. Others find some hope in the lessons of
the past.

A Lesson from History

LUO BEISHAN

Luo Beishan is the pen name of a writer and scholar in his seventies who
survived the Cultural Revolution. He went into exile in June 1989 and
writes satirical essays for the Hong Kong press.

In 212 B.C., the two "intellectuals" Hou and Lu criticized the emperor
Qin Shihuang. They were afraid of informers (though I don't know if
back in those days sisters informed on their brothers for a 500-yuan

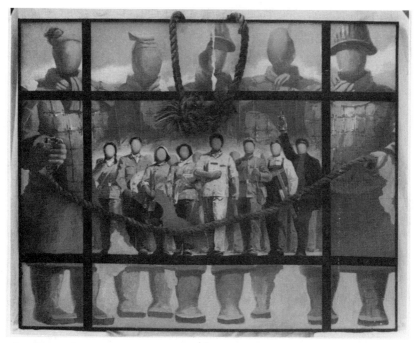

"Sacrifice," Zhang Pingjie *(Fine Arts in China)*

reward), and as there were no foreign embassies where you could take refuge, they simply ran as far as their legs could carry them.*

Qin Shihuang was furious and took his revenge on all the other scholars in the capital. The *Historical Records* state that he "had the censors interrogate all the scholars." As a result they fell about accusing one another and the emperor ordered more than 460 "counterrevolutionary hooligans" to be buried alive in a massive pit in the capital of Xianyang. It is recorded: "This was announced throughout the empire as a warning to others" and "The remainder were sent into exile in the border regions."

Actually, they began persecuting intellectuals in China two years before this, in 214 B.C., the thirty-third year of Qin Shihuang's reign. Premier Li Si presented a vicious report to the emperor stating that "scholars today have no respect for the present and emulate only the past" (translated into modern Chinese, "They don't study Marxism-

---

* Shortly after the Peking massacre the government offered rewards for students, intellectuals, and workers on their wanted lists. The sister of one student leader turned in her brother. Fang Lizhi and Li Shuxian took refuge in the U.S. embassy in Peking, and the singer Hou Dejian hid in the Australian embassy.

[Lin Biao interjects: "Qin Shihuang burned the books and buried the scholars."] So what's the big deal about Qin Shihuang? He buried only 460 Confucians alive; well, we've buried 46,000. When we suppressed counterrevolutionaries, we also killed some intellectuals, didn't we? We've debated with the democrats: They attack us for being just another Qin Shihuang. Well, they're wrong. We're a hundred times greater than Qin Shihuang. They say we're dictatorial like Qin Shihuang. Certainly, we've never denied it. It's a pity they never get it right; they need us to fill in the details for them [laughs loudly].

—Mao Zedong, 1958

Leninism but go on and on about democracy and the rule of law"). Li said, "They negate your rule and create confusion and chaos among the common people. . . . If this is not stopped, power will fall away from you and opposition parties will develop. I suggest immediate action." This led to the emperor ordering the burning of the books with an instruction that "those found discussing the *Book of Poetry* or the *Book of History* [both Confucian classics] are to be executed, and those who criticize the present by using examples from the past will have their families annihilated."

But this is the old story of "burning the books and burying the scholars," which everyone knows from Sima Qian's *Biography of Qin Shihuang*. To update it, all that is required are a few cosmetic changes: Use tanks to crush people to death instead of burying them alive, introduce machine guns to shoot people at random, employ masses of troops, carry out arrests at night, close all the borders, use the media to terrorize the nation, make up phony crimes. . . . When socialist modernization is impossible, go for fascist-feudal modernization.

The cycles of history show that China has stagnated for two thousand years. This is the tragedy of our nation.

But there are also a few encouraging historical precedents. Only two years after Qin Shihuang burned the books and buried the scholars, he died at Shaqiu, and five years later the Qin dynasty was overthrown by a military mutiny. Li Si, the running dog premier who had devised the means of dealing with the scholars, fell victim to an internal party power struggle and was sliced in two in the marketplace of Xianyang. Shortly before the sentence was carried out, he blubbered to his son: "We'll

> ## IDEOLOGICAL BAGGAGE
>
> [T]he heart of the crisis, I believe, is the fact that the Chinese Communist regime is virtually dead, and it reached this condition many years ago. Yet, it might still take some time before it is finally buried. When Qin Shihuang, the fearsome founder of the first Chinese empire, died during a voyage to the provinces, in 210 B.C., the members of his entourage were so afraid that the empire might immediately fall apart that they did not dare disclose the news of his death. Business was carried on as usual, but as it was in summer, they loaded a cargo of rotting fish in the imperial chariot, to cover up the smell of the decaying body.
>
> What amount of smelly luggage will be needed now to enable Communism to continue much further on its aimless journey?
>
> —Simon Leys, June 3, 1989

never again be able to chase rabbits at the east gate of Shangcai!" They both burst into tears, and his family was wiped out to the third generation.

I wonder if at some time in the future Yang Shangkun, Li Peng, and Chen Xitong will have cause to recall the delights of "chasing rabbits at the east gate of Shangcai"?

A Knowing Smile

In a long prose meditation on the enigmatic smile of the terra-cotta warriors interred at the tomb of Qin Shihuang near Xi'an, published in mid-1990, one writer speculated on the reasons for the frozen bemusement of the statues in a thinly disguised comment on China's modern rulers:

They smile at collapse and extinction: the proud Empire of Qin was brought low in an instant.

They smile at the greed and ambition of an emperor who, having schemed to enjoy an eternal reputation, was doomed to a short-lived reign.

They smile at feebleness and impotence: History reveals that there has never been an emperor capable of enslaving his people forever.

They smile, contemplating these fly-by-nights who believe they are the masters of history, and who do not realize that by forcing the people to bow their heads in submission they become objects of scorn. . . .

—Han Xiaohui

A Not So Clean Sweep

When the party launched its latest purge in June 1989, it didn't bury scholars alive, it just jailed them. It was reported, however, that there were book burnings in the provinces in response to the center's call to "sweep away pornography" (saohuang) and eradicate Bourgelib.

Antipornography drives were part of every major ideological campaign of the 1980s. There were also numerous local antipornography campaigns. The definition of pornography, however, changes from year to year. In the early eighties, even the innocuous love songs of Taiwan songstress Teresa Teng were deemed pornographic; by the end of the decade, punk bands performed raunchy numbers with lines like "Take off your clothes and come with me" in clubs around the capital with apparent impunity.

That was probably, however, the result more of oversight than of tolerance, for at the same time, many scholars' works, and books written or edited by Dai Qing, Liu Xiaobo, Jin Guantao, Yan Jiaqi, and others were banned. In 1988, according to unconfirmed reports in the Hong Kong press, Deng Xiaoping was so infuriated by the publication of Chinese translations of such works as Irving Wallace's Fan Club and Lovers and Gamblers by Jackie Collins that he said: "We should put some publishers on trial and execute them."

Li Ruihuan, the Politburo member in charge of ideology and cultural matters after June 1989, set the tone for the latest antipornography campaign in speeches in August and September 1989, from which the following quotations are taken:

Sweeping away pornography is a very important part of our struggle against Bourgelib. The flood of pornographic publications and audiovisual products in our society is both the insidious consequence of Bourgelib and a catalyst of the further spread of Bourgelib. An important aspect of the strategy of hostile foreign powers promoting "peaceful evolution" for China is the use of pornography, gambling, and drugs to anaesthetize our people. The fact that some of the dregs of society stepped forward to act as the aggressive henchmen in the recent counter-revolutionary turmoil in Peking clearly proves this. Making a clean sweep of such filth is the way to guarantee healthy progress for Reform and the Open Door Policy. Some comrades are concerned that the anti-pornography drive may influence the Open Door, but they needn't be worried. To wipe out pornography and get rid of the "mosquitoes" and "flies" [that have come in through the Open Door] is to create an even better environment for investment and allow the work of the Open Door to be carried out even more effectively. . . .

—Li Ruihuan, October 16, 1989

Although the [producers of tapes and videocassettes] have come up with good and relatively good audiovisual products, many other products militate to one degree or another against the construction of a socialist spiritual civilization with high cultural standards. The insightful point has been made, for instance, that music tapes whose songs are bleak in content, depressing, sentimental, filled with moaning and groaning, or simply hysterical have already corroded the souls of our young people and dissipated their revolutionary zeal. . . .

Of course, in the past we've gone a bit overboard with such things, greatly exaggerating the social effects of literature and art to the point of

"Cassette Cangue," from 1989 anti-"pornography" poster (Victoria Godfrey)

claiming that a single song, novel, or film could destroy the party and the nation. But at the same time, it is important not to underestimate the influence and effect of music tapes and videos as a means of communication in the modern age; they reach a wide audience and have a strong allure and profound influence that other media cannot duplicate. . . .

—*Li Ruihuan, September 5, 1989*

By October 18, 1989, Canton's Yangcheng Evening News *was able to report the following results in Guangdong Province alone:*

Over the last five months . . . 345,870 contraband publications of various types have been confiscated, as have 40,125 books of obscene pictures, 26,018 sets of obscene playing cards, and more than 69,000 illegal or obscene videocassette tapes. In addition, over 1,200 videocassette

In 1988 several million copies of Ni Kuang's novels, best-sellers in Hong Kong, were banned from distribution in China. Ni Kuang discussed the incident in an interview with the editor of Emancipation Monthly:

It has nothing to do with the [nature of my work] and everything to do with my political stance. I recently made it clear that just as I opposed Communism in the past, I still oppose it today and will continue to do so in the future. Some people say I've gone overboard with this. But I'm not going to change my mind just for tens of thousands of renminbi in royalties. Of course, if we were talking tens of millions I might reconsider. Every man has his price. (Laughs.)

Anyway, who's to say that writers publishing today on the mainland won't oppose Communism tomorrow? What are you going to do, get a written guarantee before you publish their books? I've said to the friends who've helped me get published in the mainland that I'm happy to go with the flow; it really makes no difference to me at all if my books can't be published now. Besides, it would be great for me if they banned all my books. Banning books is one of the stupidest things anyone can do: So you ban me for thirty years, you think you can keep banning me for three hundred? Books last forever.

—Ni Kuang

players, television sets, cassette dubbing machines, and other materials related to criminal cases have been confiscated and 2,868 people interrogated according to legal procedures.

According to a speech by Party Minister for Propaganda Wang Renzhi published in late February 1990, despite all the party's efforts to contain pornography and Bourgelib, troublemakers in the media and publishing industry were still active. Following is a brief excerpt from a very long speech:

During the previous period [before June 1989], some newspapers, magazines, publishing houses, official seminars, and conferences provided a soapbox for people involved in the dissemination of Bourgelib. Newspapers reported what these people were saying, and then other newspapers published those reports, following which excerpts appeared in many digests. In the end, a book would come out. It's a process through which those involved could garner fame and fortune; it even provided the possibility of official status and promotion. Some young people were seduced by the lure of it all. Believing that there's no future in Marxism, they chose to follow those people on the fast track to fame, promotion, and wealth. We mustn't permit this situation to continue. Our newspapers, magazines, publishing houses, and radio and television stations must never again provide a forum for Bourgelib. We must pay close attention to the fact that even today some people are continuing their activities, making exploratory moves, and getting up to their old tricks. We mustn't waver in our opposition: The moment they stick out their heads, we must beat the war drums and attack.

—*Wang Renzhi*

Wang Renzhi's was only one voice in a chorus of conservative reaction. The same propaganda hacks who attempted to crush cultural diversity during the Anti-Bourgelib Campaign at the Zhuozhou Conference of April 1987* had another chance to denounce their opponents to their hearts' content at the Baoding Conference of April 1990. The Literary Gazette *in Peking reported on the meeting:*

* See *Seeds of Fire,* pp. 403–6.

Unchecked for so long, the floodwaters of Bourgelib have inundated much of our ideological territory. The arts are a disaster area. Much work is necessary to eliminate the influence of Bourgelib, rectify people's thinking, and help Marxism occupy this lost ground once more. . . .

So some writers are refusing to write. Does this signify a cultural recession? . . . Bourgelib led some people down the wrong path—it's little wonder that, obliged to abandon their erroneous thinking, they now feel lost. For these comrades to produce good work again requires considerable intellectual and psychological realignment. To lay aside their pens and spend more time in study and reflection is not necessarily a bad thing. . . . As for those self-proclaimed members of the "cultural elite" who refuse to pluck themselves from the mire of Bourgelib, they have no desire to write for the People or for socialism anyway. It is no loss to the cultural enterprise at all if we are deprived of their talents.

As the renewed purge of Bourgelib developed in 1990, there were signs that, as in 1987, widespread opposition to Maoist-style extremism might limit the devastation. Even the Politburo's ideology chief recognized this popular resentment.

Ideological work has to be done in a way that makes people want to listen, to take notice; only then will it be effective. If they run away at the very sight of you, how are you going to achieve anything?

—*Li Ruihuan, April 28, 1990*

Moderation, however, has never been the party's strong point on ideological questions. In late June 1990, the Ministry of Culture, by then firmly under the control of narrow propagandists, published a sternly worded editorial in its weekly newspaper, China Culture. *Accompanying two pages of quotations from party leaders (except for Li Ruihuan) on ideological rectitude, the editorial was reported to be a critical response to Li's more moderate approach.*

In recent years, the destructive influence and interference of Bourgelib have stirred up an ill wind throughout the society, in particular in the ideological sphere and on the cultural front. . . . Even though the speeches of representative central leaders are still fresh in our memories, some people blatantly ignore them, interested instead in the so-called new spirit [of other factions of the party leadership]. It is as though they can always spot some cloud wafting on the horizon that might promise a new tempest. It is this type of thinking and ambience that deludes people, undermines the martial spirit, and can be extremely harmful. Such ideological confusion is the very thing that those stubborn exponents of Bourgelib who engage in political dirty tricks can seize on and exploit to their own advantage.

—June 24, 1990

Back to the Future

The new regime aimed to do more than merely "sweep away" porn and Bourgelib. The following excerpts from Party General Secretary Jiang Zemin's National Day speech in 1989, required study material for the whole nation, show that despite lip service to Reform and the Open Door, the party was also intent on recycling a number of the political aims of the Maoist era—and the rhetoric of that time as well. Jiang's comments on "national nihilism" were aimed at Liu Xiaobo, Fang Lizhi, and the authors of River Elegy.

. . . The tendency toward extreme democratization and anarchism has a broad social basis in China. It is very destructive to our cause and is liable to exploitation by a small handful of reactionaries. We must maintain sharp vigilance and resolutely prevent this trend from running rampant. We do so precisely to guarantee the democratic rights of the majority and to guarantee the healthy development of socialist democracy and the socialist legal system. Democracy toward the People and dictatorship toward hostile elements and antisocial elements are closely linked and complementary. So long as class struggle exists in some areas of life the function of dictatorship cannot be weakened. . . .

Unremitting efforts must be made in ideological education to instill the values of patriotism, collectivism, socialism, self-reliance, and hard struggle, as well as revolutionary traditions, among the masses, particularly the youth. Constant Communist ideological education should be conducted among members of the party and Youth League and among the advanced elements. We must provide Marxist and socialist ideologi-

"A Feeling I Sometimes Get When Reading the Newspaper," Hua Junwu

cal guidance for the departments of theoretical studies, propaganda and education, the press, the publishing industry, and the departments engaged in literature and the arts. . . .

Schools . . . should make moral education their priority and build up a firm, correct, political orientation. . . . We must actively absorb all the fine achievements of our country's history and culture and of foreign cultures, and resolutely discard all feudal and capitalist cultural dross and spiritual garbage. In this regard, at present we must pay special attention to combating the ideology of national nihilism that completely rejects China's traditional culture and worships everything foreign. . . .

The party and government have always considered the youth, including young intellectuals, to be the future and hope of the country and, while putting strict demands on them, have consistently treated them with love and care in the sincere hope that they will grow up healthily and quickly to become qualified citizens. We also sincerely hope that the mass of intellectuals, particularly young intellectuals, will seriously study Marxism-Leninism and Mao Zedong Thought, plunge into social realities, and work together with the workers and peasants, constantly absorbing nourishment from the people's activities as the makers of history and giving full play to their own wisdom and talents in the country's socialist construction. . . .

It should be stressed here that the international reactionary forces have never abandoned their hostility toward the socialist system or their attempts to subvert it. Beginning in the late 1950s, after the failure of military intervention, they shifted the focus of their policy to "peaceful evolution." . . . They support and buy over so-called dissidents through whom they foster blind worship of the Western world and propagate the political and economic patterns, sense of values, decadent ideas, and lifestyle of the Western capitalist world. When they feel there is an opportunity to be seized, they fabricate rumors, provoke incidents, plot turmoil, and engage in subversive activities against socialist countries. . . . The struggle between infiltration and counterinfiltration, subversion and countersubversion, "peaceful evolution" and counter–"peaceful evolution" will last a long time. In this connection, people of all nationalities, and all party members, especially leaders, must maintain a high degree of vigilance. . . .

—Jiang Zemin, September 29, 1989

A Big Confucius and Little Émiles

The wheels of education, reeducation, and indoctrination turn with each new adjustment of the prevailing ideology. The new regime may be given to displays of force—burying scholars or sending in the tanks—but it does not like to rely on them. Just as children were once imbued with the spirit of Confucianism by repeated recitation of the classics, so the citizens of China today are expected to absorb the latest party line through repetitious political study classes in which they read aloud the speeches of the leadership, the editorials of the People's Daily, and Deng Xiaoping's thoughts on everything from socialist construction to art and literature.

The message is reinforced by the slogans that are plastered, hung, and painted on every available surface, like talismans warding off the evils of pornography, Bourgelib, and counterrevolution or promoting traffic safety, population control, and proletarian internationalism.

In the Shadow of Confucius

YING-TAI LUNG

Ying-tai Lung (born 1952) is a popular Taiwan essayist and social commentator. In the following article, written in 1985 about Taiwan, she questions the mentality behind sloganizing. Although slogans are used by both the Nationalists and the Communists for different political purposes, the basic approach is the same. Confucius—that ancient master of the didactic slogan—casts his shadow over things in more ways than one.

Taiwan is a land of slogans. Walk down the street and you'll see "Two Children Is Just Right"; cross a pedestrian overpass and what greets your eyes but "Work Hard to Catch Up"; glance at a telegraph pole and be told that "Everyone's Responsible for Keeping Secrets—Beware of Spies." On the bus, you raise your eyes and you're commanded to "Revere the Aged and Honor the Wise"; in the classroom it's the familiar "Dignity and Self-Reliance; We Show No Fear in the Face of Changing Circumstances"; in the toilet you're likely to encounter "Cultivate the Good Habit of Washing Your Hands"; and on the walls of government offices you'll see "Democracy, Ethics, and Science," "Love Your Home but Love Your Country More," "To Inform on Bad People Is to Protect Good People." There are also some truly inscrutable ones: "To Risk One's Life Is to Protect Life," hung over the traffic-congested avenues, appears to encourage drivers to charge the enemy.

Has anyone ever wondered why Taiwan is so chockablock full of slogans? What is it about a nation that puts so much effort into thinking up phrases, writing them out, and plastering them over walls so that no matter where you turn you can't avoid them? What motivates it?

The answer, of course, is the desire to "solve problems." If people are dirty, you paste up a sign, "Cleanliness Is the Essence of Strength." If there are people who try to avoid military service, you hang a huge cloth banner across the street reminding them that "Military Service Is an Honor." To ward off tailgaters, you put up a sign in your car window that says "Keep Your Distance for Safety's Sake." And because the self-confidence of the Chinese people is at such a low ebb, you carve "Be a Dignified and Upright Chinese" into the pillars at school entrances. Behind every slogan is a problem waiting to be solved. Since slogans are

Ying-tai Lung is sometimes compared to Bo Yang. On a visit to the mainland in April 1989, however, Lung told a reporter from the Literary Gazette *that she and Bo Yang differed in one basic respect.*

I think Bo Yang is a fervent nationalist. He has a stronger sense of being Chinese and is more nationalistic than I am. He writes his essays with an eye to saving China. I'm not so ambitious, and not much of a nationalist, either. I always feel that I'm a human being first, then Chinese.

—Ying-tai Lung

ubiquitous in Taiwan, you can be sure that the place is seething with problems.

But do they work? How many times in the middle of a busy day have you stopped to ponder the significance of "Democracy, Ethics, and Science"? How many people, on reading "Everyone's Responsible for Combating Filth," have rushed home to clean the house? And is there anyone who has read a book just because they've seen the slogan "Let's Be a Nation of Book Lovers" on a telephone pole? I've even seen a great pile of filthy garbage right under the sign "Litterers are Swine." So how are these slogans and signs really supposed to change our lives?

Such sloganizing is only one example of the superficial, formalistic aspect of Chinese life. But there's another, far more serious question that we can use to illustrate this point. Everyone says the Chinese lack self-confidence. They have abandoned their traditions in favor of Western culture, something they have only a superficial understanding of and are unable to assimilate. The solution's simple: Slap up thousands of posters reading "Revive Chinese Culture" on the streets, in the schools, and at bus stops!

In Taipei they've come up with the idea of building a statue of Confucius that will be taller and heavier than the Statue of Liberty. Theirs is a bold vision, so much so that they plan to spend more than a hundred million [New Taiwan] dollars just to pay for the bronze to make it. The

The reactionary nature of the Chinese Communist leadership might make them value Confucius for the wrong reasons, as an additional support to the authoritarian politics, that the elders are right, young people should submit to them, subjects should submit to their rulers and so on, a kind of distorted Confucianism, the imperial Confucianism, which was used for political purposes.
—Simon Leys, June 3, 1989

Confucius was a great thinker in ancient China; his thought is part of our precious cultural heritage. We must certainly accept and study all the good things in it. Of course, due to the limitations of his time there are some unsuitable things as well. We need to select the essence and discard the dross from his thought, and use it to educate our young people so they can carry forward our outstanding national traditions.
—Party General Secretary Jiang Zemin, October 8, 1989

statue is supposed to promote Confucian thought, revive Chinese civilization, raise the people's educational level, and announce to the world that Taiwan is the bastion of Chinese culture.

I'm not making any of this up: Haven't you seen the papers? The municipal government isn't joking, either.

Once this colossus has been erected, it will probably cast a shadow over a huge area, turning a block of homes into a sunless, cheerless area. The incessant rain and pollution [of Taipei] will gradually coat the statue in a layer of filth. The hawkers will swarm around the surrounding streets like flies to meat, and the sightseers will further tie the local traffic into knots. . . . But I still can't see how some big lump of bronze is going to "Promote Confucian Thought" or "Revive Chinese Culture."

The New Émile

LAO SHE

A May Fourth writer, the great humorist, novelist, and playwright Lao She (1899–1966), gave us a memorable image of a revolutionary education in his 1936 story "The New Émile," from which the following selection is taken.

My son Émile died when he was eight years, four months, and twelve days old; but his death has never caused me to doubt the fundamental correctness of my educational methods. Of course, there were minor oversights—they were unavoidable—but on the whole my experiment was based on the soundest principles. His demise may have been the result of some small miscalculation, but that's part of the process of experimentation. Science has no reason to fear mistakes; it's people who refuse to correct their mistakes that are the danger. If I have an Émile II, I am absolutely confident he will be a total success; I have experience now, I know what to avoid and what to do. So although Émile has passed away, I feel no sense of grief; on the contrary, I look forward with considerable excitement to my future success. In the enterprise of raising children, there really is no place for displays of emotion. . . .

At birth Émile was six and half pounds, neither over- nor underweight, an ideal size in fact. The first thing he did when he entered the world was to cry. I seized the opportunity. "My friend," I admonished him, "close your mouth at once! Life is a struggle, a battle, and crying is an admission of weakness. You should know that. Very well, this was your first mistake: I command you to make sure it is your last!" He whined for a minute and then cried no more. From that moment forth, right up to his death, he never sobbed again. My brave Émile! (Please forgive me for indulging my emotions so.)

After three days I rescued him from his mother's embrace, taking upon myself the entire responsibility for his upbringing. Mothers are unreliable, no matter how well educated or talented they may be. They all have the same evil propensities, be they university graduates with diplomas in education or illiterate peasant women. The degeneration of humanity must, I fear, be blamed on the mothers of the world. Whenever I see a young woman with a bouncing, healthy infant in her arms, I think of Mother Mary and Jesus. Even if the woman is a socialist, at best the child will end up a socialist with a Christian conscience, a bearded Tolstoy who knows nothing of resistance. I couldn't allow Émile to plead for his life from his mother's breast, to be a little darling constantly petted and kissed by a woman, just like a fat little Pekinese. I wanted him to grow up to be a fighter, a man with a head and heart as hard as steel, a man to make every filthy mouth that tried to kiss him smart with pain.

I took him off milk. Blood nourished on mother's milk makes a man as flaccid as bean curd; it turns him into a pansy. Émile had to act like a man. I wouldn't let him touch cow's milk either: I didn't want him becoming a product of "milksop education." Bread, of course, was the best substitute for milk. So on his fourth day Émile started eating bread. Sooner or later he would understand the importance of bread and why one has to fight for it. I knew that bread was not as nourishing as mother's milk or cow's milk, but I felt no pity for Émile's cries of hunger. Hunger is the motivating force of revolution. He had to experience hunger if he was to learn resistance. Whenever he was hungry, I would give him a lecture on the forms and strategies of resistance. He would sit there listening to me in complete silence; after all, I was the one holding the bread. When I saw his brow break out into a feverish sweat, I would give him some—to keep him from fainting dead away. His eyes would positively sparkle every time he saw the bread. It truly pleased me, for he evidently understood its value. One of the first simple sentences Émile learned was "Give me bread!" He screamed it with such conviction and effect. He was just like a revolutionary leader shouting a slogan.

He often went hungry, and so, predictably, he started stealing food. I wasn't against this. Quite the opposite: I'd punish him for being an incompetent thief or if he admitted guilt too readily. Sometimes I even flogged him. I wanted to instill in him a sense of deception and slyness. A soldier has to be as cunning as a fox. A revolutionary who fights for justice must be sly; must use the most underhand methods to complete his important mission. . . .

By the time he turned three, other children disliked playing with him, and even adults found him utterly unlovable. For me this was profoundly satisfying.

From the moment he began to speak, I expended my energies on teaching him the precise use of language. I would not allow him to use a word unless he knew exactly what it meant. I made quite sure he did not learn any words that gave him scope for fantasy. The result was that he acquired words to describe what he knew, no more, no less; nothing vague or imaginary. For example, when I taught him the word "moon," I told him everything he needed to know about the moon: its size, age, evolution, and eventual destruction. . . . Nothing but the facts. Anything outside of this was excluded. The moon was the moon. He wasn't ex-

MORE ÉMILES

On October 13, 1989, the fortieth anniversary of the founding of the Chinese Young Pioneers, an organization for Communist cubs, Party General Secretary Jiang Zemin sent the following message of congratulation:

The Young Pioneers is a reserve force for the construction of socialist modernization in the motherland; it is also a great school in which our children and juveniles can study socialism and Communism for themselves.

The realization of our proletarian revolutionary cause requires the tireless struggle of generation after generation of people. In the twenty-first century the heavy burden of constructing the Socialist Motherland will fall on the shoulders of today's children; we must grasp the training of our successors from youth.

I hope our Young Pioneers will follow Comrade Deng Xiaoping's teaching to become successors to the proletarian revolutionary cause with ideals, morals, culture, and strict discipline.
—*People's Daily*

According to official statistics, in 1989 there were 130 million Young Pioneers in China.

"The Masses Are the Real Heroes, While We Ourselves Are Often Childish and Ignorant," Zhang Hongtu, Chairmen Mao Series

posed to any of that stuff and nonsense about "moonlight" or the "man in the moon." Everyone knows that the moon reflects the light of the sun, and that "moonlight" is nonsense. As for the "man in the moon," well, that's pure humbug, I wasn't going to let my Émile picture that dead orb with a man in it. And as for that twaddle about a hare up on the moon and the Goddess Chang'e fleeing there with the elixir of immortality, I wasn't having any of it. Legends and myths are the remnants of a barbaric antiquity; Émile was being instructed to create the culture of the future, his had to be the discourse of modern man. . . .

I really enjoyed listening to Émile. At the age of seven he was able to put together great strings of delightful expressions, and they would pour from his mouth like one great slogan: "Émile says, we must carry out revolution, we must overthrow, destroy, sacrifice ourselves to the last man. Running dogs! Blood will flow like rivers, it will drown you. . . ." With the correct knowledge he had acquired from his study of language, and with the attitude I had inculcated in him, his education was a total success. It was the most thoroughgoing kind of transformation: peeling off his flesh and draining off all of his blood. He would neither laugh nor cry but waited patiently like a machine to do what had to be done. This is the only way to train a warrior of the future. A warrior must sacrifice pleasure from infancy, must pull human nature up by its very roots. To attempt to remake man through an educational process other than this is futile.

I began teaching him the principles of politics at the age of eight. He enjoyed his instruction immensely and learned a large number of political terms. Unfortunately, it was soon after this that he fell ill. It didn't occur to me that he wouldn't recover. He'd been sick before and I treated him with medicine while continuing his instruction. One can't afford to spoil children, one shouldn't give in to them and mollycoddle them the moment they complain of feeling unwell. They get used to being pampered, and then they constantly pretend to be sick. He couldn't fool me. He knew that he'd have to keep working even if he was sick, and that playacting would get him nowhere. But this time he really did seem quite unwell, so I let him have a respite from his work. I entertained him with talks on the theory of history and revolution and gave him plenty of medicine. I never thought he'd die! . . .

I don't have the time to go into all the other details of his life. Now that I recall his death, I really don't feel like going on. I remain steadfastly confident in my educational theory and methods, but I can't help feeling a little emotional about it all. I admit that this is a weakness. Émile really was very dear to me. But my sorrow is not a sign of despair. I learned a great deal from my experience with Émile. I will forge ahead with my research and experiments. I'm sure that with Émile II my plans will come to fruition.

Much of Lao She's early work reflects the world of old Peking, and his writing is rich in the mordant wit of the Pekingese. Although not originally a supporter of the Communists—he even wrote a science fiction satire of the party in the 1940s entitled Cat City—*after 1949 he became a faithful pro-Communist writer, earning himself the title "People's Artist." He died, possibly by his own hand, after being "struggled" at the beginning of the Cultural Revolution.*

Full Circle

From Sartre to Mao Zedong

HUA MING

The "Sartre craze" first swept Peking University in 1979, and over the following ten years, along with the "fad for Freud" and the "vogue for Nietzsche," it swelled and subsided, leaving everyone quite dizzy. Cool reflection reveals that behind these crazes was a cargo cult of all manner of foreign imports. But university campuses are places that are forever trying to come up with something different. And as we enter the nineties, a new message is emanating from them.

Now, university students are "Mao crazy."

—On December 26 [Mao's birthday], 1989, more than ten universities in the capital organized a "rediscovering Mao Zedong" seminar at the Chairman Mao Memorial Hall in Tiananmen Square;

—Mao Xinyu, Chairman Mao's grandson, an undergraduate in the History Department of the Chinese People's University, is increasingly popular with his fellow students, who crowd around to hear his stories about his granddad;

—Whether at schools in the capital like Peking University, the People's University, Peking Normal University, or China Youth Political College, or at schools in the border regions like Jishou University, or Luzhou Medical College in the southwest . . . Mao Zedong's philosophical writings and poems have been exhumed from under layers of dust and are once more attracting attention. Books like *A Biography of Mao Zedong* and *Mao Zedong's Family History* are particularly popular.

—Shaoshan, Mao Zedong's birthplace, an unpopular destination for so many years, in 1989 hosted over 1.8 million visitors, 70 percent of whom were young people, and the majority of whom were middle school and university students;

—At Peking University students are organizing themselves into special groups for the study of Marxism-Leninism and Mao Zedong's writings.

What are we to make of the new fad? Everyone is talking about it. Most people are of the opinion that university students have now found the answers to China's problems in the treasury of Mao Zedong Thought. To build a new China, one has to understand China's national characteristics. . . . This writer believes this is the root cause of the "Mao craze."

What was the greatest lesson taught to us by the disturbance in the spring and summer of 1989? Intent and profound reflection has led university students to the conclusion that Western remedies can't provide cures for China's ills. . . . Over the past century of change . . . when it comes to understanding the realities of China, no one can compare with Mao Zedong; and no one achieved such successes. Mao Zedong's call to "adapt the universal theory of Marxism to the practical situation of China," together with Deng Xiaoping's formulation to "build socialism with Chinese characteristics," represents the crystallization of the living essence of Mao Zedong Thought. Since last year's disturbance, university students have spoken of "searching for Mao Zedong and being ashamed of [their] attitude to Deng Xiaoping." This is a sign of their determination to discard all Western philosophy and political thought and soberly confront the realities of China.

Over the past decade, a generation of young Chinese intellectuals has traveled the path from Sartre to Mao Zedong. It has been a tortuous journey and much time has been spent in deep thought, but they have now found the road that leads from vacuousness to relative maturity.

—*People's Daily,* March 1, 1990

What's New?

HE XIN

It's not certain that this fad for Mao meant exactly what the People's Daily said it did. After all, during the Protest Movement, students and other demonstrators frequently carried Mao's portrait during their marches. For all of Mao's excesses, many protesters seem to believe that he hadn't been as corrupt as Deng Xiaoping and his fellows, and that in any case he had been able to keep the wheels of revolution turning. The Mao cult took on more traditional trappings in the countryside, where in 1990 it was reported that he was appearing variously as a door god and the god of wealth, and that truck drivers in the south had taken to mounting little Maos in their cabs much as drivers elsewhere might carry a plastic statue of Jesus. In Peking one formerly reformist intellectual reportedly suggested in late 1990 that the party establish an official Mao cult to exploit popular sentiment.

The overall situation in China now is stable. The "independent" intellectuals have basically been obliterated. To a certain extent they brought it on themselves. (I should explain here that some intellectuals see me as a "conservative," while other, more orthodox figures regard me as an "independent." In fact, I am neither. I am nothing more than a Sinophile, that's to say, someone who loves China. The sole goal of my struggle is to find in intellectual and spiritual terms a means by which China can be revived and strengthened. In this respect I clearly belong to the traditional as opposed to the modernist camp of Chinese intellectuals. This is why it was inevitable that Yan Jiaqi, along with the "River Elegy group," and I would go our different ways.)

China is unquestionably entering a new political phase. I support some of the present policies such as the revitalization of China's national spirit and the control of discrepancies between poverty and wealth, as well as

"The Last Banquet," Zhang Hongtu, Chairmen Mao Series. This painting was excluded from the Tiananmen Memorial Art Exhibition organized by the Congressional Human Rights Foundation and Senator Edward Kennedy and held in Washington in June 1990. A committee involved in previewing exhibits reportdly found the work to be offensive on religious grounds. In response, Zhang wrote, "Eight years ago, I moved to the United States from China in order to have freedom to paint. Should I now move from the United States to . . . the moon for the same reason?"

of political corruption. However, some intellectuals will have to pay the price in this new era. In the Eastern tradition, the individual finds expression through the collective; while in the West, the collective finds its meaning in the individual. In this sense, as long as one can achieve the development of the society as a whole in exchange, and in order to renew control of the excessively inflated egos of recent years, all of this is possibly not only necessary but also in keeping with the spirit of the East.

On the international scene, the West is once more forcing China into isolation. In my personal opinion, the majority of Western politicians and intellectuals basically misread the situation this time around. In reality this is because they have let themselves be misled for some time by the emotionalism and hopes of a group of independent-style Chinese intellectuals and right-wing students. Over the next three to five years China will undoubtedly go through a period of economic hardship and also witness the outbreak of social problems. Internationally, China will be rejected and isolated. However, one should never underestimate the potential and willpower of the Chinese nation. Intellectuals such as myself will continue undaunted to concentrate our efforts on the revitalizing of our nation. . . .

—October 2, 1989, Peking

Yan Jiaqi *(l.)* and Wuer Kaixi in exile. The founding chairman and vice-chairman in late 1989 of the exiled dissident group, Federation for a Democratic China, Yan and Wuer, relinquished their posts in late 1990. *(China Spring)*

Old is the history of man; periods of order alternate with periods of chaos.

—Mencius (371–289 B.C.*)*

Whoever was in power wishes for a restoration. Whoever is now in power is in favor of the status quo. Whoever is not yet in power demands reforms. The situation is generally such. Generally!

—Lu Xun, 1927

PART V

Floating

We must harbor no illusions about there being "no change [in Hong Kong] for fifty years." Anyone who can leave has to get out of here. Those who can't have to prepare themselves psychologically for Communist rule. You can't rebel, you can't start a revolution, and you can't be independent.

NI KUANG, 1988

What does exile mean? Solitude, isolation. Spiritual exile. The courage to face defeat. Accept it. There's no other choice.

BEI LING, 1989

Floating is a feeling of rootlessness, of uncertainty about the future and even the present, of pedaling in thin air. As the theme of this section, it encompasses three broad and interrelated topics: Hong Kong, survival, and exile.

Hong Kong has always been a place where life has had an edge of precariousness: first as the southeastern tip of the Chinese empire, settled nearly a thousand years ago, later a lair for pirates, and then part of the British Empire. While Britain acquired sovereignty over the tiny island of Hong Kong and the Kowloon Peninsula outright as a result of its "gunboat diplomacy" in the Opium Wars, the largest parcel of land in Hong Kong, the New Territories, was later leased for ninety-nine years; that lease expires in 1997. Hong Kong was never more conscious of living on borrowed time than in the 1980s. Following the signing of the Sino-British Joint Declaration in 1984, in which Britain agreed to return sovereignty over Hong Kong to China in 1997, you could almost hear the clock ticking.

It was in such an atmosphere that the late satirist Hah Gong founded the *Emancipation Monthly,* which numbered its issues backward from 1997 in a countdown, and the filmmaker Shu Kei made the documentary *Sunless Days.* Perhaps nothing quite captures the insubstantiality of Hong Kong in the eighties as well as the story "The Floating City," an allegorical tale by Xi Xi, one of Hong Kong's best writers, with which we begin the section. However, until 1989, except for a few outspoken individuals, doubts and fears about the future rarely found voice in public. Ironically, it was only in 1989, during the Peking Protest Movement and following the massacre, that people in Hong Kong were shaken into a realization of what the future might hold.

By the late eighties, what had once been dubbed the "conspiracy of confidence" over Hong Kong's fate had all but broken down. To emigrate or not to emigrate, that was the question that nearly everyone who could asked themselves. The film star Deanie Ip, interviewed in *Sunless Days,* found that the Peking Massacre had deeply influenced her own views on the question of emigration—but not in a predictable way (see pp. 434–35).

Over the past four decades, the Kowloon-Canton Railway, the subject of Yu Kwang-chung's poem of the same name, has been the corridor for countless numbers of Chinese traveling into exile as well as for many who have returned to China from exile. In recent years, the international airports at China's major cities have been a more regular starting point for the trip away from the "parent body" of China. After June 1989, air, rail, road, and even the sea provided an escape route for many Chinese dissidents as they fled from a new round of repression that has created China's largest contemporary community in exile. While many chose exile, Hou Dejian and Fang Lizhi had it forced upon them a year after the massacre.

But exile on home territory is a normal state for the independent mind, the creative artist, and the individualist. These people can feel equally alienated, foreign, and strange whether at home in their birthplace or wandering the world. Many of the "old dreamers" whom we have quoted in this book felt out of step with their times and lived in a state of "internal exile."

For those who remain in China, particularly in difficult and politically oppressive times, we take "floating" to be the art of survival and the maintenance of personal integrity. It is the spiritual alternative to the political ponderousness demanded by Deng Xiaoping and his colleagues in late 1989 when they said that "stability crushes all else." Li Ao, an intellectual who has survived to speak out again and again, reviews historical techniques of self-help in his satirical essay "The Art of Survival," and Li Zongwu, a writer of the early republic, reveals the secrets of the power holders' political resilience. For Yang Jiang, the best defense is to don the "cloak of invisibility."

Those forced out of China by political persecution and cultural purges face what the Polish writer Joseph Wittlin called the "sorrow and grandeur" of exile. The sensation of floating, of being unconnected to one's environment, is particularly strong for the expatriate writer, as we see in the poet Bei Ling's essay "Exile."

One of the greatest problems faced by the latest group of Mainland Chinese cultural figures and intellectuals in the West is that of overcoming their obsession with the Chinese dilemma. Plucked out of an environment that encourages people to think in terms of Chinese exclusivity, to consider their situation unique in the world—in terms of horror as well as accomplishment—they are suddenly confronted with the fact that they are members of a larger international community. For some, this is too much, and the idea of return becomes more and more attractive.

Yet, perhaps it is only when individuals can cut themselves free from the binding networks of relationships, coteries, the unit, and Proledic itself, when they are released from the stifling Chinese "wheel of becoming"—through either actual or existential exile—that there may be a way out of the dilemma.

The Floating City

XI XI

Xi Xi is the pen name of Zhang Yan. Although her family is originally from Guangdong, Xi Xi was born in Shanghai in 1938 and moved to Hong Kong in 1950. A primary school teacher for many years, she is a novelist, poet, essayist, and editor. This story is dated April 1986.

1. THE FLOATING CITY

The floating city appeared suddenly before everyone's eyes in the middle of the sky like a hydrogen-filled balloon on a clear, bright day many years ago. Rolling clouds swirled by above; waves crashed on the swelling sea below. The floating city hovered, going neither up nor down as it maintained its position, buffeted slightly by the breeze.

Only our grandparents' grandparents witnessed how it all began. It had been an unbelievable and terrifying experience, one they recalled fearfully. There had been a violent collision of clouds lighting up the sky with flashes and roars of thunder. On the sea countless pirate vessels had run up the skull and crossbones and fired their cannon nonstop. Suddenly the floating city had dropped from the clouds and hung in midair.

Many years passed. Our grandparents' grandparents passed away, and our grandparents followed them into a deep sleep. By and by the story they had told became a mysterious legend.

The grandchildren settled in the city and gradually adapted to living there. Even its legend faded. Finally, the majority of people came to believe that the floating city had always hung in the sky, neither rising

The story was originally illustrated with a series of paintings, most of them by René Magritte.

nor sinking. Even when it was buffeted by the wind and shook ever so slightly, it was like swinging on a swing.

Many more years passed.

2. THE MIRACLE

It takes courage to live without roots: That's what it said on the jacket of a novel. To live in the floating city required not only courage, but willpower and faith. In another novel there is a nonexistent knight who is nothing more than an empty suit of armor. Emperor Charlemagne asks him, what keeps you going? Willpower and faith, he replies.

With their willpower and faith, the inhabitants of the floating city toiled to create a livable home. Within a few dozen years their efforts made the city vibrant, prosperous, and wealthy.

Buildings stood packed together in rows on the ground; highways and overpasses writhed in the air. Trains like centipedes ran underground and out to the suburbs; kidney stones were destroyed with laser beams; tumors could be located with brain scanners; people could follow the course of Halley's Comet in the observatory; and the life of the sea lion was an open book in the ocean park. Children were provided with nine years of free education, and there were unemployment benefits for the jobless, pensions for the disabled and elderly. Many arts festivals were held each year, and books from all over the world were available in the stores. If you didn't want to talk to anyone, there was absolute freedom to be silent.

People couldn't quite believe it possible that houses in the city could float in midair, that one flower grown there could fill a whole room. They all said that the floating city was a miracle.

3. SHOWERS

May to September was the windy season. The winds blew from all directions, and the floating city swayed in the sky. The residents of the floating city were used to the swaying, and they went about their business as usual, not even missing the races. They knew from experience that the floating city would never be blown upsidedown or in circles during the windy season, nor would it be blown away to some other place.

But one peculiar thing did happen in the windy season: The people dreamed. They started dreaming in May; they dreamed the same dream; they dreamed they were floating in the air, neither rising nor falling. It was as though each of them was a floating city in miniature. None of them had wings, so they couldn't fly, they could only float. They didn't speak to one another. They floated in absolute, solemn silence. Every day the sky in the floating city was full of floating people, just like rain in April.

From May on, people dreamed about floating. Even people who slept during the day dreamed that they had turned into floating people standing silently in midair. These dreams went away only in September. After the windy season people started having their own dreams once more.

Why did everyone have the same dream? Why did they all dream they were floating in the sky? One school of psychologists came to the conclusion that this was the collective expression of a "Third Riverbank Neurosis."

4. APPLES

In the summer a poster appeared in the streets of the floating city. On it was a picture of an apple with a line of French above it. It said: *"Ceci n'est pas une pomme"*—"This is not an apple." The appearance of the poster was not unusual since a large art exhibition was going to be held. This year's exhibition was being held in honor of the Belgian artist René Magritte. The apple was one of his paintings.

What did "This is not an apple" mean? The picture was obviously of an apple. What the artist had meant was that the painting of an apple was not the same as an apple you can eat. You couldn't touch it, smell it, or cut its flesh. It wasn't a real apple; it was made up of lines, color, and forms. The apple in the painting was an illusion. Didn't the Greek philosopher Plato say that even the best, most realistic painting of a bed is still only a reproduction of a bed?

Posters of Magritte's painting could be seen on every street corner, although only one or two out of every thousand people in the floating city would actually go to see the exhibition. The appearance of so many apples in the streets of the floating city was nonetheless a cause for excitement. Many people mistook it for an advertisement for the fruit market. Only a few intellectuals suddenly thought to themselves: The floating city is a stable place that neither rises nor sinks, yet it, too, is an illusion. The miracle of the floating city was not, after all, a fairy tale.

5. THE EYE

"Cinderella" is a fairy tale. The pumpkin turns into a carriage; mice turn into horses; Cinderella's rags turn into a ball gown. But at midnight everything turns back into what it was. Was the floating city just another Cinderella?

The people of the floating city didn't have defective eyes. Modern science provided them with the most accurate microscopes and telescopes. They often looked down at the sea or upward at the sky and tested the direction of the wind. Why could the floating city continue to float steadily in the sky? Was it due to the gravitational pull between the sea and the sky? Or was Fate holding countless invisible strings and putting on a puppet show?

The apple in the picture was not a real apple; the city that existed so miraculously might not remain stable forever. But could the floating city control its own destiny? The instant the pull between the sea and the sky changed, or Fate tired of its game, wouldn't the city sink, rise, or perhaps be blown off to some unknown place?

The people of the floating city opened their eyes wide and looked down. The angry waves of the sea surged beneath their feet. The city could be overwhelmed by the waters. Even if it managed to float on the water, wouldn't there be a massacre when the pirates flying the skull and crossbones fell on them in droves? If the floating city rose upward, would the shifting, airy clouds provide a stable foundation for its solid weight?

6. A PROBLEM

The floating city did not have any rivers, and the sea water was undrinkable. The city had to rely on the bounty of heaven for water. So although the people of the floating city liked brilliant sunny days, sometimes they had to pray for rain.

A teacher took a class of students to the exhibition hall of the Town Hall. They'd come for the art show. The students had pens and paper so they could record their impressions and copy down the names of the paintings. They asked: What does the picture of an umbrella with a glass full of water on it mean? And why is it called *Hegel's Holiday?* They looked through the exhibition catalogue hoping to find an answer.

People treat water in different ways at different times. Sometimes they are tolerant of it, sometimes they reject it. For example, people want to drink water when they are thirsty, they want it inside them. But on rainy days they use umbrellas to keep it out. Internal and external acceptance and rejection are things philosophers often think about. As for the problem of water, perhaps the philosopher Hegel might have been interested in giving it some thought. But it was a small problem, one he reserved for his holidays.

One student stood looking at this painting for a long time. He said: People use umbrellas to keep themselves dry. Since the water is all in the glass, there's no need for an umbrella. There's no need to reject anything. If there were a solid, reliable layer of clouds over the floating city, there would be hope for the city if it floated upward. Why reject it?

7. THE FLOWER SPIRIT

The majority of the residents of the floating city were men who wore hats—the symbol of the petit bourgeoisie. They desired a stable, prosperous society, a warm, happy home. So they worked industriously every day; they were as busy as ants or bees. Hard work can help you forget lots of things. As a result of their labors, the people of the floating city were able to build a wealthy modern society in which everyone was well fed and well dressed. But it was a society in which material attractions were so great that people threw themselves into their labors with ever greater energy. They became victims of the bottomless pit of material desire.

One painting by the Italian Renaissance artist Botticelli is called *Primavera;* it shows a goddess scattering flowers over the earth and symbolizes the return of spring. The messenger Hermes leads the way; Cupid flies above Venus; the West Wind accompanies the Flower Spirit; and the Three Graces dance around as Primavera, dressed in fine colored gauzes, scatters fragrant blossoms.

Li Gonglin of the Song dynasty painted a work entitled *Vimalakirti Preaching* that shows Manjusri with some disciples visiting the sick Vimalakirti at the Buddha's command. Despite his illness, Vimalakirti is preaching the dharma and enunciating the essence of the Great Vehicle to them. While he speaks, a heavenly spirit releases a shower of flowers. Manjusri's chief disciple is covered with the blossoms.

The citizens of the rich and populous floating city were so enamored of material wealth that they wished the heavenly spirit would cast all of her flowers onto them; they even wished they could bundle Primavera up with her flowers in a sack and carry it around with them.

8. TIME

It was an important moment, an absolute point in time. A train engine had just pulled in. A moment earlier the engine had not yet entered the fireplace; a moment later, it would have gone. It was only when the engine was steaming through the fireplace, only at this absolute point in time, that the smoke from its stack could go up the chimney. The chimney was the only suitable conduit for the smoke.

The fireplace reminded one of Christmas, a day the whole city celebrated. However, judging from the room this was not Christmas, because there were no stockings hanging in front of the fireplace, no pine tree in the room, no bright lights, no angels, no bells, no candles in bronze candle holders.

On the marble clock on the mantelpiece the hour hand was approaching one, the minute hand was approaching nine. It was unclear where the second hand was. It was after midnight. A carriage would be a pumpkin again by now, horses would have turned back into mice, and the ball gown would be rags once more.

Yes, it was after midnight. But all the fables said that Cinderella would meet her prince on a white horse before midnight. Had the prince of the floating city been waiting close by as midnight approached? Although he was riding a magic white horse, since it had only one horsepower, perhaps he had arrived late.

Zero hour always made people anxious. What would it be like at one o'clock? Could people see the future through the mirror?

9. THE MIRROR

Only people who have been to the floating city will appreciate that the mirrors there are different. In "Snow White and the Seven Dwarfs" a magic mirror hangs in the wicked queen's palace. It can answer questions and tell the queen who is the fairest of them all. It is an honest, sincere mirror: It never lies. The mirrors in the floating city are also honest mirrors. They reflect reality without fear or favor. Yet they have their limitations: The mirrors in the floating city can reflect only the backs of things.

All the mirrors, whether produced locally or imported, reflect only the reverse side of things. Whenever the people in the floating city look in a mirror, all they can see is the hair on the back of their heads. People have experimented by putting another mirror in front of the mirror on the wall, but no matter what they do, no matter how many mirrors are used and at whatever angles, they show only the backs of things. Women in the floating city always have to go to the beauty parlor to get made up because it is too difficult to do it themselves. If the men want a good shave, they have to go to a barber.

In the floating city's mirrors you can't find any answers or forecast the future. But you can know the past, and this isn't necessarily a bad thing. History can teach lessons, and this is one of the good things about the mirrors in the floating city.

10. WINGS

There are many means of transportation in the floating city: some ancient, like rope ladders and balloons, some modern, such as helicopters and parachutes. People who want to have a look in the clouds can climb the ladders or go up by balloon, while visitors to the sea can use parachutes or go by helicopter. However, over half of the people in the floating city want to grow wings themselves. All in all, these people find it scary to live in a city that floats in midair. The people who are really terrified agonize night and day, finally deciding to pack up their belongings and they behave like migratory birds, moving elsewhere to build an ideal new nest.

A novelist has recorded the following story: A man went to apply for a passport. The official asked where he wanted to go. He said it didn't matter. The official gave him a globe of the world and asked him to make his choice. The man studied it, turned it around slowly, and finally said: Don't you have another one?

It is a difficult decision to know where to go once you've left the floating city. Where can you find a city where you could live in peace forever? All those leaving the city have to have very strong wings, and they have to be very careful when in flight. If they go too near the sun, the wax that keeps the wings together melts and, like Icarus, they plummet to earth.

But the residents of the floating city are not really like migratory birds. Once they leave they do not return. Can they just go away, holding a walking stick and carrying their luggage, without ever looking back? Although the people in the floating city long to be like the pigeons that fly high in the sky, they are frustrated like birds imprisoned in a cage.

11. BIRD GRASS

In their longing to fly, the people of the floating city keep looking up at the sky. But they can't take off, nor can they create a hoist to lift them into the sky. All they can do is dream when the windy season approaches, dream that they can float silently in the air. Even in their dreams they float but cannot fly.

After the windy season all of them dream their own dreams once more. They dream of bean-curd kites, snowflakes filling the sky, butterflies, thistledown in the wind. Some people even dream that the city itself has grown wings. But they always wake up to find their feet still firmly on the ground of the floating city. And from that ground is born one of the strangest plants in the whole world, something never seen anywhere before: bird grass.

Bird grass, with its dark, lush foliage, grows everywhere—in the city and outside, on the banks of brooks, in valleys and gardens. It is a peculiar plant with large, flat, bird-shaped leaves. If you pick a leaf, it is easy to make out a bird's head, beak, and eyes. The fuzz on the leaf is like feathers. The leaves rustle in the soft breeze, like the beating of wings.

Although shaped like birds, it is still only grass. None of the bird grass has wings. People say if it grew wings it would be able to fly. The air of the floating city would be full of flying bird grass, and no one would be able to tell whether it was birds or grass, animal or vegetable.

12. THE CHILD PRODIGIES

The child prodigies appeared in the same year as the bird grass. At first they attracted no special attention; they were simply milk-guzzling babies. But they grew quickly, both physically and mentally. Before long they were healthy, precocious children.

Possibly it began with arithmetic. The mothers noticed that none of them used pen or paper to do their sums, they used colored blocks of wood. They knew to use meters to measure cloth and grams to buy rice. And what was set theory? Gradually the mothers found they couldn't understand their children's textbooks. The children didn't have to open their books to study, they just turned on the television or put earphones on their ears.

At first the children told their mothers to keep the window open when using the gas water heater to have a bath and not to use too much salt when cooking; later they took their mothers on trips, treated them to meals, and gave them presents. The mothers felt as though they were becoming the children. The children ruled the family, taking over the mother's position as the head of the family, overthrowing their traditional authority. Many mothers felt scared and didn't know what to do.

A few mothers were happy with the situation. They had been plagued by doubts and worries and had faced many unresolved problems. Now their brilliant children would, perhaps, solve all these problems for them.

13. WINDOWS

The earth is only one small planet in the universe. The floating city is only one small city on the earth. On a map it is no larger than the head of a pin, and it did not even seem to have a name. But gradually this tiny city attracted attention from afar.

The strange city floating in the air with its mirrors that reflected only the backs of things, its people who dreamed of floating in the windy season, the bird grass that grew in its soil attracted endless numbers of tourists. They came to explore, to experience, to see their reflections in the mirrors, and to dream. People who didn't come were also curious; they stood outside the city and looked in through the windows, their arms hanging by their sides. Obviously they could afford no practical assistance, but their gazing was a form of participation. Looking on was a kind of supervision.

What did the observers outside the windows see now? They saw a teacher with a group of students at Town Hall for the Magritte exhibition. Small groups of people were gathered in front of the paintings hanging on the walls. Suddenly the observers outside and the students and teachers who were looking at the paintings inside saw one another. You could follow the subtle development of events from the solemn expressions on the faces of the observers. If it was a tragedy, their faces would show sorrow; if a comedy, they would light up with a smile.

Over there, employees were putting up posters of the Mona Lisa on the announcement boards. Over here, the people in the painting and the people looking at the painting were staring at one another through an open window, all thinking their own thoughts.

Et Tu, Britain?

As it became increasingly clear that the British government had no intention of granting more than a select handful of Hong Kong citizens the right of abode in the United Kingdom, and as Peking's promises to respect Hong Kong's "prosperity and stability" and to impose "no changes for fifty years" rang more and more hollow with each act of interference in the territory's political and economic life, it seemed to some Hong Kong people that they had been sold out—even stabbed in the back—by the British. The following unsigned adaptation of Mark Antony's speech from Shakespeare's Julius Caesar appeared in the English-language South China Morning Post in July 1989.

An Appeal to British Justice

Friends, ministers, Englishmen, lend us your ears;
We are here to bury Hong Kong, not to praise it.
The evil that colonies do lives after them;
The good is oft interred with their demise;
So let it be with Hong Kong. The noble Thatcher
Hath told you Hong Kong was a burden.
If it were so, it was a grievous fault;
And grievously hath Hong Kong answered it.

Here, under leave of British freedom—
For the British is an honourable race—
Come we to speak in Hong Kong's crisis.
It was our home, faithful and just to us,

But Thatcher says it was burdensome,
And Thatcher is an honourable lady.
It hath brought many merchants home to England,
Whose fortunes did the general coffers fill.
Its sons along with British soldiers fought;
A loyal fief in turmoil and in peace.
You all did cheer when on its very soil
Her Majesty presented it her goodwill,
Which it did graciously accept.
You all did love it once, not without cause;
What cause withholds you, then, to save its people?
O Judgment, thou art fled to brutish beasts,
And men have lost their reason!

But yesterday the people of Hong Kong
Have gladly shared their glory: now lie them stricken
And none so fair to give them shelter.
O fellow subjects, if we were disposed to stir
Your hearts and minds to mutiny and rage,
We should do Howe wrong, and Howell wrong,
Who, you all know, are honourable men.
We will not do them wrong; we rather choose

"Zebra in Wonderland," Luis Chan (courtesy of Hanart 2 Gallery, Hong Kong)

To wrong the fallen city, to wrong ourselves and you,
Than we will wrong such honourable men.

But here's a parchment with the seal of Great Britain.
We saw it signed in China—'tis its will.
To every Briton and Hong Kong citizen it gives,
To every several man, fifty years of prosperity.
The dragon's open arms, and new-discovered market,
On both sides Lowu; it hath left them you,
And to your heirs forever—common riches,
To trade and seek a fortune for yourselves.
Here was a colony! When comes such another?

If you have tears, prepare to shed them now.
You all know this harbour. You heard how
The first time ever Elliot lorded over it.
'Twas on a summer's evening, upon his frigate
That year he overcame the Dowager.
Through this the much-esteemed Westminster stabbed,
And Westminster, as you know, was Hong Kong's angel.
Judge, O you gods, how deeply Hong Kong trusted them!
This was the most unkindest cut of all.

Good friends, dear friends, let us not stir you up
To such a sudden flood of anger.

FEAR AND LOATHING IN HONG KONG

If the Peking Massacre had occurred before 1984, the Joint Declaration transferring sovereignty of Hong Kong from Britain to the People's Republic of China in 1997 might never have been ratified. . . .

The crucial question for Hong Kong, and for all civilized nations and peoples, must certainly be: Should Britain still honor the Joint Declaration and hand the six million people of Hong Kong over to a Communist government that has shown itself to be no better than the murderous regime of Pol Pot? If Britain decides to betray the people of Hong Kong by doing so, then it will have to live with the crushing moral responsibility of stage-managing one of the great tragedies in the history of this tragic century.

—Lee Yee, June 1989

Lee Yee is editor-in-chief of the Nineties Monthly.

They that have done this deed are honourable.
What private griefs they have, alas, we know not,
That made them do it; they are wise and honourable.
And will, no doubt, with reasons answer you.

We tell you that which you yourselves do know;
Show you how we were cheated. Poor poor stifled mouths,
We bid conscience speak for us. As we are fellow creatures,
Would ruffle up your spirits; and put a tongue
In every man of good intent, that should move
The hearts of stone to justice and righteousness.

Future Shock: Hong Kong Satirists on 1997

A Hong Kong Absurdity

HAH GONG

Hah Gong was a popular Hong Kong columnist who died in 1987.* *Shortly before his death, he founded* Emancipation Monthly, *which was to publish many of Liu Xiaobo's essays in 1988–89. The magazine, later named* Open Magazine, *also carries regular columns by Li Ao and comments by Ni Kuang.*

THE LEGALIZATION OF RAPE

They say that in a certain civilized country there was an unwritten law that stated that a person who was raped could not cry out, offer any resistance, or go to the police for help. The victim was obliged to lie back and bear the assault in silence.

Later it was realized that this unwritten law was an offense against decency, and instead of enhancing the reputation of this civilized country, it brought disapprobation upon it. At this point, someone challenged the law. They claimed, in the first instance, that rape is a savage and barbarous act that should be outlawed; secondly, that all rapists should be punished, gang rapists most severely of all; thirdly, that victims of rape should be permitted to scream; and, finally, in cases where there is an obvious disparity between the physical strength of the victim and the rapist, making it impossible for the victim to resist without further risk, that a discussion should be held afterward in order to ascertain the precise cause and effect of the rape. For example, was the victim young and beautiful? Was

* See *Seeds of Fire*, pp. 179–88, 378–80.

her behavior in any way provocative or lewd? Did she incite the rapist in any way? Was the rapist psychologically disturbed? Should the victim receive hush money from the rapist, or should she demand a free operation to mend her damaged hymen?

(Note: This is my translation of an ancient Greek text dating from the New Stone Age. If there are any discrepancies in interpretation, the Greek text should be taken as the standard.)

I recently heard that the unwritten law quoted above now applies to Hong Kong: The Sino-British negotiations [over Hong Kong's future] have resembled a gang rape of Hong Kong by two men, with the victim being denied the right either to scream or protest. After the event, a member of a certain legislative body appeared on the scene and demanded a detailed inquiry into the background of the rape. But a number of staunch advocates of rapists' rights came forth and called for the legalization of rape, decrying the victims for being shameless. Naturally, this upset a large number of former rape victims, who have expressed support for their fellow victims.

It is said that the pro-rapists have their reasons for lobbying for the legalization of rape. They believe that the legislator mentioned above speaks only for himself and has no right to represent all rape victims, and therefore has no right to scream or protest during the act. But the

"Tanks for the Memory," Morgan Chua

opposition states that even though the legislator could speak only for himself, he too is a victim of rape and has the right to demand a discussion of and an investigation into the precise cause and effect of the rape.

Now everybody is shouting: "Rape victims of Hong Kong, unite!" As a result, the pro-rapist lobby is completely isolated, and the only course left for them is to get support from a few pseudoscholars with near-zero IQs. Having just polished off a Patriotic Chinese New Year's Eve Banquet and Patriotic Spring Festival Tea, these "scholars" can naturally be depended upon to say a few kind words and cite a few precedents to suit the occasion in support of the legalization of rape. Most curious is the fact that among them are a number of people who still have not had their political appendixes removed. Yet they make grandiose statements suggesting that everyone should simply lie back quietly and allow the rapists to get on with it, claiming that any protest would be "negative, unconstructive and in no way beneficial."

—March 1984

Today Tibet, Tomorrow Hong Kong

Ni Kuang is a former PLA soldier who fled Inner Mongolia for Hong Kong in 1957. Since then he has become one of the territory's most prolific authors, churning out science fiction, martial arts novels, romances, adventure stories, thrillers, and newspaper columns at the astounding rate of more than 10,000 Chinese characters a day. In late 1988, he was interviewed by Jin Zhong of the Emancipation Monthly *concerning Hong Kong and the Mainland.*

JIN ZHONG: [The Taiwan writer] Chen Ying-chen has said that the Communists' promise that "there will be horse racing as usual [after 1997]" is a decadent policy. . . .

NI KUANG: Hong Kong people don't consider horse racing as representative of the Hong Kong way of life. [Chen] hasn't a clue what makes Hong Kong tick. From the point of view of the sanctimonious, the general spirit of Hong Kong is one of decadence; [Chen's] viewpoint is exactly the same as that of the Communist Party. The party espouses traditional Chinese hypocrisy. Chen Ying-chen and Liu Binyan don't interest me at all, though Chen's novels are better than Liu's reportage. Liu Binyan is still waffling on about his "second kind of loyalty," but whether it's the second, third, or whatever, it's still loyalty to the party, isn't it? Fang Lizhi's better than either of them. I saw him on TV saying he would never rejoin the party—his expression of complete contempt for the Communists really deserves our respect. . . .

We must harbor no illusions about this business of there being "no change for fifty years" [after the Communist takeover of Hong Kong]. Anyone who can leave has to get out of here. Those who can't have to prepare themselves psychologically for Communist rule. You can't rebel, you can't start a revolution, and you can't be independent. The people of Hong Kong will pay the price for their apathy toward [the drafting of] the Basic Law.* No one even tried to make their feelings known to the British prime minister when she came here; it's as though the great cause of national unity were more important than anything else. But it's possible to oppose Communist rule; I don't have much sympathy for those who won't even try. What could Peking possibly do if just 500,000 of Hong Kong's five million people took to the streets, boycotted classes, and called a general strike to oppose the return of Hong Kong to China? With the Basic Law, the Communists have already managed to negate the Sino-British Joint Declaration; they're taking over step by step. . . .

What's happening to Hong Kong is exactly like what happened to Tibet when it signed the Agreement on Measures for the Peaceful Liberation of Tibet.† The Communists say the nicest possible things and then act in the most reprehensible manner. This has always been the way of the Communist Party.

—September 1988

---

* The Basic Law, finalized in 1990, lays down the structure of law and government for Hong Kong after 1997. Deng Xiaoping acclaimed the law as a "creative masterpiece," but many Hong Kong people believe it is an inadequate safeguard of their rights.
† Signed by the Dalai Lama's representatives under duress in Peking on May 23, 1951.

Take to the Seas

LEE YEE

Of all the 36 strategies, running away is the best.

—Tan Daoji, fifth century

Xu Jiatun was the head of the Hong Kong branch of the Xinhua News Agency, Mainland China's representative in the territory. It was rumored that Xu, the equivalent of a vice premier in the Chinese government, was an ally of ousted party leader Zhao Ziyang and had supported the Protest Movement. Recalled to Peking in early 1990, he returned to the territory furtively and then in May fled to the United States, where he announced he would take an unlimited stint of R & R.

How does Hong Kong feel about China a year after the Peking-based Democracy Movement was brutally crushed and hundreds, perhaps thousands, of citizens slaughtered?

One sentence can sum it up: Even Xu Jiatun has run away. . . .

Hong Kong society is renowned for being law-abiding and stable; it is widely praised for its efficiency and the quality of its service industry. The territory's capitalists, professionals, and managers are enterprising, daring, inventive, and adaptable. Hong Kong workers are famed for their industriousness, professionalism, and level of education. But all of these outstanding qualities have begun to lose their luster now that we live in the grisly shadow of June 4 and await with fear the prospects of 1997.

The genius of Hong Kong society seems to have gone into a nosedive.

Perhaps one could compare Hong Kong to a seaworthy vessel. After the 1984 Sino-British Joint Declaration, this ship set course for a volcanic island. The volcano was known to be active, but as it had remained dormant for years, many people thought it unlikely it would ever erupt again. Those who were less confident slipped away silently on small boats, paddling off with all their might. Then along came the murderous eruption of June 4. The passengers on the ship could feign complacence no longer. Disorder is now breaking out belowdecks, and the formerly confident passengers are scared that there will be turmoil on board and no lifeboats to save them. They fear that long before they reach their destination, the ship will have been scuttled by its own hands.

Xu Jiatun has already jumped ship.

—May 31, 1990

Sunless Days

In the documentary film Sunless Days, *which was released in early 1990, the Hong Kong filmmaker Shu Kei asked a number of Hong Kong people to discuss their reactions to the Protest Movement and Peking Massacre and how these events had affected their own future. One of those interviewed was the popular film actress Deanie Ip:*

The students in China didn't concern me. Who was Hu Yaobang, Yang Shangkun, or Li Peng? I didn't know, understand, or care. I didn't think it had anything to do with me. The only names I knew were Mao Zedong and Deng Xiaoping. That's all. When Hu Yaobang died, the TV showed university students mourning him. They had long hair and were filthy, and I thought to myself, yuk, how did the Chinese get like that?

I didn't think of myself as Chinese or part of what was happening at all.

In early May, I was in France. At the airport in Paris I read in a newspaper that when the PLA troops approached the city, the people of Peking showed great courage, lying down in front of the tanks to stop them from coming in and offering the soldiers food. I didn't know why, but suddenly I felt very depressed and anxious. Why had things in China turned out this way?

It was then that I realized that Chinese blood flows in my veins, too. Since June 4, I've felt that nothing is more important than the achievement of democracy in China. I still don't understand much about it, not even now, but I think things will get better. I don't know much about democracy or human rights, but since June 4, I've been going to the bookstores, thinking maybe it's not too late to learn. The events of June 4 made me want to learn more about democracy. . . .

I don't like Hong Kong because it's too crowded. I dream of going to a large, unpopulated place where I can have a little house, preferably

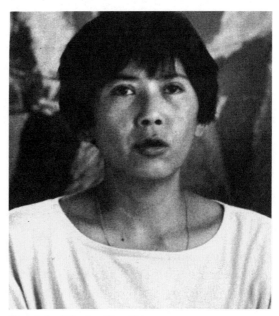

Deanie Ip ("Sunless Days")

overlooking a river, and where I can ride my bicycle to the market. A place where I could spend the rest of my life. It's not June 4 that made me want to leave. I've always dreamed of finding such a place.

I still have this dream. But now I feel more strongly about staying here. I don't know what I can do, but I think the least I can do is learn about democracy, become a person who respects other people, a person who knows about citizens' rights. That's all.

The Kowloon-Canton Railway

YU KWANG-CHUNG

Yu Kwang-chung (born 1928) is a poet and essayist who was born on
the mainland but has lived in Hong Kong for many years.

"How does it feel to be in Hong Kong?" you ask.
Holding your aerogram, I smile sadly.
Hong Kong beats with a metallic rhythm, my friend,
Of a thousand steel wheels playing on the steel tracks
To and from the border, from sunrise to sundown
Going north, coming south, playing the Border Blues again and again,
Like an umbilical cord that cannot be severed, nor crushed asunder,
Reaching to the vast endless Northland,
The parent body so familiar yet so strange,

"Breakthrough," Luis Chan (courtesy of Hanart 2 Gallery, Hong Kong)

Floating

Mother Earth joined yet long disconnected.
An old cradle rocking far far away
Rocking back your memory and mine, my friend.
And like all raw nerve ends
This railway is specially sensitive,
For right now, on the platform of a small station
Holding your aerogram, leaning against the lamppost,
Closing my eyes, just by listening, I can tell
The light knocking of the inbound passenger train,
The heavy hammering, heaven-and-earth shaking, outbound freight
    train,
And the stinking, engulfing, suffocating
Hurry, hold your breath, pig train.

Survival

hroughout Chinese history, many people have paid a heavy price for standing out from the crowd. The art of camouflage is a highly sophisticated one, each generation creating its own variations. But it was not until Li Ao composed his essay "The Art of Survival" that a Chinese writer summed up the range of survival techniques for his fellows.

The Art of Survival, a User's Guide

LI AO

Li Ao's "Art of Survival" is one science you'd better bone up on if you want to keep your head, stay out of jail, and remain free from the watchful eyes of the authorities.

It's the art of living in the chaotic world while keeping yourself in one piece. From ancient times there have been periods of turmoil. There are those people who can roll with the punches; some even thrive on chaos. The less fortunate go under; some even end up in exile. These unfortunates fall into one of three categories: one, those who find their heads no longer attached to their bodies; two, those who land in jail; and three, those who live in perpetual fear of the police.

Of these three types of no-hopers, only the third really concerns us here. The other two categories are already done for, they're losers, lost souls; let's just forget about them. The best we can do for them is pray they have more luck in the next life. Better still, get them to pray for themselves.

The third category of people, however, are ideal pupils for my correspondence course in the Art of Survival. My only regret is that I wasn't born in an earlier age: I could have given the ancients some advice on how to survive. Chinese history is full of fine men who were unjustly persecuted to death. Such a pity, and quite unnecessary, too.

Take, for example, Bo Yi and Shu Qi. These two loyal ministers refused to eat the "unrighteous grain" of the Zhou king who conquered their state. Instead they fled to Mount Shouyang, where they lived off ferns. What dopes! Didn't they realize that even the grass they were eating belonged to Zhou? If you ask me, they starved themselves to death for nothing. It wasn't worth it. Furthermore, such methods are definitely not for modern man.

Then there's the case of Tao Yuanming [fourth century]. After the world fell into chaos he changed his name to Tao Qian ["the hidden"], gave up his government job, and went to live on his neglected farm. Of course, he was lucky in that he had servants and his young sons waiting there for him, as well as a good stash of wine. His contemporary, General Tan Daoji, couldn't understand why Tao made things so hard for himself. But from our point of view Tao had it easy. Despite the chaos of the world outside he had his fields, servants, dumb kids, wine, dog meat, and chrysanthemums. At least he didn't have to worry about obtaining a residency permit, nor did he have to fear the local police— or even more endearing characters—coming to knock on his door at night. He was a damn sight better off than people today. Tao Yuanming's art of survival has no modern application.

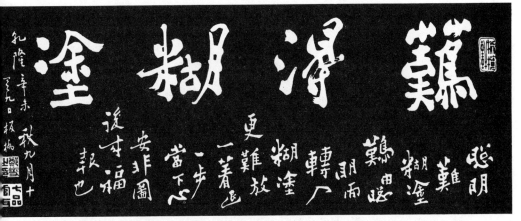

Calligraphy by Zheng Banqiao: "Hard-Won Stupidity: Hard to be clever, hard to be stupid; harder still to change from clever to stupid. Miss a move, take a step back, for immediate peace of mind, not in the hope of later reward." (1751)

The above examples illustrate survival methods of which I cannot approve. Bo Yi and Shu Qi were too extreme, too crude in their approach, whereas Tao Yuanming was too restrained, reclusive, and laid-back. Given his station in life, he was far too passive, too concerned with saving his own skin. He should have come out into the open and done something for the multitudes. Tao Yuanming's case reminds me of Feng Dao, a man who called himself the "Contented Old Man," although everyone else knows him as a turncoat who served the rulers of all the Five Dynasties. Now, Feng could have been like Tao and retired from the world, but he chose to play the shameless old man and work for his enemies. Sometimes, with a well-placed lie, he cleverly saved a town from the barbarians or got them to spare the lives of tens of thousands of people. Despite the historical verdict that he was a traitor, you can't ignore the fact that he did a great deal of good.

Methods have to change with the times. Today's survivors would be ill-advised to adopt the ways of Bo Yi and Shu Qi, or even Tao Yuanming. Thus it is necessary to review and reevaluate the details of the Art of Survival for the sake of all those people who, while not in prison, can feel the blade at their throat.

To my mind, the Art of Survival is a body of wisdom that exists in the small fissure between A: selling out body and soul to the tyrants and helping them do their dirty work, and B: having your head removed or being jailed or purged. The Art of Survival allows for self-preservation and self-expression between these two extremes. From my observations there are fifteen variations of this art all told. They are enumerated below for my comrades' reference:

1. Head for the mountains. The Bo Yi and Shu Qi method. No longer practicable.

2. Take to the sea. Confucius suggested "taking a raft into the sea" when things go badly. The modern equivalent of this is to hide out in the foreign concessions or to go to the United States. This is strictly for the inept. You're beyond the reach of the law, so you don't have to pay the price for what you say. No points for character.

3. Hide in the countryside. Tao Yuanming's method. You live off the land and write poems about flowers and weeds. No longer practicable.

4. Play mah-jongg. You devote yourself entirely to the 136 tiles of a mah-jongg set. Déclassé.

5. Practice the martial arts. You put your trust in flying swords and

(Mi Qiu)

spears that can lop off an enemy's head at a great distance. Very Ah Q,* and déclassé as well.

6. Drink. Xinling Jun was into that: "Xinling enjoyed heady wine, how many heroes has it undone?"

7. Womanize. The general Cai E [of the early republic] went in for this. But there are few women like Xiao Fengxian around today. Where are you, great ladies?

8. Play mad. Sunzi and Fan Sui both tried this. Unfortunately, today there are psychiatric hospitals. One session of shock treatment and the game's up.

---

* Ah Q is the protagonist of Lu Xun's most famous story, *The True Story of Ah Q*. He is a Chinese Everyman, proud of his ability to snatch defeat from the jaws of victory and hypersensitive about the scars on his scabby head.

9. Play stupid. It is hard to convince people you don't know what's going on. Of course, it's even harder to convince them that you do.

10. Engage in self-mutilation. Yu Rang, an assassin in the Spring and Autumn Period, disguised himself by lacquering his body to look like a leper and swallowing ashes to make himself a mute, but he was caught all the same. Gong Zizhen spoke of "illicit ejaculation," masturbation behind closed doors.

11. Feign illness. You pretend to be dizzy all day and say your legs are too weak to carry you. Complain about feeling run-down and having back pains. You'll seem impotent but only prove to people that you're also a person of no real substance.

12. Smile. Joke and laugh your way through the day, avoiding all discussion of politics; if the conversation does touch on politics, laugh it off or swear about it. Never go so far as to cause real trouble. A successful example was Ji Xiaolan [a Qing dynasty writer of ghost stories], while failures end up like Jin Shengtan [an exuberant seventeenth-century writer and literary critic who got himself killed].

13. Put on a mournful face. Look as dour as the master of a mortuary. No one will want to go near you, so of course you can't get into any trouble.

14. Go into business. Fan Li [of the Spring and Autumn Period] turned to business when he tired of politics. In his day there was no need to rely on official speculators or tax evasion to make yourself wealthy. Nowadays things aren't so simple.

15. Be like the flea. The things about fleas is that when they bite you it itches but it never really hurts, and they jump away immediately after biting, so the person bitten can never be bothered to catch them. The majority of writers today are like this; they squash a few fleas and think they're heroes.

Well, take your pick. If you want to survive in today's chaotic world, you can choose one or two of these methods. If you apply them well, you'll be okay; if you're careless, however, and you give the game away, it serves you right. . . .

—*1965*

The Cloak of Invisibility

YANG JIANG

Yang Jiang added to her Cultural Revolution memoirs, A Cadre School
Life: Six Chapters,* *in 1986. "The Cloak of Invisibility" is the author's
postscript to a volume of essays published in 1987.*
   Mocun is Yang's husband, the scholar Qian Zhongshu.

Mocun and I have jokingly discussed what type of magical powers we'd
like to have if we had a choice. We both decided on the cloak of invisibility. With it we could go traveling together and do as we wished, free
from all restrictions. Not that we'd want to do any evil or harm. But
quite possibly we'd get carried away and upset some innocent person
with our mischievousness. And finally our presence would be detected
and we'd have to flee in panic.

"Heavens, in that case we'd also need the power to travel long dis-
tances instantaneously."

"And talismans for self-protection."

The more we thought about it, the more we knew we'd need. In the
end we decided to forget about the cloak of invisibility altogether.

But you don't need supernatural powers to do things that are not
allowed in this world of ours. You can find the cloak of invisibility
wherever you are. It is a cloak made from a humble, insignificant weave.
If you occupy a lowly station in life, you're sure to be "seen through,"
to be treated as if you were invisible. People don't think of this cloak as
something precious; indeed, they are terrified that once they've put it on
it will stick to them like a wet shirt and they'll never get it off.

An old Chinese story tells of the spirit of a dead man who returns
home to find his family in mourning. They cannot see him. He speaks,
but no one hears his voice. They are seated around a table eating and he
eagerly tries to join in, only to find that there is no place set for him.
People of lowly status are like that disembodied spirit. If you are nothing
in other people's eyes, then naturally they will not see you; if they don't
acknowledge your existence in their hearts, they will look straight
through you. No matter how mortified you feel or how much you grieve
at being slighted or insulted, no one will take the slightest notice of you.

* See *Seeds of Fire,* pp. 80–87, for a chapter from these memoirs entitled "Digging a
Well."

You exist, but you feel totally insubstantial, as if you had never been born. Is not a life so spent no life at all? To don the cloak of invisibility, to proclaim its virtue and to revel in its power, is (so some might say) to play Ah Q; in other words, sour grapes.

Chinese is full of expressions about trying to be "a man among men" or seeking to put yourself "above the common herd," "enjoying the limelight," becoming "a tall poppy," or "pushing yourself to the fore." This is itself proof that most people aren't happy to be ignored. They resent obscurity, they chafe at it; they do their utmost to cast off the cloak of invisibility and to make themselves the center of attention.

In Anglo-American culture, society is compared to a snake pit. Snakes lie in a tangled heap at the bottom of a pit, each struggling to poke forth its head and thrust upward, squeezing through the mass to get on top. Heads rise to the surface and sink down to the depths again; bodies arch upward and subside; tails become entangled in an inextricable knot: You're on top, I'm on the bottom, it's a life-and-death contest, a ceaseless struggle. Unless you can get your head up and out of the heap, you will spend your whole life buried. Even if you do succeed, you'll be no better than a dancing bubble of foam on a boundless ocean, sparkling for a single moment in the sunlight. An outstanding person may realize certain ambitions, but the time spent on the crest of that wave is still only an instant. Certainly, that instant may well mark the high point of a lifetime, something to be proud of. But are you a "good-for-nothing" if you do not excel? On the other hand, will you be satisfied to spend your days subservient to others?

Heaven gives birth to all creatures, beautiful and ugly, talented and worthless. The fame of one outstanding general is built on the corpses of thousands; how else could a mere soldier become a grand hero? Some of us are born to sit in palanquins, others to carry them; there are the hosts and guests who occupy places of honor, and servants who bring them tea and food. At the banquet table there is a guest of honor and less important guests. In the kitchens a cook tends the stove while the menials add fuel. The talents with which nature has endowed humans are all so different; how can there be such a thing as equality?

People's ambitions differ vastly as well. In Chapter 26 of The Scholars* Madame Wang enthusiastically describes the magnificent feast and entertainments she has enjoyed in the Sun mansion. She was given the seat of honor, and as she was wearing a veil of giant pearls, the maids

---

* The Scholars, also known as the Unofficial History of the Literati, is a satirical novel by the Qing dynasty writer Wu Jingzi (eighteenth century).

on either side of her had to part the pearls so she could sip her honeyed tea. Sancho Panza, on the other hand, declares in Chapter 11 of *Don Quixote* that he prefers to eat a simple meal of bread and onions in a corner, free from the constraints of table manners and etiquette. Some people yearn to fly high; others are content "to drag their tails in the mud." * Each to his own.

Some people know just what they want out of life, and it is useless to try to persuade them otherwise. If, for instance, they want nothing more than to drag their tails in the mud, it's best to let them be. Then there are those who never realize their ambitions, who are forever at odds with fate. There is the mediocre fellow and his futile determination to become a "man among men." Ambition is the root of all frustration; and the higher a monkey climbs, the more clearly its shiny red behind can be seen. Blissfully unaware that he is dressed only in the emperor's new clothes, such a fellow strains to throw off the cloak of invisibility; all he does is reveal his own ugliness and perversity. Many people of moderate ability waste their lives trying to outdo others and still achieve nothing. It is all so futile.

The ancients said, "They are but human, like myself." Westerners have a similar notion. Such sayings encourage people to do their best without becoming self-destructive. In Spanish it is said that "you are what you do"—a person's worth is determined by his or her own efforts, not by birth or social position. Perhaps we should add, however, that "what you are determines what you can do." If you're a turnip, you should hope to be a juicy and crisp one; if a cabbage, the ideal is to be a solid, full-hearted vegetable. Both of these vegetables are used in daily cooking and make no pretense at being fit to join the lavish offerings in a temple.

A children's rhyme from my native place goes "On the third day of the third month, the shepherd's purse vies with the peony." One would think there was no competition. Once I saw a delicate blue flower in a patch of wild grass, and because it was so small as to be almost invisible I have often wondered if it was what Westerners call a "forget-me-not." But flowers and vegetables growing in the wild have no concept of being

---

* This is a reference to a story about the Taoist philosopher Zhuangzi, who rejected a plea by the King of Chu to manage his state. Zhuangzi, who received the king's messengers while fishing one day, said "I believe the King of Chu prizes a three-thousand-year-old supernatural tortoise shell that he keeps in his ancestral temple in a basket covered with a cloth. Now tell me, what do you think the tortoise would prefer: to have its shell thus honored, or to be alive and dragging its tail in the mud?" The messengers replied that the tortoise would rather be alive. "Quite so," retorted Zhuangzi. "Now leave me to drag my tail in the mud."

(or not being) "forgotten": They just blossom at the behest of the sunlight, the dew, and the rain. "Grasses and trees all possess a nature of their own, they wait not for a fair maiden's hand to pluck them."

I love the line by the Song dynasty poet Su Dongpo, "One can hide in the sea of humanity"; and I admire the philosopher Zhuangzi, who spoke of the sage who "drowned on dry land." Well may we compare society to a snake pit, yet in the skies above that pit birds fly free; in the ponds beside it fish swim at will. There are people who have always chosen to avoid the snake pit altogether, concealing themselves in the crowd or drowning on dry land. Their aim is to disappear like a drop of water in the sea, to be a wildflower camouflaged in thick grass, free of any aspiration to be a "forget-me-not" or to "vie with the peonies," at peace in their own niche. If people have no desire to climb to the heights, there is no need to jostle with others, no need to fear a fall. They can retain their innocence, fulfill their original nature, and concentrate on goals that are within their power.

Dressed in this cloak of invisibility, you can achieve things nobody can ever take away. Su Dongpo said, "The bright moon that floats between the hills and the clear breeze on the water are all part of the

(Mi Qiu)

inexhaustible bounty of nature." Certainly these things are to be enjoyed, and so too are man's own creations: The ways of the world and the complexity of human relations are even more delightful and intriguing than the bright moon and the clear breeze. They can be read like a book or enjoyed like a play. No matter how lifelike the descriptions in books or performances onstage may be, they are, after all, only make-believe. The real world is often stranger than fiction, so strange that it leaves us shocked and astounded. It possesses a more vital worth, a more wondrous ability to delight. Only the humble person has the opportunity of observing the reality behind the ways of the world, as opposed to the spectacle of art performed for an audience.

But I'm probably wasting my breath. Those anxious to abandon the cloak of invisibility will hardly be impressed with what I am saying, while those who were unaware of the cloak's existence will gain nothing from the knowledge of it. In all honesty, donning the cloak of invisibility, be it magical or mundane, has drawbacks and considerable inconveniences.

In *The Invisible Man* H. G. Wells describes a man who achieved invisibility by scientific means. Yet his invisibility brought him only pain. When it was cold, for example, he had to stay indoors unless he wanted to go out without any clothes on. When he did get dressed—with shoes, hat and gloves—he appeared to others as a faceless man, and if he went into the street he would cause a fearful panic. Thus he was forced to conceal his face by pulling a hat over his brow, wrapping a scarf around his mouth, and wearing a pair of dark glasses. He covered his nose and cheeks with gauze and sticking plaster. What lengths he had to go to, to conceal his invisibility!

Such are the results of a blind and mechanistic science; they cannot compare with the magical cloak of invisibility. The cloak conceals normal clothing and may be cast aside at will. But the body it disguises is one made of flesh and blood, one that feels both heat and cold, one that can be hurt all too easily. A brick, or a club, or a clumsy foot can be painful enough, but what of the agony one must endure if attacked by a knife or gun, if scalded by water or burnt by fire? If one has not the magical ability to make a timely escape, the only way to ensure safety is to acquire an adamantine body.

The cloak of invisibility has other drawbacks. The human heart it conceals is all too vulnerable, it is sensitive to heat and cold, it cannot withstand rough handling. It is an arduous process to steel oneself to this, to train oneself to be impervious to all manner of attack and insult; and to watch what happens in the world without such training may make the heart burst with indignation, it may break it. In such conditions it is inconceivable to view things like a carefree playgoer. Perhaps one should simply choose not to watch at all. After all, the world is not a variety show.

If Le Sage's "Devil upon Two Sticks" * were to invite me to go abroad with him one night, accompanying him as he lifted up the roofs of houses to peek inside, I would certainly decline. Is it necessary to see and experience everything in order to achieve wisdom? And by seeing and experiencing everything, will you necessarily obtain wisdom? How many lives does one have? The belief that on the basis of the experience of one lifetime you can achieve a unique vision and understand all human life may deservedly win no more than a furtive smile from others.

The cloak of invisibility can be found everywhere. It is no rare or magical treasure. Many people wear it. Are they all blind?

And no matter how you look at it, the cloak of invisibility is better than the emperor's new clothes.

The Thick and the Black

LI ZONGWU

We are all born with a face, and to be thick-skinned is its prerogative. God also gives us all a heart, and it can be as black as pitch. The face and heart seem to be but small physical objects, mere inches in diameter, not large enough to fill cupped hands. They seem to have no extraordinary qualities. But upon closer scrutiny you will discover there is no limit to how thick the skin on a person's face can become; and nothing can compare with the blackness a heart can attain. All things dear to man can come from being thick-skinned and black-hearted: fame and wealth, palaces, wives and concubines, clothes, chariots, and horses. How wondrous indeed is the Creator! What riches there are of which man can avail himself! To fail to do so would be the greatest of all follies.

The Science of the Thick and the Black can be divided into three levels of attainment:

---

* This is a reference to Alain René Le Sage's eighteenth-century satirical fantasy *Le Diable boiteux*.

1. To have skin as thick as a city wall and a heart as black as coal.

The skin on one's face is paper thin to start with, but it can become thicker first by inches and then feet until it is as thick as a city wall.

As for the heart, it starts off milky white, then turns gray, then blue-black until it progresses to the blackness of coal. But these are the accomplishments of beginners. For all its thickness, a city wall can be shattered by cannon fire; and the pitch-black of coal is an unpopular color, and people shy from it.

2. To develop "thickness that is impenetrable and a jet-blackness that shines." A true adept of the thick skin will remain unmoved by any salvo, while the master of black-heartedness will appear as a lacquered billboard: The darker it is, the more custom it attracts.
. . . This second stage of achievement, although a great advance on stage one, still leaves something to be desired, for both color and form remain readily apparent to the naked eye.

3. To have skin that is thick yet formless and a heart that is black yet colorless is the ultimate level of attainment. No one will have any idea of how thick and black you are. This is not easily achieved, and one finds the best examples among the sages of the past. Where, you may ask? The Confucians praise the Doctrine of the Mean as being soundless and odorless, and the Buddhists aim at wisdom that has no vessel.

Herein I have revealed the secret of the ages. To achieve a thickness of skin that is formless and a blackness of heart that is colorless is to have perfected the Science of the Thick and the Black.

Li Zongwu was born in Sichuan in 1879. Devoted to the study of the classical novel Romance of the Three Kingdoms, *which takes as its theme the political intrigues of one of the most complex and treacherous periods in Chinese history, Li based his "Science of the Thick and Black" on an analysis of the novel's protagonists. He published a series of widely read articles on the subject in the early years of the republic that again found popularity with readers in the 1930s and '40s. Editions of his collected writings have been readily available in Hong Kong for many years. Although C. Northcote Parkinson's* Parkinson's Law, or the Pursuit of Progress *was published in translation in Mainland China in 1982, and Lawrence J. Peter's* The Peter Principle *appeared in late 1988, Li*

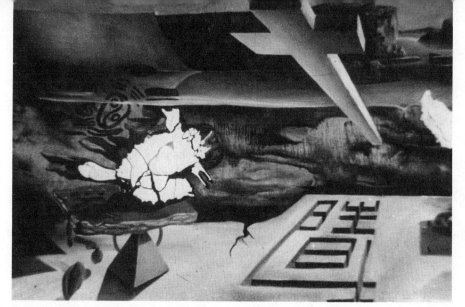

"The History of Civilization," Gu Wenda (*Fine Arts in China*)

Zongwu's writings were banned until 1989, when Hong Kong editions were pirated, and in 1990 a sequel to Li's book was published. Li observed that the true adepts of his science could be found only in the past. However, such professional survivors as the late premier Zhou Enlai must surely be regarded as modern masters.*

In a Dialogue with Nihilism

DING FANG

Too many people have experienced the cruel realities of the twentieth century; they have seen the blood and deception lurking behind all the talk of ideals and justice. No one believes anymore in the spirit of self-sacrifice; no one has faith in anything that has the power to save the soul. This fragmented and meaningless world leaves us with only a passionate sense of the absurd. It is as though only this passion can afford people a proprietorial sense of life, enjoyment, and freedom. . . . In essence, absurdist thinking aims at rationalizing the absurdity of the world,

---

* See Simon Leys's "The Path of an Empty Boat: Zhou Enlai," an excellent treatment of the man Leys calls "the ultimate Zelig of politics," in *The Burning Forest*, New York: Holt, Rinehart and Winston, 1986, pp. 152–58.

forcing people to synchronize their spirit and feelings with it. Absurdity permits people to remain unperturbed by the folly and stupidity of every-thing; they feel no pain or shame at any of the careless or harmful acts in which they take part. But the greatness of humanity is that it can come to life even in the darkness, establish a system of sacred beliefs, and find a path for the salvation and sublimation of the soul.

At the Gateway to Hell

LIU XIAOBO

To be quite honest, no matter how vicious a tyranny may be, people should not be scared, nor should they complain; all must decide whether they will subject themselves to it or rebel. Whenever the Chinese start heaping scorn on authoritarianism, they should be blaming themselves instead. How could things have reached their present state, where the most outrageous things are taken for granted, if it weren't for the Chinese being so weak-willed and ignorant? Tyranny is not terrifying; what is really scary is submission, silence, and even praise for tyranny. As soon as people decide to oppose it to the bitter end, even the most vicious tyranny will be short-lived. The only thing that is worthwhile is one's own choice and the decision to accept the consequences of that choice. Why the long face of the suffering martyr when you make a plaintive criticism of the violence of tyranny? Do what everyone else does: Either stay silent or give in entirely. Move ahead cautiously, cover the hilly terrain slowly, follow the serpentine course of the river tena-ciously. You won't upset the autocrats, and you'll win the highest acco-lade of traditional Chinese morality: You'll be known as "subtle." . . . What good fortune! If you're already aware of how pitiless the autocrats are and you know that any opposition to them will only be begging disaster to fall from the skies, and still you go ahead and bash your head against a brick wall, then you've got no one to blame but yourself if you split your head open. You can't blame the people who are watching you, nor can you blame the autocrats. If you want to enter hell, don't com-plain of the dark; you can't blame the world for being unfair if you start on the path of the rebel. If all you do is complain, you'll never get anywhere.

—November 1988

Doors: Essays on the Open Door

The Open Door

QIAN ZHONGSHU

*The following passage comes from the introductory essay Qian Zhong-
shu, one of China's greatest scholars and Yang Jiang's husband, wrote
for a series of books published by Zhong Shuhe in Hunan in the early
1980s. The* Bound for the World *series, as it was called, included the
travel diaries of leading late Qing dynasty figures who traveled overseas
and saw for themselves the simultaneously threatening and enticing realities of Western civilization.*

China is "bound for the world"; you could also say the world is bound
for China. The reason we've opened the door and gone out is that people
outside have been pushing on the door, knocking, and crashing into it,
even breaking it down or jumping in through the windows. Stereotyped
expressions such as "closing the door to the outside world" or "opening
the door" are simple and neat, easy to remember. As headings or slogans
they are convenient and sound good. But it would appear that history
cares little for the convenience of the historian, and it is unwilling to
unfold in a clear or orderly fashion.

In everyday life the door is sometimes wide open. Sometimes only a
window is open, or half open, while the door is closed. Sometimes both
doors and windows are firmly shut, a crack in the window or a keyhole
being the only way for a little outside air to get in. When both the door
and windows are fully open, it's hard to ensure that the old and the
young won't catch cold. If there are too many people in the room and
the doors and windows are shut tightly, it can be stifling, even suffocating. If the doors and windows are only partially opened, in practical

terms [the relationship between the inside and the outside] is like that of lovers who are both eager for and shy of intimacy.

—March 1984

Passports and Freedom

WU ZUGUANG

When Zhao Ziyang and his four besuited Politburo colleagues did the rounds at a special press conference held in Peking at the closing of the Thirteenth Party Congress on November 2, 1987, wineglasses in hand, many foreign reporters seemed to be falling all over themselves to hail what many presumed to be a "new era" in Chinese political life. The international press corps was presented with the squeaky-clean new Politburo. Factional differences supposedly laid aside, they stood there smiling, joking, and within handshake range.

But what to outsiders may have appeared to be Zhao Ziyang's wit and candor as he responded to the journalists' questions left many Chinese groaning in disbelief that their Marxist-Leninist rulers could get away with such obfuscating doublethink in front of supposedly tough-minded foreign journalists. For example, when one asked whether there is freedom of expression in China, Zhao responded; "There certainly is. However, there is no absolute freedom. There is no such thing as absolute freedom in any country. Don't you still need a passport to travel overseas? You can't enjoy absolute freedom either, can you?"

According to the Xinhua News Agency, this reply resulted in peals of merry laughter. Zhao's comment inspired the following essay by Wu Zuguang, which remained unpublished until it appeared in the Hong Kong press in early 1989.

Although that reporter hadn't said anything about "absolute freedom," it's not unreasonable that Zhao Ziyang should use passports to illustrate that there is no such thing as absolute freedom anywhere. Zhao's response does show, however, just how sensitive we are to the word "freedom." Throughout history many brave and upright individuals have died in the quest for freedom. Yet the tragic reality is that almost without exception, when they manage to become rulers themselves, freedom fighters tend to lose all interest in freedom for their subjects.*

Progress has brought ceaseless change in its wake, and life drags us all into its vortex. Although I haven't consulted any documents or statistics on the subject, my own observations lead me to believe that the net result of human ingenuity is that individual freedoms are lessened with each passing day, and that people go to great lengths to restrict their own freedoms.

When I was a boy, China controlled its people by means of a "household system." A headman and his assistant were put in charge of groups of families. While the headmen reveled in the system that gave them power, for the people it simply represented another layer of repression. But let's return to the question of passports. I asked two friends of mine who are familiar with the subject to tell me something about the history of passports. Although they were a bit fuzzy on the details, they did recall that they'd needed passports when they traveled overseas in the 1920s. In *Journey to the West* even Xuan Zang, the Tang dynasty monk who voyaged to India to obtain the Buddhist scriptures, is said to have taken a travel document with him. Perhaps it was the equivalent of a modern-day passport and visa. You can see how far back the idea goes.

In the 1920s, however, it was easy to obtain a passport. If you know anything at all about modern Chinese history, you know how many revolutionaries and progressives were able to flee overseas to escape persecution at the end of the Qing dynasty or during the warlord era. Liang Qichao and Sun Yat-sen were among them . . . later the writer Guo Moruo and many others were always running off to Europe, Japan, and other countries to avoid arrest. Today that would be impossible; not only must you have a passport, you also need a visa from the country you're headed for. A passport without a visa is useless, and to get a visa in China, applicants have to ask their work units or local Public Security Bureaus to apply at the relevant embassy or consulate on their behalf.

In 1946, a year after the Japanese surrender, the eight-year wartime alliance between the Nationalists and the Communists was strained to breaking point. When in 1946 and 1947 two satirical plays of mine were performed in Shanghai, they so infuriated the government that I was forced to escape to Hong Kong. I was following in the footsteps of many other people in the arts. Even though Hong Kong had been a British

* See Bo Yang, "Democracy Is a Way of Life," pp. 46–7.

"Giant Fish Boat," Luis Chan (courtesy of Hanart 2 Gallery, Hong Kong)

territory for nearly a century, there were no travel restrictions between the colony and the mainland, and no documents were required. All you needed was a plane ticket. The return trip, whether you chose to go by air, sea, or train, was just as simple.

But things are very different today. To get to Hong Kong or Macao is the same as traveling overseas; you need both a passport and a visa. I have no idea when this system was introduced, though I do know that after the founding of New China there was a period during which travel was still unrestricted. In 1997 Hong Kong will return to the motherland and become part of Chinese territory once more. I wonder what type of travel restrictions will be put into place then? If it is going to be anything like Shenzhen [the Special Economic Zone next to Hong Kong], then you'll need to apply to the Public Security Bureau for a special travel permit. It looks like travelers will still face numerous restrictions.

So what does all of this mean? Simply that our freedoms are being eroded away day by day due to human interference. Why? Because people don't trust one another; they suspect others' motives and constantly think the worst of each other. They set up barriers and put everything under heavy guard. This type of mistrust has been increasing over the

EVERYBODY OUT

Reading *Science News* today, I came across an article on the craze for going abroad. It said that at first it was young people who were trying to get out, but now even middle-aged and older people with established careers are lining up as well. These people are willing to go despite the knowledge that they'll have to take jobs beneath their abilities. This is a painful but incontestable reality. How did things come to such a pass? Why is it that in the 1950s, when China was still desperately poor, everyone was returning from abroad, but today it's the opposite? This is the psychology of a nation that is falling apart.

Another thing—recently the bulletin board at Peking University carried a notice saying there was a shortage of math and physics teachers in American high schools and Chinese university lecturers in these fields would be welcome to apply for the positions. As soon as the news got out, lots of people, including full professors, began hankering after these jobs. Why? Because while everyone feels that there's so much to be done [in China], under the present circumstances it's difficult to do anything at all.

—*Fang Lizhi, December 1988*

past fifty years. It sends a shiver up my spine to think of what kind of world, what kind of country, we will have in the future. The thought of it leaves me hopeless and depressed. Frankly, I think humanity is on the decline.

I should make one concluding point: Although the above reflections were inspired by Zhao Ziyang's response to that reporter, Zhao is in no way responsible for my meditation. Nonetheless, I would be very interested to know his views on the subject. What it all boils down to is the question: Is it better to have greater freedom or more passports?

—*December 9, 1987*

Tibet: A Spiritual Exile

In 1989 *the fourteenth Dalai Lama had been in exile from his homeland for thirty years. During that time he worked tirelessly for the peaceful resolution of the conflicts between the Tibetan people and the Chinese government.* In March 1989, Lhasa was put under martial law following protests against the Chinese occupation of Tibet. At the time a few observers noted that the use of martial law in Tibet had a cautionary value as well: It was a signal to the rest of China. The Dalai Lama followed the 1989 Protest Movement closely. Later that year he was awarded the Nobel Peace Prize.*

Remarks by His Holiness the Fourteenth Dalai Lama, on Being Awarded the Nobel Peace Prize

I am deeply touched to be chosen as this year's recipient of the Nobel Peace Prize. I believe my selection reaffirms the universal values of non-violence, peace, and understanding among all members of our great human family. We all desire a happier, more humane, and harmonious world, and I have always felt that the practice of love and compassion, tolerance and respect for others is the most effective manner in which to bring this about.

* For more material on Tibet, see *Seeds of Fire*, pp. 413–53.

I hope this prize will provide courage to the six million people of Tibet. For some forty years now Tibetans have been undergoing the most painful period in our long history. During this time, over a million of our people perished and more than six thousand monasteries—the seat of our peaceful culture—were destroyed. There is not a single family, either in Tibet or among the refugees abroad, that has gone unscathed. Yet our people's determination and commitment to spiritual values and the practice of nonviolence remain unshaken. This prize is a profound recognition of their faith and perseverance.

The demonstrations that have rocked Tibet for the past two years continue to be nonviolent despite brutal suppression. Since the imposition of martial law in Lhasa last March, Tibet has been sealed off, and while global attention has focused on the tragic events in China, a systematic effort to crush the spirit and national identity of the Tibetan people is being pursued by the government of the People's Republic.

Tibetans today are facing the real possibility of elimination as a people and a nation. The government of the People's Republic of China is practicing a form of genocide by relocating millions of Chinese settlers into Tibet. I ask that this massive population transfer be stopped. Unless the cruel and inhuman treatment of my people is brought to an end, and until they are given their due right to self-determination, there will always be obstacles in finding a solution to the Tibetan issue.

I accept the Nobel Peace Prize in a spirit of optimism despite the many grave problems that humanity faces today. We all know the immensity of the challenges facing our generation: the problem of overpopulation, the threat to our environment, and the dangers of military confrontation. As this dramatic century draws to a close, it is clear that the renewed yearning for freedom and democracy sweeping the globe provides an unprecedented opportunity for building a better world. Freedom is the real source of human happiness and creativity. Only when it is allowed to flourish can a genuinely stable international climate exist.

The suppression of the rights and freedoms of any people by totalitarian governments is against human nature, and the recent movements for democracy in various parts of the world are a clear indication of this.

The Chinese students have given me great hope for the future of China and Tibet. I feel that their movement follows the tradition of Mahatma Gandhi's *ahimsa*, or nonviolence, which has deeply inspired me ever since I was a small boy. The eventual success of all people seeking a more tolerant atmosphere must derive from a commitment to counter hatred and violence with patience. We must seek change through dialogue and trust. It is my heartfelt prayer that Tibet's plight may be resolved in such a manner that once again my country, the Roof of the World, may serve as a sanctuary of peace and a resource of spiritual inspiration at the heart of Asia.

I hope and pray that the decision to give me the Nobel Peace Prize will encourage all those who pursue the path of peace to do so in a renewed spirit of optimism and strength.

A Chinese Reaction

CHEN RUOXI

Chen Ruoxi, a writer from Taiwan, set up the Tibet-American Cultural Exchange Association after her first trip to Tibet in 1987. She enlisted the support of a number of prominent Taiwanese and other writers, but by early 1990 the association had still not achieved official recognition in China despite protracted negotiations that included a demand that they change their name to the Tibetan Buddhist Research Society.

In 1988, at a meeting with Yan Mingfu, then head of the United Front Ministry, which deals with overseas personalities, Chen remarked that the Dalai Lama had been nominated for the Nobel Peace Prize. She added that the Chinese government would be wise to start negotiations with him before he received the award, as he would be in a much better bargaining position afterward. Yan Mingfu responded emotionally, "Our position won't change even if he gets three Nobel Prizes!"

I never imagined that just one year later the Dalai Lama would be awarded the prize. It is richly deserved, and it is also a message of peaceful protest aimed at the Chinese. It gave me a renewed sense of hope for both Tibet and China.

Now, after the tanks have crushed our compatriots in the Tiananmen Incident, who but a religious man could save Tibet and China? People are but flesh and blood, they are no match for tanks and bullets. Only those who are possessed of a religious spirit can look on death with equanimity; for the rest there is no choice but to grovel and submit to the authorities. . . .

I hope that the award of the Nobel Peace Prize has strengthened the determination of the Dalai Lama to return to Tibet and not just given him an advantage in negotiations with the Communists. The liberation of a people cannot rely on outside force, nor can democracy and freedom be bestowed on China by another nation. Although freedom fighters in exile can be propagandists and keep the message alive, the real battlefield remains at home, in their own country.

Voices from the Outside

Exile

BEI LING

You can see the Hudson River from my window. Its enchantingly misty surface is smooth, and on clear days it seems you can even smell its breath, a calm, majestic air. I'm living in New York now.

But this is as far as my imagination ever takes me. Other things force themselves in on me in all their rawness. They surge out of my memory, and when they appear before me, I can find no peace.

These unsettling things were part of the ambience of everyday life I once considered the spring of creativity, an ambience I nurtured carefully but enjoyed carelessly, an all-embracing, even suffocating atmosphere. It exists in my homeland, especially in Peking.

Let me try to describe it. An apartment in the residential quarters of a university, far from the city; simple but comfortable. As I lived by myself, I picked up both lunch and dinner from the school canteen. When I got too bored, I'd visit Ah Xian and make a nuisance of myself at his place.* He's an artist who lived only about a hundred meters away. He always had a worried look on his face as he inspected a newly stretched canvas, while outside the wind rustled in the trees.

Each night I'd walk over to my parents' apartment to watch the seven o'clock news. About once a week I'd ride my bike over to see my old friend Zhou Duo.† He lived ten minutes away. I'd put off visiting until late at night. His light was always on, and I'd find him reading at his desk. He'd stand up to greet me with reluctance, but having resigned

---

* Ah Xian was an independent Peking artist. His work has appeared in *Seeds of Fire*, p. 240. In September 1990, he moved to Sydney, Australia.
† Zhou was an employee of the Stone Corporation *(Sitong gongsi)*. Active during the 1989 Protest Movement, he participated in the June 2 hunger strike led by Liu Xiaobo and Hou Dejian. He was detained by police in June 1989, released in May 1990, and with Hou petitioned for Liu's release in May 1990.

himself to my visit he'd try to entertain me. Come on, let's make something to eat, he'd say, kneading his [tired] face. Then we'd start talking. His crazy father, an old professor, would be howling in the next room like some wild prophet of doom. We never took any notice.

Late at night the wide streets of Peking's western suburbs were lonely and dignified, like a grave old man listening silently for the occasional crisp laughter of girls passing on their bicycles.

There's more. The wild all-night parties in the diplomatic compound on the weekends—smoking, drinking, and the loud talk and laughter of the artists; the deafening rock 'n' roll music; the suspicious glances exchanged by Chinese meeting for the first time; the games people play when drunk, going wild. The poets would usually be in a room of their own, holding serious discussions about literature, excited perhaps by the publication of some new book or lost in vague imaginings about the outside world.

It was a kind of underground life; within our limited environment, we enjoyed it unreservedly, nervously, but with verve, thinking it would go on forever. Only with the stimulation of the outside world did we find things somehow tolerable. Short bursts of enchantment inspired us to write clearheaded or perhaps not such clearheaded poetry. Sometimes we'd recite our work in the dim light of the salons. But this gave birth to an illusion, and we became increasingly self-inflated. A comic interlude in a tragedy, allowing us momentarily to forget history. But the baneful net of history had already been cast wide.

Now I'm adrift in a foreign land, the apartment of an American friend my temporary abode. Lying on the sofa, I examine the densely printed "for rent" columns of the *Daily World*. I'm into details; life won't let me ignore the fine print. "An inexpensive room is approximately $250. Best look for a basement. Better still, it should be out of Manhattan. Places in town are too expensive. Maybe Queens, lots of Chinese, that's good, only ten minutes from the subway station. A woman in the local grocery store speaks Chinese." I talk to myself as I read.

I've finally admitted to myself that I'm in exile. It's involuntary exile, though I chose it voluntarily. Faced with the agonizing realities of home and considering what I've done, I've been left with no other choice.

The four walls of my room have nothing on them. I've been to five American cities. I went to a bookstore, but only once, because there's no joy left in browsing: In this country I'm an illiterate. Every morning for the past ten months I've woken up fully aware that my ability to think is in decline. I try to remember the books I've read; I have to rely on my memory. At home in Peking I have a whole wall of books, they reach up to the ceiling, maybe a thousand volumes in all. One desolate and rainy autumn evening last year, the wind was blowing through the leaves in a way that could break your heart. I was yearning for the sudden, startling knock of a friend. No one came. I dragged my chair over to the bookshelves, climbed up, and took a book from the very top: *The Sound and the Fury*. Faulkner's novel had been sitting there for five years; I'd never finished it. It's written in a stream-of-consciousness style, set in the author's [imaginary] homeland, Yoknapatawpha County, and uses dialogue and interior monologue to follow the psychological relations among the idiot Benjy, his sister, and his family. It's a subtle tale; the language is complex and pure. Astounding how a master can use language that way. It depicts a psychological history. I was too young the first time, too full of my own sound and fury. But in the company of the autumn wind I felt I could enjoy a dialogue with Faulkner's creations.

Books. To buy a good book and to start reading it eagerly on a crowded bus; the wind and the falling leaves. These pleasures, so hard to describe, were all part of the ambience of my life in Peking.

Now I'm in New York; my sole occupation is recollection.

What does exile mean? Solitude, isolation. Spiritual exile. The courage to face defeat. Accept it. There's no other choice.

On one excited afternoon in late May [1989] I rang an Australian writer friend in Peking. (As luck would have it, Xiaobo was at his place.)* I told him I wanted to go back, I was returning. I had booked a ticket; I didn't want to go on wasting my time in America.

"What can you do back here? It's virtually all over. Bei Ling, there's nothing you can do; don't come back," he said.

I was silent. Neither of us spoke for a long time. He was waiting for my response. Xiaobo may have been standing next to him. But what could I say? There was too much to say, but I couldn't speak. To return meant too much, far too much. It didn't only mean participating in the Democracy Movement. Perhaps it would be no more than being able to read a book, to hear my own language, to listen to the sound of those rustling leaves, returning to the familiar environment of home. It's impossible to express what I mean in such simplistic terms. In May there was a yawning "jet lag" between New York and Peking. Peking was the focal point of the world's attention, the forces of light and darkness were

---

* The Australian writer friend is Nicholas Jose, whose report "And the Beat Goes On" can be found in Part III, "Red Noise." Xiaobo is Liu Xiaobo. In his novel *Avenue of Eternal Peace* (Melbourne: Penguin Books Australia, 1989), Jose uses the party and salon scene of the Peking diplomatic compounds from 1985 to 1987 as a backdrop to the story of an Australian's personal quest.

> Even when we Chinese admit we are hopelessly backward and must learn from the West, we don't face the rest of the world in a spirit of equal competition but, rather, see ourselves as future masters of the universe. When we're forced to admit defeat, we genuflect before foreigners, happy to be their slaves, but deep down these slaves are motivated by a desire one day to become the masters of the Westerners. . . . Even among extreme antitraditionalists in China today, the dream of "China as the center of the world" still obviously informs the psychology of the defeated—China has always seen itself as the center of the world, and its backwardness in recent times is no proof that it doesn't want to be the center of the world once again. To put a positive gloss on it, you could say the Chinese have a "Messiah fixation," or, to describe it in less charitable terms, you might say it is wild hegemonistic ambition. . . . All of the prohibitions on contact between Chinese and foreigners in China today are in essence no different from the sign in the park on the Bund in Shanghai all those years ago: "Chinese and dogs forbidden." If, one day, China really does become a strong nation, it is not unimaginable that in the Chinese concessions in Paris, London, or New York a sign will appear reading "Caucasians and dogs forbidden." The most important thing I learned on my first trip overseas was that race and nationality are irrelevant to interpersonal relations; I am faced with an individual human being, not a foreigner of some description. . . . First and foremost, we Chinese must learn to think of other people as our equals. From this perspective we will see that humanity has common weaknesses; in the West there are also those who think of other people as their slaves.
>
> —Liu Xiaobo, 1988

fighting for time. Perhaps the Democracy Movement would be defeated, but could that really prevent me from returning home? I know now that it could.

It's too late, all that's in the past now. My friends are in jail, and that "jet lag" made me a survivor. I'm in exile, and perhaps I will end my days as an exile. A daydreamer like me has to be patient, to engage in endless reverie.

Every morning I pass through Columbia University. The buildings are large and impressive. Lively young students are hanging around or rushing to class. The girls are pretty in the morning light. I buy a Chinese paper at the newsstand on Broadway. Others buy their English papers and hurry on their way. I can't read those papers, papers with reports on the rest of the world, more varied, more objective and accurate, than those in my paper. But they're beyond my reach. The world is too vast, and my experiences lie too heavily on me.

It's been twenty-one years since the Prague Spring. The survivors are still in exile. When they fled, like me they fantasized about returning in two or three years. Things would be turned around, the young people who had blocked the Soviet tanks would be rehabilitated. But twenty-one long years have passed without any basic change.

Milan Kundera continues to write in Paris, his hair now gray. This is the "unbearable sin of being." Khrushchev was purged in 1964, and the Brezhnev era lasted twenty years. It appears that nothing can turn back the tide of reform under Gorbachev, but Solzhenitsyn is still in exile in America. He has said he will not return to the Soviet Union before his books do. No one can tell what tomorrow will bring; crystal ball gazing is not a writer's task. A writer merely tries to express the unique reality of his own world.

Your life as an exile has begun. You can't make time pass any faster. Life becomes a mosaic of endless concrete details. Your job teaching at a university in China is apparently over. Tomorrow you have to start work as a kitchen hand. Nine hours a day up to your elbows in dishwater bleaches your hands, but you've no right to complain. Here you're an outsider. They've accepted you, and you have to do what you must to survive, even though your hand was made to hold a pen or a piece of chalk.

I often ask myself, is it possible for a Chinese writer to exist in exile in the West? Is a Chinese literature in exile possible? The cultural difference between East and West is so massive. You have to make a much greater effort than the exiles from Eastern Europe, greater strength is required. Starting with the language, you must endure a life of spiritual poverty. You're no longer young; the first enemy you must confront is yourself, your temperament that has been conditioned by an authoritarian environment, your physical weakness, and all the habits born of the slow-paced society from which you come.

This is exile, a life without a sense of belonging, one made up of difficulties. It's not only a matter of life-style, it is something that touches on the very essence of existence. Even while you examine it, exile examines you and may draw its own conclusions.

You need determination, belief, and all your painful memories to bear it. Because you still haven't lost the ability to look out at the world.

—*September 1989*

Bei Ling (the pen name of the poet Huang Beiling) was born in 1959 and had contact with the Today *writers in Peking in 1978–79. He was an ubiquitous member of the semiunderground literary and party scene in Peking up to his leaving for the United States in 1988. Originally from Shanghai, he was able (as a journalist and then a university employee) to devote himself to poetry and the literary scene. Although he was a poet in a country awash with aspiring poets, Bei Ling was a Peking liaison for out-of-town young writers, finding accommodations, transportation, and useful contacts for the provincials. In this way he built up a wide network throughout the country. His intimate knowledge of the alternative literary scene inspired him to start work on a history of post-Mao underground writing in 1989, which he continued while in residence at Brown University in 1990.*

He was invited to the United States by Yan Li, a poet and artist, formerly of the Stars, to help edit First Line, *a small Chinese literary journal based in New York. He became friendly with Liu Xiaobo when the latter visited New York in March–April 1989.*

People fly off to distant parts, flee this impoverished land in search of a new world, paradise.

It is the physical manifestation of a spiritual longing. This great migration gives form to a sense of national hopelessness, it's a new superstition with the outside world as its totem. Postindustrial society appears as a terrestrial refraction of some heavenly blueprint, enticing troubled souls to venture forth and enjoy. . . .

Taken from another angle, these neighboring peoples will be devastated as they witness yellow-skinned ETs descending on every corner of the globe, invading their streets and pillaging their wealth, culture, and women. People take upon themselves the style of the exile, undertaking a crusade of the weak, casting a net of gentle terror over the world as the process of colonization in reverse unfolds. This is the ironic revenge of the descendants of Genghis Khan. . . .

[Exile] is certainly a moral process suffused with shame and pangs of conscience. The writer in exile must learn to be thick-skinned and shameless, to bow his head as he stands beneath the eave of his patron's magnanimity, to accept the downward gaze and ridicule of new divinities. People must first understand that they are the descendants of a fallen tribe—only then can they become citizens of the world.

—Zhu Dake, 1988

The parties Huang describes continued in increasingly lackluster form in late 1989 and the early nineties. After the massacre many were farewell gatherings as both Chinese and foreigners connected with the salon scene drifted overseas.

Mainland Chinese writers generally see themselves as the first of their race to be forced into exile. Forgetting about the exile of many writers who fled overseas or to Taiwan in the 1930s and '40s (such as Lin Yutang and Hu Shi), they also tend to ignore the fact that many prominent and talented Taiwanese writers like Chen Ruoxi, Pai Hsien-yung, and Nieh Hua-ling, as well as numerous outstanding academics, were also more or less forced overseas in the 1960s by a repressive political regime on the other side of the Taiwan Strait.

Although this essay was written during a period of depression not long after the June massacre, Bei Ling later said that the events in Eastern Europe in the last months of 1989 had made him more hopeful.

Early in 1990, Chen Ruoxi and the mainland author Kong Jiesheng, exiled from Canton since 1989, started a new literary journal, Culture Square, *in the United States to provide a forum for émigré Chinese writers. Also in 1990, Bei Dao and a number of other exiled writers revived the literary magazine* Today *in Oslo, Norway.*

A Poignant Season

The poet Duo Duo spent much time on Tiananmen Square during the Protest Movement. He had earlier been invited to England for a visit and had a passport and ticket in June when he went into exile. Shu Kei interviewed him in London some months later for his film Sunless Days:

I flew to London from Peking on June 4. It's early autumn now in London. The ground is covered with fallen leaves; it's a poignant season. September was always my favorite month in Peking. The weather was fresh and cool; it made me feel content.

Every year I start writing seriously in September and October. But now I'm in a foreign land. Originally, I'd planned to visit the U.K. for ten days to take care of some publishing business. With the present political situation, I have no home to return to now. As a poet, a writer, I face an alien linguistic environment and a society with a completely different culture and history. How can I continue to create and develop?

Duo Duo ("Sunless Days")

It won't be easy. Suddenly, all your habitual support systems—psychological and sensual—are gone. Lots of things here may impress you, but nothing stimulates you. That's because I left China when I did and in a traumatized state. If it were last year, I'd be thrilled to be here. But now I'm a bit numb.

In China I was one of those "wholly Westernized" types; but outside China, I've discovered I am very Chinese.

You worry about becoming passé, that no one will pay attention to you anymore. These days most people call me to discuss work. "We want to interview you," that sort of thing. After a while, you're like any other rootless person, facing the world alone.

In May 1990, a group of three quixotic figures attempted to continue the 1989 appeals for liberalization of government policies and the release of political prisoners. They were the Taiwan-born pop singer Hou De-jian, Zhou Duo, and Gao Xin, all of whom had joined Liu Xiaobo in his hunger strike on Tiananmen Square (see pp. 70–72). After the massacre, Gao Xin was jailed but freed in December and Zhou, also jailed, was released in early May. From late December 1989, Hou had provided the sole voice of public protest in Peking, speaking frequently to the foreign press about the massacre and the state of affairs in China. In late May 1990, shortly after Zhou's release and timed to coincide with the first anniversary of the Peking Massacre of June 4, Hou suggested that they write a petition to the government reiterating the line they had adopted with Liu Xiaobo during the last days of the student movement, that is, one of "rationalism, tolerance, and nonviolence." In it they said:

> . . . Our greatest concern is how to bring an end to hate, violence, and confrontation. When will there be an end to the ceaseless violent revolutions that define the blood- and tear-stained history of our nation?
>
> At the very time that the majority of socialist countries have peacefully engaged in basic social reforms, the people of China have experienced the most bitterly silent and repressive year of the Open Door and Reform decade . . .

They called for the release of Liu Xiaobo and other political detainees. However, even before this petition could be released to the media, Hou and his comrades were detained by the authorities. While Zhou Duo and Gao Xin were eventually let go with no more than a warning, Hou was "exiled" on a fishing boat back to Taiwan, where he was prosecuted by the KMT government for illegal entry.

In late 1990, Liu Binyan, himself an exile, praised Hou's action and observed that it marked a significant departure from the cowed silence that is the typical response of Chinese intellectuals to oppression.

In early 1991, Gao Xin went to the United States and Liu Xiaobo was released from jail. Hou applied to immigrate to Australia on humanitarian grounds.

Epilogue

The poet Bei Dao once wrote: I—do—not—believe!*
Today, I too declare: I do not believe. . . .

I do not believe that the Chinese will forever refuse to think for
   themselves;
I do not believe that the Chinese will never speak out through their
   writings;
I do not believe that morality and justice will vanish in the face of
   repression;
I do not believe that in an age in which we are in communication
   with the world "freedom of speech" will remain an empty
   phrase.

           —*Dai Qing, February 8, 1989*

* See *Seeds of Fire*, p. 236.

What's the Nineties Gonna Bring?

XIE CHENGQIANG

Xie Chengqiang is a rock singer in his late thirties who lives in Canton. "What's the Nineties Gonna Bring?" written and sung by Xie, was released in Hong Kong on a cassette, Shake the World (Fantian fudi), *in mid-1990. It was also made into an underground music video—a Chinese "video-izdat"—in Canton with the help of Hong Kong MTV producers. The video features images of Sun Yat-sen, China with a red flag burning over it, and the singer gagged and blindfolded, then breaking free of his bonds and knocking down a wall with his guitar (a reference to Pink Floyd's film* The Wall, *pirate copies of which have circulated in China since 1986). Although the video was broadcast in Hong Kong, Canton Television declined to air it on the mainland.*

The thirties was a laid-back melody
The forties a poignant threnody
The fifties had that vigorous feel
As all the nation smelted steel
The sixties sang "going down to the country"
The seventies' model operas were revolutionary
The eighties was break dance, but that's not all
There was a fever for rock 'n' roll
Still there's many songs to sing—
What's the nineties gonna bring?
What's the nineties gonna bring? . . .

List of Translators

Beijing Review: Deng Xiaoping, a comment on education in China to the Ugandan President; Jiang Zemin, "Speech at the Meeting in Celebration of the Fortieth Anniversary of the Founding of the People's Republic of China." *

Don J. Cohn: Chen Ruoxi, "The Old Man" (with Diane Cornell); * Hah Gong, "A Hong Kong Absurdity." *

Diane Cornell: Chen Ruoxi, "The Old Man" (with Don J. Cohn). *

David Hawkes: Qu Yuan, "A Lament for Ying."

Brigette Holland: Xu Xing, "Variations without a Theme" (with Jonathan Hutt); * Wang Shuo, "Hot and Cold, Measure for Measure" (with Jonathan Hutt). *

Jonathan Hutt: Liu Yiran, "Rocking Tiananmen;" * "Variations without a Theme" (with Brigette Holland); * Wang Shuo, "Hot and Cold, Measure for Measure" (with Brigette Holland). *

W. J. F. Jenner: Zheng Banqiao, "Hard-won Stupidity."

Simon Leys: Three quotations from Lu Xun, "My 'Origins' and My 'Department' " and "Minor Random Thoughts."

John Minford: "The Howl" (with anonymous); Xi Xi, "In the First Light of Dawn" (with Pang Bingjun).

Pang Bingjun: Zhou Zuoren, "An Encounter with Mounted Troops at Qianmen"; * Xi Xi, "In the First Light of Dawn" (with John Minford).

Gary Snyder: Han Shan, poem.

Stephen C. Soong: Yu Kwang-chung, "The Kowloon-Canton Railway."

Yang Qinghua: Feng Jicai, "Three-Inch Golden Lotuses." *

Yang Xianyi and Gladys Yang: Two quotations from Lu Xun, "My Views on Chastity."

---

* All translations not listed here have been done by one or both of the editors. Selections marked with an asterisk have been reworked by the editors.

Further Reading

PART I: THE CRY

Amnesty International: *China: The Massacre of June 1989 and Its Aftermath,* London: 1989.

Asia Watch: "Asia Watch Work on China, March 1989–June 1990," New York: Asia Watch, 1990.

———: "The Case of Wang Juntao," New York: Asia Watch, March 11, 1991.

Bei Dao (Zhao Zhenkai): *The August Sleepwalker,* trans. Bonnie S. McDougall, London: Anvil Press, 1988.

Buckley, Christopher: "Science as Politics and Politics as Science: Fang Lizhi and Chinese Intellectuals' Uncertain Road to Dissent," *The Australian Journal of Chinese Affairs,* January 1991.

Canetti, Elias: *Crowds and Power,* London: Penguin Books, 1973.

Cooper, John F., and Ta-ling Lee: *One Step Forward, One Step Back, Human Rights in the People's Republic of China in 1987/88,* Occasional Papers/Reprint Series in Contemporary Asian Studies, 92:3, 1989, Baltimore: University of Maryland School of Law.

Fang, Lizhi: *Bringing Down the Great Wall: Writings on Science, Culture and Democracy in China,* New York: Alfred A. Knopf, 1991.

———: "China's Despair and China's Hope," *The New York Review of Books,* February 2, 1989.

Fathers, Michael, and Andrew Higgins: *Tiananmen: The Rape of Peking,* London/New York: *The Independent* in association with Doubleday, 1989.

Hawkes, David: *The Songs of the South, An Anthology of Ancient Chinese Poems by Qu Yuan and Other Poets,* London: Penguin Books, 1985.

None of the books listed in the bibliography of *Seeds of Fire* is repeated here.

473

He, Xin: "A Word of Advice to the Politburo," trans. G. Barmé, *The Australian Journal of Chinese Affairs,* January 1990.

Hicks, George, ed.: *The Broken Mirror: China after Tiananmen,* London: Longman, 1990.

International League for Human Rights and the Ad Hoc Study Group on Human Rights in China: *Massacre in Beijing: The Events of 3–4 June 1989 and Their Aftermath,* New York: 1989.

Kahn, Joseph F.: "Better Fed Than Red," *Esquire,* September 1990.

Kent, Ann: "Human Rights in the People's Republic of China," Canberra: Department of the Parliamentary Library, 1989.

Kwok, D. W. Y., ed.: *Protest in the Chinese Tradition,* Honolulu: University of Hawaii, Center for Chinese Studies Occasional Papers, No. 2, 1990.

Leys, Simon: "The Curse of the Man Who Could See the Little Fish at the Bottom of the Ocean," *The New York Review of Books,* July 20, 1989.

Lin, Zi-yao, ed.: *One Author Is Rankling Two Chinas,* Taipei: Sing Kuang Book Company Ltd., 1989.

Link, Perry: "The Chinese Intellectuals and the Revolt," *The New York Review of Books,* June 29, 1989.

Oksenberg, Michael, Lawrence R. Sullivan, and Marc Lambert, eds.: *Beijing Spring of 1989—Confrontation and Conflict: The Basic Documents,* Armonk, N.Y.: M. E. Sharpe, 1990.

Parkes, Graham, ed.: *Nietzsche in Asian Thought,* Chicago: Chicago University Press, 1991.

Sabatier, Patrick, Romain Franklin, and Patricia Zhou: *Chine: Le Printemps de Pékin de la liberté au massacre,* Paris: Libération, 1989.

Saich, Tony, ed.: *The Chinese People's Movement: Perspectives on Spring 1989,* Armonk, N.Y.: M. E. Sharpe, 1990.

Schell, Orville: "An Act of Defiance," *The New York Times Magazine,* April 16, 1989.

Schneider, Laurence A.: *A Madman of Ch'u: The Chinese Myth of Loyalty and Dissent,* Berkeley: University of California Press, 1980.

Shen, Tong, with Marianne Yen: *Almost a Revolution,* Boston: Houghton Mifflin Company, 1990.

Simmie, Scott, and Bob Nixon: *Tiananmen Square,* Vancouver: Douglas & McIntyre, 1989.

Strand, David: "Protest in Beijing: Civil Society and Public Sphere in China," *Problems of Communism,* May–June, 1990.

Turnley, David and Peter: *Beijing Spring,* Hong Kong: Asia 2000 Ltd., 1989.

Unger, Jonathan, ed.: *The Pro-Democracy Protests in China: Reports from the Provinces,* Armonk, N.Y.: M. E. Sharpe, 1991.

PART II: BINDINGS

Balazs, Etienne: *Chinese Civilization and Bureaucracy, Variations on a Theme,* trans. H. M. Wright, New Haven: Yale University Press, 1964.

Brugger, Bill, and David Kelly: *Chinese Marxism in the Post-Mao Era,* Stanford, Calif.: Stanford University Press, 1990.

Chang, Hao: *Chinese Intellectuals in Crisis: Search for Order and Meaning, 1890–1911,* Berkeley: University of California Press, 1987.

Cheek, Timothy: "Habits of the Heart: Intellectual Assumptions Reflected by Mainland Chinese Reformers from Teng T'o to Fang Li-chih," *Issues & Studies,* March 1988.

Chou, Chih-p'ing: *Yüan Hung-tao and the Kung-an School,* Cambridge: Cambridge University Press, 1988.

Cohen, Paul A.: *Discovering History in China: American Historical Writing on the Recent Chinese Past,* New York: Columbia University Press, 1984.

———, and John E. Schrecker: *Reform in Nineteenth-Century China,* Cambridge, Mass.: East Asia Research Center, Harvard University, 1976.

de Bary, William Theodore: *Self and Society in Ming Thought,* New York: Columbia University Press, 1970.

Dirlik, Arif, and Maurice Meisner, eds.: *Marxism and the Chinese Experience: Issues in Contemporary Chinese Socialism,* Armonk, N.Y.: M. E. Sharpe, 1989.

Dutton, Michael: *Policing and Punishment in China: From Patriarchy to "the People,"* Cambridge: Cambridge University Press, [in press].

Goldman, Merle: *China's Intellectuals: Advise and Dissent,* Cambridge, Mass.: Harvard University Press, 1981.

Graham, A. C.: *Chuang-Tzu: The Inner Chapters,* London: Unwin Paperbacks, 1986.

Harbsmeier, Christoph: *The Cartoonist Feng Zikai: Social Realism with a Buddhist Face,* Oslo: Universitetsforlaget, 1984.

Hegel, Robert E., and Richard C. Hessney, eds.: *Expressions of Self in Chinese Literature,* New York: Columbia University Press, 1985.

Hsiao, Kung-ch'üan: "Li Chih: An Iconoclast of the Sixteenth Century," *Tien Hsia Monthly,* April 1938.

Kane, Daniel: "Jin Guantao, Liu Qingfeng and Their Historical Systems Evolution Theory," *Papers on Far Eastern History,* March 1989.

Kwong, S. K.: *A Mosaic of the Hundred Days: Personalities, Politics and Ideas of 1898*, Cambridge, Mass.: Council on East Asian Studies, Harvard University, 1984.

Levy, Howard S.: *Chinese Footbinding: The History of a Curious Erotic Custom*, New York: Bell Publishing Company, 1967.

Lin, Yutang: *My Country and My People*, London: Heinemann, 1938

———: *The Importance of Living*, London: Heinemann, 1938.

———: *The Importance of Understanding*, London: Heinemann, 1960.

———: *The Pleasures of a Nonconformist*, London: Heinemann, 1962.

Lipman, Jonathan N., and Steven Harrell, eds.: *Violence in China: Essays in Culture and Counterculture*, New York: State University of New York Press, 1990.

Liu, Binyan: *A Higher Kind of Loyalty: A Memoir by China's Foremost Journalist*, trans. Zhu Hong, New York: Pantheon, 1990.

Liu, I-ch'ing: *A New Account of Tales of the World*, trans. Richard B. Mather, Minneapolis: University of Minnesota Press, 1976.

Ma, Shu Yun: "The Rise and Fall of Neo-Authoritarianism in China," *China Information*, Vol. V, No. 3, Winter 1990–1991.

Munro, Donald J., ed.: *Individualism and Holism: Studies in Confucian and Taoist Values*, Ann Arbor: The University of Michigan, 1985.

Pollard, David E.: *A Chinese Look at Literature: The Literary Values of Chou Tso-jen in Relation to the Tradition*, Berkeley: University of California Press, 1973.

Pye, Lucien, W.: *The Mandarin and the Cadre: China's Political Cultures*, Ann Arbor: Michigan Monographs in Chinese Studies, No. 59, 1988.

Qian, Wen-yuan: *The Great Inertia: Scientific Stagnation in Traditional China*, Beckenham, Kent: Croom Helm, 1985.

Saari, Jon L.: *Legacies of Childhood: Growing Up Chinese in a Time of Crisis, 1890–1920*, Cambridge, Mass.: Council on East Asian Studies, Harvard University, 1990.

Smith, Arthur H.: *Chinese Characteristics*, New York: Fleming H. Revell Co., 1894, facsimile reproduction Singapore: Graham Brash (Pte.) Ltd., 1986.

Sun, Lung-kee: "Contemporary Chinese Culture: Structure and Emotionality," *The Australian Journal of Chinese Affairs*, July 1991.

Wakeman, Frederic: "The Price of Autonomy: Intellectuals in Ming and Ch'ing Politics," *Daedalus*, No. 2, Spring 1972.

Waldron, Arthur: *The Great Wall of China: From History to Myth*, Cambridge: Cambridge University Press, 1990.

PART III: RED NOISE

Bao Lord, Bette: *Legacies: A Chinese Mosaic,* New York: Alfred A. Knopf, 1990.

Barmé, Geremie: "The Chinese Velvet Prison: Culture in the 'New Age,' 1976–89," *Issues & Studies,* August 1989.

Chan, Anita: *Children of Mao: Personality Development and Political Activism in the Red Guard Generation,* Seattle: University of Washington Press, 1985.

Davis, Deborah, and Ezra F. Vogel, eds.: *Chinese Society on the Eve of Tiananmen: The Impact of Reform,* Cambridge, Mass.: Council on East Asian Studies, Harvard University, 1990.

Goldblatt, Howard, ed.: *Worlds Apart: Recent Chinese Writing and Its Audiences,* Armonk, N.Y.: M. E. Sharpe, 1990.

Havel, Václav: "Stories and Totalitarianism," *Index on Censorship,* 1988:3.

Honig, Emily, and Gail Hershatter: *Personal Voices: Chinese Women in the 1980's,* Stanford; Calif.: Stanford University Press, 1988.

Hooper, Beverley: *Youth in China,* London: Penguin, 1985.

Huang, Ray: *1587, a Year of No Significance,* New Haven: Yale University Press, 1981.

Hui, Ching-shuen, ed.: *The Stars: 10 Years,* Hong Kong: Hanart 2 Ltd., 1989.

Jaivin, Linda: "It's Only Rock 'n' Roll but China Likes It," *Asian Wall Street Journal,* October 12–13, 1990.

———: "Sexology: New Word in the Chinese Dictionary," *Asian Wall Street Journal,* December 21, 1990.

Jose, Nicholas: *Avenue of Eternal Peace,* Melbourne: Penguin Books Australia, 1989.

Link, Perry, Richard Madsen, and Paul G. Pickowicz, eds.: *Unofficial China: Popular Culture and Thought in the People's Republic,* Boulder, Colo.: Westview Press, 1989.

Liu, Binyan: *China's Crisis, China's Hope: Essays from an Intellectual in Exile,* trans. Howard Goldblatt, Cambridge, Mass.: Harvard University Press, 1990.

Liu, James J. Y.; *The Chinese Knight-Errant,* London: Routledge & Kegan Paul, 1967.

Liu, Xinwu: *Black Walls and Other Stories,* ed. Don J. Cohn, Hong Kong: The Chinese University of Hong Kong, 1990.

Louie, Kam: *Between Fact and Fiction: Essays on Post-Mao Chinese Literature and Society,* Sydney: Wild Peony, 1989.

Pelc, Jan: "It's Gonna Get Worse," *Index on Censorship,* 1986:6.

Renditions, Special Issue: Contemporary Women Writers, Spring and Autumn 1987.

Schell, Orville: *Discos and Democracy: China in the Throes of Reform,* New York: Pantheon, 1988.

Shi, Nai'an, and Luo Guanzhong: *Outlaws of the Marsh,* trans. Sidney Shapiro, London: Unwin Paperbacks, 1986.

Terzani, Angela: *Chinese Days,* Hong Kong: Odyssey Productions Ltd., 1988.

Van Gulik, R. H.: *Sexual Life in Ancient China: A Preliminary Survey of Chinese Sex and Society from ca. 1500 B.C. till 1644 A.D.,* Leiden: E. J. Brill, 1961.

Yao, Ming-le: *The Conspiracy and Murder of Mao's Heir,* London: Collins, 1983.

PART IV: WHEELS

Buckley, Christopher: *A New May Fourth: The Scientific Imagination in Chinese Intellectual History, 1978–1989,* unpublished thesis, Sydney University, 1989.

Chow, Tse-tsung: *The May Fourth Movement: Intellectual Revolution in Modern China,* Cambridge, Mass.: Harvard University Press, 1960.

Cohen, Paul A., and Merle Goldman, eds.: *Ideas Across Cultures, Essays on Chinese Thought in Honor of Benjamin I. Schwartz,* Cambridge, Mass.: Harvard University Press, 1990.

Elvin, Mark: *The Pattern of the Chinese Past,* Stanford, Calif.: Stanford University Press, 1973.

Fang, Lizhi: "The Chinese Amnesia," *The New York Review of Books,* September 27, 1990.

Furth, Charlotte, ed.: *The Limits of Change: Essays on Conservative Alternatives in Republican China,* Cambridge, Mass.: Harvard University Press, 1976.

Geist, Beate: "Lei Feng and the 'Lei Fengs of the Eighties'—Models and Modelling in China," *Papers on Far Eastern History,* September 1990.

Goldman, Merle: *Literary Dissent in Communist China,* Cambridge, Mass.: Harvard University Press, 1967.

Goodman, David, and Gerald Segal, eds.: *China in the Nineties: Crisis Management and Beyond,* Oxford: Clarendon Press, 1991.

Grieder, Jerome B.: *Hu Shih and the Chinese Renaissance: Liberalism in the Chinese Revolution, 1917–1937,* Cambridge, Mass.: Harvard University Press, 1970.

————: *Intellectuals and the State in Modern China: A Narrative History*, New York: The Free Press, Macmillan, 1981.

Hay, Stephen N.: *Asian Ideas of East and West: Tagore and His Critics in Japan, China, and India*, Cambridge, Mass.: Harvard University Press, 1970.

He, Xin: "Letter from Beijing," trans. and reply by G. Barmé, *The Australian Journal of Chinese Affairs*, July 1990.

Hollander, Paul: "Ideological Noise," *Encounter*, December 1989.

Jaivin, Linda: "Learn from Lei Feng? No, Thanks," *Asian Wall Street Journal*, May 30, 1990.

Jenner, W.J.F.: *The Tyranny of History: The Roots of China's Crisis*, London: Viking Penguin [in press].

Kohn, Livia, ed.: *Taoist Meditation and Longevity Techniques*, Ann Arbor: Center for Chinese Studies, University of Michigan, 1989.

Kuhn, Philip A.: *Soulstealers: The Chinese Sorcery Scare of 1768*, Cambridge, Mass.: Harvard University Press, 1990.

Kwok, David: *Scientism in Chinese Thought, 1900–1950*, New Haven, Conn.: Yale University Press, 1965.

Ladany, Laszlo: *The Communist Party of China and Marxism, 1921–1985, a Self-Portrait*, London: C. Hurst & Company, 1988.

Lee, Leo Ou-fan: *The Romantic Generation of Modern Chinese Writers*, Cambridge, Mass.: Harvard University Press, 1973.

Levenson, Joseph R.: *Confucian China and Its Modern Fate: The Problem of Intellectual Continuity*, London: Routledge & Kegan Paul, 1958.

Lévi, Jean: *The Chinese Emperor*, Melbourne: Penguin Books Australia, 1990.

Lifton, Robert Jay: *Thought Reform and the Psychology of Totalism: A Study of "Brainwashing" in China*, London: Pelican Books, 1967.

Lin, Yü-sheng: *The Crisis of Chinese Consciousness: Radical Antitraditionalism in the May Fourth Era*, Madison: University of Wisconsin Press, 1979.

Meissner, Werner: *Philosophy and Politics in China: The Controversy Over Dialectical Materialism in the 1930s*, trans. Richard Mann, London: C. Hurst & Co., 1990.

Nathan, Andrew J.: "Chinese Democracy in 1989: Continuity and Change," *Problems of Communism*, September–October 1989.

————: *China's Crisis: Dilemmas for Reform and Prospects for Democracy*, New York: Columbia University Press, 1990.

Pye, Lucien W.: *Asian Power and Politics: The Cultural Dimensions of Authority*, Cambridge, Mass.: Harvard Univesity Press, 1985.

Schwarcz, Vera: *The Chinese Enlightenment: Intellectuals and the Legacy of the May Fourth Movement of 1919,* Berkeley: University of California Press, 1986.

Schwartz, Benjamin I., ed.: *Reflections on the May Fourth Movement: A Symposium,* Cambridge, Mass.: East Asia Research Center, Harvard University, 1973.

Shen, Rong: "Snakes and Ladders—or Three Days in the Life of a Chinese Intellectual," trans. G. Barmé and Linda Jaivin, in *At Middle Age,* Peking: Chinese Literature Press, 1987.

Spence, Jonathan D.: *The Gate of Heavenly Peace: The Chinese and Their Revolution, 1895–1980,* New York: Viking Press, 1981.

——: *The Search for Modern China,* New York: W. W. Norton & Company, 1990.

Wang, Y. C.: *Chinese Intellectuals and the West, 1872–1949,* Chapel Hill: University of North Carolina Press, 1966.

Wilhelm, Hellmut: *Change: Eight Lectures on the "I Ching,"* trans. Cary F. Baynes, New York: Harper & Row, 1964.

Wilhelm, Richard: *"I Ching" or Book of Changes,* trans. Cary F. Baynes, London: Routledge & Kegan Paul Ltd., 1970.

Wright, Arthur F., ed.: *Studies in Chinese Thought,* Chicago: University of Chicago Press, 1953.

——: *The Confucian Persuasion,* Stanford, Calif.: Stanford University Press, 1960.

PART V: FLOATING

Aksyonov, Vassily: *The Island of Crimea,* London: Abacus, 1986.

Barmé, Geremie: "Travelling Heavy: The Intellectual Baggage of the Chinese Diaspora," with a translation of Liu Xiaobo, "The Inspiration of New York: Meditations of an Iconoclast," *Problems of Communism,* January–April 1991.

Chan, Anita: "Self-deception as a Survival Technique: The Case of Yue Daiyun," *The Australian Journal of Chinese Affairs,* January/July 1988.

Cheng, Joseph, ed.: *Hong Kong in Transition,* New York: Oxford University Press, 1986.

Conrad, Joseph: *Under Western Eyes,* London: Penguin Books, 1957.

Duoduo: *Looking Out from Death: From the Cultural Revolution to Tiananmen Square,* trans. Gregory Lee and John Cayley, London: Bloomsbury, 1989.

Havel, Václav: *Living in Truth,* London: Faber and Faber, 1989.

Limonov, Edward: *His Butler's Story,* trans. Judson Rosengrant, London: Abacus, 1989.

Liu, Zongren: *Two Years in the Melting Pot,* Hong Kong: Joint Publishing Company, 1985.

Pan, Lynn: *Sons of the Yellow Emperor: The Story of the Overseas Chinese,* London: Secker & Warburg, 1990.

Renditions, Special Issue: Hong Kong, Spring and Autumn 1988.

Rueschemeyer, Marilyn: "The Emigration Experience of Soviet Artists in the United States," *Canadian Slavonic Papers,* September 1982.

Schell, Orville: "Children of Tiananmen," *Rolling Stone,* December 14–28, 1989.

————: "The Liberation of Comrade Fang," *Los Angeles Times Magazine,* October 7, 1990

Siklová, Jirina: "The 'Gray Zone' and the Future of Dissent in Czechoslovakia," *Social Research,* Summer 1990.

Skilling, H. Gordon: *Samizdat and an Independent Society in Central and Eastern Europe,* Columbus: Ohio State University Press, 1989.

Tabori, Paul: *The Anatomy of Exile: A Semantic and Historical Study,* London: George G. Harrap, 1972.

Tenzin Gyatso: *Freedom in Exile: The Autobiography of the Dalai Lama of Tibet,* London: Hodder & Stoughton, 1990.

Tsang, Steven: *Democracy Shelved,* New York: Oxford University Press, 1988.

Waks, Raymond, ed.: *Civil Liberties in Hong Kong,* New York: Oxford University Press, 1988.

Wittlin, Joseph: "Sorrow and Grandeur of Exile," *The Polish Review,* Spring–Summer 1957.

Wong, Jan: " 'No One Can Twist the Truth Again,' " *The Globe and Mail* (Toronto), January 13, 1990.

Xi Xi: *A Girl Like Me and Other Stories,* Hong Kong: The Chinese University of Hong Kong, 1986.

Yang, Jiang: *Lost in the Crowd: A Cultural Revolution Memoir,* trans. G. Barmé, Melbourne: McPhee Gribble Publishers, 1989.

Yang, Lian: *The Dead in Exile,* trans. Mabel Lee, Canberra: Tiananmen Publications, 1990.

Zinoviev, Alexander: *Homo Sovieticus,* trans. Charles Janson, London: Paladin Books, 1986.

Sources

(The romanization of Chinese sources is given in *Hanyu pinyin*.)

INTRODUCTION

p. xv: Lu Xun, "Wu ti," *Nanqiang beidiaoji, Lu Xun quanji*, Vol. IV, Beijing: Renmin wenxue chubanshe, 1981, p. 487.

p. xxiv: Li Ao, "Yizhong shichuanlede yanlun daoju," *Li Ao quanji*, Vol. V, Taipei: Siji chuban shiye gongsi, 1980, p. 79.

p. xxvi: Zhang Hongtu, from a letter dated December 21, 1989.

p. xxvi: Liu Xiaobo, "Hunshi mowang Mao Zedong," *Jiefang yuebao*, 1988:11, p. 31.

PART I: THE CRY

p. 1: Lu Xun, "Zagan," *Huagaiji, Lu Xun quanji*, Vol. 3, Beijing: Renmin wenxue chubanshe, 1981, p. 50; Dai Qing, "Peidiao yidai jing-ying," ed., *Lianhebao, Tiananmen 1989*, Taibei: Lianjing chuban shiye gongsi, 1989, p. 262.

pp. 5–22: Liu Yiran, "Yaogun qingnian," *Qingnian wenxue*, 1988:10, pp. 4–11, 29. Boxes: p. 8: Liu Yiran, "Yaogun qingnian," p. 4; p. 15: Deng Xiaoping's comment on education to the Ugandan President, *Beijing Review*, July 17–23, 1989, p. 19; p. 18: Wei Chao and Xiao Bai, eds., *Piliwu zai Zhongguo*, Beijing: *Guangming ribao* chubanshe, 1989, p. 115.

p. 23: Liu Xiaobo, "Beiju yingxiongde beiju—Hu Yaobang shishi xian-xiang pinglun zhi san," *Jiefang yuebao*, 1989:5, pp. 33–34.

pp. 24–26: Ouyang Bin, "Qiqu minzhulu," *Mingbao yuekan,* 1989:4, p. 4.

p. 26: Xinhua, "Sifabu youguan fuzeren fabiao tanhua—jiu Chen Jun deng ren xiexin zhengji qianming shi," *Renmin ribao,* February 23, 1989.

pp. 27–28: Bei Dao, "Zhizhengzhede erduo bixu xiguan butongde shengyin," handwritten manuscript dated February 27, 1989.

p. 29: Lee Yee, "Qianming yundong yiyuelaide fazhan," *Jiushi niandai yuekan,* 1989:4, p. 18.

p. 29: Langlang, "Daibiao yizhong daoyide husheng," *Jiushi niandai yuekan,* 1989:4, pp. 24–25.

p. 30: Ni Kuang in "Dui Fang Lizhi shijiande fanying," *Jiefang yuebao,* 1989:3, p. 20.

pp. 31–32: Wang Dan, "Lun fanduipaide yanlun ziyou," *Jiushi niandai yuekan,* 1989:9, pp. 72–73.

pp. 33–48: Liu Xiaobo, "Beiju yingxiongde beiju—Hu Yaobang shishi xianxiang pinglun zhi yi, er, san," *Jiefang yuebao,* 1989:5, pp. 30–34. Boxes: pp. 39–41: "Yaobang huo zai women xinzhong—benbao yu *Xin guancha* zazhi zai jing juxing lianhe daonian huodong," *Shijie jingji daobao,* April 24, 1989; p. 42: Sun Shixian, "Deng Xiaoping zhenya xueyunde qianyin houguo," *Jingbao yuekan,* 1989:7, p. 46; pp. 46–47: Bo Yang, *Jiayuan,* Taibei: Linbai chubanshe, 1989, pp. 102–4.

p. 34: Lin Yutang, *My Country and My People,* London: Heinemann, 1938, p. 343.

p. 48: Chen Jun, "He Liu Xiaobo zai yiqide rizi," *Jiefang yuebao,* 1989:7, p. 26; Liu Binyan in Jin Zhong, "Cong heima dao heishou," *Jiefang yuebao,* 1989:7, p. 60.

p. 49: Simon Leys, "The Curse of the Man Who Could See the Little Fish at the Bottom of the Ocean," *The New York Review of Books,* July 20, 1989, p. 29.

pp. 50–53: Wang Ruowang, "Wei yanshi yige cuowu buxi fan shige cuowu?—Wang Ruowang 4 yue 25 ri zhi Deng Xiaoping shu," *Tiananmen 1989,* Taibei: Lianjing chuban shiye gongsi, 1989, pp. 330–33; illustration caption p. 67 from Qu Yuan, "Jiuzhang: Ai Ying," ed. Nie Shiqiao, *Chuci xinzhu,* Shanghai: Shanghai guji chubanshe, 1980, p. 103, "Nine Pieces: A Lament for Ying," trans. David Hawkes, *The Songs of the South, An Anthology of Ancient Chinese Poems by Qu Yuan and Other Poets,* London: Penguin Books, 1985, p. 164.

pp. 53–58: Xinhua, "Zhongguo shehui kexue yuan fu yanjiu yuan He Xin dui dangqian xuechao fenxi ji xingshi yuce," published internally by Xinhua, provided by He Xin; trans. G. Barmé, "A Word of Advice to the Politburo," *The Australian Journal of Chinese Affairs*, January 1990, pp. 65–70, 76.

pp. 58–59: Li Honglin et al., "Wenhuajie bufen zhiming renshi 'Jinian Wusi shenhua gaige changyishu,' jianchi gaige, queli minzhu yu fazhide quanwei, 1989 nian, 5 yue 12 ri," p. 322.

pp. 60–61: Bei Cun et al., "Zhongguo zuojia renquan huyushu, 1989 nian, 5 yue 13 ri, Shanghai," unpublished pamphlet.

p. 62: Yan Jiaqi, Bao Zunxin, et al., "5.17 xuanyan," ed. *Mingbao, Beizhuangde minyun,* Hong Kong; *Mingbao* chubanshe, 1989, p. 66.

pp. 62–63: Lung-kee Sun, *Zhongguo wenhuade "shenceng jiegou,"* Hong Kong: Jixianshe, 1983, pp. 420–21.

pp. 63–64: Wang Peigong et al., "Xia juexin he xuesheng zhijie duihua," *Wenhuibao*, May 18, 1989.

pp. 64: Ba Jin, "Zhongguode xiwang zai tamende shenshang," *Wenhuibao*, May 19, 1989.

pp. 65–66: Li Ximing, "Guanyu Beijing xuechao qingkuangde tongbao," *Jiefang yuebao*, 1989:6, pp. 96–97.

p. 67: "Liudian yijian," distributed on Tiananmen Square as a Peking University pamphlet on May 19, 1989.

pp. 68–69: Liu Xiaobo, "Womende jianyi," Zheng Wang and Ji Kuai, eds., *Liu Xiaobo: qiren qishi,* Beijing: Zhongguo qingnian chubanshe, 1989, pp. 133–34, 135–36.

p. 69: Bing Xin's calligraphic inscription from *Mingbao,* June 1, 1989.

pp. 70–72: Liu Xiaobo et al., "Jueshi xuanyan," *Jiefang yuebao,* 1989: 6, pp. 48–49.

pp. 71–72: Yuan Zhiming, "Heishou yu qishou," *Xinwen ziyou daobao,* January 20, 1990.

p. 73: Lu Xun, "Kongtan," *Eryiji, Lu Xun quanji,* Vol. 3, p. 281.

pp. 74–97: Wei Shaoen, "Tiananmen suiyue," *Junzi zazhi* (*Esquire,* Chinese edition), 1989:7, pp. 138–48. Boxes: p. 79: Hou Dejian, "Xiaqubu!" from a handwritten manuscript provided by the author; p. 80: "Dui jinqi Xianggang mouxie ren yixie huodongde kanfa—Quanguo renda changweihui fazhi gongzuo weiyuanhui ba ming gongzuo renyuan," *Renmin ribao,* June 15, 1989; p. 85: Yang Shangkun, "Yang Shangkun tongzhi zai junwei jinji kuoda huiyishangde jianghua yaodian," a computer-typeset pamphlet version of a secret speech distributed by Peking University students on Tiananmen Square in late May 1989; p. 85: from written records provided by Chinese observers.

p. 96: "Chai Ling yishu tusha jingli," *Beizhuangde minyun*, Hong Kong: *Mingbao* chubanshe, 1989, p. 123; Xie Chi and Shi Lu, "Pingbao 'beiwanglu,' " *Renmin ribao*, July 26, 1989.

p. 97: "Beijing zhe yiye," *Renmin ribao*, June 4, 1989.

pp. 98–9: Zhou Zuoren, "Qianmen yu madui ji," *Zhitang wenji*, Shanghai: Tianma shudian, 1933, pp. 89–91.

pp. 100–5: Anonymous, "Ku ba . . . ," from a handwritten manuscript from China.

p. 104: Yang Lian, from a handwritten manuscript dated October 11, 1989, Auckland.

pp. 106–7: Xi Xi, "Tianse weiming," *Xiangdao wanbao: xingqiri zazhi*, June 11, 1989.

p. 108: Chen Xitong, "Guanyu zhizhi dongluan he pingxi fangeming baoluande qingkuang baogao," *Xuechao, dongluan, fangeming baoluan zhenxiang: ziliao xuanbian*, ed. Zhonggong Beijing shiwei xuanchuanbu, Beijing: Zhongguo qingnian chubanshe, 1989, p. 1; Wang Bingyun, "Quanshi jiedao banshichu zai pingbaozhong gongxian tuchu," *Beijing wanbao*, August 3, 1989.

pp. 109–10: Chen Yingzhen, "Dengdai zongjiede xiezi," *Renjian*, 1989:7, pp. 72–73.

pp. 111–15: Zhang Langlang, "Wojia jiu zai Tiananmen pangbian," *Jiushi niandai yuekan*, 1989:7, pp. 15–16.

PART II: BINDINGS

p. 117: Tan Sitong, "Renxue," *Tan Sitong quanji*, Beijing: Sanlian shudian, 1954, p. 73; Jin Zhong, "Wentan 'heima' Liu Xiaobo," *Jiefang yuebao*, 1988: 12, p. 61.

pp. 121–26: Feng Jicai, "Sancun jinlian," *Shouhuo*, 1986:3, pp. 7–9. Box p. 124: Gu Hongming, quoted in Zhou Zuoren, "Baijiao shangdui," *Zhou Zuoren zaoqi sanwen xuan*, Shanghai: Shanghai wenyi chubanshe, 1984, p. 47.

pp. 126–27: Shi Shuqing, "Feng Jicai tan tade wenge shinian," *Jiushi niandai yuekan*, 1987:2, pp. 96–97.

p. 127: Hu Shi, "Kexue fazhan suo xuyaode shehui gaige," *Zhuanji wenxue*, 55:1, p. 39.

p. 128: Lin Yutang, "Lun dazu," *Renjianshi*, No. 13, October 5, 1934, pp. 8, 9.

pp. 128–30: Li Ao, "Cong *Chuantongxiade dubai* dao *Dubaixiade chuantong*," *Li Ao quanji*, Vol. 5, Taibei: Siji chuban shiye youxian gongsi, 1980, pp. 12–13.

p. 129: Lung-kee Sun, *Zhongguo wenhuade "shenceng jiegou*," Hong Kong: Jixianshe, 1983, pp. 254–55.

p. 131: Ba Jin, *Jia*, Beijing: Renmin wenxue chubanshe, 1977, p. 18.

pp. 131–32: Li Zhi, "Bie Liu Xiaofu shu," *Fenshu Xufenshu*, Beijing: Shangwu shuju, 1975, p. 48.

pp. 132–33: Lu Feng, "Danwei: yizhong teshude shehui zuzhi xingshi," *Zhongguo shehui kexue*, 1989:1, p. 79.

p. 134: Michael Dutton, *Policing and Punishment in China: From Patriarchy to "the People*," Cambridge: Cambridge University Press [in press].

p. 135: He Xin, "Tongzhang ehua ji jinggai shibaide yuanyin," *Mingbao yuekan*, 1989:2, p. 63.

pp. 136–37: Gong Zizhen, "Bingmeiguan ji," *Gong Zizhen quanji*, Shanghai: Shanghai renmin chubanshe, 1975, pp. 186–87.

p. 137: Su Xiaokang, Wang Luxiang, et al., *Heshang*, Beijing: Xiandai chubanshe, 1988, p. 54.

p. 138: *Ibid.*, p. 22.

p. 140: *Ibid.*, p. 114.

pp. 141–42: *Ibid.*, p. 287.

p. 142: Su Xiaokang, *Ziyou beiwanglu*, Hong Kong: Sanlian shudian, 1989, p. 283.

p. 143: He Xin, "Ping 'Heshang' de mingming," *Beijing ribao*, September 25, 1989.

p. 144: Zhuangzi, "Qiushui," *Zhuangzi qianzhu*, ed. Cao Chuji, Beijing: Zhonghua shuju, 1982, p. 237.

p. 145: Su, Wang, et al., *op cit.*, p. 19.

pp. 146–47: *Ibid.*, pp. 80–81.

p. 147: *Ibid.*, p. 79.

p. 148: *Ibid.*, p. 66.

pp. 148–49: *Ibid.*, pp. 66–68.

pp. 149–51: *Ibid.*, pp. 88–93.

p. 151: *Ibid.*, p. 36; p. 35.

pp. 151–52: *Ibid.*, pp. 52–53.

p. 153: *Ibid.*, p. 12.

pp. 153–54: Hou Dejian, the 1989 version of "Longde chuanren," from a handwritten manuscript by the author.

p. 154: Su, Wang, et al., *Heshang*, p. 20.

p. 155: Su, Wang, et al., *op. cit.*, p. 11; Bo Yang, quoted in Su Xiaokang and Wang Luxiang, eds., *Heshang: Zhongguoren zui shenchende changtan,* Taibei: Fengyun shidai chubanshe and Jinfeng chubanshe, 1988, p. 209.

p. 155: *Ibid.,* pp. 98–104.

pp. 155–56: *Ibid.,* pp. 107–8.

p. 156: *Ibid.,* pp. 108–9.

p. 157: *Ibid.,* p. 106.

pp. 157–58: *Ibid.,* p. 102; p. 110.

p. 158: Lin Ching-wen and Lina Hsu, *The Free China Journal,* January 11, 1990.

pp. 158–59: Wang Xiaodong and Qiu Tiancao, "Jiqingde yinying—ping dianshi xiliepian 'Heshang,' " *Zhongguo qingnianbao,* July 10, 1988; Wei Minglun, " 'Heshang' you xing shui bu xing," *Renmin ribao,* September 2, 1988.

pp. 159–60: Su, *op. cit.,* p. 285; Gao Wangling and Wu Xin, " 'Heshang' fanyingle yizhong shiheng xintai—Gao Wangling, Wu Xin tan wenhua fanxing wenti," *Heshanglun,* ed. Cui Wenhua, Beijing: Wenhua yishu chubanshe, 1988, p. 183.

p. 160: Lin Yü-sheng, quoted in Su Xiaokang, *Longniande beichuang,* Hong Kong: Sanlian shudian, 1989, p. 50; Chen Yingzhen, "Dengdai zongjiede xiezi," *Renjian,* 1989:7, p. 72.

pp. 160–61: Diao Xiaoli's letter is from viewer's responses collected in an internal reference booklet by China Central Television in mid-1988; Su *op. cit.,* p. 285.

pp. 161–64: Liu Xiaobo quoted in Jin Zhong, "Wentan 'heima' Liu Xiaobo," *Jiefang yuebao,* 1988:12, p. 61; He Xin, "Wode kunhuo yu youlü," *Xuexi yuekan,* 1988:12, p. 37.

p. 163: Lee Yee, "Zhongguo yao jiesan?—zhuanfang Fang Lizhi," *Jiushi niandai yuekan,* 1988:10, p. 74.

p. 165: Xu Yinong, "Zigui yeban you ti xie, bu xing dongfeng huan bu hui—bianzhe xinsheng," *Shan'aoshangde Zhongguo,* Guiyang: Guizhou renmin chubanshe, 1989, p. 4.

pp. 166–69: quotations from He Bochuan, *Shan'aoshangde Zhongguo,* Chapter 1, p. 17; Chapter 2, pp. 38, 56–57; Chapter 3, p. 77; Chapter 4, p. 118; Chapter 5, p. 142; Chapter 6, p. 179; Chapter 7, p. 215; Chapter 8, p. 255; Chapter 9, p. 310; Chapter 10, p. 326; Chapter 11, p. 349; Chapter 12, p. 365; Chapter 13, pp. 394–95; Chapter 14, p. 424; Chapter 15, pp. 454–55; Chapter 16, p. 486; Chapter 17, p. 499; Chapter 18, p. 529.

p. 169: "Weiji yishi yu Zhongguo wentixue," *Dushu,* 1989:4, pp. 35, 44.

p. 170: Wu Jianguo, "Pouxi *Shijie jingji daobao Qiuji* taolunde zhengzhi daoxiang," *Renmin ribao,* November 26, 1990.

p. 171: Li Honglin, "Jiushinian hou kan Wuxu," *Xin guancha,* 1988:22, p. 3.

p. 173: Bao Zunxin, quoted in *Heshang,* pp. 106–7.

p. 174: Dai Qing, "Kexue yu wenhua luntan dierci huiyi ceji," *Shijie jingji daobao,* October 3, 1988.

pp. 174–75: Ge Yang, "Heimeng," *Shijie jingji daobao,* June 2, 1988.

p. 175: Hu Jiwei, "Meiyou xinwen ziyou jiu meiyou zhenzhengde anding," *Shijie jingji daobao,* May 8, 1989.

p. 176: Jin Guantao, "Yishujiade shiminggan," *Dazhong dianying,* 1989:5, p. 9.

p. 176: Li Honglin, "Weiji yu gaige," *Xin qimeng (2),* 1988, p. 53.

p. 177: Li Zehou, interviewed by Sun Shangyang, " 'Wusi' de shishi feifei—Li Zehou xiansheng dawenlu," *Wenhuibao,* March 28 and April 11, 1989.

pp. 177–78: Liu Binyan, "Liu Binyan da *Jiefang yuebao* wen," *Jiefang yuebao,* 1988:8, pp. 9, 14.

p. 178: Liu Zaifu, "Liangci lishixingde tupo—cong 'Wusi' xinwenhua yundong dao xinshiqide 'xiandai wenhua yishi,' " *Renmin ribao,* April 25, 1989.

pp. 178–79: Qian Jiaju, "Yinggai bushang 'de xiansheng,' 'sai xiansheng' zhe yike," *Qunyan,* June 7, 1989, pp. 26–27.

p. 179: Qin Benli in "Jianshou yanlun lichang diyige bei zhengsu," ed. *Lianhebao, Tiananmen 1989,* Taibei: Lianjing chuban shiye gongsi, 1989, p. 214.

pp. 179–80: Su Shaozhi, "Zai 'Jinian dangde shier jie sanzhong quanhui zhaokai shi zhounian lilun taolunhui' shang fayan," *Shijie jingji daobao,* December 26, 1988.

p. 180: Su Xiaokang, quoted in Liu Menglan, "Wan Huanghe kuanglan yu chensi zhi zhong—fang Su Xiaokang," *Renmin ribao,* July 4, 1988.

p. 181: Wang Ruoshui, unpublished transcript of a speech on the second day of the "China '89 Symposium" held at Bolinas, California, April 28, 1989.

p. 181: Wen Yuankai, quoted in Zhang Weiguo, "Ningjuli he xinxin wenti bi jingji xingshi geng yanjun: Wen Yuankai dui dangqian xingshide fenxi," *Shijie jingji daobao,* January 9, 1989.

p. 182: Yan Jiaqi, quoted in Zhang Weiguo, "Yan Jiaqi tanhualu," *Shijie jingji daobao,* November 7, 1988.

p. 182: Yu Haocheng, "Renmen ying you mianyu kongjude ziyou," *Xin qimeng (3)*, 1989, p. 23.

p. 183: Liu Xiaobo, "Zai diyude rukouchu—dui Makesizhuyide zaijiantao," *Xinwen ziyou daobao*, September 30, 1989.

pp. 184–90: Dai Qing, "Cong Lin Zexu dao Jiang Jingguo," *Xin quanweizhuyi—dui gaige lilun ganglingde lunzheng*, ed. Liu Jun and Li Lin, Beijing: Beijing jingjing xueyuan chubanshe, 1989, pp. 86–90. Box p. 187: Timothy Richard, *Forty-five Years in China*, London: T. Fisher Unwin, 1916, p. 2.

p. 188: Wu Jiaxiang, "Xin quanweizhuyi shuping," *Xin quanweizhuyi —dui gaige lilun ganglingde lunzheng*, p. 36.

p. 188: Yu Haocheng, "Zhongguo xuyao xin quanweizhuyi ma?" *Xin quanweizhuyi—dui gaige lilun ganglingde lunzheng*, pp. 165–66.

p. 192: Zhuangzi, "Zeyang," *Zhuangzi qianzhu*, pp. 395–96.

pp. 193–94: Ruan Ji, "Daren xiansheng zhuan," *Ruan Ji ji*, Shanghai: Shanghai guji chubanshe, 1978, pp. 64–65.

pp. 194–95: Ji Kang, "Yu Shan Juyuan juejiaoshu," ed. Xiao Tong, *Wenxuan*, Vol. 2, Beijing: Zhonghua shuju, 1977, pp. 601–2.

p. 195: Li Ao, "Kuai kan *Dubai xiade chuantong*," *Li Ao quanji*, Vol. 5, pp. 16–17, 18.

p. 196: Liu Ling, quoted in Liu Yiqing, *Shishuo xinyu*, Vol. 1, Shanghai: Shanghai guji chubanshe, 1982, p. 381.

p. 196: Han Shan, *Kanzan*, annotated by Iriya Yoshitaka, Tokyo: Iwanami shoten, 1981, p. 72, trans. Gary Snyder, *Riprap & Cold Mountain Poems*, San Francisco: Four Seasons Foundation, 1969, p. 60.

p. 196–97: Li Zhenjie, "Hanshan he tade shi," *Wenxue pinglun*, 1983:6, p. 100.

p. 197: Li Zhi, "Zashu: Yuyue," *Fenshu Xufenshu*, pp. 185–86.

p. 198: Yuan Hongdao, "Qiu Changru," *Yuan Hongdao ji jianjiao*, Vol. 1, Shanghai: Shanghai guji chubanshe, 1981, p. 208.

pp. 198–99: Zheng Banqiao, "Weixian shuzong yu shedi Mo diershu," *Zheng Banqiao quanji*, ed. Bian Xiaoxuan, Jinan: Qilu chubanshe, 1985, pp. 190–91.

p. 199: Chen Duxiu, "Ouxiang pohuai lun," *Xin qingnian*, 1918:5, 2, p. 91.

p. 199: Lu Xun, "Wode 'ji' he 'xi,'" *Huagaiji, Lu Xun quanji*, Vol. 3, Beijing: Renmin wenxue chuabanshe, 1981, pp. 82–83, trans. Simon Leys, *The Burning Forest*, New York: Holt, Rinehart and Winston, 1986, pp. 217–18.

p. 200: Zhou Zuoren, "Liangge gui," *Zhou Zuoren zaoqi sanwen xuan,* pp. 98–99.

p. 200: Lin Yutang, "Youbuweizhai congshu xu," *Yuan Hongdao ji jianjiao,* Vol. 2, pp. 1734–35.

pp. 201–2: Feng Zikai, "Du 'Du Yuanyuantang suibi,' " *Feng Zikai suibiji,* ed. Feng Yiyin, Hangzhou: Zhejiang wenyi chubanshe, 1983, pp. 277–78.

p. 203: Li Ao, *Dubai xiade chuantong,* Beijing: Renmin wenxue chubanshe, 1989, back cover.

pp. 203–4: Liu Xiaobo, "Zailun xinshiqi wenxue mianlin weiji," *Baijia,* 1988:1, p. 18; Jin Zhong, "Wentan 'heima' Liu Xiaobo," *Jiefang yuebao,* 1988:12, pp. 62, 64.

pp. 204–5: Zhu Dake, "Kongxinde wenxue," *Zuojia,* 1988:9, pp. 73–74.

p. 206: Hou Dejian, quoted in Peter Ellingsen, "Dissident Speaks Out on Tiananmen," *The Age* (Melbourne), February 8, 1990.

pp. 207–9: Liu Xiaobo, "Lun gudu," *Baijia,* 1988:2, pp. 5–6.

p. 208: He Xin, "Wode kunhuo yu youlü," *Xuexi yuekan,* 1988:12, pp. 36–37.

p. 210: Bo Yang, *Zhongguoren, ni shoule shenme zuzhou?* Taibei: Linbai chubanshe, 1987, pp. 249–50.

pp. 211–12: *Ibid.,* pp. 19–20, 23.

p. 212: Zhou Zuoren, "Dai kuaiyou," *Zhou Zuoren sanwen xuan,* p. 62.

PART III: RED NOISE

p. 213: Lung-kee Sun, "Contemporary Chinese Culture: Structure and Emotionality," from the unpublished version of this paper, 1989, p. 38; He Xin, "Gudu yu tiaozhan—wode fendou yu sikao," *Zixue zazhi,* 1988:10, p. 39.

pp. 217–26: Zuo Shula, "Buru 'liu' zide qile, xiexie Wang Shuo," *Dangdai* (Taibei), 1989:4, pp. 129–33.

p. 225: *Ibid.,* p. 136.

pp. 227–44: Wang Shuo, "Yiban shi huoyan, yiban shi haishui," *Xin shiqi zhengming zuopin xuan,* ed. Zhongguo dangdai wenxue yanjiuhui jiaoyu fenhui, Xi'an: Xibei daxue chubanshe, 1988, pp. 198–216. Box p. 235: Zuo Shula, p. 133.

pp. 244–45: Chen Yishui, "Xing fanzuide jiaokeshu ping 'Yiban shi huoyan, yiban shi haishui,' " *Xin shiqi zhengming zuopin xuan,* pp. 299, 300, 307.

p. 245: Zuo Shula, p. 135.

pp. 248–49: John Minford, "Picking Up the Pieces," *Far Eastern Economic Review,* August 8, 1985, p. 30.

pp. 250–51: Wang Zheng, "Shusheng zhi qing jiyu shu," *Renmin ribao,* March 3, 1989.

pp. 251–53: Yi Shuihan, "Wuchan jiejide liumang yishi weihai shehui," *Chaoliu yuekan,* No. 25, March 15, 1989, p. 22.

p. 252: Anonymous, "Guan da chihe," in Yu Jiwen, "Beijingde xin yaogun," *Jiushi niandai yuekan,* 1989:6, pp. 104–5.

pp. 253–54: He Xin, "Gudu yu tiaozhan—wode fendou yu sikao," *ibid.*

p. 254: Lu Xun, "Wo zhi jielieguan," *Fen, Lu Xun quanji,* Vol. 1, p. 116, trans. Yang Xianyi and Gladys Yang, "My Views on Chastity," in *Lu Xun Selected Works,* Vol. 2, Beijing: Foreign Languages Press, 1980, p. 13.

p. 255: Lee Yee, "Zhongguo yao jiesan?—zhuanfang Fang Lizhi," *Jiushi niandai yuekan,* 1988:10, p. 75.

pp. 256–59: Xu Xing, "Wuzhuti bianzou," *Renmin wenxue,* 1985:7, pp. 29, 32–33, 36, 37.

pp. 260–64: He Xin, "Dangdai wenxuezhongde huangmiugan yu duo-yuzhe, du 'Wuzhuti bianzou' suixianglu," *Dushu,* 1985:11, pp. 4, 5, 6, 7, 10–11, 11, 12. Boxes: p. 263: He Xin, "Dui Zhao wende jidian dafu," *Yishu xianxiangde fuhao—wenhuaxue chanshi,* Beijing: Renmin wenxue chubanshe, 1987, pp. 162–63; p. 264: Zhu Dake, "Kongxinde wenxue," *Zuojia,* 1988:9, p. 68.

pp. 265–78: Liu Xinwu, "5.19 changjingtou," *Duhui yongtandiao,* Beijing: Zuojia chubanshe, 1986, pp. 3–5, 6, 6–10, 10–16, 16–17, 19, 19–20, 23–27, 30; "Zooming In on 19 May 1985," trans. G. Barmé in Liu Xinwu, *Black Walls and Other Stories,* ed. Don J. Cohn, Hong Kong: The Chinese University of Hong Kong, 1990, pp. 149–51, 152, 152–54, 154–55, 155–56, 156–57, 157–60, 161–62, 164–65, 168–72, 174–75. Boxes: p. 268: Su Xiaokang, *Heshang: Zhongguoren zui shenchende changtan,* Taibei: Fengyun shidai chubanshe and Jinfeng chubanshe, 1988, p. 8; p. 274: Su Xiaokang, "Longniande beichuang —guanyu 'Heshang' de zhaji," *Ziyou beiwanglu,* Hong Kong: Sanlian shudian, 1989, p. 267.

p. 277: Lung-kee Sun, "Contemporary Chinese Culture: Structure and Emotionality," unpublished manuscript, p. 38.

p. 279: Wu Shanzhuan, "Guanyu 'da shengyi,' " *Zhongguo meishubao,* 1989:11, March 13, 1989.

p. 280: *Ibid.*

p. 281: Li Xianting, "Liang sheng qiangxiang: Xinchao meishude xie-muli," *Zhongguo meishubao,* 1989:11, March 13, 1989.

pp. 282–83: Yi Ming, "Xiandaizhan yubo wei jin," *Zhongguo meishu-bao,* 1989:14, April 3, 1989.

p. 283: Wang Zhong, "Ping 'meishu xinchao,' " *Renmin ribao,* December 13, 1990.

pp. 284–85: Yang Yu, "Ziyou yu shizhong," *Wenyibao,* April 16, 1988.

p. 286: Miklós Haraszti, *The Velvet Prison: Artists under State Socialism,* trans. Katalin and Stephen Landesman with the help of Steve Wasserman, New York: Basic Books, 1987, p. 78.

p. 287: Xinhua, "Xinwen chubanshu fuzeren tan 'wenge' ticaide wen-zhang zuopin chuban wenti," *Renmin ribao,* April 4, 1989.

pp. 288–90: Mei Xinsheng and Gao Xiaoling, *Wo, Linfu, yinsi, mu-jizhe: yige Lin Biao mishude huiyi,* Beijing: Zhongguo wenlian chuban gongsi, 1988, pp. 348, 354–55, 355–56. Box p. 290: Lee Yee, "Zhongguo yao jiesan?—zhuanfang Fang Lizhi," *Jiushi niandai yuekan,* 1988:10, p. 74.

p. 291: Zhang Weiguo, "Ningjuli he xinxin wenti bi jingji xingshi geng yanjun: Wen Yuankai dui dangqian xingshide fenxi," *Shijie jingji dao-bao,* January 9, 1989.

pp. 291–92: Zhang Zhenglong, *Xuebai xiehong—Liao-Shen zhanyi juan,* Beijing: Jiefangjun chubanshe, 1989, pp. 614–15, 5.

pp. 293–309: Dai Qing and Luo Ke, "Xing 'kaifang' nüzi," *Zhongguo nüxing xilie,* Shenyang: Liaoning renmin chubanshe, 1988, pp. 24–41.

p. 295: Lu Xun, "Wo zhi jielieguan," *Fen, Lu Xun quanji,* Vol. 1, p. 118, trans. Yang Xianyi and Gladys Yang, "My Views on Chastity," pp. 15–16.

pp. 309–11: Zhang Mingduo, "Daodede lunsang, shouyude xuanxie: Xing 'kafaing' nüzi duhou," *Zuopin yu zhengming,* 1988:12, pp. 73–75.

pp. 312–13: Sun Xiaogang, "Hei pifu chengshi," *Chengshiren,* ed. Song Lin et al., Shanghai: Xuelin chubanshe, 1987, pp. 154–56.

p. 313: Song Lin, "Shiyede qiutu," *Chengshiren,* p. 11.

pp. 313–14: Zhu Dake, "Ranshaode mijin," *Shanghai wenyi,* 1989:4, p. 56.

pp. 314–15: Sun Xiaogang, "Makesi diaoxiang liji," *Cheng zhi meng: Zhongguo nanfang chengshi shi xuan,* ed. Li Hong et al., Guangzhou: Xinshiji chubanshe, 1986, pp. 35–37.

pp. 316–19: Nicholas Jose, "China: What Is Going On?" *The Independent Monthly,* October 1989, pp. 14–15.

p. 318: Jaime Florcruz, "A Rebel's Words and Music," *Time,* January 8, 1990, p. 34.

pp. 319–20: Hou Dejian, "Huoxiaqu," handwritten manuscript by the author.

PART IV: WHEELS

p. 321: Lu Xun, "Xiao zagan," *Eryiji, Lu Xun quanji,* Vol. 3, p. 532, trans. Simon Leys, *The Burning Forest,* p. 222; Li Ao, "Kuai kan Dubaixiade chuantong," *Li Ao quanji,* Vol. 5, p. 20.

pp. 326–27: Liu Yazhou, *Guangchang—ouxiangde shentan,* Hong Kong: Tiandi tushu youxian gongsi, 1990, pp. 235–36.

p. 328: "Zhuangyan mianmao kaishi huifu—qingchanghoude Tiananmen guangchang jianwen," *Beijing ribao,* June 8, 1989.

pp. 328–334: Chen Ruoxi, "Laoren," *Laoren,* Taibei: Lianjing chuban shiye gongsi, 1978, pp. 33–36, 41–45, 50; "The Old Man," trans. Diane Cornell and Don J. Cohn, in Chen Ruoxi, *The Old Man and Other Stories,* Hong Kong: The Chinese University of Hong Kong, 1986, pp. 28–31, 34–38, 42–43.

pp. 334–37: Fang Chuanming, "Zhege an fanbuliao," *Beijing ribao,* August 3, 1989.

p. 336: Liu Xiaobo, "Pingfan! Zhongguo zuidade beiju.' *Tiananmen, 1989,* p. 277.

pp. 338–39: Bo Yang, *Jiayuan,* Taibei: Linbai chubanshe, 1989, pp. 152–53.

p. 340: Pierre Ryckmans, *The Chinese Attitude Towards the Past, The Forty-seventh George Ernest Morrison Lecture in Ethnology, 1986,* Canberra: The Australian National University, 1986, p. 17, note 19.

pp. 341–43: Cai Yuanpei, "Hongshui yu mengshou," *Xin qingnian,* 1920:7, 5, pp. 1–2.

p. 343: Ding Shisun, interviewed in "Beida zhuanji," in Zhang Zhaotang's television documentary *Tamen zhengzai xie lishi,* Zhongguo dianshi (CTV), Taibei.

pp. 344–45: Li Ao, "Zailun Wusi," *Jiefang yuebao,* 1989:5, p. 29.

pp. 345–50: Xu Jilin, "Xiandai wenhuashishangde 'Wusi guaiquan,' " *Wenhuibao,* March 21, 1989. Box p. 348: Lin Yü-sheng et al., *Wusi: Duoyuande fansi,* Hong Kong: Sanlian chubanshe, 1989, p. 242.

pp. 350–53: Fang Lizhi, "Cong Beijing tianwentai kan Zhongguo min-zhu jincheng: jinian 'Wusi' qishinian," unpublished paper.

pp. 353–54: Jiang Zemin, "Aiguozhuyi he woguo zhishifenzide shiming —zai shoudu qingnian jinian Wusi baogaohuishangde jianghua (1990 nian 5 yue 3 ri)," *Renmin ribao,* May 4, 1990.

pp. 355–57: Ah Cheng, "Guancha," *Jiushi niandai yuekan,* 1990:2, p. 12.

p. 358: Dai Qing, "Chu Anping yu 'dang tianxia,'" *Mingbao yuekan,* 1989:1, p. 45.

pp. 359–60: Dai Qing, *Chu Anping yu "dang tianxia,"* Beijing: Zhong-guo huaqiao chubanshe, 1989, pp. 43, 46–47.

pp. 360–61: *Ibid.,* p. 126.

p. 361: *Ibid.,* p. 107.

p. 362: Kuang Yan, "Dongluan 'jizhe' Dai Qing," *Guangming ribao,* September 13, 1989.

p. 362: Dai Qing, *Wode ruyu,* Hong Kong: Mingbao chubanshe, 1990, p. 36.

pp. 363–66: Wu Zuguang, "Qiantan 'guoqing,'" a speech made at the Second Session of the Seventh National People's Political Consultative Congress, Peking, March 22, 1989, unpublished manuscript.

p. 367: Dai Qing, ed., *Changjiang Changjiang—sanxia gongcheng lun-zheng,* Guiyang: Guizhou renmin chubanshe, 1989, pp. 169–70.

pp. 368–69: Qian Liqun, "Fansi santi," *Wenyibao,* May 20, 1989.

p. 369: He Xin, "Lun jingying taotai," *He Xin ji—fansi, tiaozhan, chuangzao,* Haerbin: Heilongjiang jiaoyu chubanshe, 1988, p. 268.

pp. 370–71: Li Ao, "Gei tan Zhongxi wenhuade ren kankan bing," *Li Ao quanji,* Vol. 4, pp. 36–37.

pp. 371–72: Li Xiaoshan, "Xiaaide minzuzhuyi—Zhongguo xiandai yishu," *Zhongguo meishubao,* 1989:16, April 17, 1989.

p. 373: Yi Dian, "Liuxing ganmao," *Cheng zhi meng: Zhongguo nan-fang chengshi shi xuan,* ed. Li Hong et al., Guangzhou: Xinshiji chu-banshe, 1986, pp. 26–27.

p. 374: Ke Yunlu, *Da qigongshi,* Beijing: Renmin wenxue chubanshe, 1989, pp. 8–9.

p. 376: Li Rongxia, "Yijing: The Chinese Calisthenics," *Beijing Review,* October 22–28, 1990, p. 33.

pp. 377–80: *Ibid.,* pp. 236–39.

pp. 380–81: Ke Yunlu, pp. 430–31.

p. 382: *Ibid.,* p. 339.

p. 383: *Ibid.,* pp. 262–63.

pp. 384–85: Liu Xiaobo, "Zai 'qigongre' de diceng," *Jiefang yuebao,* 1988:10, pp. 57–59.

p. 386: Bo Yang, *Jiayuan,* p. 103.

pp. 386–89: Luo Beishan, "Jiushi chongwen," *Mingbao ribao,* August 3, 1989. Box p. 388: Mao Zedong, "Zai bada erci huiyishangde jianghua, di yici jianghua (1958 nian 5 yue 8 ri)," *Mao Zedong tong-zhi shi dangdai zui weidade Makesi-Lieningzhuyizhe,* Beijing: no publisher given, 1969, p. 195.

p. 389: Simon Leys, interviewed by Greg Sheridan, "A Waterfall Changing Course," *The Weekend Australian,* June 3–4, 1989.

pp. 389–90: Han Xiaohui, "Bingmayong qiande chensi," *Shiyue,* 1990:3, p. 218.

pp. 390–91: Li Ruihuan, "Zai nanfang sisheng 'saohuang' gongzuo zuotanhui shangde jianghua," *Yangcheng wanbao,* October 16, 1989.

pp. 391–92: Li Ruihuan, "Ticha minyi, renzhen 'saohuang': cong zhili yinxiang chuban shiye tanqi," *Renmin ribao,* September 5, 1989.

pp. 392–93: "Guangdong 'saohuang' chengxiao chujian," *Yangcheng wanbao,* October 18, 1989.

p. 392: Jin Zhong, "Weishenme yao tongyi? Moming qimiao!—zhuanfang Xianggang zuojia xiehui huizhang Ni Kuang," *Jiefang yuebao,* 1988:9, p. 35.

p. 393: Wang Renzhi, "Fandui zichan jieji ziyouhua," *Yangcheng wanbao,* February 23, 1989.

p. 394: "Renzhong daoyuan, zhandou weiyou qiongqi," *Wenyibao,* April 28, 1990.

pp. 394–95: Xinhuashe, "Li Ruihuan tan wending dangqian daju," *Yangcheng wanbao,* April 30, 1990; "Quan dang fucong zhongyang," *Zhongguo wenhua bao,* June 24, 1990.

pp. 395–97: Jiang Zemin, "Speech at the Meeting in Celebration of the 40th Anniversary of the Founding of the People's Republic of China, September 29, 1989," *Beijing Review,* October 9–15, 1989, pp. 20, 20–21, 23, slightly revised with reference to the Chinese original.

pp. 399–401: Ying-tai Lung, "Buyao zhezhu wode yangguang," *Ye-houji,* Taibei: Yuanshen chubanshe, 1985, pp. 73–75. Boxes: p. 399: Ying Hong, "Yici wuzhuti caifang; zai Beijing ting Long Yingtai liaotian," *Wenyibao,* May 6, 1989; p. 400: Simon Leys, "A Waterfall Changing Course"; "Jiang Zemin huijian Kongzi taolunhui Zhongwai pengyou," *Renmin ribao,* October 9, 1989.

pp. 401–5: Lao She, "Xin Aimier," *Lao She wenji,* Vol. 7, Beijing: Renmin wenxue chubanshe, 1984, pp. 264–67, 271–72.

p. 403: "Jiang Zemin zhixin quanguo shaoxianduiyuan, shaoxiandui gongzuozhe zhuhe shaoxiandui chengli sishi zhounian," *Renmin ribao,* October 13, 1989.

pp. 406–7: Hua Ming, "Cong 'Satere' dao 'Mao Zedongre,' " *Renmin ribao (haiwaiban)*, March 1, 1990.

pp. 408–9: He Xin, from a letter to G. Barmé dated October 2, 1989, see He Xin, "Letter from Beijing," trans. G. Barmé, *The Australian Journal of Chinese Affairs,* July 1990, pp. 343–44.

p. 410: Yang Bojun, *Mengzi yizhu,* Vol. 1, Beijing: Zhonghua shuju, 1960, p. 154; Lu Xun, "Xiao zagan," *Eryiji, Lu Xun quanji,* Vol. 3, p. 531, trans. Simon Leys, *The Burning Forest,* p. 222.

PART V: FLOATING

p. 411: Jin Zhong, "Weishenme yao tongyi? Moming qimiao!—zhuanfang Xianggang zuojia xiehui huizhang Ni Kuang," *Jiefang yuebao,* 1988:9, p. 36; Bei Ling, "Liuwang," *Xinwen ziyou daobao,* November 20, 1989.

pp. 416–24: Xi Xi, "Fucheng zhiyi," *Shoujuan,* Taibei: Hongfan shudian, 1988, pp. 1–18.

pp. 425–28: Anonymous, "An Appeal to British Justice," an advertisement in English in the *South China Morning Post,* July 11, 1989.

p. 427: Lee Yee, "Fear and Loathing in Hong Kong," *The Asian Wall Street Journal,* June 20, 1989.

pp. 429–31: Hah Gong, " 'Qiangjian hefahua' lun," *Mingbao,* March 2, 1984, trans. Don J. Cohn, *Renditions, Special Issue: Hong Kong,* Spring and Autumn 1988, pp. 326–27.

pp. 431–32: Jin Zhong, *op. cit.,* pp. 34, 36.

p. 433: Lee Yee, "Hong Kong Slides to Xu Jiatun Solution," *The Asian Wall Street Journal,* May 31, 1990.

pp. 434–35: Ye Dexian, interviewed in Shu Qi, *Meiyou taiyangde rizi,* film script lines 112–45, 597–613.

pp. 436–37: Yu Kwang-chung, "Jiu-Guang tielu," *Renditions,* Autumn 1975, p. 78.

pp. 438–42: Li Ao, "Bihuoxue dagang," *Li Ao quanji,* Vol. 6, pp. 7–11.

pp. 443–48: Yang Jiang, "Yinshenyi," *Jiang Yincha,* Beijing: Sanlian shudian, 1987, pp. 183–89.

pp. 448–50: Li Zongwu, "Houheixue," *Qishu Houheixue,* Hong Kong: Baicheng chubanshe, no date, pp. 8–9.

pp. 450–51: Ding Fang, "Yu xiandai xuwuzhuyide duihua," *Zhongguo meishubao,* 1989:11, March 13, 1989.

p. 451: Liu Xiaobo, "Zai diyude rukouchu—dui Makesizhuyide zaijiantao," *Xinwen ziyou daobao,* September 30, 1989.

pp. 452–53: Qian Zhongshu, "Qian Zhongshu xu," in Zhong Shuhe, *Zou xiang shijie: jindai Zhongguo zhishi fenzi kaocha Xifangde lishi,* Beijing: Zhonghua shuju, 1985, p. 2.

pp. 453–56: Wu Zuguang, " 'Huzhao' yu 'ziyou,' " *Wu Zuguang xianwen xuan,* Hong Kong: Mingbao chubanshe, 1989, pp. 153–56.

p. 456: Lee Yee and Fang Su, "Aiguozhuyi bu ying fang zai diyi wei—dianhua fangwen Fang Lizhi," *Jiushi niandai yuekan,* 1989:1, p. 97.

pp. 457–59: "Remarks by His Holiness the Fourteenth Dalai Lama, on Being Awarded the Nobel Peace Prize," from the Bureau of His Holiness the Dalai Lama.

pp. 459–60: Chen Ruoxi, "Dalaide diyige Nuobeierjiang," *Xinwen ziyou daobao,* November 20, 1989.

pp. 461–67: Bei Ling, "Liuwang," *Xinwen ziyou daobao,* November 20, 1989.

p. 464: Liu Xiaobo, "Danyuan Xianggang yongyuan shi shijiede ziyougang," *Zhengming,* 1989:1, p. 60.

p. 466: Zhu Dake, "Kongxinde wenxue," *Zuojia,* 1988:9, pp. 74–75.

pp. 467–68: Duo Duo, interviewed in Shu Qi, *Meiyou taiyangde rizi,* film script lines 480–516.

p. 469: Hou Deijian, Zhou Duo, and Gao Xin, "Zhi Zhongguo lingdaorende gongkaixin," in Hou Deijian, *Huotouzi zhengzhuan,* Taibei: Lianjing chuban shiye gongsi, 1990, pp. 261–62.

EPILOGUE

p. 470: Dai Qing, ed., *Changjiang changjiang—sanxia gongcheng lunzheng,* Guiyang: Guizhou renmin chubanshe, 1989, p. 172.

p. 471: Xie Chengqiang, "Jiushi niandai zenme yang?" *Fantian fudi,* Hong Kong: Yongsheng yinyue chuban youxian gongsi, 1990.

Index

Index

ABOUT THE EDITORS

Geremie Barmé is a research scholar at and Linda Jaivin is an associate of the Australian National University in Canberra. Geremie Barmé is the coeditor (with John Minford) of *Seeds of Fire: Chinese Voices of Conscience*. Both have lived in China and have written and lectured on Chinese culture, politics, and history.